ONE AND ALL

D0312046

The Real Meaning of Money

BY THE SAME AUTHOR

Choosing Not Losing
The Courage to Live
Depression: The Way Out of Your Prison
Living With the Bomb: Can We Live Without Enemies?
Beyond Fear
The Successful Self
Breaking the Bonds
Wanting Everything
Time On Our Side: Growing in Wisdom, Not Growing Old
Dorothy Rowe's Guide to Life

The Real Meaning of Money

DOROTHY ROWE

HarperCollins*Publishers*

HarperCollins*Publishers*
77–85 Fulham Palace Road,
Hammersmith, London W6 8JB

Published by HarperCollins*Publishers* 1997
1 3 5 7 9 8 6 4 2

A catalogue record for this book
is available from the British Library

ISBN 0 00 255329 5

Set in Postscript Linotype Minion by
Rowland Phototypesettting Ltd
Bury St Edmunds, Suffolk

Printed and bound by
Caledonian International
Book Manufacturing Ltd, Glasgow

CONTENTS

Acknowledgements vii

Preface ix

1 The Logic of the Illogical 1

2 What Does Money Mean? 11

3 The Public Meaning of Money 40

4 The Private Meaning of Money 115

5 The Value of Money 178

6 The Market and Its Experts 259

7 Money and Morals 342

8 A Choice of Futures 382

Notes 431

Index 441

ACKNOWLEDGEMENTS

The author and publishers should like to thank the following for their permission to reproduce copyright material:

For the cartoons:
American Scientist, David Austin, *Australian Business Monthly*, Steve Bell, *The Cartoonist*, Les Gibbard, Michael Leunig, Alton Mort, Universal Press Syndicate

For the written excerpts from:
The Audi Magazine and Geoff Howard, *Australian Business Monthly*, Ian Aitken, Dan Atkinson, George Ball, Michael Billington, Alex Brummer, the *British Journal of Psychiatry*, *Changes*, Daniel Dennett, Mark Douglas, the *Economist*, Roy Greenslade, Paul Flynn, the *Guardian*, Simon Hoggart, Will Hutton, the *Independent*, Ben Laurance, *New York Times*, the *Observer*, *Private Eye*, Ian Stewart, *Telegraph* Group Limited, Richard Thomas, Francis Wheen, Martin Woollacot

Alan Unwin for Edna Carew's *Paul Keating* and *The Language of Money*
John Brockman Associates for Colin Tudge's *The Day Before Yesterday*
Curtis Brown for Andrew St George's *The Descent of Manners*
Edward Elgar for Samuel Brittan's *Capitalism with a Human Face*
Faber & Faber for Paul Omerond's *The Death of Economics*
Georges Borchardt, Inc. for Fred Kaplan's *Dickens*
Robert I. Ducas for Michael Lewis's *Liar's Poker* and *The Money Culture*
Harvard University Press for Jeffrey Masson's *The Complete Letters of Sigmund Freud to Wilhelm Fliess*
HarperCollins, New York, for Jack Schwager's *Market Wizards*

and *The New Market Wizards*, and for Bryan Burrough and John Helyar's *The Barbarians at the Gate*

HarperCollins, London, for Hamish McRae's *The World in 2020* and for Steve Jones's *The Language of the Genes*

John Wiley for Peter L. Bernstein's *Against the Gods*

Laurence Pollinger Limited for Thomas Merton's *The Way of Chuang Tzu*

Little Brown for Nick Leeson's *Rogue Trader*

Macmillan for John Maynard Keynes *The Collected Writings of John Maynard Keynes*

Martin Brian and O'Keefe for Hugh McDiarmid for *Complete Poems*

New Directions Publishing for Thomas Merton's *The Way of Chuang Tzu*

Oxford University Press for Kevin Jackson's *The Oxford Book of Money* and for Robert R. Locke's *The Collapse of the American Management Technique*

Penguin Books Ltd for J. K. Galbraith's *A Short History of Financial Euphoria* and *A History of Economics*, John Allen Paulos's *Innumeracy*, and Daniel Dennett's *Consciousness Explained*

Andrea Pistolesi for Vito Albergo and Andrea Pistolesi's *San Galgano*

Random House, New York, for David Lamb's *The Arabs*

Random House, London, for Terry Smith's *Accounting for Growth*

Rogers, Coleridge and White Ltd for Oliver Sacks's *An Anthropologist on Mars*

Simon and Schuster for Jeffrey Robinson's *The Laundrymen*

Sinclair-Stevenson for J. K. Galbraith's *The Culture of Contentment* and *The Good Society*

Transworld for Gregory Milman's *Around the World on a Trillion Dollars a Day*

Verso for Noam Chomsky *Deterring Democracy*

Victor Gollancz for David Barchard's *Asil Nadir and the Rise and Fall of Polly Peck*

Weidenfeld and Nicolson, London, for Bernard Lewis's *The Muslim Discovery of Europe*

Weidenfeld and Nicolson, New York, for Lewis L. Lapham's *Money and Class in America*

PREFACE

Money alone sets the world in motion.

Publilius Syrus, first century BC[1]

You, oh money, are the cause of a restless life! Because of you we journey towards a premature death; you provide cruel nourishments for the evils of men; the seed of our cares sprouts from your head.

Propertius, first century BC[2]

With money in your pocket, you are wise and you are handsome and you sing well too.

Yiddish Proverb[3]

Such is the power of money. It makes the world go around. It is the source of all evil. If makes life worth living, or at least it cushions misery.

Money's power has been recognized ever since it entered the human world and now there is no part of that world where it has not penetrated. Isolated tribes who have no use for money now find that the effects of money – the demand for land and the land's products – are stealing their land from under their feet and bringing misery. Money's effects can be found even where there are no people. A seal in the Antarctic that has never seen a human being now has traces of man-made pollution in its blubber.[4]

Deploring money and its effects is a treasured occupation for those people who like to feel virtuous. Doing so is as useful as deploring the fact that we need air to breathe. We cannot go back to living without money any more than we can go back to living without telephone connections and computers. Computers nowadays communicate with one another more frequently than people communicate with one another. World trade depends on computers talking to one another. Close down all the computers and we'll starve. Try to abolish money and we'll perish in chaos.

Money is now quite beyond human control. Governments do not control their country's money, though they like to pretend they do. True, there are some immensely wealthy individuals and international corporations whose actions briefly can have some noticeable effects on the world economy, but there is no one individual or corporation who can claim to understand, much less direct, the universal, changing pattern of money and its effects.

We all worry about money. Most of us worry about money solely in personal terms. We think, 'Where can I get some money?' or 'Have I got enough to last to pay day?' or 'How can I make myself financially secure?' An increasing number of us put our personal worries about money into an international context. As well as worrying whether we're using our money wisely we've learned how to worry about the derivatives market and what the big players in this market might be up to.

People who see themselves as big players want to believe that, while they may not be able to control the money markets, they do have the experience and guile to predict which way the markets will go. Some people, like those called Market Wizards,[5] do do well, but such skill cannot be based solely on a good head for numbers and a thorough knowledge of statistics. Movements in the money market cannot be encapsulated in those statistical methods based on the notion that one or two events go on to cause one or two effects. Such methods can demonstrate that if the coffee crop fails prices of coffee are likely to rise. But if other events occur, such as a tribal war in central Africa, a revolution in Brazil, a research finding in the USA linking coffee and cancer, and a drugs cartel investing heavily in coffee in order to launder its money, predicting changes in the price of coffee becomes a much more chancy business.

The only statistical methods which seem to offer the possibility of reflecting the world movements of money are those developing out of the mathematics of chaotic systems and fractal geometry. The definition of a chaotic system as one where the slightest change in starting conditions leads to completely different results applies remarkably well to the movements of money in the world markets. Sadly, such an understanding does not help those people who wish to predict such movements. Scientists used to believe that if they could identify all the starting conditions and measure them absolutely accurately, then feed their figures into the right equations, they would discover the history of the universe and its future. Now they know that they can never measure accurately all the starting conditions of a large system, be it physical or economic, yet the slightest inaccuracy in measurement can lead to wildly inaccurate predictions. Even if it were possible to identify all the factors that played a part in the market at any one time, it would take months, perhaps years, to measure them accurately, and by then different factors would be playing their part.

Predicting the money market means searching for regularities, yet as researchers in chaos theory know, in many chaotic systems the randomness in the occurrence of events is something to be cherished because when randomness turns into regularity disaster results. A regular pattern of brain waves can precede an epileptic fit. A very regular heartbeat can precede a heart attack. When everyone in the market runs in fear in one direction the market crashes.

Perhaps the only contribution chaos theory will be able to make in the understanding of the money markets is in persuading more people to think of cause not as a line from A to B to C but as an interlinked network of many factors. Unfortunately thinking in this way requires a considerable tolerance of uncertainty, a talent few people possess.

Meanwhile, experts on money – politicians, economists, financiers, bankers, money men, journalists – agree on only one point. Things are bad and going to get worse. Just what they consider to be really bad and what remedies might work depend on which political and economic theories they have espoused, but they do agree that something must be done.

Many of these complaints and cures aren't worth considering because they are so deeply embedded in political prejudices. Here blame is laid at the opposing political party's door and cures attributed to the favoured political party's manifesto. However, there are a few commentators upon our plight who do try to examine the evidence with rigorous honesty. Four such people are the political economists Will Hutton, Hamish McRae, J. K. Galbraith and Samuel Brittan.

Nowadays publishers will call any book that sells more than two copies a best-seller, but in 1995 Will Hutton's *The State We're In*[6] really was one. In his preface to the revised edition Will Hutton writes,

> When it was published in hardback, *The State We're In* struck more of a chord with a wider range of British readers than I had ever imagined possible. There is plainly an untapped reservoir of concern about our country – and a hunger both for a different explanation of our predicament to that offered by conservative orthodoxies and for a different way forward.[7]

Perhaps this was all that most of Will Hutton's readers wanted, an explanation. However, I for one wanted something more. Complaining is fine, but if out of complaints, however well-informed and analysed, no plan of action emerges, complaining achieves nothing but momentary emotional relief. So I searched *The State We're In* for a plan of change which had a chance of successful implementation.

A preface to a book should be where the author tells the reader what the book is about. In the preface to the first edition Will Hutton shows that he sees his book as offering more than an explanation.

> My greatest hope is that the book will offer a way forward that is neither a return to the bastardised Keynesian corporatism of the 1960s and 1970s, nor the forced march towards a wholly deregulated market. There are other options besides becoming a huge version of Hong Kong with American levels of wages for the millions at the bottom of the pile. Our people deserve better than that. What is required is a creative institution-building and a democratic opening – and confidence that men and women can shape their world.[8]

For creative institution-building to succeed old institutions have to change. Will Hutton identifies the old institutions as the City of London, Whitehall, Westminster, the Crown, the Bank of England, the legal profession, the judiciary, the Establishment, the Conservative hegemony, private education, and rentiers who live off what others produce. All of these are bound together in what he calls 'a fundamental amorality'.

> It is amoral to run a society founded on the exclusion of so many people from decent living standards and opportunities; it is amoral to run an economy in which the only admissible objective is the maximisation of shareholder value; it is amoral to run a political system in which power is held exclusively and exercised in such a discretionary, authoritarian fashion. These exclusions, while beneficial in the short-term to those inside the circle of privilege, are in the long run inefficient and ultimately undermine the wealth generating process.[9]

What is needed, he says, is 'a moral economy'.

All that needs to be done is for the amoral members of the privileged institutions to recognize their amorality and change, so that 'a written constitution; the democratisation of civil society; the republicanisation of finance; the recognition that the market economy has to be managed and regulated, both at home and abroad; the upholding of a welfare state that incorporates social citizenship; the construction of a stable international financial order beyond the nation state'[10] can be brought into being.

Will Hutton's theory about how people can change has a structure which is very popular with theoreticians in politics, economics, sociology, religion, psychiatry and the wilder reaches of humanistic psychology. It is the 'then a miracle occurs' theory (see over).

Such theoreticians rarely manage to be more explicit. Indeed it would be difficult for Will Hutton to be more explicit because there are very few examples of people enjoying privilege, power and wealth who relinquished these for the benefit of others. Certain individuals might choose to behave in saintlike ways, but as a group the privileged hang on to their privileges. Revolutions might wrench their privilege, power and wealth away from them, but, as ever, *Plus ça change, plus c'est la même chose*, the more things change the more they stay the same. The original owners of privilege might disappear but there are always people willing and able to take their place.

Just how jealously the privileged defend their privileges was clear

"I THINK YOU SHOULD BE MORE EXPLICIT HERE IN STEP TWO."[11]

in the months following the publication of *The State We're In* when, to Conservative politicians and the right-wing media, Will Hutton was transformed from a serious but ignored left-wing journalist to a dangerous demagogue advocating a return to the evils of socialism and union power.

Hamish McRae in predicting the state of the world in 2020 is remarkably optimistic, though he has assumed that 'there will be no collective "nervous breakdown" such as struck the German people in the 1930s, no domination of a giant nation by a wicked emperor such as Joseph Stalin.'[12] There could be, he says, a great natural or environmental disaster such as an earthquake in Tokyo. That nuclear proliferation has increased the dangers has to be taken into account, as have the large flows of cross-border migration and racial and social tension. There could be an easily transmitted killer virus, while old enemies like tuberculosis have made their reappearance.

Against these dangers he puts what could go right. He feels that it is probable that 'most countries will be far better governed than in any previous period of history'.[13] He is optimistic about the market. 'The triumph of the market system over central planning means that the world economy will be far better run than any time before.'[14] Added to this people are becoming better educated and healthier. There are, he admits, some 'intractable problems – of crime, drugs, family break-up, poverty, and, in some parts of the world, hunger, danger and despair'.[15] The fact that people are better educated, better informed and healthier does not necessarily mean that they are wiser, but he does have the formula for ensuring that they do improve. It is his 'economic case for good behaviour'.

> Enduring prosperity requires societies which are stable, ordered and honest. Countries can manage a burst of growth based on the exploitation of cheap labour and natural resources, and stomach a fair degree of corruption while they do so. But as the experience of a country like Argentina shows, it is hard to maintain prosperity amid chaos . . . There is a powerful economic case (quite aside from the social arguments) for wanting to try to persuade citizens to behave in an orderly way – not to rob people on the street, have children they cannot look after, waste the time of the courts by suing on absurd pretexts, drive dangerously, take drugs, fiddle their taxes or claim social security benefits to which they are not entitled – because as it becomes tougher to increase the productivity of a country simply by improving its manufacturing industries, the standard of living of the next generation in the developed world will depend very much on whether the present generation behaves with civic responsibility. For this to happen, ordinary people have to want to sustain the balance between order and individualism which leads to societies which are both efficient and humane. Put bluntly, if countries wish to carry on becoming richer, their people will have to learn to behave better.[16]

(Curiously he does not suggest that the wicked members of the rich and powerful should change their ways. Do the crimes of the rich and powerful have no effect on the economy?)

Now we come to the nub of the problem – changing people's behaviour. Hamish McRae has two suggestions.

First, 'Politicians have a duty to explain the choice: that it will be hard to increase living standards over the next generation unless people are prepared to accept in the first instance a greater degree of self-discipline, and on occasion a greater degree of external discipline too.'[17] (A case, I fear, of 'do what I say, not do what I do'.)

Second, 'there may indeed be a fundamentalist revolution in the West. This may not take the form of Christian fundamentalism – it is more likely to be driven by secular populism – but it could have the same effect: aggressive assertion by the majority of its values which are then imposed on the various minorities. Such a process could be benign: a grass roots movement where ordinary people revive their faith in the Protestant ethic of honesty, hard work and family values.'[18]

Well, there we have it. Like an Old Testament prophet and every revivalist preacher since, Hamish McRae urges us to recognize our sins and sin no more.

As a method of changing human behaviour the repentant sinner theory has shown itself throughout history to be quite ineffective. Repenting of sins has always been a popular pastime and backsliding even more so. The promise of heaven and the threat of hell have never ensured good behaviour, so the promise of a possible share in economic prosperity is hardly likely to entice us to change our wicked ways.

J. K. Galbraith's great clarity, wisdom and pertinent wit have provided me with good cheer for many years. Time and time again he has shown how self-interest conquers virtue, but he is always hopeful that enlightened self-interest will prove an adequate substitute for virtue, a hope which he makes explicit in his most recent book, *The Good Society*.[19] Here he defines not a perfect utopian society but one which could be achievable if only we chose to be wise. His definition is one with which I agree and so, I guess, would Will Hutton, Hamish McRae and Samuel Brittan.

> The essence of a good society . . . is that every member, regardless of gender, race or ethnic origin, should have access to a rewarding life. Allowance there must be for undoubted differences in aspiration and qualification. Individuals differ in physical and mental facility, commitment and purpose, and from these differences

> come differences in achievement and economic reward. This is accepted.
>
> In the good society, however, achievement may not be limited by factors which are remediable. There must be economic opportunity for all . . . And in the preparation for life, the young must have the physical care, the discipline, let no one doubt, and especially the education that will allow them to seize and exploit that opportunity. No one, from accident of birth or economic circumstance, may be denied these things; if they are not available from parent or family, society must provide effective forms of care and guidance.
>
> The role of economics in the good society is basic; economic determinism is a relentless force. The economic system in the good society must work well and for everyone. Only then opportunity will match aspiration, either great or small.
>
> Very specifically, the good society must have substantial and reliable economic growth – a substantial and reliable increase in production and employment from year to year.[20]

Such a good society 'must distinguish between enrichment that is socially permissible and benign and that which is at social cost'.[21] In Chapter 5 of this book I have elaborated on this distinction by contrasting what I have called intelligent trades and stupid trades.

J. K. Galbraith goes on to set out very succinctly what changes in society need to be made. Then he comes to how we can do this. Here he notes that

> Books of this mood and genre, as I have previously had occasion to suggest, almost always end on the same note. Having defined what is good and achievable, they assume that the necessary political response will follow, if not soon, then in time. People have an instinct, immediate or eventual, for what is right. Having specified this, the writer's task is done; action proceeds from there. It is this optimism that sustains the toil of thought and authorship.[22]

He allows himself 'no such fragile optimism'. Instead he notes that 'In the political turnover in the United States in the autumn of 1994, those opposing aid to the poor in its several forms won their stunning victory with the support of fewer than one quarter of all eligible voters, fewer than half of whom had gone to the polls.'[23] His solution to the problem of how to create the good society is that the poor should vote. 'Only when all vote – all but the eccentric few – will the good society achieve its urgent goals.'[24]

He notes that in Belgium and Australia voting is compulsory, but does not elaborate just what actually has happened in these countries. As I write the people of Belgium are amazed and enormously distressed to discover that a large group of murderous paedophiles have been operating in their midst with the passive and, in some cases, active connivance of the police force maintained by the negligence of the politicians.

Meanwhile, the Australians have trooped to the polls and elected a Federal Labor Government, first under Bob Hawke and then under Paul Keating, which gave great succour to a group of financial buccaneers without a moral scruple between them, and created the greatest division between the rich and the poor that that country had ever seen. Then the Australian voters, growing tired of Labor, elected the Liberals under John Howard. These Liberals, many of whom lack the wit to come in out of the rain, are pursuing policies which do nothing but deepen the divide between the rich and the poor.

The poor, whether they vote or not, have to think in their own short-term interests of 'Where is my next meal coming from?' They are possessed of no greater wisdom than the rich. I believe that everyone should be involved in politics, at the very least by knowing what is happening and by voting, but this alone is not enough to create the good society.

It was not until I began reading the writings of Samuel Brittan that I discovered that I was a methodological individualist. If ever Samuel Brittan should read this book he'll discover that he is a personal construct theorist. Different labels, similar ways of making sense of the world. Economics and psychology are not sciences, though they adhere (or should adhere) to scientific methods. They are, in Samuel Brittan's words, 'ways of looking at the world'.[25]

A personal construct theorist is concerned with how individuals make sense of what happens to them. A methodological individualist, Samuel Brittan explains, 'insists that any satisfactory explanation of the working of complex wholes must be capable of being expressed in terms of the actions of individual members. He or she will not be so foolish as to believe that in practice we can get along without convenient collective nouns referring to groups. But when there is acute controversy, tension, difficulty or ambiguity he will want to analyse what is being said by translating it into possible statements about individual men and women.'[26] In the emphasis of italics he wrote, '*but in the last analysis, even in the most embattled "them versus us" situations, it is individuals, not collectives, who feel, exult, triumph or despair. It is this which distinguishes individual people from trees and makes the individual person the ultimate end of political and moral discourse.*'[27]

Of course we are never individuals operating totally autonomously. We are always interacting with and responding to other people and our environment. We always think of ourselves as being an individual and being a member of different groups.

When our starting-point in economics or psychology is an examination of individual experience we can soon see that the meanings which individuals create are all moral judgements. The judgement might be narrowly selfish – 'good for me' – or altruistic – 'good for others'. If we look out of the window and judge that it is raining we include moral judgements like, 'Blast, I'll get wet,' or 'The farmers will be pleased'.

Samuel Brittan has pointed out that although 'more thoughtful economists have always known that markets need a background not only of formal laws, but of accepted rules of behaviour, if the invisible hand is to work,'[28] the relation between moral evaluation and economic analysis 'went underground in the heyday of the belief in economics as a purely technical guide to action; but it has now resurfaced.'[29]

There is never any shortage of people ready to claim that they are the keepers of society's conscience and that to be good we must all be unselfish. Often these moralists espouse the view that only a religious faith can engender such moral behaviour. Whenever I discover I am in the company of such a moralist I get very nervous lest the moralist suddenly suffers a loss of faith and falls to rape, murder and plunder. I suspect that Samuel Brittan feels the same. He writes, 'People in the grip of greed often do much less harm than people in the grip of self-righteousness, especially when that righteousness is harnessed to the supposed needs of a collectivity or given some theological or metaphysical justification.'[30]

'Moralists,' he points out, 'have long been upset by Adam Smith's invisible hand doctrine, epitomized by the well-known quotation: "It is not from the benevolence of the butcher, the brewer, or the baker that we expect our dinner, but from their regard of their own advantage." '[31] Where economic theory has always ended and where my brand of personal construct theory starts is in examining what meaning an individual gives to 'his own advantage'. An examination of any act which can be praised as being altruistic will reveal that the person has interpreted the situation along the lines of 'If I behave selfishly I shall be unable to live with my conscience,' or 'I am not the kind of person who behaves in mean, selfish ways,' or 'It is in my long-term interests to take other people's welfare into account.' This last interpretation is what Samuel Brittan, following Bertrand Russell, advocates as 'enlightened self-interest'.

I share his view. But what is enlightened self-interest?

There's no doubt we're in a perilous situation. The world economy is under no one's control, scientists agree that the climate is changing with the Greenhouse Effect, and the world's population is still increasing. Wars continue, land mines kill and maim thousands and prevent agriculture. The biggest growth industry is in illicit drugs. There's pollution, crime and starvation. No one, no matter how rich, is safe.

What's to be done? The advice we get from three of these well-read, well-informed, thoughtful, humane, intelligent specialists in economics is that the rich should be unselfish, the poor good and everyone vote.

Of course Will Hutton and Hamish McRae are quite right in advocating improvements in our morals. If we were all unselfish and honest our world would be a better place. But it's a waste of time telling people that they should be good. Advice and exhortation change no one.

Let's assume, for the sake of argument, that you and I are what Will Hutton calls amoral and that we have never adopted the Protestant ethic of honesty, hard work and family values (whatever they may be). This is a very wild assumption. No matter how wicked we are we all like to tell ourselves that we are highly moral and that we work hard. Nevertheless, let's assume that the veil of self-deception has slipped from our eyes. We see our wickedness and decide to change. It is possible to claim to be a better person and still go on doing what you've always been doing, but no one will believe that you are now a virtuous person. To become virtuous we have to change what we do. That is, we have to change how we order our priorities and make our decisions. No longer when we worry about money will we think about fiddling our taxes. Instead at the head of our priorities goes, 'I shall pay every penny I owe.' Now we check our change before we leave the shop in case we've been given too much and we seek out the bus conductor, no matter how crowded the bus may be, and pay our fare.

If it is true that the problems and suffering which beset us can be changed only if we change the way we order our priorities and make decisions, then our starting-point must be to understand the processes by which we order our priorities and make decisions. In short, we need to understand ourselves and thus arrive at an understanding of what are our long-term interests.

Unfortunately this is an area of study which has failed to excite the interest of most of those people who pontificate upon our plight. Understanding ourselves is a no-go area, ignored or dismissed as 'subjective' or of interest only to a certain type of woman and simple-minded men. Real men, like real intellectuals of all gender persuasions, have far more important things to think about than to wonder why they have certain priorities and make certain decisions. They would claim that their decisions are made on the grounds of logic and reason, but such an argument does not stand up to inspection. The decisions we make about money, whether our personal money or other people's money, whether in the world of international finance, or in politics and government, or in trade, or gambling, are often far from a logic and reason on which all people would agree. Rather, our decisions arise from a private logic hidden from others and often hidden from ourselves.

Our private logic is concerned with what is for each of us our top priority, the maintenance of ourselves as the person we know ourselves to be. This immediate need to maintain oneself as a person (what might be called personal pride) often takes precedence over what wisdom would see as one's long-term interests. Unfortunately, most of us act in this way without any awareness of what we are doing or any awareness that other people's actions are also determined by their need to survive as a person. We are capable of such awareness, and out of that awareness choosing more beneficial ways of behaving, but we rarely choose to exercise our capability. Alas, tertiary education and a high IQ are not contra-indications of such stupidity.

What follows here is my attempt to make a bridge between economics and an understanding of how we create meaning. I am not attempting to create my own economic theory, nor to offer a blueprint for the solution of all our problems. I want to show how the meanings we create, our own individual meanings, are fundamental to our economic life. I have read a great many analyses of what is wrong with various economies – of different countries and worldwide – and how the economy in question should be put right. I was struck by how little account is taken of a group of trades which occupy a major sector of the world's economy, thus affecting all of us and, one way or another, causing injury to many millions of people. These are the arms trade, the pharmaceutical industry's trade in mind-altering drugs, prostitution, pornography, slavery, the illegal drugs trade, and the money laundering which arises from this and other illegal activities. If we want to understand the role money plays in our lives these trades must be taken into account.

In the course of writing this book I talked to a great many people covering a wide spectrum. Only a few of them actually appear in the book, but I am very grateful to all those who talked to me so personally and/or introduced me to parts of the world of money which I had never encountered before. I have read incessantly about money in a wide variety of books, magazines and newspapers, but my constant companions over the last four years have been the *Economist* and the *Guardian* which between them cover a wide range of opinion. I have a special debt to two friends, Andy Beven and Toby Raymond, who helped me in the writing of this book. Each of them in his own way is involved in the money market, but each, one a writer and one with a passion for the theatre, is concerned with how we live in this world.

Understanding money is a matter of understanding ourselves.

1

The Logic of the Illogical

If everything on earth were rational, nothing would happen.

Dostoevsky[1]

The love of money, so Saint Paul told Timothy, is the root of all evil. If this is true then most of us are evil because most of us do love money.

Not that we love money in the way that we love our family and friends, or beauty or music, or winning a game, or feeling confident, or being loved, or driving a great car, or enjoying a splendid meal. Each of these loves is different, a special kind of love. Some people love money just for itself but most of us love money for what it can get us, be that the satisfaction of our needs, the envy of those who covet our power and wealth, or the pleasure of making other people happy.

What I've just said is quite banal. Everyone knows that we love, or at least like, money because money gets us what we want. It may not buy happiness but it can assuage the pain of unhappiness. What is contradictory is that we would all say that everyone loves money when we are speaking generally about people at large, but we would not say it in particular about ourselves. We would not set out in detail how much money we had, what we did with our money and what fantasies we had developed about getting and spending money. Where money is concerned most of us are very secretive.

From what I have read it seems that people have always been secretive about money. The code of manners in Victorian times forbade any discussion of money within the home,[2] which must have created as many problems as the Victorian's secretiveness about sex.

Now we live in an era when we encourage one another to be open about relationships. Every day someone offers to share their thoughts and feelings with me! Back in the early sixties my dear friend Warwick was thought to be a little eccentric because he would greet a friend whom he had not seen for a while with, 'Who are you fucking now?' He always asked with such genuine concern for your welfare that you could not possibly take offence. Warwick must have been ahead of his time, for now his question is commonplace amongst friends and acquaintances.

Yet do we, when we're greeting friends, ask, 'What are you earning now?' or 'How much is your mortgage?' No, we don't. Money matters are secret.

Why?

I put this question to many of the people I interviewed. They gave lots of reasons and all very true. I shall discuss these later in this book. However, no one gave the reason which is part of the theme of this book.

One of the reasons we are secretive about our own money is that we want to present ourselves to the world as being very sensible and rational about money, but in fact we are not. Or rather, what we do about money relates not so much to what is called logical, scientific thinking but to the logic of our own individual structure of meaning. This meaning structure is an interrelation of the beliefs, attitudes, conclusions and expectations which has developed out of our experiences since the time we were conceived. It is your meaning structure which makes sense of what you encounter and which decides upon your future action. No two meaning structures are ever identical. That is, each of us is an individual.

Your individual structure uses the kind of logical, scientific thinking which everyone knows only in so far as it suits your purposes. Private logic makes your decision.

Suppose, for example, you've been living in rented accommodation for the first ten years of your working life and you've now reached a point where you're earning good money and have some savings. The financial consultant at your bank advises you to take out a mortgage and buy a home. His arguments are eminently logical and sensible. However, one of your abiding memories from childhood is of you and your family being evicted from your home after your father became ill and fell behind with his mortgage payments. It is an intensely painful memory. As a child you drew from this experience the conclusion that you would never put yourself in your father's position. You would never have a mortgage.

You don't tell your financial adviser this because you know he'll pooh-pooh your fears. He'll say that times have changed, your financial situation is different from what your father's was, and so on. You know all this. What you have to work out is whether you can ignore your private logic which creates in you such foreboding, or whether you must let your private logic prevail.

The method you use in resolving this dilemma is something which every salesperson in the world wants to discover. Every sales director, every marketing manager, every advertising and public relations consultant, every banker, every financier, every trader on the financial and commodity markets, and every owner of a corner shop wants to find out how people make decisions about money. Many frustrated economists and money traders have tried ignoring all these private decisions and have developed theories about the economy and the markets which disregard the reality that we buy, sell and save according to our own private logic. Such theories fail to work in practice, the fate of all theories which ignore reality. Some economists and money market traders are now trying to develop theories which incorporate this private logic. I hope they will find this book useful, but I should warn them about trying to incorporate real people into theories. People ruin theories. They never conform to what the theorist wants.

Everyone is a theorist. Our meaning structure is busy creating theories about everything it encounters. We talk publicly about some of our theories but other theories we keep private.

Everyone has a theory about politics and few of us hesitate to present our theory even though we might in doing so reveal our complete ignorance of political matters. Everyone has a theory about how money operates, but we are much more circumspect about presenting this theory in case we reveal our ignorance of complex financial matters. We are prepared to hazard some statements about what the government should do, but this is always in terms of what is in our interests. People who see themselves as being badly off favour increased taxes on the rich while those who want to hang on to what they've got and who are not dependent on help from the government favour reductions in public spending. However, while we are all prepared to air our views about the relative merits of capitalism and socialism, few of us would do the same about monetarism and Keynesian economics. Most of us like to think that economics and high finance are matters which only a certain kind of intelligent person could understand. Such people look after the business of money and are, we hope, looking after our interests.

What little we used to know about economics and high finance we picked up in the course of studying British history, as summarized by Sellar and Yeatman in their 1930 treatise, still in print today, *1066 and All That*. They explained how

> It was William and Mary who first discovered the National Debt and had the memorable idea of building the Bank of England to put it in. The National Debt is a very Good Thing and it would be dangerous to pay it off, for fear of Political Economy.[3]

However, our views started to change when the events of the late eighties and the early nineties suggested that perhaps these intelligent people who were supposed to understand money didn't know what they were doing. The blessings of monetarism were not arriving as predicted. Live television coverage of the events of Black Wednesday, 16 September 1992, when the pound was forced out of the Exchange Rate Mechanism, showed a worried Chancellor of the Exchequer, Norman Lamont, scuttling past the rubbish bins outside the Treasury while the Prime Minister, John Major, hid at Number Ten. Power seemed to reside in the hands of tense, perspiring young men clutching telephones and yelling. No wonder many of us decided that we should stop trusting the experts and instead learn something about how money operates. We might not be able to make ourselves safe but at least when the blow came we would know why.

Writing at the time of the 1992 currency crisis the financial journalist Ben Laurance described the change in attitudes to money.

> Fifteen years ago (money's) place in the public consciousness was confined to pay packets and a particularly awful song by Abba. Now, anyone who seriously aspires to be part of the chattering classes has to be financially literate. The ugly argot of economists – PSBR, ERM, DM – has, as it were, become common currency.
>
> The change within no more than a generation is astonishing. One has a vague recollection from the 1960s: one's parents were shocked to learn that the couple up the road were borrowing a huge amount of money (a thousand or so) to buy a house. This bordered on delinquency.
>
> Harold Wilson appeared in glorious 405-line black and white on the screen of the second-hand Murphy television perched on the sideboard to lecture us about the pound in our pockets. Folk either nodded sagely or simply kept quiet. They certainly didn't scoff. They couldn't. They lacked the scalpels of economic analysis which their offspring, less than 25 years later, felt they could wield with such confidence.[4]

Tim Gardam, head of weekly current affairs programmes on BBC radio and television, described how journalism changed.

> From the late seventies, it wasn't possible to cover politics properly if you weren't economically literate. A lot of us weren't. From that moment, a generation of TV journalists lost their edge. Oxford Union repartee couldn't cope with supply-side economics and the PSBR. It cut through the clubbiness, the sense that politics was just about personalities.[5]

With the privatization of public utilities people who'd never given share owning a second thought learned how to buy and sell shares. By 1987 all the tabloid newspapers, including the *Sun*, were running a City page and lists of share prices. Money was news.

Changes just as great occurred in the one country where people were long used to owning shares. In the *New York Times* Thomas L. Friedman explained that whether the dollar is up or down, it's always bad news.

> The dollar story is the ultimate investor Rorschach test: How you interpret it depends entirely on where your money is.
>
> But what's new today is how many more people find themselves

reading those inkblots. The dollar story used to be read by exporters, Wall Street types and tourists about to go to Europe who wanted to know whether they would get a bargain on Lacoste shirts in Spain.

No more. Millions of Americans are now invested in global stock and bond markets, either directly or through their pension funds and mutual funds; this is where the highest yields are now. But fluctuations in the dollar exchange rate affect their portfolios every day. 'During the cold war, when there was a disturbance somewhere, the first question that people asked was: "Are we going to send troops?" said a top Clinton economic adviser. 'Today the first question is: "How is an invasion of Haiti going to affect my Argentine bond fund?"'[6]

Politicians now felt that they had to explain money matters to the public. Not that that meant telling the public the truth. When Kenneth Clarke as Chancellor of the Exchequer went on television[7] to explain that day's rise in interest rates, he warned of the dread disasters. His and his hand alone kept the ravening beast inflation in his iron grasp. This is a delusion of grandeur, as Will Hutton would be the first to tell him.

> Inflation has fallen world wide[8], and Britain's performance has only improved marginally against the average; nor is it clear that the improvement can be sustained if the country's economic weakness provokes an inflationary fall in the value of sterling. Low inflation is earned through economic strength; that is not the British position.[9]

Britain's manufacturing industry might be small and ailing but a whole new industry has been created, that of television economic punditry. These are the experts who can be seen day and night on the box telling us what the world economy is going to do. They tell us how inflation will go up, or perhaps down. The Bundesbank will put interest rates up – some time. Share prices will go up, or they mightn't. Some of their cold-hearted colleagues keep a tally of their successful predictions, and always come up with the same score – no better than chance. If you're planning to make a killing on the stock market, you might as well have your own theory about the future or toss a coin. These experts are always ready to create predictions on inadequate evidence, so why don't you? After all, the best prediction economic experts can ever come up with is to say just before the mob of investors makes a move, which way they'll run.

The mob move when they're frightened. The market turns on fear. Traders in the money markets know this. Of recent years some traders have been experimenting with using the theories of chaos and neural learning as predictors of the market. These theories are far more applicable to human behaviour driven by fear than are traditional statistics. However, few traders, if any, are aware of just what this fear is that drives the market and how it is the deciding factor, not just in the decisions we make about money but every decision we make because it relates to the operation of a person's private logic. If you want to find out why a person does what he does, find out what he fears the most.

Fear breeds insecurity, and insecure people try to make themselves secure. This is why money was invented, and then bills, cheques, insurance, pensions and now derivatives. Whether derivatives will save the world economy or destroy it has been fiercely argued in money centres all around the world. Why is it that every attempt to make ourselves more secure with regard to money results in greater insecurity? Are we being illogical and irrational when we try to make ourselves perfectly secure?

In the early eighties, like many other people, I was writing about the threat of nuclear war and of the industrial pollution which was fast rendering the planet incapable of sustaining human life.[10] Since then, and despite many valiant efforts by some brave people, matters have only got worse. The vast industries of the arms trade and drug trafficking have skewed the world economy, possibly beyond repair. The people in power who might have prevented this happening have failed to do so. Will Hutton describes such behaviour as amoral.[11] I call it stupid.

Did you know that cockroaches are impervious to radiation? Now it's been found that rats are much more resistant to pollution than are humans. What should we call a species which makes the world safe for rats and cockroaches? 'Logical' and 'rational' hardly spring to mind. Yet, as Dostoyevsky pointed out, it's the illogical, the irrational which makes things happen. This seems to have been a part of the functioning of the universe right from the beginning. The Big Bang burst, going from zero to infinity (or near-infinity) in an instant. What physicists now know is that, if that occurrence had been without aberration, space-time would be so smooth and featureless that no galaxies, no stars, no earth and no people could have ever evolved. There must have been tiny imperfections at that initial fraction of a second which created 'wrinkles' or ripples in space-time and out of these evolved the universe we know today.[12]

Perhaps we shouldn't call illogical, irrational behaviour 'amoral' or 'stupid' but try instead to understand the private logic which informs and determines what each of us do. Aristotelian, scientific logic is just one form of logic, albeit a logic of paramount importance. However, there are other logics, often ones where A can simultaneously be not-A. As Kevin Jackson, in the introduction to his *Oxford Book of Money*, noted,

> It is honourable to earn one's living; it is venal to make money the sole object of work. Artistic labour done without a view to money is an indulgence; artistic labour done for money is hack-work, and so on. 'Inconsistencies,' says the sage Imlac in Johnson's moral tale *Rasselas*, 'cannot both be right, but, imputed to man, they may both be true.'[13]

When we use public logic publicly we can be called to account if we break any of the rules of Aristotelian logic and scientific method. Our private logics are not only private but within them, while we can use the rules of public logic, we can make use of some very different rules.

Aristotelian logic states very firmly that if something is something it cannot simultaneously be its opposite. A cannot be not-A. In private logic A and not-A exist together. This arises from the fact that we cannot perceive anything unless that thing stands in some contrast to something else. If we lived in a world where nothing and nobody ever died we would not know that we were alive. If we lived in a world where everybody always behaved in a friendly manner we would have no word for 'friend' because we would lack the concept 'enemy'. To know anything you must know its opposite. So our private logic is full of examples of the simultaneous existence of opposites. After all, who can you hate more than those you love!

Aristotelian logic makes a firm distinction between identity and similarity. The fact that two things are similar does not mean they are the same. Whereas in private logic similarity is often seen as identity. If you see your boss as being just like your father you can well respond to your boss as you did to your father.

Aristotelian logic and scientific method have to be expounded in language, either in words and sentences or in mathematics. Private logic can operate in words and sentences but it often operates in images. These might be pictures, or sounds, or bodily feelings such as being sick in your stomach every time your boss/father raises his voice. Much of the process of therapy, or of simply trying to be clear in your own mind about what you think and feel, is the process of turning images into sentences. (I say 'sentences' rather than 'words' because words relate only to individual objects whereas linguistic meaning is found in sentences.[14])

In public logic there is supposed to be a consistency across the whole body of what is being argued. Each of our individual private logics is one indivisible whole, but we can perform a number of private operations so as to delude ourselves that we have a split in our private logic and that one thing can be argued in one place and another in another. Many people believe that they can split emotions from thought or sexual interests from all other interests.[15] Only a small part of private logic is conscious at any one time, so the rest of the private logic is considered to be forgotten. People differ greatly in what they forget and what they remember.[16]

Of course, public and private logics do not operate separately from one another. The exercise of public logic takes place in the space occupied by private logic – our brains. We can be trying to think in terms of public logic and rationality, but our private logic often interferes. A simple example of such an interference is how being happy or being sad interferes with thinking through different kinds of tasks. When you're happy you perform well on creative tasks calling for a flow of divergent ideas but you'll do less well on analytic tasks. When you're miserable the opposite applies.[17] So cheer yourself up before a brain-storming session and make yourself miserable before doing your tax return.

Private logics differ in their degree of flexibility and openness to change. Many of these private logics turn on beliefs that allow no modifications. Many politicians and journalists would have us believe that whenever something goes wrong with the market it's always the fault of the Bundesbank. Many of these logics turn on magic. There's the talisman in the pocket, the putting of the right shoe on before the left, the special, private prayer.

All these private logics turn on pride. When Marty Schartz, a very successful Market Wizard, was asked, 'Why do most traders lose money?' he said,

> Because they would rather lose money than admit they're wrong. What is the ultimate rationalization of a trader in a losing position? 'I'll get out when I'm even.' Why is getting out even so important? Because it protects the ego. I became a winning trader when I was able to say, 'To hell with my ego, making money is more important.'[18]

So, if you want to understand how money functions you need to understand the logic of the illogical.

2

What Does Money Mean?

> If everyone forgot what money was, there wouldn't be any money any more; there would be stacks of engraved paper slips, embossed metal disks, computerised records of account balances, granite and marble buildings – but no money: no inflation or deflation or exchange rates or interest – or monetary value. The very property of those variously engraved slips of paper that explains – as nothing else could – their trajectories from hand to hand in the wake of various deeds and exchanges would evaporate.
>
> Daniel Dennett[1]

Money means a great deal to every one of us. We're not likely to forget what it is.

We work for it, we think about it, we worry about it, we dream about it, we want more of it. We spend it, we hoard it, we give it away.

We scheme, lie, even kill for it.

Some people say they think nothing of money, but they don't say that when they're homeless or starving. When people have got money they might despise it so they can feel virtuous, and feeling virtuous can be as important to us as being greedy.

Money is power. Money is comfort, security, contentment, freedom, just as it is imprisonment, filth, disgust and degradation.

Money binds us together and splits us apart. It is a golden thread that knits us together, tentacles that strangle us, an explosive force that blasts us apart. It is as common as dust and stranger than a will o' the wisp.

We recognize money but we don't know what it means. We, alone of all the animal species, use money, but we don't understand it. How could we, when money has for us so many different meanings?

Only human beings know about money. We invented it. Moreover, only human beings can recognize money when we see it. Fish once swimming in tropical seas didn't realize that cowrie shells were money. Rabbits burrowing into a hillock didn't recognize that the rocks with a yellow glint are money. The rats which gnawed the paper under the bed of Sheikh Shakhbut, the ruler of Abu Dhabi who was deposed in 1966, didn't know that they were working their way through two million dollars' worth of banknotes.[2] The city pigeons who tap their beaks on stockbrokers' windows don't know that the changing patterns on the screens in the room represent millions of pounds, dollars, francs, yen and marks. Only human beings are intelligent enough to know about money.

So how is it that we know that that bit of paper is good only for lighting the fire while this bit of paper will pay your gas bill? How do we know that that bit of rock is good only for throwing, whereas this bit will buy you several jet fighters? How do we know that those figures on your computer screen mean that your hard disk has just crashed while those figures mean that you've just made yourself a million dollars?

Is it because we with our exceptional intelligence have the power to divine the true essence of objects, and so we know that some objects are, in their very essence, money while others are not? After all, many philosophers have argued that everything that exists has an appearance, which is not real, and an essence or perfect form which is real. Have we the ability to perceive the real, at least where money is concerned?

Would that it were so! Then we would have something firm, solid and real on which to base our transactions. Every object for sale, every piece of work would have a real price. Friends might betray us, our health may fail us, but where money was concerned we would know where we stood.

If only life were like that!

Instead, as Benjamin Franklin said, the only things we can be certain of are death and taxes, and even with death and taxes there are uncertainties. With death the questions are When and How, but with taxes the terrible question is always, 'How much?' To that question comes a wide range of answers.

Why is this so?

It is because cowrie shells, lumps of metal, bits of paper and numbers on a computer screen do not have an essential, immutable value. All they have are the values we choose to give them, and we are always changing our minds. We call some objects money one day and another day we say they are not. Something else is money and the first set of objects is worthless. How many two bobs are you still keeping in the hope that one day the Bank of England will announce that they are again legal tender? Do you even remember what a two bob was?[3]

We can decide that an object in one situation is very valuable and in another situation it is not. At the time I am writing this £100 will get you a night's accommodation in a very ordinary hotel in London but in Sydney it will buy you the best room with a harbour view in a posh hotel. By the time you're reading this these two situations could have been reversed.

Even worse, people don't agree on what money itself is worth. In Moscow the banks will give you one amount of roubles for your ten-dollar bill, but around the corner, down the lane you'll be offered many more.

The sad truth is that money means what we want it to mean but that each of us has our own idea of what money means, and no two of us agree on a meaning. You think that your house is worth £225,000 while I think it's worth £175,000. You sell me your house for £200,000, a compromise which leaves both of us feeling cheated.

If money is no more than the meanings we create and if financial exchanges are compromises between different meanings, it is impossible for money to provide us with a secure basis on which to order our lives. Buying and selling will always be a chancy business.

Why don't we change this? Instead of having all these different meanings for money relating to different people and different situations, why don't we construct some absolute rules and values which will exist outside our personal situations and our needs and wishes?

These rules and values could be like those rules and values called absolute truths which, so some people believe, lie outside the realm of lived human experience but which influence it directly. Some people believe that the statement 'God exists' is an absolute truth. Others believe that 'My country is the best country in the world' is an absolute truth. Many men believe that 'Life is all about competing and winning' is an absolute truth.

Absolute truths are very different from relative truths where rules and values are different in different situations and mean different things to different people. According to the journalist Michael Lewis, many Americans believe that the meanings they give to money are absolute truths.

> If you really want to get under someone's skin you write about what he's carrying in his wallet. You can write a thousand editorials in praise of nuclear holocaust and you won't receive as many hysterical letters from readers as when you write the piece arguing that all good citizens should tear up their American Express cards. Or fire their favourite stockbrokers. Or chuck their most cherished get-rich-quick schemes into the waste basket where they belong. Americans, unique in their tendency to confuse personal finance with matters of faith, grow especially heated on the subject.[4]

If there can be absolute truths about money, why can't politicians, bankers and financiers get together and devise some absolute standards for money? Why can't money be reliable, consistent and unchanging?

In those centuries when the control of the currency was the prerogative of the king few monarchs could resist tampering with it in order to fund their favourite projects like building palaces and waging wars. The king owned the mint and could order other metals to be mixed with gold or silver, thus debasing the coinage. Inflation followed with its attendant miseries. Henry VIII should be remembered not so much for his six wives as for the million-pound profit he made out of his debasement of the currency.

Henry VIII, like monarchs before and after him until the unfortunate Charles I who lost his head, laid claim to the Divine Right of Kings. Monarchs were appointed by God and so if they fiddled the currency no subject could complain. When in 1695 the philosopher

John Locke recommended that the currency should be so organized that it had an enduring value, the sheer novelty of this idea caused considerable interest. In 1717 Sir Isaac Newton established the Gold Standard by defining the gold value of the pound and the monarch became no more than the keeper of the weights and measures.

The Bank of England maintained a strict relationship between the notes in circulation and the money in its vaults until 1797 when Britain went to war against revolutionary France. During a war governments try to hang on to their precious metals while individuals interested in personal, not national, survival try to move them to a safe haven. When Napoleon had been vanquished and the French monarchy restored, Britain returned to the Gold Standard.

By 1880 all the major countries of the world had adopted the Gold Standard which did keep the value of money fairly stable until 1914 and the outbreak of the First World War. However, a stable value for money did not mean a stable economy. Boom followed bust and bust followed boom. And who bore the brunt of these economic cycles? The poor, the politically disenfranchised. The Gold Standard did not produce universal prosperity.

Between 1880 and 1914 the bankers in charge of the central banks in each country created a special fraternity, a kind of international old boys' network, helping each other in time of need. Like most people who find themselves in positions of power, they assumed that being powerful necessarily implies being especially wise. By 1918 the governor of the Bank of England, Montagu Norman, felt that his special wisdom led him to the conclusion that the only way forward was for the central banks to separate from the state and become autonomous, thus ruling the financial markets. As the Bank of England was then the most important of the central banks, Montagu Norman would become the world's most powerful person. He had no doubt that he knew what was best for all of us.

Not surprisingly the various governments were not prepared to give their central banks such power. However, these banks did have the power to affect international finance. An intervention by the US Federal Reserve Bank in 1929 precipitated the greatest stock market crash in US history.

Not that this brought an end to the Gold Standard.

Here was the point where for me history became lived experience. I must have first heard the words 'Gold Standard' when I was a babe in my father's arms. He soon made quite clear to me that Montagu Norman was far more wicked than the devil. My father would describe to me in tones of great derision how gold was dug out of one hole and dropped down another, the one under Fort Knox where the US government stored its gold. Meanwhile barges loaded with fresh fruit were towed down Sydney Harbour and the fruit dumped at sea, in Happy Valley near my home people lived in humpies made from hemp sacks, and my aunts told me how lucky I was because my father had a job.

The numbers of those who remember the Great Depression are steadily decreasing, but the photographs and films of that time are often seen by younger generations and must reinforce the fear that so many people have of unemployment. In the thirties the unemployed numbered some 14 million in the USA, 6 million in Germany, 3 million in the UK. In Australia the rate was higher than that in the USA and the UK. In each country people were supposed to fend for themselves with little help from the government, and the suffering was immense. Such extremes of experience produce extremes of reaction. Erstwhile peaceful, obedient citizens went on hunger marches, and political parties of the extreme right and the extreme left emerged, making the Second World War inevitable.

The miseries of the Great Depression continued while Montagu Norman stuck to the Gold Standard. He was one of those people whose private logic could not admit of a mistake. Whenever we admit we've made a mistake we're admitting that our private logic has got it wrong. Then we can't help thinking, 'If I was wrong in that I could be wrong in everything else,' and that idea is very scary. People who can never admit that they are wrong are frightened people who cannot or will not find the courage to confront the source of their fear, which is usually that someone will discover how worthless and useless they really are. Instead they go on trying to force the world to be what they want it to be, and in the course of such futile attempts inflict great misery on others. Later in life Montagu Norman became increasingly paranoid, the logical outcome for reasoning which will admit of no mistake. If you insist that you cannot possibly be wrong in any respect yet the world refuses to conform to your ideas, you can only draw the conclusion that you have enemies who are conspiring against you. Thus being too frightened to admit that you have made a mistake leads you to become increasingly frightened of the world around you. Still, being paranoid does have one advantage. It means that no matter how alone you might be, someone, somewhere is thinking of you.

After September 1939 the miseries of the Great Depression changed into the miseries of the Second World War. Soon we were being told that after the war all the ills of society would be cured. No more poverty. No more ill health. An economically secure world. Plans would be drawn up to create all this.

The United Nations Monetary and Financial Conference, known as the Bretton Woods Conference, took place in July 1944. Representatives of 44 nations attended, but the driving force of the conference was the band of economists, the brightest and the best, headed by John Maynard Keynes from the UK and Harry White from the USA. Argue though they might, they did not doubt their ability to plan a better world. They, of course, were experts, and experts in the various professions, in my experience, are always expert in using the most reliable defence available to private logic, that of intellectualization. This defence depends on minimizing the significance of human waywardness and maximizing public logic and reason even when such logic and reason might have few underpinnings in reality.

> The Bretton Woods designers began with a cracked world and painted on it their own hyperrational construction, abstracted from the messy unreasonableness of ordinary living . . . they really wanted their machine to work. Their plan had no technical flaws. Unfortunately the world had many.[5]

The Bretton Woods Conference attempted to create an international currency regime maintaining more or less stable exchange rates between currencies. Such a system did not produce the full employment, price stability and free trade the conference had hoped for and was broken by all the speculation in the markets after the oil price rises in 1973.

Over recent years the desire for a stable currency has expressed itself in the need to control inflation. Certainly the inflation of prices and the corresponding devaluation of the currency cause tremendous uncertainty and the loss of hard-worked-for gains. Changes in the prices of ordinary commodities over the past five decades are hard to believe unless you were there. In my first year at university in 1948 I was shocked by a friend's scandalous extravagance when she told me she had paid *two pounds* for a pair of shoes. It is sensible that we have a system which keeps prices and the value of money within certain limits. However, the pain that is inflicted when a government decides to control inflation is not evenly spread across the whole population. Australians were told that the needs of the economy were paramount. Michael Leunig showed what many Australians felt in his cartoon.[6]

The idea that money could be made to be totally reliable, consistent and unchanging contains two major errors.

The first error is the belief that things can stay the same. Nothing stays the same. We are part of a universe where everything is moving and changing all the time. We might like to think that institutions and ideas stay the same, but they do not. The institutions of the Church and of Royalty in the 1990s are very different from those institutions in the 1590s or even in the 1930s. Ideas like 'socialism' or 'free trade' have different meanings for different generations. Not even scientific laws are absolute and unchanging. Our vast technologies developed using scientific laws which are always approximate in their applications. As Einstein explained,

> As far as the laws of mathematics refer to reality, they are not certain; and as far as they are certain, they do not refer to reality.[7]

The second error lies in the belief that there are, or could be, absolute truths and absolute values which, omnipresent and eternal, lie outside human lived existence, impervious to human interference but nevertheless able to influence our lives.

Perhaps there are some absolute truths and values and perhaps we sometimes bump into them, but if we do we cannot know for certain that they are absolute. We do not possess the capacity for such knowledge. Of course there are many people who claim to be in possession of an absolute truth, but examination shows that there are as many different absolute truths as there are people claiming to know them. Every religion lays claim to a clutch of absolute truths. The faithful of different persuasions go into battle with the cry, 'Mine is an Absolute Truth. Yours is a lie!', but all this activity simply suggests that the beliefs that are held are not absolute truths at all, just the different answers that people have devised for the questions that life poses for each of us.

The answers we give to life's questions are part of what Xenophanes, the ancient Greek philosopher, called 'a woven web of guesses'.

> The gods did not reveal, from the beginning,
> All things to us; but in the course of time,
> Through seeking we may learn, and know things better.
>
> But as for certain truth, no man has known it,
> Nor will he know it; neither of the gods,
> Nor yet of the things of which I speak.

And even if by chance he were to utter
The final truth, he would himself not know it;
For all is but a woven web of guesses.[8]

Being a human being means that, although we are part of everything that exists, we do not have the kind of sensory perception which allows us to perceive the reality of which we are part. All we are able to do is to construct a model which to some greater or lesser degree may represent the reality which lies beyond the reach of our receptors. What we perceive of the world and ourselves is what we've learned to perceive. As Oliver Sacks said, 'We are not given the world: we make our world through incessant experience, categorization, memory, reconnection.'[9]

Frequently I am called upon to talk about such an understanding of ourselves to groups of people, many of whom would regard themselves as well educated. I find that very few people, educated or not, have sufficient knowledge of their own physiology to understand how everything they perceive and know is what they have learned to perceive and know. It is possible, so I have discovered, to be medically qualified and to practise as a general practitioner or psychiatrist and be unaware of what research in our physiological makeup has revealed.

Some people, ignorant of physiology but not philosophy, assume that I am dogmatically taking one side in an old argument. From the time of the ancient Greeks there have been metaphysical philosophers, who believe that we can have knowledge which isn't derived from sensory experience, and empiricist philosophers, who believe that all knowledge comes from observation and measurement. The metaphysical philosophers have claimed that it is possible to make discoveries about the world, not by observation but simply by thinking. Thus Plato considered vision to be a result, not of light entering the eye, but of particles shot out of the eyes. It seems never to have occurred to Plato to do a few simple experiments to check his hypothesis.

The trouble with experiments is that they can ruin the greatest theories. Plato and many of the philosophers who followed him preferred to claim to have the power to discover the truth by thought alone because then they could claim to be in possession of some great absolute truth. The empiricist philosophers of Plato's time, the Sophists, lost the propaganda war which Plato and his followers waged against them. Thus philosophy students study Plato, not Xenophanes, and, lacking a scientific education, are unaware that the arguments between the metaphysicians and the empiricists is now as relevant as the argument over whether the world is round or flat. Not that this advance in our scientific knowledge has silenced the metaphysical philosophers, theologians and politicians. From their pronouncements it can be seen that the forces of unreason are still alive and well and preventing us from understanding ourselves and thus becoming the wondrously clever and successful people we all could be.

If you're unaware that Xenophanes was right, read Oliver Sacks, or Susan Greenfield's *Journey to the Centers of the Mind*,[10] or Richard Gregory's *Eye and Brain*, where he wrote,

> The senses do not give us a picture of the world directly; rather they provide evidence for the checking of hypotheses about what lies before us. Indeed, we may say that the perception of an object *is* an hypothesis, suggested and tested by sensory data . . . When a perceptual hypothesis – a perception – is wrong we are misled, as we are misled in science when we see the world distorted by a false theory. Perceiving and thinking are not independent.[11]

What we make is not an accurate picture of the world but a set of interpretations, 'a woven web of guesses'. If we do not test our theories about life against what is actually happening we are soon misled.

The results of our interpretations can show us how accurate they were. For example, because our visual sensory equipment is responsive to only a small portion of the electromagnetic spectrum, that which we call light, when you walk down the stairs in the dark you have to guess when the next step you take will reach the floor. If you're right you'll proceed smoothly, but, if you're wrong, at the following step you'll stumble or fall. On the other hand, you can misinterpret the evidence you are given. For instance, you might believe that you are a superb manager and that all your staff love you and admire you. Actually your staff neither love nor admire you. You interpret their smiling obedience as evidence of their affection when all they care about is keeping their jobs. At Christmas time you might be puzzled why the staff party is arranged at a time when the staff know you cannot attend. It can be inconceivable to you that the world is not what it seems.

Those people who have learnt about philosophy but not about physiology tend to criticize people like me by saying that we claim that all the alternative constructions of reality are equally good. Such critics are speaking from the depths of their ignorance. The fact that different people create different interpretations does not mean that all interpretations are equally good. If you create interpretations without careful observation and thought, if your interpretations arise solely from your desires and fantasies, if you do not try to get as close as possible to the reality you cannot reach directly, your interpretations will get more and more out of touch with that reality and disasters will follow as night the day.

We create our interpretations out of our past experiences, and since no two people have exactly the same experiences no two people create exactly the same interpretations. (Even identical twins do not have the same experiences. They occupy different positions in the womb, they are born one after the other, and from the moment of

SUBTITLES: SILVER LININGS

David Austin

birth they see the world from a different perspective and are treated differently by other people.)

Communicating with other people is possible only when our methods for forming interpretations are similar to those of another person, when we see things in much the same way. Thus, amongst those of us who speak English mutual understanding can be quite good with statements like 'Half a dozen Grade 3 free-range eggs cost eighty-six pence'. Statements like 'The Abbey National is offering a fixed-rate mortgage', 'The Bundesbank has cut the Lombard rate by half a per cent', 'The dollar fell sharply against leading currencies', 'The Footsie jumped more than 100 points to reach its intra-day peak of 3115', and 'I'm interested in an IBM April 130 call' do not command a universal understanding.

The meaning of each of these statements could be discovered by recourse to dictionaries and reference books, but, no matter how precise the definition of terms may be, no one explanation could capture all the meaning which a particular statement has for the person who utters it and for the person who hears it. To the degree to which the two people share meanings they can communicate, but it is the private meaning which each person holds which determines what that person does. For instance, you, as a building society salesperson, might see your company's offer of a fixed-rate mortgage as the best offer I could get, but I might be wondering whether I would even buy a used car from you.

If you and I were discussing the merits of a film we had seen we might be prepared to reveal some of our most private thoughts – how much we fancied one of the actors or how we can't stand the sight of blood. But when we're talking about money we keep our private thoughts to ourselves. Revealing the private meanings we give to money renders us vulnerable. If you reveal that you don't think I'm intelligent enough to understand the implications of variable interest rates and I reveal that I don't trust you where money is concerned, we'll both be offended.

Moreover, we might not want to scrutinize our private meanings too closely for fear we see something we don't want to see. You might pride yourself on being a good judge of character, particularly in relation to financial matters, and so you ignore the substantial evidence which shows that you are not, while I might like to think of myself as being an amazingly tolerant and generous person, but actually I regard anyone who tries to sell me something as a crook.

Nevertheless, you believe that, in dealing with money, you are sensible and rational. Similarly I believe that I am sensible and rational.

And so do the Chancellor of the Exchequer, the President of France, the Prime Minister of Australia, the President of the Federal Reserve Bank of the USA, the executives of every business great and small, every economist, every financial journalist, every market trader, and everyone who has to handle money. Even those people who say, 'I'm a fool with money' believe that their way is the best way to handle money. They secretly despise people who are 'good with money'.

We couldn't be more wrong. We think that we are being logical and sensible about money and so we are, but the logic we are using is not the Aristotelian logic which everyone can agree is sensible and realistic. Instead we are using our own private logic, a logic which is always logical to the individual but rarely to other people. We use our private logic in order to survive not just as a physical body but as the person we know ourselves to be.

Money and Survival

We all like to think of ourselves as being sensible with money. Just what 'sensible' means depends on the individual using the word.

Some people think it is sensible to make money the central focus of all their planning. They build their life around getting and spending money. Others push money to the periphery of their lives and concentrate instead on their relationships or on art or science or technology or simply on doing nothing. Some people always know to the last penny what money they have, while others never know what their debts and credits are. Some people always pay their Visa account within the month, while others consistently pay a small fortune in interest charges. Some people like to give their money away to friends or charities, while others like to hoard it. For some people money is real only when it is turned into possessions, while for others real money is the bottom line of their bank statement. Nevertheless, no matter how great the variety of ways in which people deal with money, everybody is using money for the same purpose.

We all use our money in order to survive.

Obviously we use our money to keep ourselves alive. We buy food and shelter and protect ourselves from harm. But there is another form of survival, and one equally or even more important to us. We want to survive as a physical body and we want to survive as a person.

We all talk about being a person, having an identity, a self, and we know that 'myself as an identity, a person' is tremendously important to us even if not to anyone else. To understand why this is so it is necessary to understand how this sense of being a person comes about. It arises from how we are constructed physiologically.

No doubt while you are reading this it seems to you that this book and your surrounds are outside you. You might possibly be thinking that you are taking an objective view of this book and its contents. But this is not what is really happening. Your brain is playing a trick on you.

> The problem is that human beings cannot obtain an objective view of the universe. Everything we experience is mediated by our brains. Even our vivid impression that the world is 'out there' is a wonderful trick. The nerve cells in our brains create a simplified copy of reality inside our head, and then persuade us that we are inside it, rather than the other way around.[13]

Sometimes, under certain conditions, the wonderful trick fails to work.

On one occasion I gave a talk where I quoted this passage about the brain. Afterwards I was talking to an old friend, now a distinguished psychologist but once a child of the sixties. He told me how the passage I had quoted had reminded him of something which had happened to him.

> Some years ago I was given some Vietnamese weed – really high quality stuff. I was sitting looking at a lit candelabra. As I watched

the image of the candelabra came towards me and seemed to rest on my eyes. Then it came inside. I was around it. I was huge. I was the whole world. When I pushed the image outside – it seemed that my brain was doing this – I became my usual size again.

It is when our brain's trick fails to work that we can become aware of how what we perceive is what we've constructed and not what might actually be there. Our brain's trick can fail to work when, like my friend, we've ingested certain substances, or when we're extremely tired, or when we've lost all confidence in ourselves and feel overwhelmed by the chaos of what is happening in our life. If we don't understand what is happening to us we can think that we are going mad.

All the constructions we create are meanings. The function of our brain is to create meanings. A meaning like, 'Your windpipe is partly blocked so have a good cough' might not be conscious if you're sound asleep, for example, while a meaning like, 'If the base rate goes up so will my mortgage payments' is likely always to be conscious; but, conscious or not, both are meanings. Feelings are meanings. Feeling angry is an interpretation. So saying, 'I'm furious because that person jumped the queue' is an interpretation of an interpretation.

The essence of our being is that we are meaning-creating creatures. Every moment of our lives, asleep or awake, drunk or sober, conscious or unconscious, we create meaning. We live in a world of meaning like a fish lives in water. *We cannot conceive of the opposite of meaning.* This is why defining meaning is so difficult. Everything else we encounter we can define in terms of its opposite. 'Peace' is an absence of war. 'Happiness' is an absence of sadness. However, 'meaningless' is still a meaning. It can mean, 'I can't readily find a sensible meaning for this,' or, 'Any meanings I can give for this are unacceptable to me,' or, 'I don't approve of this.'

We begin creating meaning from the moment our brain develops the capacity to do so, which is somewhere between 18 and 23 weeks' gestation. Babies while still in the womb are making sense of much of what is happening to them. Even though they aren't thinking, 'I'm happy', or 'Ouch, that hurt', they do have feelings of pain and pleasure. They are also capable of connecting one event to another and using the occurrence of the first event to predict the second. Just as you connect the sight of black clouds to the likelihood of rain, so have thousands of babies connected the theme tune of the television programme *Neighbours* to the sense of pleasure. It's so much more comfortable in the womb when mum sits down to rest! Once born, such babies respond with happy anticipation when they hear the music they like best.

The physiology of how we create meaning is far from being understood, but we are all familiar with the process of drawing conclusions from our experience. Every moment of your life you are encountering a new situation. Even if you've walked into your office on a thousand occasions the next occasion you walk into your office will be the first occasion you've walked into your office at that singular date and time. Immediately you encounter a new situation you make sense of it. You give it meaning.

There is only one way you can do this. You draw on your past experience. You have nothing else to use.

Suppose two people walk on to the floor of the London International Futures and Options Exchange (LIFFE) in London at precisely 11.23 on 1 February 1995. One of the two is a LIFFE trader. The other has never seen a trading floor before. To the first person the activity on the floor and on the computer screens forms an understandable pattern. To the second the scene is a confusing swirl of frenetic activity and noise. What they see is what they're learned to see.

While we are making sense of the new situation we are also passing through it and drawing a conclusion about that situation. Of the two people encountering the LIFFE floor the first might be drawing the conclusion, 'I shouldn't have left the floor. I've missed something very important,' while the second might be drawing the conclusion, 'This is exciting. It's what I'd like to do.'

The conclusions we draw from our experiences become the meanings which we use to predict the future and to guide our decisions. All these meanings accumulate to form a meaning structure. Many of the meanings in our structure change over time while others remain very much the same. Some people in their youth have drawn the conclusion that it didn't matter if they were careless with their money, but once they take on the responsibilities of married life they conclude that they must be careful with their money; other people never change their views that money is made to be spent.

Whenever I try to explain how we create meaning the way that the English language functions forces me to say some things which are not strictly true. I might say, 'Over time you change your meaning structure,' and thus give the impression that I am talking about two separate things, you and your meaning structure.

This isn't the case. You and your meaning structure are one and the same. What you experience as you, your person, self, identity, is the structure of meaning which has developed ever since your brain became capable of creating meaning. I could say, 'Your meaning structure creates itself' or 'You create yourself', but both statements mean the same. You are your meaning structure. Your meaning structure is you.

Current research in brain function suggests that the meanings we create could be analogous to the brain states which Susan Greenfield calls 'gestalts' and defines as 'a highly variable aggregation of neurones that is temporarily recruited around a triggering epicenter'.[14] Some of these gestalts might occur only once while others recur frequently, and often in conjunction with other gestalts. In presenting her theory of consciousness she draws on the work of Daniel Dennett who suggests that

> our mental states are a kind of ecosphere of ideas, tunes, catchphrases (dubbed by the biologist Richard Dawkins as 'memes') that harmoniously blend. In this way the mind is constituted of elements presumably more flexible and labile than those that make up the original idea of a rigid and constant self. These memes organize themselves, according to Dennett, as an ever adapting ecosystem where all the participants altruistically aid and abet the well being of the whole. There is no need to invoke a boss to organize this inner world any more than a super-ant is needed to organize an anthill.[15]

Philosophers and scientists of past generations have usually assumed that where there is order there must be some super-being who created the order within a system. Thus the individual must have a self or a soul or a spirit, and the world must have a God.

God presumably created the various selves, souls and spirits, but then the problem arises as to whether there was a God who created God, and so on into infinity. Eschewing such a futile line of questioning, many quantum physicists and biologists have developed another way of understanding how complex systems operate. The behaviour of subatomic particles, the evolution of species and the behaviour of the brain are so complex that they appear to be random, but they actually contain an underlying order which 'arises naturally and spontaneously because of the principles of self-organization – laws of complexity which we are just beginning to uncover and understand.'[16] (It may be that the world economy will one day be understood in terms of the laws of complexity, but for that to happen economists and market wizards will probably need a working knowledge of quantum physics!)

You, your meaning structure organizes itself. The aim of such self-organization is to maintain the meaning structure's survival. You, your meaning structure is in the business of surviving as a person.

At New York University Rodolfo Llinás and his colleagues have suggested that in the brain 'it is the dialogue between the thalamus and the cortex that generates subjectivity',[17] that is, the sense of being a person. In 'comparing the electrophysiological properties of the brain in waking and dreaming, (they) postulate a single fundamental mechanism for both – a ceaseless inner talking between the cerebral cortex and thalamus, a ceaseless interplay of image and feeling, irrespective of whether there is sensory input or not. When there is sensory input, this interplay integrates it to generate waking consciousness, but in the absence of sensory input it continues to generate brain states, those brain states we call fantasy, hallucination, or dreams. Thus waking consciousness is dreaming – but it is dreaming constrained by external reality.[18]

What Rodolfo Llinás and his colleagues call 'dreaming' could well be what I call 'creating meaning'. When we are asleep we are oblivious to the sights, sounds, smells, and tactile sensations which we can choose to be aware of when we are awake. I say 'choose' because when we are awake we can still be oblivious to what is going on around us if we are lost in a daydream or a meditation. Even when we are aware of our surroundings we are still choosing to pay attention to one thing rather than to another. When we do decide to pay attention to something we choose just how closely we shall examine it. You might be skimming through the daily paper when a certain item catches your eye. You stop skimming and read the item carefully.

Actually, we can get through our lives without paying too much attention to the world around us, but if we try to ignore it totally we can come a cropper. We can fall under a bus, or destroy our marriage, or lose a fortune.

The way we are constructed physiologically is really a cruel irony. We are made incapable of knowing reality directly, yet if we don't try to get to know reality as well as we possibly can we jeopardize our survival. Fail to pay sufficient attention to reality and you can die, not just as a physical body but as a person.

I don't need to describe how a failure to pay sufficient attention to reality can lead to physical death. You can remember incidents in your life when, by failing to pay attention to something, you nearly died. Remember how shaky you felt after your close shave! Now remember something even worse. Remember when you made a huge error of judgement. Perhaps it was when you thought a certain person loved you and would stay with you for ever, and you discovered you were wrong. Perhaps it was when you believed that your home had an infallible security system, and burglars cleared it out. Perhaps it was when you gambled a lot of money on a rise in share prices, and you lost.

Do you remember how you felt that you were falling apart? You felt that you were shattering, crumbling, even disappearing. You felt that you as a person were about to be annihilated. Do you remember how frightened you were?

That fear is worse than the fear of death. After all, with the thought of death you can always comfort yourself that some important part of yourself will continue on, perhaps your soul or spirit, or perhaps that you'll continue on through your children, or the memories your friends have of you, or through your work.

Why do rich men make charitable bequests? Not just to salve their consciences. Many of them seem to lack this particular faculty.

The object of their bequests is never a disinterested choice but relates closely to their wishes and needs. When Michael Milken, the American investment banker and junk bond specialist imprisoned for fraud in 1990, was released from gaol in 1993 he found that he had prostate cancer. When no satisfactory treatment was forthcoming he set up an organization called CAPCURE to increase public awareness of the problem and to stimulate research. (Drug companies prefer to look for cures for diseases well known to the public than for diseases which have attracted little fame despite the suffering they cause.) Milken gave between 3 and 5 million dollars of his own money to this cause.[19]

Rich men make bequests not simply out of the goodness of their hearts or to repay their debts to society. The purpose of their bequests is to overcome their death. They might die, but they won't be forgotten and people will speak well of them, or so they hope.

However, there's no bequest, no soul, no spirit, no children or memories which will ensure that you will survive the annihilation of you as a person. With this death you disappear like a wisp of smoke in the wind or a ripple on the water. It will be as if you never existed. Or at least this is how it seems when you face this kind of threat.

Photographs of people going through this experience show how the threat of annihilation has changed them. Compare the photographs of Michael Milken, Martin Siegel, Ivan Boesky and David Levine[20] when they thought they were invincible and when they had found that they were wrong. The first group of photographs shows each man occupying space in the manner which says, 'The world is mine.' In the second group the three men seem to be shrunken, unsure of their right to occupy any space. It was not surprising that Michael Milken developed cancer. The threat of annihilation of a person has a profound effect on that person's body. Research shows that the stress and the often accompanying depression following a serious error of judgement interrupt the efficient functioning of the auto-immune system, thus making the person vulnerable to noxious influences in the environment or latent in the person's body.

We are faced with the annihilation of ourselves as a person whenever we discover that there is a serious discrepancy between what we thought our life was and what it actually is. That is, when there is a serious discrepancy between our meaning structure and what is actually happening. Remember how, when you discovered you'd made a serious error of judgement you questioned every judgement you had ever made. If you were wrong about one important issue you could be wrong about everything else. As you doubted yourself you felt yourself falling apart.

It feels as though you are falling apart, but remember, you are your meaning structure. Your meaning structure is falling apart and of course it has to fall apart in order that it can be reorganized into a better fit with what is happening. If you understand this you can ride out the storm. If you don't understand this the dread you feel can lead you to think you are going mad. You might behave in ways which other people consider to be mad.

When we were toddlers our simple meaning structure was often out of kilter with what was happening and so we had many experiences of falling apart. (Adults call these episodes 'temper tantrums' and often make these experiences even worse by punishing the child.) So unpleasant were these experiences of falling apart we had to find ways of avoiding them or of protecting ourselves against them. As a result, much of what we each do, from our simplest domestic arrangement to the whole project of our lives, is aimed at preventing the annihilation of ourselves as a person.

People don't usually think in terms of preventing the annihilation of themselves as a person, but they do think in terms of personal pride. We use pride to hold ourselves together and to fend off the threat of annihilation. Unfortunately, the logic of personal pride can run counter to the scientific logic of what Bertrand Russell called 'enlightened self-interest', that is, the ability to examine closely what is actually happening and, without being misled by the fantasies which arise from pride, to make your plans accordingly.

When Norman Lamont became an ex-Chancellor in 1994 he did not act with enlightened self-interest but with personal pride. If he had accepted quietly and politely the less important post in Cabinet the Prime Minister offered him he would have been rewarded quite quickly with a secure seat in parliament (his Kingston-on-Thames seat was due to disappear in the next boundaries reorganization) or a place in the House of Lords. Instead he made a bitter resignation speech, telling the government that it was 'in office but not in power', and, in the following March, he voted with the Opposition on a Labour motion criticizing the government's policy on Europe. The next day he justified his behaviour to journalists by saying that the government, principally the Prime Minister, were ignoring him, and he wished everyone to know his views. If being noticed saves you from annihilation, what matter if nothing but criticism and punishment follow?

(What did follow showed that wickedness brings its own reward. The Prime Minister was reminded of Lyndon Johnson's advice about pissing in and out of tents and Norman, after many anxious months, was rewarded with what he hoped was a good Conservative seat.)

The media offer many opportunities for people to protest against their fate and thus ward off the terror of annihilation. This is why so many people offer themselves and their story to the media even though it would be prudent to be silent and unapproachable.

When I first came to England in 1968 I was amazed to find that there were many working-class people who voted Tory. I discovered that they did this out of pride. They felt that voting Tory distinguished them favourably from the common, rough working class people who tended to vote Labour. (Now we have a Labour Party which is busy distinguishing itself from the common, rough working-class people.) One of the saddest sights I ever saw on television was a working-class Tory, having suffered some personal betrayal at the hands of the Conservative government, saying, 'I've been working hard ever since I left school and I've voted Tory all my life. I'll never vote for them again.' At last he'd discovered that it's never sensible for the chickens to vote for the fox.

Alas, we all have habits and hold ideas which other people might regard as illogical, but such habits and ideas are completely logical to us within the realm of our own private logic.

If in your early life there is some area of experience which you found very painful you might decide not to acknowledge that such an area of experience exists. The philosopher Daniel Dennett called this behaviour 'neglect' and described his own particular form of neglect.

My most serious form of neglect is my bad case of finances neglect. So little do I like balancing my checkbook, in fact, that only some truly awful alternative, such as grading student exams, can force my attention to the topic. This neglect has serious consequences for my welfare, consequences I can readily be brought to appreciate, but, in spite of this alarmingly unsuccessful appeal to my underlying rationality, I manage to persist in my neglect, unless some fairly drastic measures of self-manipulation are brought into play.[21]

Other people, having encountered an area of very painful experience, decide the safest way of dealing with it is never to take their eyes off it. They might even make it the centre of their lives.

When I was staying in a holiday cottage on Fire Island, New York, some years ago I discovered a book by an economist, Catherine de Camp, called *The Money Tree*. This was a book of extremely detailed advice on how to manage your money. In her Introduction Catherine de Camp wrote,

I still have complete record books going back to my college days. As an economics major, I gave much thought to a statement by Professor (later Senator) Paul Douglas. He said that few middle-class people really knew where their dollars went. He believed they could live much better if they supervised and recorded their expenditures. I have found that he was right.

Not long ago an inspector for the Internal Revenue Service undertook to review a tax return that was three years old. I was able to answer promptly and accurately all the questions he asked in a three-hour investigation by using materials collected in one paperboard file box. My record box, or Day Book as I like to call it, listed all the money received in the course of the year in question and showed how most of it was spent. I supported these records with canceled checks, paid bills, receipts, earning vouchers, and statements from the brokerage firm with which I deal.

At the end of the interview, the inspector – a thorough but fair young man – said: 'Mrs de Camp, I want to tell you that I have never seen records like these in all my years with the Service. If my boss were here, he would say so too.'

More to the point, he passed the return as it stood. There was no question of guesswork on my part. No additional taxes were due.[22]

Although I wrote to Daniel Dennett, he was too cunning to disclose to me what experiences in his life had led him to financial neglect. Catherine de Camp's secret was given away in the foreword to her book, written by an old friend, the science fiction writer Isaac Asimov. He explained,

> It seems that her own family, which had wealth to begin with, managed to lose its money through sheer carelessness when Catherine was still quite young. Being a creature of grit and determination, she grittily determined that it would never happen to her. She might never become wealthy, but, whatever money she did earn, she was going to be careful with.[23]

If money were something which served no purpose other than to maintain our survival as a physical body, we would be entirely rational in our dealings with it. Indeed, it would occupy a very small part of our lives in the way that the air which we breathe might rarely become an object for our attention much less our concern. Those of us who are old enough to remember the days before pollution will know how we just took fresh air for granted. Even now when we worry about pollution we are usually thinking in terms of physical survival.

Of course we can only go on thinking of air solely in terms of physical survival as long as someone in power does not devise a way of packaging and marketing it. (I'm sure the Conservative Think Tank has been working on this.) Make air marketable and we'll think about it very differently.

Even in the days before water became a marketable product we saw it as providing something far more than mere physical survival. With water we can do more than quench our thirst and wash the dirt from our bodies. Water, so each religion would have us believe, can wash the dirt from our souls and transform us into a member of a religious community. The religious acts of washing and being baptized have the aim of assuring us that even though we die as a body the person that we are does not perish but has eternal life or, as in Buddhism and Hinduism, returns to the world in another physical form.

People who simply eat without worrying about being too fat or too thin, who enjoy food but who have no compulsive hates or fancies about different types of food, treat food simply as being necessary for physical survival. However, there are many people who use food in order to survive as a person. When they feel themselves falling apart they hold themselves together by eating a great deal, or they deny themselves food in order to feel in control of their chaotic lives, or to win admiring attention from other people, the attention which assures them that they exist. Some people constantly succumb to the lure of foods which they see as comfort foods, while other people avoid certain foods which create a sense of revulsion which is far more than a physical revulsion.

The relationship between food and bodily survival is clear. I eat, I live: I don't eat, I die. The relationship between money and bodily survival is not so clear. Even if you have no money you might still survive because other people feed you. Even if you have money you can still die if there is no food to be bought.

In the history of our species money was created relatively recently. Western society has made physical survival without money quite difficult, but, as many thousands of people have found, not impossible. There is always theft, begging and the charity of others. If you are now saying, 'But I would never steal, beg or accept charity,' you are making a statement not about the conditions for your physical survival but about the conditions for your survival as a person. You are saying, 'I am the kind of person who would never steal, beg or take charity.'

Money isn't necessary for physical survival but in most societies today many if not most people regard money as essential for the survival of their person. This is what makes understanding money in all its various contexts so very difficult. We use money to conduct the daily business of our lives and, simultaneously, to maintain our sense of being a person.

In our everyday lives we might try to use the shared logic of rational, sensible thought. However, conducting the daily business of our lives always involves interpreting new situations, predicting the future, assessing risks and making decisions on inadequate data. Such activities draw far more on our private logic, which is devoted to the maintenance of ourselves as a person, than on shared, rational thought.

A simple example. Most people know that all the research shows that air travel is the safest form of transport. Yet many people refuse to fly or fly only when forced to do so and then in a state of great anxiety. Their fear comes from a conclusion drawn by them following some unhappy experiences in childhood. These experiences usually have to do with being betrayed, or rejected, or shamed by the adults on whom the child depends. Accordingly, such children decide that they should never put themselves in a situation where other people are totally in control of their welfare. They feel safe only when they are in control of the situation. Thus they would be prepared to hurtle down the motorway at the wheel of a car doing 100 mph, but they would not trust even the pilots of Qantas, the world's safest airline.

In every decision we make about money we try to ensure that we are keeping ourselves physically safe and maintaining ourselves as a person. However, situations often arise where we are prevented from making a decision which would achieve both aims. What we always do then is choose to survive as a person and to put our physical survival in jeopardy.

Perhaps you are one of those people who regard generosity as being one of the greatest virtues. To be seen to be mean would fill you with shame. You have a limited income. One day when you have barely enough money to keep you fed until pay day you are asked to contribute to a well-liked colleague's leaving present. You decide that it's better to go hungry than be shamed in the eyes of others. Or perhaps you are one of those people for whom never showing fear and always winning are the standards you have set yourself. Competitive colleagues offer you a gamble and make it clear that to refuse would be cowardice. You know that the size of the stake is more than you can sensibly afford. Are you sensible? No.

In every decision we make about money, even though we might try to be sensible and logical in the ways which most people would agree are sensible and logical, our choice is always based on the private logic of our own individual meaning structure. No two people have identical meaning structures. Even when two people arrive at the same conclusion, they have used quite different logical paths. People can do exactly the same thing for very different reasons.

The theories which economists have devised to explain how an economy works are all based on an assumption about the needs of those men who are part of the economy because they buy and sell. (The part played by women in the economy was usually ignored, there having been a notable shortage of women economists.) It was assumed that all men wanted to maximize their profits. When in the eighties the idea of 'the market' became what the idea of 'the Kingdom of God on Earth' was in the Middle Ages, 'maximizing profits' was referred to simply as 'winning'.

For many men the meaning of life is winning. If they hear a woman saying, 'There are more important things in life than winning,' her words don't make sense. To them winning is everything. They don't always realize that even winning has different meanings for different men.

I've encountered a great many men who knew beyond a shadow of a doubt that there is an Absolute Law of the Universe which says, 'If you don't win your balls drop off.' Nothing frightens them more than losing, so their every action is aimed at winning, be they engaged in a multi-billion dollar hostile takeover or a game of draughts with their eight-year-old son. I've met other men, equally keen on winning, but who know that sometimes you win by losing. It depends on what you want to win – money and power, or your son's love.

For some men winning, or in some way having a sense of satisfactory achievement, is what life is about. For others winning is of vital importance because being a winner ensures that other men admire you and the tenuous thread which holds balls to body remains intact.

Of course, many people who buy and sell, men and women, simply want to earn some money, buy what they need and not feel cheated. As in Margaret Thatcher's oft-used phrase, they want 'value for money' but, as Margaret Thatcher never seemed to realize, we each assess value for money in our own individual way. People engage in buying and selling for all kinds of different reasons based on all kinds of different values. These values are part of the individual's meaning structure which has its own private logic.

Whenever we present our arguments to other people we usually make out that our logic is such that everyone must agree with us. ('Be reasonable. See it my way.') After all, our private logic is always logical to us. This is why no politician is ever a liar. In your logic and my logic he might seem to be lying, but in his logic he isn't. Most politicians have a private logic which, with individual variations, goes

* *To survive as a person I must be a member of the government.*
* *To be a member of the government I must be loyal to the party in every way.*
* *Being loyal to the party means presenting everything to the public in a way which shows the party in its best light.*

In such a system of logic, truth and lying are irrelevant.

Taking account of private logic makes understanding why people behave as they do very complicated. It requires a great deal of thought, and thinking is the hardest work of all.

It is only by taking account of private logic that we can come to understand the function of money in its many guises. To do this we need to understand how we create, maintain, extend and defend our sense of being a person.

We can begin by discovering the immense variety of meanings individuals and societies can give to money.

3

The Public Meaning of Money

For security against robbers who snatch purses, rifle luggage, and crack safes,
One must fasten all property with ropes, lock it up with locks, bolt it with bolts.
This (for property owners) is elementary good sense.
But when a strong thief comes along he picks up the whole lot,
Puts it on his back, and goes on his way with only one fear:
That ropes, locks, and bolts may give way.
Thus what the world calls good business is only a way
To gather up the loot, pack it, make it secure
In one convenient load for the more enterprising thieves.
Who is there, among those called smart,
Who does not spend his time amassing loot
For a bigger robber than himself?

Chuang Tzu[1]

Of all the animal species ours, it seems, is the only one that uses money. No zoologist has as yet discovered another species which uses money. Chimpanzees and gorillas turn objects into tools and all species seem to have ways of communicating with one another, but we create objects to use as tools, and we communicate using the complex medium of language. Other animals share and exchange, and so do we, but often by using objects which symbolize something else. Money is part of our language.

We develop language because, quite early in our life, we create an extraordinary assumption about the world into which we have been born. For the first four or five months after birth we see our surroundings as a passing phantasmagoria of present moments. For the rest of our lives all we ever experience and all we can ever experience is a passing phantasmagoria of present moments. However, provided our developing brain has not suffered some destructive assault, at around six or seven months we start to create an assumption about this phantasmagoria. We realize that some parts bear a resemblance to other parts which we have already seen. There's a string of faces that look much the same and are accompanied by certain smells and sounds that are always much the same. We ask ourselves, 'Could it be that instead of having an infinite array of mothers which appear one at a time I have one mother who comes and goes? Could it be that the passing phantasmagoria is made up, not of an infinity of objects but of certain single objects which go on existing when they are out of my sight?' To these questions we then assume that the answer is 'Yes.'

This is an extraordinary assumption. We can never be absolutely sure about what is happening in places which we cannot directly experience. Other people can assure us that certain things are still existing out of sight, but how can we be absolutely sure that they are telling us the truth? Perhaps parts of the passing phantasmagoria can tell us that they are the same parts which we have already seen, but couldn't there be an infinite array of parts that look alike and claim that they are the same? How can I be absolutely sure that you are the same person I met last week? How can you be absolutely certain that I am the same person you met last week?

Life would be unlivable if we kept this doubt in the forefront of our mind. So we continue to operate on the assumption which we created in the early months of our life, that objects go on existing when they are out of the range of our sensory perceptions.

Psychologists call reaching this developmental milestone the gaining of object permanence. Babies develop this assumption about the world before they acquire language, but it is this assumption that makes language a possibility and a necessity. If everything we experience is just one thing after another and nothing ever recurs, then there's nothing to remember or anticipate. But if objects do go on existing even when they're not passing by, it is worth having some words to refer to them when they're not around. Language allows us to remember and anticipate. Language creates a past and a future. Language creates time.

Scientists and philosophers used to think that time was an attribute of the universe which exists in an absolute state outside human experience. Many people still believe this, but in fact time is our creation. Physically constituted as we are, all we can experience is a string of present moments. We create a sense of time passing. What has passed we call the past, and what is to come we call the future, and we see ourselves moving in only one direction into the future. (Isn't it curious that we can go back and forward in space but only forward in time?)

If we had never created time we could never have created money. Money is embedded in our language of time. Those lumps of metal, pieces of paper and figures on a computer screen are, in a string of present moments, nothing more than lumps of metal, pieces of paper and figures on a computer screen, but seen in terms of past and future they accept the symbolic meanings we want to impose on them. When you examine the coins and notes in your pocket or purse you ask yourself a question about the past and a question about the future. 'What have I spent all that money on?' and 'Have I got enough to buy what I want to buy?'

The future is far more important for money than the past. What's gone is gone, and, while some people learn from their mistakes with money, many do not. The investors and speculators who move the market never seem to learn from history. J. K. Galbraith commented on 'the extreme brevity of the financial memory'.

> Financial disaster is quickly forgotten. In further consequence, when the same or closely similar occur again, sometimes in only a few years, they are hailed by a new, often youthful, and always supremely self-confident generation as a brilliant innovative discovery in the financial and larger economic world. There can be few fields of human endeavour in which history counts for so little as in the world of finance. Past experience, to the extent that it is part of memory at all, is dismissed as the primitive refuge of

those who do not have the insight to appreciate the incredible wonders of the present.[2]

Money exists because we believe we have a future. We spend our money so that we shall go on living. We invest our money so that in the future it will be worth more. Even though we know our individual future is limited by our death, we can see our money going on, giving worth to our children or to our favourite charitable institution. Without a future our money is worthless. Members of religious sects who believe that the end is nigh give away their possessions. The year 2000 will prove a bonzana to those unscrupulous but charismatic leaders of sects who, while preaching that the end of the world is imminent, are selfless enough to take care of all the goods and money owned by their followers.

The worth of money is embedded in our creations of language and time. Language is based not just on our assumption that objects go on existing outside our awareness but also on our need for other people.

Our survival both as a body and as a person is always trapped in a paradox that we are for ever alone in the individual world we have each created yet other people are as necessary to us as air, food and water. Babies who are adequately fed and kept warm but never cuddled turn grey and still and soon die. Children who are deprived of all close contact with caring adults never manage to enter the world of human relationships in any satisfactory way although they might manage to form relationships with animals or objects. Adults living alone, without even contact with animals which can be transmuted into human-like friends, create an extremely idiosyncratic way of living which other people call insane. As much as we are alone we need to be with other people.

Babies develop language through their relationships with other people. The sounds babies make in their first weeks cover the full range of the sounds our vocal equipment can produce. However, gradually certain sounds disappear and what remains are the sounds that the babies hear around them. It's not just that English babies babble in English but that Yorkshire babies babble in Yorkshire and Texan babies babble in Texan. Out of the babies' relationships comes language.

Although we need relationships they can always be dangerous. Other people are a threat to our survival, both as a body and as a person. They can maim and kill us. They can press their ideas upon us and take away the conditions necessary for our survival as a person. We keep ourselves safe by developing and maintaining rituals. These might be the simple rituals of 'please' and 'thank you' or the complex rituals of university, parliament or church.

'Money,' wrote the anthropologist Mary Douglas, 'is only an extreme and specialised type of ritual.'[3]

The rituals of relationships, of which money is one, try to remove the uncertainty which is always part of relationships. Other people can be so unpredictable. Money was created so as to remove the uncertainty inherent in trading transactions. As we shall see, it has not proved to be very successful in this at all. However, money has been most successful in removing one of the great dangers of relationships, the necessity to be close and committed to the other person.

Leo Tolstoy hated money. He wrote, 'Money is a new and terrible form of slavery, and, like the old form of personal slavery, it corrupts both the slave and the slave-owner, but it is even much worse because it frees the slave and the slave owner from personal relations.'[4] Paying someone for a service allows us to distance ourselves from that person.

Personal, as against impersonal, relationships are presented as being rare in the world of high finance and international trading. Many men like to be seen as objective and rational in their business relationships. Where personal relationships are supposed to matter most – in the family – money can wreak havoc.

Much sentimental tosh is talked about the family with the unspecified virtues of 'family values' and being 'a close family'. Sentimentality is cruelty in pretty colours, for in both the person is not treated as a person but as an object. 'Family values' can mean 'Anyone who isn't family doesn't count.' 'A close family' can mean tyranny and exploitation.

From about the middle of the fifteenth century to the middle of the eighteenth most manufacture went on in the home. J. K. Galbraith wrote,

In later centuries the factory system, with its myriad of organized and regimented workers, would evoke a powerful image of exploitation. Over household or cottage industry down to our own time would hover, by contrast, an impression of family independence and benign parental responsibility and command – a socially tranquil scene. Men and women of vulnerable tendency think even now of homely arts and crafts when they yearn for an escape from the more rigorous disciplines of the economic world. In India all governments and nearly all politicians are required, in the Gandhian tradition, to seek the revival of the cottage industries, including the spinning and weaving that brought the traders and the great trading companies to Madras, Calcutta and Bengal in the era of merchant capitalism. Forgotten, at least by many, is the terrible exploitation forced on men and women by the threat of starvation and thus on children by their parents. Nor is management by the head of a family always at a high level of efficiency or intelligence. More of those who have described or endorsed the homely romance of household industry over the centuries should have personally experienced its rigours when it was the sole source of income.[5]

The financial value of the family is the one value which family firms seem to hold dear, though not so dear that they will always co-operate with one another in order to maintain the profits and share price. Gucci, founded by Guccio Gucci in 1906, passed to Investcorp, an investment corporation owned by wealthy Arab investors in 1993 after ferocious fights between family members.[6] In a drama worthy of the soap operas *Dallas* and *Dynasty*, Herbert Haft, a self-made millionaire, fired his son Robert with whom he had worked happily for sixteen years, put another son Ronald in his place and split the family into bitter factions.[7] In 1994 the Dunne family, who own Ireland's largest retailer Dunnes Stores, ended in the High Court their long-running dispute which began with an argument over who should be chairman. Factional fighting between the Spear family and the board led to the loss of independence for the Scrabble game manufacturer J. and W. Spear with the firm being taken over by the American toymaker Hasbro.[8]

Lewis H. Lapham saw that in wealthy American families money and feeling had the same public meaning.

> The equivalence between money and feeling becomes increasingly apparent in the upper reaches of income and net worth. People who define their lives as functions of their wealth display their affection, or lack of it, by withholding both the substance and symbolism of money. Between a rich man and his estranged son (or a rich mother and her alienated daughter) the *casus belli* almost always can be reduced to a precise sum: the inheritance the son expected but didn't get, the wife's fee for being cheated of her youth, the father's price for mortgaging what he thought was his own happiness to the speculation of his daughter's future. I sometimes think that the only American story is the one about the reading of the will.[9]

Not that money isn't important in less wealthy families. Acuma, the financial arm of American Express, surveying 988 professional adults found that money was the biggest cause of domestic strife.[10] The problem is that our nearest and dearest do not usually give to money the private meanings which we do, even though we share the public meanings for money. Is the breadwinner's money 'his' money, or 'her' money, or 'their' money?

Not that public meanings are universal in all societies. There are many national differences.

The British might scorn what they sometimes call filthy lucre, but not so much as the Japanese do.

> Japanese bankers, it seems, are about to develop a new line of business: money laundering. Hitachi, an electrical-appliance manufacturer, has started making automatic teller machines (ATMs) that not only dispense banknotes, but press and disinfect them first. One of Japan's big banks is already giving the machines a spin.
>
> Prompted by the country's finance ministry, Hitachi thinks it has spotted a gap in the market. The Japanese are finicky about dirt and mess. They also like to settle debts in cash, often carrying large quantities of notes around in order to do so. And they give presents of money on occasions such as weddings and births. Carrying dirty money is unpleasant; giving it to your friends is somewhat rude. But the supply of freshly printed yen is hardly equal to the demand. Thus, reckons Hitachi, any bank that can deliver reconditioned second-hand notes should be on to a winner.

It might also prolong the useful life of the notes, which would please the finance ministry.[11]

Start a conversation about the UK lottery and soon you'll be talking about magic, all kinds of magic, which, so its believers hope, will determine which numbers will win the prize. Just what kind of magic is a matter of individual choice. One person might favour using birthdays or marriage anniversaries. Another might throw dice or count the number of starlings on each branch of a tree. No matter how often on television a mathematician might explain that there is no connection between the winning numbers in one draw and the numbers in another draw, many people keep a count of how frequently each number is drawn and use this count to predict what the next winning numbers will be. The problem is in deciding whether a number which has been drawn frequently is a lucky number likely to be drawn again or an unlucky number not likely to be drawn again. The fact that the chances of choosing the winning number are one in fourteen million deters very few people.

In contrast to these individual forms of magic the Chinese have a national magic. They value raw fish (in Chinese *fu cai yusheng*, meaning prosperity fish) mainly for auspicious symbolism. At the New Year at table everybody joins in with chopsticks to toss a salad of vegetables and raw fish. Tossing is *lo hei* which sounds the same as the Cantonese for 'ever increasing wealth'. The black seaweed strands of *fat choy* are very popular at the Chinese New Year because their name echoes part of the traditional New Year's Eve greeting, *Kung Hei Fat Choy*, meaning 'grow in riches'.

The Chinese in Hong Kong celebrate both the Chinese New Year and the Western 31 December. I arrived in Hong Kong on the evening of 31 December 1993 and found myself in the middle of great celebrations, not just because it was New Year's Eve but because the Hong Kong stock market had ended the year on a most auspicious note, closing at 11,888.38. As Johnny Cheung of Harper-Collins, Hong Kong, later told me, 'The name of 8 in Cantonese echoes "easy to get great fortune". People like treble 8 or double 8 or quadruple 8 because it will be money, money, money.'

The *Hong Kong Standard* commented, 'The significance of the

(Hang Seng) figure is not likely to be lost by Hong Kong's many small investors. Indeed it was the smaller retail buyers who erased the morning's early losses to push the index up to the magic figure.'[12]

Such auspicious times did not last. There were rumblings from China which made the investors nervous. By 7 January the Hang Seng had dropped to 11,142 by the close of the London market.[13] There was the dreaded number 4 which, said Johnny, 'In Cantonese means death, or something related to death or debt.'

Alistair, an executive at a leading bank in Hong Kong, told me, 'The Chinese are extremely canny with managing their own money. Many Chinese run their businesses in a very conservative way, so extremely conservative that someone with an MBA from a European or US university would look at it as being almost anachronistic as we push toward the twenty-first century. However, with their own money they will be much more speculative. With the money that they have beyond the needs of the family they are very, very active in the way they use it. Many people here deal in foreign currencies as an ordinary part of their own financial management. It is not unusual at all to see people walking down the streets and staring at screens in the bank windows looking for currency ratings to see which currency they should be keeping their money in. I used to go to a tailor when I was working as a financial journalist here. Every time I walked home from work I would pass his shop and he inevitably would be waiting for me to call me inside the shop. He would ask me, "What should I do with my money?" I would give him my general ideas and say, "Well, why don't you look at X Y Z company", which would be a very small company that I didn't think he would have heard of. I'd find that not only would he have heard of it but he would be able to cite for me the number of the company in the Stock Exchange registry. When he would ask me about currencies he would be able to quote me a dollar/Deutschmark rate down to 2 or 3 decimal points. You see many people here walking around with little pagers that don't just forward them their telephone calls, but also the foreign exchange rates or stock market rates.'

Joseph Kwan of the Federation Australian Alumni Associations of Hong Kong had described to me how people there needed money to provide education for their children and as provision for their old age. 'The Chinese concept,' he said, 'is very much "Look after yourself".' Joseph had spent much of his childhood in Australia, so he drew a contrast between the Australian and Chinese attitudes to gambling. 'In Australia not everyone goes to the races but here almost everyone does, and particularly working-class men and women do because they don't earn that much money. They think, "If I'm lucky I'm going to win that million dollars and that will set me up for the rest of my life." Australians go to the races or bet on the lottery partly for fun and partly believing in luck, whereas here gambling is essential.'

Being astute and keen in business yet using superstitions to determine business decisions seemed to be quite incompatible characteristics. I asked Alistair why the Chinese were so superstitious. He said, 'The Chinese of southern China have for thousands of years been subject to great whimsics, events that they have had no control over. Terrible political events, cataclysms in terms of weather, flooding and typhoons which whip along this coast very regularly during the summer months. Perhaps the inability to control one's own destiny gives rise to a greater belief in superstition. I think the reason why people are so fascinated with money and its potential here is because people have been so poor in China for so long and they have been subject to such deprivation and so many spasms of oppression by their government, not just since 1949 with the various strange twists and turns that Mao's China would take but even before that. I think that the people here do feel that they live within a largely malevolent world and anything they can do to shield themselves from these winds of malevolence they will try to tap into.'

The explanation for inconsistencies in people's behaviour can usually be found in the way our private logic, our structure of meaning, operates.

Traditional Chinese culture gives power to the oldest people in the community. To criticize in public one's elders and those perceived as one's betters is unthinkable. P.E.H., an industrial scientist who has lived in Hong Kong for many years, told me that it was very difficult at the end of a lecture to persuade the audience to question the speaker, especially if he were nominally 'eminent', in the way that would be commonplace with a European or American audience. He added that this may be due also to a reluctance to appear not to have understood the speaker properly or, in Hong Kong, to be diffident about speaking in English; in either case laying oneself open to loss of face.

This was consistent with what I had found in discussions I had had with various people when I visited China. If you live in a culture where it is dishonourable to disagree with much less disobey your elders, where it is dangerous to disclose views different from those of your government and where you are at the mercy of a cruel climate and unexpected and disastrous events, you are always facing the threat of annihilation of you as a person. You have to find power from somewhere to protect yourself, and what better place than in the realms of magic. The Chinese of Hong Kong, on the whole, receive an education which is strong on obedience and conformity and weak on the skills of critical analysis and they live with the uncertainties and dangers of Communist China so it is not surprising that, even though they might be economically well off, they still feel the same need for magic as their forebears.

The very popular *South China Morning Post* leaves nothing to chance. At the top of the page headed 'Information' is a matrix which sets out the current foreign banknote rates for 21 countries so that each currency can be compared with every other one. (This table is much more informative than those lists of currency rates given in British and American newspapers.) Immediately under the table is 'Lady Luck', what British papers call 'Your Stars', but with the additional information about what is the 'lucky number' for today and the 'lucky encounter'. Just to be on the safe side, included in this same piece is the day's text from the Bible.[14]

However, people can change. Alistair said, 'There are many idiosyncrasies here in Hong Kong with people's attitude toward money, but I wonder if in a generation or two they will cease to exist because the forces that are current will have dissipated. I think that the world is homogenizing at a very rapid rate and that these idiosyncrasies will be sort of buffed out. I think that one of the most powerful social phenomena in Asia right now is Star Television, the network that Rupert Murdoch recently bought. It is based on satellite broadcasting with footprinted satelliting, which means that the area that satellite reaches extends from the Middle East to northern Japan and from Australia up to northern China. The reason it is so important socially is that where it is watched most is in places where people don't have very much to do, where there is a shortage of entertainment, places like rural India and China. There are some countries that have banned it, like Singapore and Malaysia, because they are scared of the influence that it may have on the people. When I was in India recently this television was just coming in. It was astounding to see how people who were living in very modest circumstances would go to the communal television in the village and watch US soap operas about people who have lots of money and live in California and drive fancy cars. I think that this is shaping very strongly people's attitude towards money.

'From a marketing point of view it is very interesting. The reason the media exist, at least in the capitalist world, is to sell advertising. Now it is based on the assumption that people all over Asia want more or less the same things. They want basic consumer goods that in India might just mean cheap little cameras or dishwashers or black and white televisions. As the country gets richer it may need cars or trips to Europe or whatever, but I am not sure that people really want some of these things necessarily. But they are shown in such a seductive way, using the highest technology available, that people become seduced by it. And I think that it threatens to warp a lot of people's values, especially in places like India where these things have been pushed down the throat so quickly that traditional values don't have a contest against them.'

The values which Alistair fears are being pushed down the throats of Indians and others are those of developed countries. Yet these countries themselves have differing attitudes to money.

Anyone who listens regularly to BBC Radio 4's morning programme *Today* often hears in 'Thought for the Day' various church people warning against the contaminating effects of money. Not so in the USA. Michael Lewis wrote,

> God and money have never been as far apart in America as they are in most places. Partly this must be because selling is a form of ecstasy in America. But there is also a long history of American preachers aiming to reconcile the moral precepts of the Bible with

> the making of money. (Peale is one example, as was Russell Conwell, the author of the world's most successful success pamphlet, based on a sermon, called *Acres of Diamonds*.) With the clergy dragging God towards the market, it seems only practical for the laity to pick up the market and drag it towards God. Thus the new breed of success merchants laces its language with pulpit-speak and references to Christian values.[15]

But then God is infinite, and in America, so Lewis H. Lapham wrote, money is seen as an infinitely expanding resource.

> Even the more cynical and well-travelled Europeans, accustomed to seeing strange sights in Paris or the Malaysian Archipelago, admit to a degree of surprise when introduced to the American faith in cash. Perhaps this is because the Europeans still tend toward a mercantile rather than a capitalist understanding of money. They think of the stuff as a finite commodity: any addition to the substance of A implies a subtraction from the substance of B. Americans take a more transcendent view. We construe money as an infinitely expanding resource, like helium or greeting-card sentiment or leaves on eucalyptus trees. In support of our faith we can offer so many miraculous proofs – of fortunes gained almost overnight in anything from Californian real estate to chocolate chip cookies – that it becomes easy to think of money not as a means but as an end.
>
> Throughout the nineteenth century immigrants of all nationalities found it difficult to comprehend the American uses of money. Their letters and diaries express their confusion in a commercial society that wasn't held together by the ties of family, by a monarchy, by tradition, by the secret police. They felt threatened in a capitalist dynamic that could so easily overturn moral certainties and so readily dissolve the stability of the land.[16]

Such migrants, or their descendants, must have come to understand that what holds the vast diversity of people in the USA together are three moral certainties. The first two are God and America, ideas in which all Americans must claim belief lest they be declared to be un-American, the greatest crime of all. The third idea is the market. No American is in danger of not believing in that. When in 1841 a grain broker and an elevator operator, W. I. Whiting and Thomas

Richmond, formed the Chicago Board of Trade they probably did not realize that they had created the third supreme idea.

> The futures exchanges provided a central point where the prices of a whole nation's crops could be determined not by fiat but by what hundreds of traders, in the purest Adam Smith fashion, decided. Chicago's futures exchanges set the price of corn from Minnesota to Mississippi, for beef driven from Abilene to the east-bound trains of Dodge City railhead, and for soyabeans in the Ohio, Illinois, and the Missouri River bottomlands. In Chicago, America's widely dispersed farmers were drawn into one economic unit.[17]

The British do not have a concept of un-British, but many imbue their unit of currency, the pound, with a strongly patriotic quality as the furore over a single European currency shows. Indeed, when I listen to the anti-European rhetoric of some politicians I get the impression that they believe that, back in the mists of time when this most noble race first set foot on this sceptred isle, God gave the British the pound for their own special use. Actually the history of money is somewhat different.

The History of Money

In the debate about the origins of language there is one line of argument which says that our early ancestors began talking to one another and then they discovered they could talk to themselves, that is, think. Be that as it may, it's highly likely that the first sounds whose meaning was shared with other members of the tribe included the sounds for 'mine', 'yours' and 'let's swap'. There was probably another set of sounds which meant 'value for money', as in 'My mammoth haunch is worth more than your three stone axes.' Language and the market developed together.

However, bartering is an extremely cumbersome process. The solution was readily at hand because every language speaker understood the principle of a symbol, that one thing can be used to represent another thing which might not be actually present. So money was born.

Money, so my computer dictionary tells me, is 'any medium of exchange that is widely accepted in payment for goods and services in settlement of debts. Money also serves as a standard of value for measuring the relative economic worth of different goods and services.'[18] As a medium of exchange money can be anything a group of people decide to call money. The seventeenth-century settlers in America soon used up the supply of coins they had brought with them and resorted to commodities like dried fish, furs, gunpowder and shot, grain and wampum, which was Indian beads made from the inner whorl of seashells. Lonely male settlers in Virginia paid for their brides' passage from the Old World at the rate of 100–150 pounds of tobacco per bride.[19] When the supply of coins ran short in the early years of the British settlement in Australia the settlers turned to a much prized possession, rum, to serve as money.

Being able to define what money is in your community gives a certain amount of autonomy and power. In Britain in the eighties, when rising unemployment and plummeting job security made many people feel that they were losing what autonomy and power they had over their lives, groups of people got together to trade services – 'I'll babysit your children if you'll paint my kitchen'. These groups set up Local Exchange Trading Systems (LETS) and developed their own money, each with its own distinctive name. In Manchester it was 'bobbins', in Bath 'olivers', in Reading 'readies', in Exmouth 'cockles'. Such names reflected a wit which was perhaps not readily appreciated by the officers of the Inland Revenue who felt that some taxable income was escaping their net.

Objects which can be used as money need to be fairly durable and transportable. The metals gold, silver, lead, copper, iron and bronze had these properties and could be divided into lumps of much the same size. In China as far back as 1100 BC miniature bronze knives and axes were circulating as money. The Greek historian Herodotus recorded that in the latter part of the eighth century BC the kings of Lydia coined gold and silver into money. By 500 BC every Greek city state not only had its own coinage but competed with each other state to produce the most beautiful coins. The design of coins became a prized art form.

Some surviving specimens cannot be viewed without a quick intake of breath at their beauty. After Alexander the Great the custom of depicting the head of the sovereign on the coins was less, it has been suggested, as a guarantee of the weight and fineness of the metal than as a thoughtful personal gesture by the ruler to himself. It was one that could work in reverse. According to Suetonius, after the death of Caligula his money was called in and melted down so that not only the name but the features of the tyrant might be forgotten.[20]

Coins which contain an amount of metal which has a value close to that given to the coin are called commodity money. Some early coins stayed constant in their value, like the drachma issued by Athens in the sixth century BC and the copper Chinese *qian* (cash) which was introduced in the fourth century and remained standard for some two thousand years. However, gold and silver coins always represented a temptation to those who were less than honest. It is said that as far back as 540 BC Polycrates of Samos cheated the Spartans with coins which contained less gold than was claimed for them. He set the precedent for kings to debase the coinage, while the rest of the populace, at least until milling the edges was introduced, could clip or shave the coins to their advantage.

Another problem with commodity money was the supply of the commodity itself. In the fifteenth century Europe ran out of gold and silver to make money. People had to melt down their household gold and silver or resort to barter. This bullion famine increased the appetite for gold, hence the enthusiasm for the Inca gold, but as the gold of the Americas flooded into Europe a famine turned into a glut.

> In fact, the easy availability of money destroyed the old feudal order. Instead of paying obligations to one's lord by spending time in his service, a vassal could pay a tax in coin instead. The abundance of gold and silver dissolved the old feudal ties, eroded the very basis of society, and indirectly set the stage for the revolutions that occurred three centuries after Columbus.[21]

Commodity money could be debased; it was heavy to carry, though not so heavy that a thief could not carry it away. The solution seemed to be credit money, pieces of paper on which the person or institution which had issued them promised to pay the bearer a certain amount of commodity money. The Tang dynasty in China in the ninth century issued paper money as cash certificates. In Europe in the sixteenth century banks began issuing promissory notes against the money deposits which they held. The use of paper money proliferated.

There were practical problems. Paper money wears out. In the UK every day six tons of banknotes are disintegrated into fine particles and used as fertilizer. Worse, unscrupulous people could copy the notes. In the UK between 1797 and 1829 some 618 unlucky people were hanged for counterfeiting.[22] The lucky ones were transported as convicts to New South Wales where some of their number are now national heroes.

When a government does not have sufficient precious metals in its coffers it can issue fiat money simply by fixing the value the notes represent. There is always the temptation to print more money than the government can sustain. The stormy history of the American greenback began with the Continental Congress which directed the American War of Independence issuing in 1775 notes called Continentals with the promise to redeem them in Spanish silver dollars after the war. When the war did end some 241 million dollars' worth of paper notes were in circulation, much more than the government could redeem. The Continental became worthless.

With fiat money, money leaves the realm of tangible objects and enters the world of ideas. The realm of objects always places limits on what we can say and do, but the realm of ideas easily seduces us with promises of freedom and power. So it is not surprising that, despite the fact that history is littered with examples of the dangers of fiat money, by the second half of the twentieth century the world's currencies had become fiat money. The UK left the Gold Standard in 1931 and the USA severed its link with gold in 1971.

Money became numbers on a computer screen and pieces of plastic in our wallets. In the history of money and commerce every innovation brought with it new opportunities for thieves and scoundrels. When in the fifteenth and sixteenth centuries the Vatican, in order to fill its coffers, sold papal dispensations, some rogues, instead of taking this opportunity to save their souls, set about creating forged papal dispensations. The universal blessing of cellular telephones now produces four billion dollars worth of fraud each year. Credit card fraud is now eight times larger than frauds with counterfeit currency.[23]

No matter how complex the credit card companies made their cards counterfeiters successfully copied them. Even the introduction of holograms on the cards held up the counterfeiters for no more than three or four years. No doubt they are studying the Mondex card designed to overcome the one drawback of telephone banking. The phone cannot deliver cash. Just as a telephone card holds credits so the Mondex card holds cash and can be used both to pay and receive money. There will be counterfeiters hard at work right now uncovering its secrets so as to be able to reproduce them.

The Internet offers unlimited opportunities for buying and selling, but how to safeguard the payments for such transactions? Microsoft and Visa International got together to develop software so people can make purchases using coded credit card numbers.[24] Then Visa and MasterCard agreed to develop jointly a secure online payment system. Kelly Knutson, a senior Visa executive, 'said that his company expected to handle transactions worth up to $700 billion (£475 billion) this year, and that Visa and MasterCard together would handle more than $1,750 billion by the end of the century . . . He accepted that no system could be 100 per cent secure but added, "We are striving to be more secure than today's physical payments."'[25] Whatever this system might be, electronic money, or e-money or e-cash, is full of possibilities, not least those which are being explored by computer literate crooks.

At every step in the history of money something new is created in order to increase the sense of security and each step is inevitably accompanied by some new insecurity. Who indeed does not spend his time amassing loot for a bigger robber than himself?

Perhaps the solution is to have a world without money.

Moneyless Worlds

When in 1935, in the middle of the Great Depression, Hugh McDiarmid wrote his poem 'On the Money Monopolist Being Like Hell' he was presenting an idea which has been voiced by writers and philosophers down the centuries.

> There was no competition for riches
> When God made the world and men were few,
> All was in common, with no thought of fortune
> In good times or bad, until avarice grew.
>
> The world has grown greatly in men and cattle,
> When men started to use the curst trick of money,
> Peace departed then. War developed on every side,
> Thrusting out all love, making common goods private property.[26]

The idea is simple. Money creates wickedness. To get rid of wickedness, abolish money. Like Hugh McDiarmid, some people pictured a return to a golden age before money was invented. Others pictured a future Utopia where a society had evolved which needed no money.

Plato described a Utopia where, under the beneficent rule of the philosophers, people worked at and received what was appropriate for their station in life. Plutarch in his *Lives* described how Lycurgus, king of Sparta, defeated his subjects' avarice by calling in all the gold and silver and issuing coins made of iron which were worth very little and weighed a great deal, making it not worth the effort to amass it or steal it. Such coinage was like modern day LETS, a shorthand reference to show who owed whom what.

It is always said that Henry VIII had Sir Thomas More put to death because More refused to support Henry's request to the Pope for a divorce from Catherine of Aragon. However, some eighteen years before, in 1516, More had written his account of life on the island of Utopia where people lived in happiness because money had been abolished.

> For who knoweth not that fraud, theft, ravine, brawling, quarrelling, brabbling, strife, chiding, contention, murder, treason, poisoning, which by daily punishments are rather revenged than

> refrained, do die when money dieth? And also that fear, grief, care, labours, and watching, do perish even the very same moment when money perisheth? Yet poverty itself, which only seemed to lack money, if money were gone, it would also decrease and vanish away.[27]

In his quarrel with More it would have already been clear to Henry that if he broke with the Church of Rome he would not only have the riches of the Church at his disposal but that he, as head of the Church, could make his own rules. More died in 1535. Seven years later Henry bought up the nation's silver and began the Great Debasement. Perhaps he feared More's moral views with regard to money as much as he feared his views on divorce.

Three centuries later the entrepreneur and philanthropist Robert Owen, like Will Hutton and Hamish McRae, saw the resolution of all economic problems as requiring a profound change in morality. He described his vision of the New Moral World.

> Money, which has hitherto been the root, if not of *all evil*, of great injustice, oppression, and misery to the human race, making some slavish producers of wealth, and other wasteful consumers or destroyers, will be no longer required to carry on the business of life: for as wealth of all kinds will be so delightfully created in greater abundance than will ever be required, no money price will be known, for happiness will not be purchaseable, except by a reciprocity of good actions and kind feelings.[28]

In the second half of the nineteenth century art, politics and economics came together in the work of the poet, designer and reformer William Morris who described a commonwealth where people had 'cast away riches and attained wealth'.[29] When I was a child my father used to read to me from a book which had been popular for forty years but is little heard of now, Edward Bellamy's *Looking Backward* which described a nation where buying and selling was irrelevant. One character, Dr Leete, explained,

> The nation is rich, and does not wish the people to deprive themselves of any good thing. In your day, men were bound to lay up goods and money against coming failure of means of support and for their children. This necessity made parsimony a virtue. But now it would have no such laudable object, and, having lost its

> utility, it has ceased to be a virtue. No man any more has any care for the morrow, either for himself or his children, for the nation guarantees the nurture, education, and comfortable maintenance of every citizen, from the cradle to the grave.[30]

For my father, who as a soldier had seen the horrors of the First World War and who was battling to survive the horrors of the Great Depression, Bellamy held out hope. So did one of the few economists who earned my father's approval: John Maynard Keynes, who in 1930 wrote,

> When the accumulation of wealth is no longer of high social importance, there will be great changes in the code of morals. We shall be able to rid ourselves of many of the pseudo-moral principles which have hag-ridden us for two hundred years, by which we have exalted some of the most distasteful of human qualities into the position of the highest virtues. We shall be able to afford to dare to assess the money-motive at its true value. The love of money as a possession – as distinguished from the love of money as a means to the enjoyments and realities of life – will be recognized for what it is, a somewhat disgusting morbidity, one of those semi-criminal, semi-pathological propensities which one hands over with a shudder to the specialists in mental disease.[31]

None of these books proved to be a great financial success, unlike the most popular of all moneyless Utopias, the television series *Star Trek*. By 1991, 'not only was *Star Trek* now the most successful science-fiction series of all time, it was the most successful dramatic syndicated series of all time, and, when the millions of dollars of additional revenue from books and toys and posters and dozens of other merchandising licences were added in, perhaps the most successful entertainment franchise of all time, science fiction or not.'[32]

In his writers' and directors' guide the originator of the series, Gene Roddenbury, makes quite clear that, as the Star Fleet on which the adventurers were boldly going can make almost anything that might be needed, money no longer exists. On Earth most of the problems and difficulties which beset us in the present have been solved and the planet has become a human paradise for a population of people who are literate and compassionate. Earth is part of the

Federation where many worlds, human and otherwise, have joined together in mutual co-operation.[33]

Brian Aldiss and David Wingrove have argued in their book *Trillion Year Spree*[34] that the reason science fiction stories are often set in times and places where money plays no part is because the typical reader of these fantasies is an adolescent who, like most adolescents, is short of money. This may well be so in the case of science fiction writers who just want to spare themselves the difficulties of fitting some kind of economy into their stories, but for Gene Roddenbury the choice of a moneyless economy for *Star Trek* came from far more profound reasons.

When Roddenbury was trying to establish himself in the early sixties as a television dramatist he was writing plays which were set in present time and which explored the issues that caused great public concern, issues to do with politics, race and the functioning of a capitalist economy. The television companies to whom he sent his work made it clear to him they had no room for dramas about real life. So he wrote what appeared to be just what the television companies wanted, action drama, and set it in the future because science fiction stories were becoming popular. The first series was seen by its producers as just another cheap, slick entertainment which an unthinking public likes. But what *Star Trek* had which similar programmes lacked was a set of interesting, believable characters who formed the kind of team with which people want to identify, and stories which, while full of suspense and dramatic incidents, actually made telling comments about issues which directly concerned those people watching. Roddenbury had got on to the screen the stories he wanted to tell, and these stories questioned some beliefs which Americans are supposed to hold dear.

Even though the captain of the Starship *Enterprise*, James T. Kirk, and all his crew had sworn to obey the orders of their more senior officers, what the stories reveal is that

> Authority was seen as anathema to original and independent thought. Kirk's goal was to get the residents of these societies thinking for themselves, to get people of these planets to stand on their own two (or however many) feet. Phaser fire usually got the oppressed citizenry on the road to their full potential.[35]

In present-day America research on religious beliefs shows that 96 per cent of Americans profess a belief in God. In *Star Trek V: The Final Frontier* Kirk meets God and challenges his judgement. Kirk's challenge saves the *Enterprise* and its crew and reveals that this particular God was a fraud.

According to Shakespeare, Jack Cade, when rebelling against Henry VI, promised that when he became king, 'There shall be no money; all shall eat and drink on my score; and I will apparel them all in one livery, that they may agree like brothers and worship me as their lord.' The butcher in his audience replied, 'The first thing we do, let's kill all the lawyers.' Such sentiments are echoed in the jokes Americans tell about lawyers. *Star Trek* is much kinder to lawyers. They still exist in the twenty-third century but they believe in truth and justice, not money.

Americans also profess a belief in possessions, unlike the inhabitants of the USS *Enterprise* where no one seems to collect things. Their cabins are remarkably bare. However, their computers are stuffed full of data. The *Enterprise* crew care about knowledge.

If Americans are supposed to believe in God they are also supposed to believe in money. Gene Roddenbury didn't banish money totally from his stories. He created one group of people to whom money meant everything – the Ferengi.

Not all the worlds in the universe belong to the Federation. The Ferengi had formed with a number of planetary systems the Ferengi Alliance which they ran in ways well understood today. The first, last and only principle of the Ferengi was profit. The Ferengi Rules of Acquisition make this clear. Here are some:

> Rule 1 Once you have their money you never give it back.
> Rule 6 Never allow family to stand in the way of opportunity.
> Rule 9 Opportunity plus instinct equals profit.
> Rule 18 A Ferengi without profits is no Ferengi at all.[36]

All the stories show the Ferengi to be insensitive, mean, devious, untrustworthy and childish. They are also very ugly.

What greater criticism of capitalism could there be? Yet, much as *Star Trek* audiences admire, even idolize the heroes of the USS *Enterprise*, the Ferengi have proved to be so popular that when a series, *Deep Space Nine*, set on a space station near a stable wormhole, was conceived, the Ferengi characters were given very prominent roles.

This is an example of how we are all able to hold simultaneously two opposing ideas. We can long for the calm and security of a well-organized world where money is irrelevant, while at the same time being amused by, even identifying with characters who exhibit lawlessness, cunning and greed. Underlying this juxtaposition of opposites is a universal juxtaposition of opposites, a condition of life which prevents us from ever creating an ideal world. It is the juxtaposition of security and freedom. The more you have of one the less you have of the other. You cannot be simultaneously secure and free. To be secure you have to conform to the conditions of your security. You are not free to do as you like.

If you ask people to describe their ideal world, whatever the image, it will appear to have as a basic feature a world which gives the individual both security and the freedom to make and act upon choices. However, if you question the person about what kind of choices are available in this ideal world it soon becomes apparent that the choices are limited by the rules which create the security.

Communist leaders have always insisted that the Communist 'ideal worlds' of the USSR and China gave people freedom from hunger and unemployment. They ignored the fact that 'freedom from' is very different from 'freedom to'. The only things people in totalitarian countries can do is what they're told.

If you grew up in a secure family home, as you approached adulthood you had to choose between continuing to obey the family rules and enjoying security or the insecurity and freedom of independence.

The Christian Church teaches that believers enjoy both the security of God's love and freedom. However, a father, whether heavenly or earthly, who says to his children, 'You are free to behave however you choose,' and then proceeds to get upset or angry or to punish the children when they do not choose to do what he wants is not giving freedom at all.

Hamish McRae's solution to our economic woes, that we should all adopt the Protestant work ethic, sets up a set of stringent rules which, as any renegade Presbyterian can confirm, greatly restrict freedom. Whatever system Will Hutton would create for the sensible regulation of our society it would not contain the freedom for buccaneers to make their fortunes in the city. There'll be no Ferengi in Will's world.

Freedom, like hope, requires uncertainty. If all the conditions of our lives are certain and our future is fixed we would have no hope and no freedom. We would be prisoners serving life sentences in a vast jail.

Fortunately for us, this can never happen. Life is always uncertain and the unexpected can always happen. This happens in every aspect of our lives but especially when we try to create security through money.

Money: Secure and Insecure

Money in history shows a progression from the real to the increasingly imagined. In the beginning what was traded were objects and actions which all people present could see as existing in the world around them. They could agree that this was a goat, that a sheep and that a pile of firewood. When it was services that were being traded all could agree that this woman is doing the washing for that man who is building her house. However, even in these very real trades there was a degree of the imagined, namely the value that people put on the goods and services that were being traded. These values were simply ideas in people's minds, and, since each of us has our own way of seeing things, people could differ very much in those ideas they called values.

The next increasing degree of the imagined occurred when objects like shells, tobacco and rum were deemed to be able to symbolize the value of actual objects. There were the ideas about the value of such objects in themselves (drinkers no doubt valued rum more than did teetotallers) and ideas about the value of the objects being bought and sold which was represented by the objects which were both themselves and a symbol for something else (how much rum is this sheep worth?).

When gold and silver became the coinage a whole new realm of ideas invaded the market place. If gold and silver were valued simply for their usefulness they would cost a great deal less than they do, because their usefulness is quite limited. True, the gold leaf used on the world's most expensive production car, the McLaren F1, is not there for decoration but, unseen, to provide a heat shield in the engine, but other uses of gold, like fillings for teeth, are not so special that other compounds cannot be used. Silver is used as silver salts in some medicines and in photography. Gold and silver have become really valuable for practical reasons only in this half-century when because of their good conductivity they can be used in computer chips. However, they have always been valued for that most intangible of ideas, beauty, and beauty always resides in the eye of the beholder. They are valued for ideas about being special, different, powerful or wealthy. Some people wear gold jewellery because they believe that it enhances their beauty or their position. Others scorn the wearing of gold because they think it is cheap and showy. Thus gold and silver coins did not just bear the ideas about the worth they symbolized in terms of other objects but the fantasies that people hold about gold and silver.

Because gold and silver were the object of some very commonly held fantasies about their values, if the government was overthrown or the coinage debased the owner of gold and silver coins was left with something which still had some value. But when non-intrinsically valuable coins and paper notes were used there was no residual value. In one situation they would have an imagined value and in another they were nothing but sheets of paper and lumps of metal. Their value lay in the realm of the imaginary.

If in the realm of the imaginary I decide that I have a million pounds in my bank account and you, my banker, imagine that I have not I am likely to be defined by others as being mad or bad and dealt with accordingly. But if I imagine that I have a million pounds in my bank account and you, my banker, also imagine that I do then I am deemed not to be mad or bad but simply rich. Business confidence resides in people holding much the same ideas.

The invention of what are now called *financial products* took money even further into the realm of the imaginary. Such products include shares, bonds, pensions and insurance. Here interest (extra value) was given to non-intrinsically valuable paper and coins. When words have an extremely tenuous connection to the actual world they often change their meaning. A product used to be something which we could see and touch. Financial products are simply ideas. They take on a kind of 'reality' only when a number of people hold the same ideas.

The next step further into the imaginary was the abandonment of paper and coins. Money was now represented on computer screens. When I visited Dow Jones in New York the financial journalist showing me around said, 'Money isn't real. It's just shifting noughts on a computer screen.'

These computers allow currency traders to shift the ideas pertaining to some one trillion dollars around the world each day. Some of this money represents the buying and selling of objects that actually exist. Some of it represents the values of objects which do not exist but are expected to exist some time in the future. The future, of course, does not exist. The future is no more than an idea in our minds. So futures trading relates to non-existent commodities or non-existent values for financial products. Most of the one trillion dollars appearing and disappearing from the computer screens around the world relates to the buying and selling of certain figures on certain screens in order to create other figures on other screens. Some of this particular activity is to secure a good price for certain currency in the future and some of this activity is simply for profit. This is the currency market.

Denis Healey once described these changing figures on computer screens as an 'atomic cloud of footloose funds'. The cartoonist Steve Bell pictured these footloose funds as having no contact with the real world (see over).[37]

The history of money illustrates the intractable and continual insecurity of our existence. The way we are constructed physiologically means that everything, absolutely everything we know is mediated by our brains, that is, exists as ideas. If we are wise we try to get as close as possible to a reality we can never know directly by using the ways of thinking and acting which we call the scientific method. Nevertheless, in everything we know there is always an element of uncertainty.

Along with the uncertainty of what we know goes the uncertainty about the outcomes of our actions. We act in order to achieve a certain result and sometimes we are successful, but, successful or not, our actions always have more effects than we expect and often very different ones from what we expect.

This is inevitable because we live in a universe where everything is connected to everything else and everything is in constant motion. Whether this 'everything' is described in terms of sub-atomic physics or of geology or of climate or of human behaviour, the chaos theory 'butterfly effect' is easily demonstrated. A shower of neutrinos, an earthquake in Peru, a hurricane in Texas or the sale of a building in Lower Manhattan can set off a multi-dimensional network of effects which will ripple through the universe until the end of time.

No matter how much information you might gather in order to predict the outcome of a certain action you can never gather enough to be absolutely sure of one outcome, much less the infinite number of outcomes of any one action.

Some people find the intractable and continual uncertainty of our existence too terrifying to contemplate. So they hide from it, protected, they think, by ideas which they believe are absolute certainties. The most popular of these ideas is the belief that there is an over-arching Grand Design of the universe called the Just World where goodness is rewarded and badness punished. In the Just World if you're good you'll be safe. A belief in the Just World is popular with the rich. Are not their riches proof of their goodness? Some people refuse to think and instead focus their attention on small practicalities. Many believe that they can buy security with money. All are mistaken.

The history of money shows that attempting to acquire a certain and reliable security through the use of money always results in greater insecurity. There's always a bigger robber ready to carry away your loot.

Gurus down the ages have advised anyone who cared to listen that possessions breed insecurity. Get rid of your possessions and

17 25-9-92
©Steve Bell 199

you'll be secure. You'll also be uncomfortable, and most of us prefer comfort.

When recently I moved from a large three-bedroom house in Sheffield to a two-bedroom flat in London I was confronted with the huge volume of my possessions. One day when I was sorting them into that which I needed or especially treasured and that which could go to Oxfam I went, memory by memory, through every piece of furniture and every cupboard in my parents' house. I remember the house in great detail, but until then I had never thought of my parents as having very few possessions. I also recalled that the only locks in that house were a Yale lock on the front door and a single little bolt on the back. Nowadays neither would be regarded as adequate security. In my London flat every outside door and window has a set of complex locks and there's a security alarm linked to the police. I spend a small fortune on insurance for the contents of my flat. More possessions and less security. But at least my flat is more comfortable than was my parents' house.

Acquiring possessions requires money, and many people acquire money in order to feel secure. However, having money doesn't ensure security.

I always think about this when I'm holidaying on Fire Island. On that strip of sand facing the Atlantic north-east of New York are some very beautiful houses owned by some very beautiful people. Every year, and in some years more than others, the winds and the sea whisk away much of the sand and often some of the houses.

The house where my friends and I were staying was set in a garden filled with stubby, spreading pine trees. There was a clearing set with a barbecue fireplace and a large hammock swung between two trees. But we never stepped off the path or veranda to light the barbecue or rest in the hammock. This garden, like the lands around Chernobyl, was a killing ground containing not radiation but the deadly lyme disease tick carried by the beautiful deer which frolicked through the undergrowth.

Money can't protect us from the vagaries of nature but it can keep us fed, sheltered and physically safe. So we try to acquire money in order to feel safe.

We try to acquire the pieces of paper and numbers on a computer screen which tell us we have lots of money, but so many things can spoil our plans. Due to matters entirely beyond our control the amount of goods available nationally for purchase goes down or the amount of money available nationally goes up, so prices go up and the value of our money goes down. What is inflation but greater insecurity? Again, due to matters beyond our control, the government embarks on policies which lead to the loss of our jobs or, worse, to war and we lose everything we own. To protect ourselves from such calamities we can use our money to buy more security. What we actually purchase is the possibility of greater insecurity.

Safe as a Bank?

At home in Australia in the thirties on weekday mornings my mother used to check the household clock with the radio announcement, 'It's ten o'clock and the Commonwealth Bank is open for business.' I loved this announcement. It was so solid, so reassuring, a point of absolute fixity in a world of change and uncertainty. I could rely on 10 o'clock and the Commonwealth Bank.

This was how the banks presented themselves – solid, reliable, cautious. Their behaviour did not belie their image. Apart from three bank collapses in 1931 at the beginning of the Great Depression no bank in Australia had failed since the end of the 1890s. It might be hard to get a loan from a bank but you knew that your savings were safe and accruing interest.

For many people interest is seen as occurring naturally like rain, and, like rain, it comes in varying amounts. Interest, however, isn't like rain. It's an idea and not one that is held universally. Aristotle defined the giving of interest, usury, as the birth of money from money and called it unnatural. The three monotheistic religions, Christianity, Judaism and Islam, each prohibited usury. The historian R. H. Tawney summarized the arguments against it:

> It is contrary to nature, for it is to live without labour; it is to sell time, which belongs to God, for the advantage of wicked men; it is to rob those who use the money lent, and to whom, since they make it profitable, the profits should belong; it is unjust in itself,

> for the benefit of the loan to the borrower cannot exceed the value of the principal sum lent him; it is in defiance of sound juristic principles, for when a loan of money is made, the property in the thing lent passes to the borrower, and why should the creditor demand payment from a man who is merely using what is now his own?[38]

Usury was not wholeheartedly condemned by the Christian Church until 850 when the Paris Synod decreed that usurers should be excommunicated. Medieval depictions of hell usually include the moneylender with a bag of money around his neck. It is said that what saved usury and allowed the development of modern banking was the adoption by the Catholic Church in 1253 as doctrine Saint Augustine's idea of purgatory where after death everyone, except saints, martyrs and the incorrigibly wicked, went.[39] Thus wealthy moneylenders could ensure that sufficient prayers were said for their soul to enable them to escape from purgatory into heaven.

The Judaic prohibition against usury included an instruction in Deuteronomy 'Unto a stranger thou mayest lend upon usury; but unto thy brother thou shalt not lend upon usury.'[40] Some Christians saw this as allowing Jews to lend to Christians. Some Jews were prepared to oblige and of course there were many people who wanted to borrow.

The Quran makes it quite clear the Allah has forbidden usury and that the fate of moneylenders is not to arise from the dead but to burn in hell for eternity. However, the Prophet Muhammed was himself a merchant and trade must go on. The Quran points the way. 'Allah hath blighted usury and made alms-giving fruitful.' David Lamb in his study of the Arabs wrote,

> Instead of the traditional creditor–debtor relationship between a bank and its clients, the two parties become partners under the Islamic system, and the bank's function, in addition to making a profit, is to help build society and assist the needy . . .
>
> If you are poor and want to buy a house, the bank will give – yes, *give* you – the necessary money. It provides numerous college scholarships and donates 2.5 percent of the shareholders' profits to charity each year (a tithe known as *zakat*). You want to build a factory or start a business? The bank may write you a check,

> interest free, that will make you a partner. You and the bank share the profits or losses of the venture.
>
> At the heart of the system are the Muslim beliefs that wealth is transitory, that money is not a commodity and that those blessed with abundance have an obligation to share with the less fortunate. The Koran urges individuals to labor and increase production, thus endorsing capitalism and fair profits. It encourages the acceptance of risk but forbids speculation . . .
>
> To apply Koranic principles, Islamic banks have devised enough regulations and plans to fill a mosque: *Murabaha* encourages banks to buy commodities for clients, then sell them back to the same client at a higher price. Under *muamalat*, the bank purchases goods for a customer and is paid back in instalments. When loans are made, commissions and fixed fees are involved, all of which sounds like just another name for points and interest. Indeed, many of the differences between Western and Islamic banking are cosmetic, but having been told how unsavory interest is, Arabs feel psychologically comfortable doing business in a religious environment. And governments encourage the presence of Islamic banks as a harmless way of appeasing the fundamentalists' call for a society based on the Koran.[41]

In effect, in Islamic banks equity takes the place of interest. There is a downside to this seen in the performance of Islamic unit trusts. 'They don't invest in gilts, naturally, nor, usually, in A-shares, which are a little too close to IOUs for comfort. They also don't buy bank shares and this means that the returns are unlikely to be the best on offer. But when it comes to banks – Islamic or otherwise – you can't have everything.'[42]

The first attempt to set up a bank based on Islamic principles was in Egypt in 1962, but President Nasser, who wanted to undermine Islamic principles, closed it down two years later. After his death in 1970 came the oil boom which left much of the Arab world awash with petrodollars. Much of this money was going into the usurious Western financial system so the idea of an Islamic bank became very attractive to many Muslims.

Islamic banks are now flourishing all around the world. But they cannot exist in isolation from the Western system. When the Institute of Islamic Banking and Insurance wanted to organize a seminar on the development of an accounting system in Islamic banks they co-opted the financial firm Price Waterhouse and advertised the seminar in the standard bearer for traditional capitalism, the *Economist*.[43] Even Iran has recognized the necessity for contact with the West. Private banks have been allowed to do business there since 1994.[44]

One of the many problems that beset the Malaysian prime minister Dr Mahathir Mohamad was that the Chinese in Malaysia were far more commercially-minded than the Malaysians themselves. Confronted by the implacable attitudes of the religious right he had tried to outwit them by being holier than thou. When that did not succeed he set about trying to interpret Islam as 'a religion for success in this world as well as in the next'.[45] So Malaysia became the first country to establish a fully Islamic financial system with an inter-bank money market which operates on a profit-sharing concept of *Al-Mudharabah* where the provider of funds earns profit from his investments instead of being paid interest. The managing director of Bank Islam Malaysia explained that if you wanted to buy a house, 'The bank will buy the house on your behalf and then sells the house to you at a cost which includes the cost and a margin for profit but still allows you to make deferred payments. That extra amount that you pay will be more or less equal to the extra amount that you will pay when borrowing from commercial banks.'[46]

So, equity or interest, you're as safe with an Islamic bank as you are with a Western bank.

It does seem as though Islam is managing to accommodate itself to usury just as several centuries ago the Christian Church managed to do. How long, I wonder, will it take the Islamic banks to abandon alms-giving in the way that Western banks gave up service in favour of sales?

The banks that most of us know are the retail or commercial banks. These is where we keep our savings, get a loan and a credit card, buy travellers' cheques, get investment and tax advice and perhaps buy insurance. In most countries there are retail banking chains so we can usually find a branch of the bank we use. This isn't the case in the USA because banks have been forbidden by law to operate in more than one state. However, in 1985 a Supreme

Court ruling allowed interstate mergers approved by the states concerned. In the USA, as in the UK and Australia, where the regulations which controlled the banks have been relaxed, the structure and functions of the commercial banks have changed, not necessarily for the better.

Is the purpose of the commercial banks to help people or to make money? When these banks were tightly regulated they seemed to strive for a balance between public service and profitability. Somehow it seemed that the bank manager was there to look after your interests. (Offering advice is regarded in the Christian West as a respectable form of alms-giving.) His view of what was in your best interests might differ greatly from yours, but your relationship with your bank manager was analogous to the relationships you might have already encountered with a stern but responsible father or headmaster. The bank manager mightn't give you any money, but you could feel secure though misunderstood.

Constrained by regulations, these banks formed a kind of cosy cartel. Then in the eighties the prime ministers Margaret Thatcher in the UK and Paul Keating in Australia decided that everything would be much better if banks were deregulated so that they could compete with one another. Now the sole purpose of their existence was to make profits for their shareholders. Mary Carryer, the general manager, product management of the Australian bank Westpac, said, 'Everything has changed for banks in the economics of their business but, because they were regulated until relatively recently here, the way the public wants to think of them is very much what they were in regulated days. There is an expectation that they provide social services.'[47]

Much of the 'social services' which the banks do is in handling small bank accounts. 'Most bank accounts are small. About two thirds of Westpac's 1.8 million accounts would go below $500 each month. The proportion of the Commonwealth's 6 million accounts may be even higher, as it has traditionally been the "people's bank".'[48]

Handling small accounts is the most unprofitable business in banking. Since deregulation many people have found that the bank which they saw as their bulwark against chaos no longer wanted their business. The banks introduced all kinds of charges, often unbeknownst to their customers. It rapidly became clear that what seemed to be the most profitable enterprise a bank could undertake was writing letters to customers. All this was done under the pretext that we would all be happier now the bank gave us salesmanship instead of service.

In the UK people with limited funds might seek sanctuary in building societies which had a reputation for probity and caring for their customers. But when in the nineties the government changed the rules so that building societies could become banks, many ceased to be sanctuaries. Banks and building societies might be happy to hold your savings and pay interest, but ask for credit and you will be set a test. If you fail it, you may never know why. Banks and building societies determine your credit rating by investigating your past and applying their non-disclosable evaluation to it. You can get a copy of the file about you held by the credit reference agencies (you have to pay for it) but you have no control over how various people have interpreted this file. Does that make you feel secure?

Banks no longer take responsibility for checking the accuracy of their work. Eddie Wetherill of the Independent Banking Advisory Service commented, 'Everybody used to think that banks checked themselves to make sure that mistakes didn't happen, but now customers are totally responsible for checking to make sure they have not been sold short. Unfortunately the recent shedding of staff at the banks is likely to mean mistakes happen more often.'[49]

Feel secure about your bank balance?

My mother wanted me to get a good, secure job and as far as she was concerned there were only two such jobs – bank clerk or schoolteacher. Now neither is secure. In banking jobs are disappearing because banks are 'streamlining' their services. This means closing many branches and encouraging customers to use telephone banking. I find telephone banking very convenient when I want to do something simple like check a bank balance or move some money from one account to another. It's quite a different matter when I want to discuss possible options about, say, avoiding immense overdraft charges if a direct debit is drawn on my business account before a cheque to cover it has been cleared.

When I lived in Sheffield I became increasingly concerned about my bank, the Midland, when it was having an on-off courtship with the Hongkong & Shanghai Bank and whenever more evidence of its involvement in the arms trade was forthcoming, but I felt that moving my accounts to another bank would be an insult to the staff at my local branch who knew me and who were unfailingly kind and helpful. When I moved to London I changed to the Co-operative Bank which so far has proved efficient but I have no personal relationship with any of their staff. There's an anonymous voice on the telephone who makes it clear that there's no time to chat and a computer screen giving me instructions. Neither makes me feel that I have a secure relationship with my bank.

However, at least I'm with a bank where the directors seem not to reward themselves with immense pay rises and perks irrespective of the quality of their work. Commenting on the way in which directors of privatized industries and of banks have done this Will Hutton said, 'Commercial mistakes of the first magnitude have been made, without any apparent impact on the salaries and career prospects of those who made them. The clearing banks, who lent massively on property during the later 1980s property boom, have seen few heads roll despite collectively writing off more than £20 billion of bad debts.'[50] This spectacle does not increase the sense of security and well-being felt by those whose income will never rise to such dizzying heights.

A sense of security is not engendered by the activities of the merchant or investment banks. These banks act as intermediaries between organizations with money to lend and organizations who want to borrow. Such banks will underwrite an issue of shares, and advise on mergers and acquisitions and management buyouts. In the UK the terms merchant bank and investment bank are often used interchangeably whereas in the USA a distinction is made, as a director in the Investment Banking Division of Smith Barney in New York pointed out to me.

He said, 'Investment bankers work more with companies in terms of providing them with avenues to access the capital markets, either the public capital markets or the private markets, to raise capital for the firm, either equity issuance and/or debt issuance. Also to provide financial advisory services to companies that are perhaps seeking to divest a subsidiary, or wanting to acquire a company in the same line of business or a different line of business, so they act more as a conduit to the capital markets for a company to raise additional capital and also as a financial adviser to companies in matters of acquiring and divesting companies of businesses. A merchant banker is somebody who is an individual or a group of individuals that have a pool of capital available to them to invest in a company, and buy a particular company on a leveraged basis. In other words they put up very little equity or they put up the smallest amount of equity they can and they raise a large amount of debt and then they acquire a company with the hopes of improving the profitability of the company and some time in the future selling that company to a private buyer at a much higher price or taking the company public through public offering at a much higher price and then profiting from that transaction. A merchant banker would be more of a principal, meaning that they take ownership, investment bankers, and I am giving you the general definition, typically do not take a principal position in a transaction, we merely facilitate the transaction.'

I had thought that being a merchant or investment banker was a position of considerable prestige and importance until I read *Barbarians at the Gate*, the gripping account by Bryan Burrough and John Helyar of the eventually successful attempt by Henry Kravis of Kohlberg Kravis Roberts to achieve a leveraged buyout of the tobacco and food giant RJR Nabisco, headed by Ross Johnson.[51] Both sides of this long-drawn-out battle had posses of merchant bankers at their beck and call. These poor chaps had to spend their days either frantically scrambling to assemble the contracts and reports the contenders wanted or waiting hour after hour for the next orders to come from their bosses. Still, they were probably well paid for their work.

Did they wonder, at the end of their labours, whether it was worth while? Burrough and Helyar conclude their book,

> The founders of both RJR and Nabisco would have utterly failed to understand what had happened to their companies. In the mind's eye, it is not hard to see R. J. Reynolds and Adolphus

Green wandering through the carnage of the LBO war. They would turn to each other, occasionally, to ask puzzled questions. Why did these people care so much about what came out of their computers and so little about what came out of their factories? Why were they so intent on breaking up instead of building up? And last: What did all this have to do with doing business?[52]

Not that this was the end of the story which the *Economist* sees as having 'a symbolic dimension'.

In the past decade RJR Nabisco has been put through the wringer by several of America's legendary financial engineers, including Ross Johnson, the chairman who tried to buy it; Henry Kravis, the leader of Kohlberg Kravis Roberts, which took RJR Nabisco private in America's biggest leveraged buyout; and now by Messrs Icahn and LeBow. Their activities have not always been popular – except with the grateful shareholders who sold out to Mr Kravis.[53]

And, of course, the merchant bankers and the lawyers.

In the UK the merchant banks had a long history and had acquired a reputation for probity and reliability. They were pillars of the community, part of the society of the Great and the Good known as the Establishment. If you banked with Coutts or Barings you knew that you had a prestigious place in the fabric of society.

The merchant banks had earned their reputation for probity and reliability, not because they were intrinsically so, but because they were tightly regulated. Their special quality, Alex Brummer wrote, 'is, as a sage once put it, they "live on their wits rather than their deposits." They are essentially people businesses, where the lifeblood is ruthlessness in the fray, creativity in deal making, innovation in the market place and most importantly of all, confidence.'[54]

Confidence, our own and other people's in us, can always so easily vanish.

Nigel Lawson, Chancellor of the Exchequer in 1986 and once himself a merchant banker, had every confidence that the deregulation of the City, known as the Big Bang, would produce outstanding results. The merchant banks would flourish. They did not.

Instead of flourishing after the Big Bang, Britain's investment banks have been floored . . . All of the banks that have surrendered

> to foreign ownership have done so for different reasons; Barings because it went bust; Warburg because in the end it did not have the capital or the management to fulfil its ambition of becoming a global player; and Kleinwort because it believed itself too small to survive in a fast-consolidating industry. The circumstances might be different, but each reflected a failure of management . . . Shareholders in investment banks just as often lose their money as make it, and transferring ownership overseas might legitimately be considered as much a blessing as a curse.[55]

Writing in the *Independent on Sunday* in 1993 Jason Nisse listed some 16 merchant banks each with a set of deals totalling 87 which 'bankers would rather forget'. These deals included notorious ones involving Lonrho, the Fayeds, Eurotunnel and Asil Nadir's Polly Peck. At least three of these banks had enjoyed relationships with the infamous Robert Maxwell.[56]

Things were no better in Australia following deregulation. The escapades of people like Alan Bond, Christopher Skase and John Spalvins with the support of a plethora of bankers makes hilarious reading – so long as you forget the people who suffered at their hands. The eminent financial journalist Trevor Sykes called these villains 'the bold riders'[57] and gave a warning,

> Today, the banks are the most hated and ridiculed sector of enterprise in Australia – and they deserve it. In the 1970s and 1980s they betrayed our trust, and we are still paying for their follies and what in some cases came close to crimes . . . between 1989 and the end of 1992 Australian and foreign banks wrote off more than £28 billion in bad debts . . .
>
> Many a good, old-fashioned Australian business was taken over and raped so that a bank could collect a fat up-front fee. And so we saw businesses such as Elders, Tooth and Fairfax transformed from proud, solid old businesses into debt-ridden wrecks. Half the time the banks didn't even collect the fee. They capitalised it as part of the loan and eventually had to write the whole lot off . . .
>
> The vital question now is whether the banks have learned anything. The answer is that they do seem to have learned from their mistakes. But it took them a long time to learn, they have only learned recently, and there is no guarantee they won't forget again the next time greed overtakes them . . .

> In science and engineering, progress is cumulative. On all the evidence, however, progress in finance is cyclical. Each generation seem incapable of learning from the successes and failures of its predecessors.
>
> Whatever was wrong with banking in the 1980s, it was not technology. They had computers everywhere, automatic teller machines, smart card credit cards and the world's most mature bond trading software programs. What was not mature was the judgement of the people making the loans and allegedly vetting the deals. Their forebears, who worked with quill pens, were better bankers because they were better judges of risk, and of character.[58]

To learn from history we have to listen to our elders. Bankers, being human like the rest of us, are always torn, as we all are, between the protection offered by the conservatism of their elders and the freedom of striking out on their own. Again it's the dilemma of freedom and security. The more you have of the one the less you have of the other. Our favourite way of trying to reconcile security and freedom so as to have both is to use the model of the family. There are the parents, strong, unchanging, eternal and wise, providing the backstop and haven for the young who are independent and free. When people praise 'family values' this is the model they have in mind. On a larger scale God the Father provides a backstop and a haven. In banking it's the central or reserve banks.

It's a lovely model and how wonderful it would be if it were an accurate representation of real life. Alas, it is not so. When we're small children we see our parents as all-wise, all-powerful and all-good, but no matter how much we want them to be just so, we soon discover that they are but flawed and limited ordinary human beings. We find too that when disaster strikes us God turns out to be, at best, absent-minded. Central banks do no better than parents and God.

In Australia the Reserve Bank, which took over the central banking functions from the Commonwealth Bank in 1950, limited the state banks' freedom by ruling that no bank could lend more than 33 per cent of its capital in any one transaction, loans over 10 per cent had to be reported to the Reserve Bank and loans over 25 per cent had to be approved by it. However, foreign banks were not bound by these rules and by the 1980s state banks found other ways, usually by equity issues, of getting around the rules. After deregulation of the financial system in 1983–4 there were no controls over how much money the banks could inject into the system. The only power the Reserve Bank had was to vary interest rates. 'The heavy-handed use of interest rates in 1989–90 was a prime cause of the recession which afflicted Australia for the following three years.'[59]

However, back in Britain everyone knew that while your parents might let you down and God forget you, the Bank of England stood between you and chaos.

Or did it?

The Bank of England was set up to stand between the English and the chaos their kings might create. Charles II stole the gold which the goldsmiths, who also operated as bankers, had deposited in his Exchequer for safekeeping. When Charles died and his brother James II was deposed in the Revolution of 1688 the government of William III desperately needed money and hit upon the idea of borrowing £1,200,000 at 8 per cent interest from the public. To make the lenders feel important they were incorporated by the name of the Governor and Company of the Bank of England. The creation of the Bank of England and the National Debt meant that the Stuarts could never be allowed back on the throne lest they repudiate the National Debt. Of course, William III could have saved his government and every successive government millions of pounds had he decided to let the Irish govern themselves. Had there been no Battle of the Boyne England and Ireland would be much richer. But what ruler has ever let sound economic sense stand between him and glory?

Still, Britain had the Bank of England and the English could feel secure – up to a point.

The role of the Bank of England developed over time. It acts as banker for the government and it manages the government's debt. The role of the Governor of the Bank of England is very important. He advises the government on economic matters, especially on the control of inflation. It would be nice to think that in his dealings with the government the Governor remains objective, concerned only with the welfare of the country. In fact, what happens to the advice he gives depends on something very personal, the relationship between the Governor and the Chancellor of the Exchequer.

That this is being more commonly recognized is seen in the closeness with which political commentators and the media followed the relationship between the Governor Eddie George and Kenneth Clarke when Chancellor. Both presented themselves as bluff, no-nonsense men who'd stand their round at the pub, but, as we all know, appearances can be deceptive. We are all friendly and easy to get on with when we are not under threat. It's when we feel threatened that we can behave in ways which others might not predict. If we have a Governor and a Chancellor each of whom believes that he must win every contest, no matter the cost, or that he and he alone is privy to the Absolute Truth, the rest of us are in trouble.

We are also in trouble when the Governor holds the view that it's always best to let people get on with their jobs, or that other chaps like him are always decent and honest, or that if you ask too many questions you'll get answers you don't like. Such attitudes can cause disasters, because another important part of the Bank of England's work is to supervise other banks, both UK and foreign banks.

Take, for instance, the Bank of Credit and Commerce International (BCCI) which came to be known to many as the Bank of Crooks and Criminals. It was set up by Agha Hasan Abedi who began a career in banking in Bombay in the Habib Bank which had been created by the Muslim Chamber of Commerce. This bank followed the Islamic code of banking, a philosophy which Abedi espoused but, while he was always seen to be lavish in his alms-giving, 'in fact BCCI represented a quite different eastern banking tradition, that of the pavement money lender and the "chop shop", with minimal paperwork and scant regard for capital ratios and the like.'[60]

Abedi set up BCCI with the help of Arab backers who bought the first shares in the bank and were rewarded with loans which they never had to pay back. The money for these loans came from small and large shareholders, first in the Third World and then from richer countries. Much of the bank's money came from money laundering deals with drug traffickers and from the dictators Marcos in the Philippines, Duvalier in Haiti and Noriega in Panama. The US Central Intelligence Agency maintained secret accounts in BCCI. The bank 'had billed itself as a Third World bank, as the financial tool that would help developing countries pull themselves out of poverty and starvation. It disguised itself through numerous charitable operations, and hired influence peddlers and respected politicians world wide to embellish that image. Yet in the end, it was the money of the honest depositors that would disappear in the ruins of the bank. The bank would turn out to be a reverse Robin Hood, stealing from the poor and giving to the rich.'[61] Indeed, by 1996 investigators had established that BCCI 'was much more than a bank. It was deeply involved in the international arms and drug markets – acting as a financier and facilitator, cloaking itself in the friendship of top-level politicians and duping them into serving its own ends.'[62]

When in July 1991 BCCI was shut down by worldwide regulatory action the liquidators found fraud totalling £17 billion, the largest in history. Thousands of depositors faced losses of £6 billion and the Bank of England lawsuits for alleged negligence.

Several of the bank's officials were arrested and served prison terms, but its president Abedi remained safe in Pakistan where he died in 1995. No serious attempt was ever made to extradite him to the UK or the USA. British investigators in 1996 disclosed that the Foreign Office refused a police request to draw up extradition papers on the grounds that this would have a bad effect on British diplomats in Pakistan.

However, one of the bank's officials did extremely well. Syed Ziauddin Ali Akbar, the head of BCCI's treasury division, strolled out of Brixton prison in November 1996, after three years in custody. The US prosecutors had wanted him extradited for trial on blackmail charges, but somehow the Home Office had not actioned this request within the time allowed. The Home Office blamed the American officials for a mix-up of the necessary papers, but the BCCI investigators were not convinced. 'Akbar's release, they say, was not the result of incompetence, self-destructing documents, or random acts of either God or the devil, but part of a scenario, choreographed by powerful men and women we shall never hear about. For all his years in jail, Akbar remains a protected species, rumoured to have salted away huge sums of money, extorted from the bank in exchange for his silence.'[63]

When Akbar left the prison looking, as the photographs showed, happy and relaxed, the Conservative government was in the midst of a campaign to improve the morals of the populace, particularly the morals of children who had been issued with a government Code which urged them to be upright, honest and truthful. In this endeavour the Labour Party Opposition competed with the government for the high moral ground. The Liberal Democrats did not stand aside from this competition. Their leader, Paddy Ashdown, joined John Major and Tony Blair in declaring, like them, he was a Christian. Politicians, thy name is Hypocrite.

Simple-minded people like myself would think that if a central bank were supervising another bank, no matter how widespread that bank's interests might be, the central bank would want to see a consolidated financial statement. Yet for years the Bank of England was satisfied to see just bits of information from BCCI. We can all do creative accounting if we know that no one is going to ask to see all our accounts. The Bank of England, unlike the Federal Reserve Board or Office of Comptroller of the Currency in the United States, does not have its own staff of examiners. It has to rely on outside auditors who can be the same auditors for the bank it is regulating. Nevertheless, the Bank of England under British law could have taken control over BCCI's financial operations but instead the bank left that task to those havens for bank secrecy, Luxembourg and the Cayman Islands.

It would be unkind to conclude that the officials of the Bank of England were not greatly concerned about BCCI because after all it was full of foreigners. It must be only by chance that the Bank of England has shown itself most assiduous in arranging a 'lifeboat' for those British banks which were facing destruction after the lending boom of the late 1980s. Lord Spens, having been cleared of charges of conspiracy and false accounting in relation to the 1986 Guinness bid for Distillers and returning to the House of Lords to campaign for improvements in fraud prosecution, claimed that up to sixty banks were on the verge of collapse in the summer of 1991 and had to be bailed out by the Bank of England.[64] Heart-warming stuff, but a trick which the Bank of England could not repeat in 1995 when Barings Bank collapsed under the weight of trading losses run up by one trader, a twenty-eight-year-old called Nick Leeson.

Some years ago Barings Bank celebrated its success in the City by pulling down a quite adequate building and replacing it with what the political journalist Ian Aitken called a 'horrible glass tower'. He recalled that when another firm decided to celebrate their own extravagance with a new building they invited 'that ultra-troublesome trouble-shooter' Sir John Harvey Jones to open it. Always ready to give some pertinent advice, Sir John said, 'I have always made it a rule that whenever I see an apparently successful company moving into plush new offices, I go straight out and sell their shares.'[65] If only he'd given that advice to Barings' depositors!

Who would have thought that with its long history Barings would have allowed one of its traders to run up losses of £827 million, more than the bank's entire capital? Founded in 1762 by Francis and John Baring, by 1818 the bank had become so strong that the Duc de Richelieu commented that in Europe there were six great powers, France, England, Prussia, Austria, Russia and the Baring Brothers. Descendants of the brothers married into the aristocracy and acquired titles for themselves. Not that the bank wasn't capable of making mistakes. Involved in a share issue in Brazil in the late 1890s the bank faced bankruptcy, but it was far too important for the Bank of England not to step in to save it.

Nick Leeson's losses were not a secret in Singapore but somehow the directors of Barings were the last to know. The chairman Peter Baring placed the blame solely on Nick Leeson but on the publication of the report by the Board of Banking Supervision the leader in the *Daily Telegraph* was not so sparing of the directors.

> Mr Leeson is neither a victim nor a hero, merely the latest in a long history of young men entrusted with responsibilities for which they proved unfit. But it is those who sat on the board of Barings who emerge from this story as almost sublime incompetents, blithely counting their own booty on the promenade deck, oblivious of the torrent cascading into their ship below the waterline.

> The public are bound to ask whether the standards prevailing at Barings are typical of those prevailing elsewhere in the City of London, or represent merely a unique theatre of folly . . .
>
> There will always be cats who seek to catch canaries. But those who leave cage doors open for years on end are also gravely culpable. If Mr Leeson goes to prison while the former board of Barings continues going to Glyndebourne, this sorry saga will leave the bitterest of tastes.[66]

As it turned out poor Nick was found guilty and sentenced to six and a half years in Changi Prison, Singapore. The Securities and Futures Authority (SFA) which regulates the City investigated the matter and decided that the two most senior executives, Peter Baring, the chairman of Barings group, and Andrew Tuckey, chairman of its investment banking arm, were not responsible for the insolvency of the group. In return the two men assured the SFA that they would not seek senior management positions in the investment industry. Nine other executives were found to have failed to show 'due skill, care and diligence' and were guilty of 'misconduct'. These nine were barred from working in the investment industry for one to three years and charged costs of £10,000. Not one of these eleven will be prevented from attending Glyndebourne.[67]

The greatest beneficiaries from this sorry affair will be the lawyers. Barings bondholders sued three stockbrokers – Hoare Govett, Barclays de Zoete Wedd and Cazenove – and a number of former Barings directors. Barings' administrators Ernst & Young issued a £1 billion writ against Coopers and Lybrand, Barings' former auditor, and, on the first anniversary of Nick Leeson's imprisonment, Coopers and Lybrand issued a £1 billion writ on nine former executives of Barings. 'The legal fall-out from the February 1995 crash is likely to drift well into the next century and consume millions of pounds in lawyers' fees.'[68]

Who was it that said, 'It's the rich what makes the money and the poor what takes the blame'? The *Daily Telegraph*, which the Barings directors might think would support them, headlined its analysis of the Baring Report with 'How could it happen? The answer is greed', and went on to point out that Nick Leeson contributed a third of the entire profits of Barings. He was paid a good bonus, but nothing like the bonuses the directors of Barings paid themselves. 'When Peter Baring, the last of his line in the chair, plodded round to the Bank on that fateful day in February, perhaps he wondered whether his own £1 million bonus had been fully earned, and whether he could bank on it. In the end, the answer to both these questions was no.'[69]

The Barings Report could only leave an observer with the impression that the higher reaches of banking are inhabited by fools and liars, rather than by men and women who enjoy clarity of thought and a sense of responsibility and honesty.

Brian P. Moss, writing to the *Guardian*, was puzzled by the evidence given to the inquiry that two months' trading by Barings' Singapore office was missing. 'Every transaction is recorded to the nearest second and even if the bank burned down, half an hour later all discs are backed up by other areas and it is absolutely impossible for data to be irretrievably lost. Or is that just what the banks tell us when we query phantom withdrawals or erroneous statement entries?'[70]

Private Eye described in its inimitable way another curiosity of the report, concerning the large amount of money Barings London had been sending to its Singapore office.

> 'It is,' boasted (Eddie) George at the (parliamentary) select committee about the new fiasco at Barings, 'a criminal offence not to inform us, to advance this money without notifying us.' Very well, then why has no one in Barings been prosecuted for not notifying the bank of their advances to Singapore? The answer is barely credible. It is that the bank had given Barings an 'informal concession', waiving for nearly two years its iron rule banning 'exposures' of more than 25 per cent of the bank's capital. Barings of course took advantage of the 'concession' – and poured a cool and ultimately calamitous 73 per cent of the bank's capital into the bottomless pit dug by their blue-eyed 'expert trader', Nick Leeson.
>
> How was the 'informal concession' granted? The recent inquiry by the Board of Banking Supervision could not find out. Not a single letter, document or memorandum, inside or outside the bank or Barings, can be found to prove it. Mr Christopher Thompson, a relatively junior manager at the Bank of England, told the

inquiry that he personally had authorized the concession. He has hastily resigned with every prospect of a good pension. But the bank's guidelines for managers which he failed to follow at his peril specifically insist that any such concession must be referred, at least, to a head of division. The head of division regulating all British banks was, and is, Carol Sergeant.

Thompson said he'd 'mentioned the informal concession' to her. She said she couldn't remember any such thing . . .

The inquiry managed to satisfy itself and the Chancellor (but no one else) that poor little Mr Thompson took the full burden of this vast decision on his own puny shoulders and that no one else was responsible. Then the entire City of London united to reassure the public that the Barings scandal was due to some minor incompetence among junior officials, and had nothing to do with the City's old boy network.[71]

The old boy network of the City and the Establishment is often the subject of sneering remarks, but surely the men in this network are exhibiting that great virtue, loyalty to one's kind. In the East such loyalty is highly regarded. When Agha Hasan Abedi died he was wanted for trial in the US and to serve an eight-year sentence for fraud in Abu Dhabi, but in Pakistan he was a hero. When Imelda Marcos returned to the Philippines she was greeted rapturously by those thousands who had given her their undying loyalty. But at least Imelda had gone as a penitent to church to give thanks when a court in New York found in her favour. She crept to the altar on her knees, a sight which brought tears to many people's eyes. One wasn't entirely sure what Imelda was sorry for (neglecting to take all her shoes with her when she fled the Philippines?), but the spectacle of someone saying sorry is a rare one for those who watch the political and financial processes in the UK.

The fall of Barings Bank showed that the Bank of England no longer had the power it once had to deal with chaos. The bank's officials sought the help of the Sultan of Brunei, usually a good friend of the UK, and then tried to persuade their Japanese colleagues to close Leeson's open accounts, all to no avail. Barings collapsed, its investors faced heavy losses and eventually its assets were taken over by the Dutch financial institution ING. The failure of the Bank of England to regulate the activities of Barings was greatly criticized. At the time the Governor, Eddie George, called such criticism 'a witch hunt', but in the following year he said that he would accept the report by an outside team of consultants which recommended that there should be more bank staff to police what is an increasingly sophisticated financial system. However, he rejected the 'super regulator' methods used in America. He said, 'The tighter the regulation the greater the costs – not just the direct costs of regulation . . . but the constraints imposed on the ability of intermediaries to compete by offering cheaper and more innovative products.'[72] The tighter the security, the less the freedom.

Still, as my mother always said, it's an ill wind that blows nobody any good. The Barings débâcle might undermine our sense of security, but Will Hutton saw signs of hope.

> Every bank is now aware that the Bank of England can no longer stand guarantor if it makes mistakes. Moreover if lessons are learned – about the need for proper regulation and the importance of a strong industrial hinterland to support any financial centre with international ambitions – Barings' collapse could prove the first milestone in a British industrial renaissance.[73]

The trouble is that even if the banks do at last get their act together they now have to face the rise of the 'non-bank'.

With some notable exceptions, banks around the world have been trying to put their house in order after the excesses of the 1970s and 1980s. However, while they have been doing this the demand for their services has been decreasing. In the US depositors have been taking their money out of banks to invest in mutual funds while in the UK unit trusts and Personal Equity Plans or PEPs, which are similar to mutual funds, have become very popular. Borrowers too are turning away from banks to borrow direct from the capital markets. When George Soros, now a philanthropist as well as a spectacularly successful money markets trader, wanted to raise $2.5 billion to build power plants in the developing world he went to GE Capital Services, the financial services arm of General Electric. Ford now owns Ford Financial which is among America's top ten issuers of credit cards. General Motors through its financial corporation GMAC sells insurance and mortgages. From Marks and Spencer you can get food, clothing, personal loans, unit trusts, life insurance and pensions.

Banking regulations used to keep banks quite separate from financial institutions but now across the world the barriers between these two kinds of institution are coming down. Since 1990 mutual funds have been available from most of the large American banks while in Europe the banks have tended to invest in insurance and pension plans.

Meanwhile the Internet is entering banking.

> A survey of Internet banking by Booz-Allen and Hamilton, international management consultants, has found that 154 European banks already have sites on the World Wide Web, with sites increasing at a rate of nearly 90 per cent a year . . .
>
> The survey found the cost of an average transaction on the Internet was 13 cents or less. This compares with 26 cents for a personal computer banking service using the bank's own software, 54 cents for a telephone banking service and $1.08 for a bank branch . . .
>
> Booz-Allen says the Internet poses considerable threats to traditional banks, both because it costs them more to set up Web services and because it neutralises many of their competitive advantages.[74]

Drawing on Robert Litan's book *What Banks Should Do*[75] the *Economist* concluded its survey of international banking,

> Though it has lost its monopoly, the class of businesses known as banks is unlikely to disappear.
>
> Many individual banks, on the other hand, will indeed go under. Robert Litan has been charting the progress of financial disintermediation for many years. At the end of the second world war, he says, banks controlled more than half of the American financial-services industry. Now their share is down to a quarter, and it continues to decline steadily as consumers put their wealth in other places. With spreads contracting, corporate lending is clearly a dying business. But even Mr Litan has no doubt that banks will survive, albeit in a much-changed shape. More of banking's revenues will come from fee-based services such as cash and information management, trading and derivatives. For the sur-

vivors and innovators, there are still huge profits to be made.[76]

How many of these survivors and innovators will be the equivalent of the directors of Barings Bank?

Rely on a Pension?

My neighbour, a man in his seventies, was always kind and helpful but inclined to be critical of those whose skins were darker than his own. When the pictures of yet another famine in Africa were filling our television screens he would say that the Africans had too many children. They should, like him, limit their family to two. One day I sought to enlighten him. I said, 'These people have lots of children in the hope that enough of the children will survive to look after them in their old age. They don't have pensions so they have children instead.'

My neighbour had been born at a time when the old age pension in the UK had been established and accepted. With a period in the forces during the Second World War he had been in full employment all his working life and he retired on a secure, adequate pension. He regarded pensions as part of natural life, like the sun and the rain that made his garden grow. He did not know that he had lived in a rare, brief moment of history when his government saw it as its duty to provide for the old and his country was rich enough to do so.

Now the situation is very different. Will Hutton, who has made a special study of the future of pensions and done much to alert the public to the dangers, summed up the situation:

> More than ever people are on their own – left to the tender mercies of the scarcely regulated labour, capital, annuity and pension markets. They don't know it yet – but the old age they face will be remarkably less affluent than that which their parents enjoyed. For that they can thank Britain's gentlemanly capitalists and the New Right accomplices in government.[77]

Part of the problem lies in the demographic changes in the population in developed countries into the twenty-first century. There will be far fewer workers to support a larger number of old people. Just what the ratio will be is still a matter for debate, but it is agreed that there will be changes in the age composition of the population which will necessitate changes in pension provision if all the population is to be adequately supported in old age. This is actually a big if. In the UK the Conservative Party would have us believe otherwise, but the question is not actually whether enough money could be found to support the entire elderly population – only whether such support is desirable. Just how this question is phrased immediately reveals the speaker's own prejudices. I could say, 'Is it not our duty to care for those who cannot care for themselves?', or, 'Why should people who are working hard support those who aren't working?'

Not that working hard all your life will ensure a sufficiency in old age. Margaret Thatcher presented self-reliance and thrift as the greatest virtues, but many hard-working and thrifty people are finding in old age that what they have achieved is being taken away from them because the state will not provide the care they had expected. The infirmities of old age can be defined as illnesses or as social problems. One way to save National Health Service money is to define such infirmities as social problems, not as illnesses in need of medical care. Thus, if you are old and infirm and you become the responsibility of the Social Services you can be required to spend on your care all that you have built up over decades of work. You can lose your savings and your home.

It could be argued that this is appropriate, that one of the reasons we work is to provide for those times when we cannot work. But in the case of the old something else, I feel, ought to be taken into consideration.

Every stage in our lives presents us with some special task. As little children we have to master certain skills and learn how to fit into society. In adolescence we have to face the task of becoming independent adults. And so on. The special task of old age is to face our own death with a degree of equanimity.

The only way we can do this is to review our lives and reassess our past so that we can come to feel that our life has been satisfactory, that we have not lived in vain and that we have somehow left our mark upon the world. There are a multitude of ways in which we can achieve such an assessment of our lives. Some people seek fame and some riches, but by far the most popular and available way is to have children and to leave them your property. Thus you can feel that you have overcome death because some important part of you continues on. It is as cruel to force old people to sell their homes as it would be to forbid Margaret Thatcher or George Soros to set up foundations in their names.

So, if you want to be able to face your old age and death with equanimity you will have to decide what you are going to do about a pension. Have you or are you going to take out a private pension? Not that whatever you decide to do will make you feel secure.

Will Hutton succinctly described how private pensions work.

> Regular premiums are paid to a company which invests them – typically in shares in the leading 200 companies at home and in other industrialised countries, as well as in a mixture of government securities and property assets. On retirement a fund is accumulated which is then used to buy an annuity, which gives a pension until death. The size of the pension depends upon the level of payments, the size of the fund, the performance of the stock market and the competence with which the assets have been managed – and of course the prevailing annuity rate on retirement.[78]

And that's all the uncertainties – providing there's been no major disaster in your lifetime, no Tokyo earthquake, no stock or financial market crash, no major war in the Middle East.

When the Conservative government in the late eighties made it increasingly clear that the way forward was that people should cash in their rights to the state earnings related pensions (SERPS) and buy personal pensions the insurance companies were given a gold mine. Their salesmen, who earn a commission not a wage, were sent out on the road selling pensions which for some 400,000 people who cashed in their SERPS to buy personal pensions proved to be fools' gold. What the insurance companies did was to 'sell policies they know are unsuitable and calculate their profits on the certainty that buyers will cash in their inappropriate policies early, for a fraction of the proper value . . . The fact that some of the most famous names in British insurance have been shown to be shysters and tricksters casts yet a deeper pall of uncertainty and fear over the vast majority of people who are not rich enough to face the future without careful planning.'[79]

It's not just the people who sell pensions who create uncertainties and untoward outcomes. There are also the pension fund managers.

Pension funds have grown enormously and will continue to grow. 'Once savers realise that they can no longer count on a state-financed safety net, they tend to increase savings dramatically. Dutch pension funds had assets equivalent to 73% of GNP in 1991; since then the figure has risen to almost 85%, according to the European Federation for Retirement Provision.'[80]

It is the job of the pension fund managers to invest these funds so as to ensure a good return on the money. Changes in the patterns of pension fund investments are having a profound effect on the market. Initially in European countries pension fund managers invested in their own country's bonds and similar assets, but now the trend is towards equities because over the long run they tend to give higher returns. At first pension fund managers favoured their own country's equities but now the investment is becoming more international.

The *Economist* sees the growth of the pension fund industry as a force for good. There'll be greater competition between funds, which themselves will demand that the countries in which they invest improve the transparency and efficiency of their stock markets with an improvement in the market's regulation. Such funds will also 'create a new constituency of voters with a vested interest in sound economic policies . . . Some Dutch pensioners have already formed pressure groups to persuade politicians to follow sensible policies.'[81]

Such a constituency of voters might not yet have discovered their power. Some pension fund managers will not risk upsetting any company which might give them the contract for the company's pension but others are well aware of their power and will use it when they feel it appropriate to do so. It was a pension fund manager who successfully deemed Maurice Saatchi unfit to run the firm he had co-founded, Saatchi and Saatchi. Not that pension fund managers are privy to truths which the rest of us are denied. One pension fund manager told me how he had been so convinced that the Labour Party would win the General Election in 1992 that he saw no reason to hedge his bet. This had an unfortunate effect on his fund when the electoral result was announced.

Pension fund managers might be inspired by the extraordinary success of money managers like William Buffett who over four decades consistently outperformed the stock market and who in February 1996, with a surge in the value of the shares in his company Berkshire Hathaway, became the world's richest man. All the research shows that in the long term the odds against consistently beating the market are astronomical. From the work of Harry Markowitz and of William Sharpe, economists who shared the Nobel Prize in 1964, it is clear that the person who buys a representative cross-section of the market and hangs on to it for a long time has a better chance of finishing ahead of the person who is constantly looking for high returns in the market, the kind of trading which carries high risk. William Buffett's method was to invest over a long period in companies with a proven track record for making profits. However, just as many people involved in the world of finance never seem to learn from history, they never learn from science either. The chief executives of pension funds are often prepared to spend vast sums of money in the effort to find money managers who can beat the market.

In the USA pension funds own over a quarter of all American stocks (28.6 per cent in 1992). In 1994 the Pension Fund Guarantee Corporation published a notice which showed that private pension plans were underfunded by about $53 billion. This means that these pension funds don't have the money to pay out the pensions which their members expect. Some of this underfunding comes from too little investment in the fund and some from the poor performance of the investments made by the fund managers. A study in 1992 by the Brookings Institution showed that fund managers, who had been hired at enormous cost to the fund, had not done as well as the stock market by an average of 1.3 per cent per year.[82]

And then there are the proprietors who plunder the pension funds for their own benefit. The most notorious of these is Robert Maxwell upon whose death in 1991 it was discovered that some £440 million of these assets were missing. Less spectacular but just as reprehensible are those company executives who regard any surpluses in their company's pension fund as theirs to use in the company's interests, not in the interest of the fund itself or its pensioners. Surplus pension funds is one of the reasons that a company is seen by company raiders as a suitable object for their depredations.

In some countries there have been attempts to find new and effective ways of caring for an elderly population. The Australian Federal Government under Paul Keating developed a method of co-operation between individuals, businesses and government which was based on the idea of superannuation, a concept known and trusted by generations of Australians. For Australians paying your 'super' out of what you were earning was as much a part of life as having a shower. You could do all sorts of things with your super. At the time of my divorce in 1965 I was utterly penniless except for my monthly salary, but I had been paying superannuation. I drew what I had and escaped with my young son to England to start a new life. A large proportion of the Australians who are abroad at any one time are enjoying the benefits of their superannuation. The Keating solution also contained the provision that all the superannuation funds had employee representatives on their boards of trustees. This reflects the essentially classless nature of Australian society. A favourite Australian activity is reducing to average size anyone who might attempt to be what in Australia is known as 'a tall poppy'.

Singapore arrived at a method which develops from the tradition of caring for one's parents in their old age. There is a Central Provident Fund into which workers are compelled to pay and from which they cannot draw until they are aged fifty-five. There is also legislation which obliges families to support their parents in their old age.

Such filial devotion is not so common in the West. Here instead people need to develop what the financial journalist Joanna Slaughter called survival strategies. She listed these as:

Expect state pensions, unemployment benefits and long-term health care to be privatized – and make provision for yourself.
Take responsibility for your own finances. Become your own DIY financial planner.
Plan for frequent job switches and periods of unemployment.
Don't be afraid of cashless transactions. Plastic 'chip' cards and telephone banking will soon be the norm.
If in doubt, rely on traditional financial common sense. Minimize debt, be suspicious of get-rich-quick schemes and don't put your eggs all in one basket.[83]

If all else fails, have lots of children and teach them that it's their duty to look after you.

Insure Against Risk?

Sod's law of insurance is that if you insure against a disaster it won't happen but if you don't it will. Thus many people, once they've insured against risk, behave carelessly. They insure against risk and then they increase the risk. On the whole we aren't very good at assessing risk. Houses in certain parts of Britain are much affected by the naturally occurring radon gas which is strongly linked to cancer. Although the government offers significant help in making these houses safe, many of their owners discount the danger and refuse help. It seems that we assess risk, not in terms of probabilities but in terms of whether we can imagine an event actually occurring in our life. No matter how carefully insurance companies draw up risk tables of probabilities, how individuals interpret these tables depends on personal attitudes.

Many people see insurance companies as bottomless pits of money to provide recompense. A car accident or the loss of possessions causes no concern because the insurance company will pay. Such a way of thinking leads easily to the idea of a deliberate 'accident' or 'loss'. Stage a break-in at your home, set fire to your factory, and thus get a new television or dispose of the factory you can't sell and still end up financially ahead. Insurance fraud is vast and often cruel. In 1993 a man was arrested in Florida for breaking the leg of a horse and later confessed to killing 13 horses by electrocuting them. For these deeds he earned more than $150,000. '"People get paid less for killing people," Mr Burns said, adding that he hated the job so much he always got drunk first. "When these millionaires get tired of them, they throw the horses away like broken toys."'[84]

Insurance now has a major role in the economies of most countries. It provides some restitution when we are beset by loss, illness, injury or death. The vast sums which insurance companies acquire from the premiums paid are invested, thus making insurance companies big players in the market like the pension funds. Prudential Corporation owns an average of 3 per cent in every quoted company, while Hermes, on behalf of its members in the Post Office and British Telecom pension funds, has invested £30 billion. Such big investors own about 70 per cent of the stock market.[85]

In recent years there has been an enormous increase in the amount of money spent on insurance policies. 'The average family now spends just under £1,000 on insurance every year, in real terms more than twice the level of expenditure of 10 years ago.'[86]

It was not always so. Andrew St George, writing about attitudes to money in the nineteenth century, described the debate about life assurance.

> Assurance in God meant promise of the afterlife; assurance between two people meant trust; life assurance meant something between the two.
>
> The 1850s and 1860s saw heated debate about the morality and usefulness of life assurance. On the one hand, why provide for an eventuality which was already divinely plotted, why play God? On the other hand, why leave needy dependants with no support when prudence could store up earthly treasures and pass them on? John Scoffern's *The Philosophy of Common Life* (1857), written in the thick of market activity, included a chapter on the 'The Nature, Objects and Tendencies of Life Assurance'. It was a prominent feature of the age; important to the individual, and powerful in moulding the characteristics of the family.
>
> For Scoffern, all who believed in the possibility of human moral and material advancement were called upon to map out the principles on which it was based:
>
> *When the practice of life assurance was first established, religious*

> *objections were urged against it. The argument was used that bargaining, during life, for a sum of money, payable at death, partook of irreligion, if not immorality; that it was impious to attach a pecuniary value to so portentous an event in the existence of man, as death. That feeling, happily, has long since given away to a more rational faith; and the practice of life assurance is now advocated by members of every Christian religious denomination.*[87]

When one remembers how stern Jesus was with the rich young man who wanted to follow him, telling him that to do so he would first have to sell all his property and give the money to the poor, one might wonder how Jesus would have responded if that same young man had tried to sell him life assurance.

By the 1880s what was now called life insurance was seen as a good and wholesome discipline for the young. In his book *Talks with Young Men* (1884) J. T. Davidson advised,

> It would be easy to apply those principles in a practical way to the subject of *life insurance*. It is a good and wholesome discipline for a young man, as well as wise and right in the interest of dear ones whom the future may raise up around him, to set apart a sum out of his yearly income for this purpose, and, of course the sooner it is done the better. Sternly, determinately fight the battle with the self. If you conquer this foe, you will be a nobler victor than Alexander, or Caesar, or Bonaparte.[88]

Today a young man seeking life insurance needs the combined courage of an Alexander, a Caesar and a Bonaparte. No matter if he is earning an excellent salary in a secure job, to get a mortgage and/or insurance he will have to answer questions about his sex life. If the answers he gives do not show that he is a confirmed heterosexual who has never taken part in any kind of sexual activity which would put him at risk of contracting AIDS, his request will be refused or accepted only with the payment of an excessive premium. John Ryle, pondering what might happen if, in filling in the application form, you failed to disclose what the insurance company calls 'all material facts', commented,

> That's the deal. They need to know about your sex life. If you want the money you've got to tell them the story. Then they'll let you know. Once such matters were the prerogative of the Church;

you made your confession to save your soul. These days you do it to get a loan. Instead of absolution, insurance; instead of penance, premiums. In the Church of the Latter-Day Underwriter the only sin is to be mortal.[89]

Just as the Church has often fallen below the standards of conduct it advocates, so insurance companies have not maintained a standard of behaviour commensurate with that which they require from those members of the public who seek their services. In the UK in 1994 alone four large insurance companies, Legal and General, Norwich Union, Scottish Widows and the Guardian Royal Exchange, were fined for offences ranging from misleading advertising to poor records. The insurance regulator Lautro told Norwich Union that its training of the sales force was inadequate, something which purchasers of their private pensions were discovering. In the same year in the USA the Prudential Insurance Co was under investigation by the Securities and Exchange Commission.

One would expect that any insurance company which called itself 'Prudential' would indeed be prudent. Not so the Prudential in the UK. It went into the estate agency business in the property boom of the eighties and managed to lose some £340 million. The Pru was not alone. Altogether the building societies who went into the estate agency business between 1985 and 1992 lost some £1 billion between them. Tom Rubython, editor of *Business Age*, quoted the Abbey National as saying, 'Frankly we went into it because others were doing it,' and remarked that it seems 'that most big businesses are not managed by the principles of Tom Peters or Peter Drucker or Harvard Business School but by the lemming strategy which states that if someone else is doing it, we must do it too. Not only that. We must also do it to the death.'[90]

No matter what sensible business principles Tom Peters, Peter Drucker and the Harvard Business School might devise, such principles cannot circumvent the decisions made by those executives who feel safe only when they are doing what others are doing. Needing to go with the crowd rather than stand out on your own relates to individual feelings of self-confidence and self-worth, aspects of ourselves which can subvert the most sensible and efficient of business planning.

Feelings of self-confidence and self-worth play a vital part when a business is undergoing change. Change in the insurance industry became inevitable with, amongst other factors, the success of Direct Line which ignored the traditional insurance sales methods to use the latest technology to set up what was essentially a telephone sales job. Imitators quickly followed, and the large insurance companies shed staff and offices. No longer would a boy or girl leaving school in Norwich look forward to a secure job with Norwich Union. However, there were even more threats to the insurance industry than the use of a telephone to sell insurance.

There's an old saying in the market that there is no such thing as a bad risk, there are only mispriced risks. In the insurance industry over the last ten or so years there have been a great many mispriced risks.

Part of this problem stems from the vagaries of nature. The Earth has always been plagued by earthquakes, hurricanes and erupting volcanoes, but the number of such catastrophes has been rising since the early 1960s. The blame for these disasters cannot be laid entirely at nature's door. There is now considerable agreement amongst scientists that a warming of the planet, called the Greenhouse Effect, is occurring and that these changes affect the climate. The increase in the world's population means that people and industries now occupy land which is at threat from earthquake, volcanic eruptions and flood. The cost of such catastrophes has also been rising. Between 1960 and 1993 the cost rose from $1 billion to $12 billion. Added to this are the costs of urban warfare when terrorist groups deliberately choose targets like the City of London, Canary Wharf and New York's World Trade Center in order to do the maximum damage to the country's economy. Moreover, the costs of dealing with the sins of the past are increasing. Cleaning up polluted industrial sites and paying compensation for industrial diseases like asbestosis will run into many billions. Insurers on the whole have not shown themselves as adept at assessing the risk of such catastrophes. A Los Angeles earthquake had been estimated to cost about $1 billion but in the event cost some $7 billion. The most expensive catastrophe up to 1994 was Hurricane Andrew which cost nearly $16 billion. 'No one knows what Hurricane

Andrew would have cost had it hit Miami instead of missing it by a whisker.'[91]

Insurance companies deal with risk by paying a premium to other insurers (called reinsurers) to assume part of the risk. Or as Patrick, a very successful reinsurer, defined it for me, 'It's quite simple – you get an electric fan, put it in the middle of a table, switch it on, get a lump of insurance and drop it on the fan.'

The most famous firm of reinsurers is Lloyds, and what a sorry tale there is to tell of Lloyds of London.

In the eighteenth century the gentlemen of the City of London met one another in various coffee houses to do business and to gossip. Edward Lloyd, who had a coffee house, realized that if he provided his customers with paper and ink they would stay longer to drink coffee. His premises became popular with merchants, ship owners and businessmen who were prepared to offer insurance for ships and cargoes. Such businessmen did not want to bear the full risk by themselves so they shared it out amongst several colleagues who wrote their names under the name of the lead insurer – hence the term 'underwriter'.

Lloyds outgrew the coffee house and in 1871 was incorporated by an Act of Parliament. Membership expanded over the next hundred years as Lloyds competed successfully with insurance companies around the world. Today the Lloyds building in Lime Street represents the twenty-first century but the practices that go on in the building are far more traditional.

The Lloyds market is made up of about 230 syndicates and each syndicate is made up of individuals known as Lloyds Names. To be a Name once meant that you were part of the financial elite, but no longer. The great thing about being a Name was not just that you had to be very special to be selected, but that you could invest your money twice over. All you had to do was to put up a mere 30 per cent of the full premium required to join. The remaining money could be invested elsewhere. Provided the professionals who ran your syndicate did their job well, all you needed to do was to draw your profits.

However, grand though Lloyds might be, it still kept to the rule that there are no free lunches. Profits for the Names are high in the good years, but in the bad the Names are liable, not just for the full amount of the money that they each had offered on joining but for the full cost of the venture the syndicate was insuring. That is, the Names had accepted unlimited liability. Limited liability didn't exist in the insurance market until the nineteenth century and Lloyds, mired in the past, kept to the original unlimited liability.

In all the Names over the last three hundred years have done rather well, but Nemesis caught up with a significant number of them when the reinsurance bills for the increasing number of disasters started coming in. It seemed also that there was some insider dealing by some of the Lloyds professionals and less than excellent action by the governing body. Not all the syndicates were affected, but the losses certain syndicates and Names suffered have been estimated to be £1.1 billion. When in 1994 three key underwriters were taken to court, Mr Justice Phillips ruled that they had failed to exercise the skill and care to be expected of reasonably competent underwriters and so had breached their duty of care to the Names.

Patrick was harsher in his judgement. He told me, 'These disasters are entirely predictable. The thing that was not entirely predictable was that they were a bit bigger than was expected and a bit more close together than expected. But you are supposed to plan your underwriting to be able to withstand such events. You are not expected to go totally bankrupt. The real reason that they had such terrible losses was that they were greedy. They competed among each other for the same business. It got cheaper and cheaper and they bought more and more of it. It was destined to blow up.'

Many of the Names are now bankrupt or living in reduced circumstances. Some thirty have committed suicide. Various rescue packages have been devised by Lloyds to assist the Names affected, although even as I write in March 1996 a rescue package has been 'unveiled' but not yet acted upon. Meanwhile certain syndicates have discovered that underwriting the activities of Barings Bank was not such a great idea, and six American states have sued Lloyds for fraud and another six are considering doing the same.

No doubt the insurance industry will continue but there are certain to be changes. It is now possible to buy 'hurricane futures' from the Chicago Board of Trade which specify the time and place of the hurricane damage. Or there are 'Act of God' bonds which give insurers some protection whenever God decides to move in one of his mysterious ways and kills people who seem not to have done anything special to deserve his wrath. In the future there could be some difficulty in defining just what is a simple Act of God. If, say, the increase in size and frequency of hurricanes is linked to the Greenhouse Effect, should not the blame for the hurricane's devastation be laid at the door of those industries which have made a major contribution to global warming?

Insurance firms have more to worry about than simply the defining of an Act of God. Claims for industrial illnesses will continue to come in for many years ahead, while the bill for cleaning up polluted sites has been put at a figure which would wipe out the world's entire insurance market. The armaments industry has made it possible for terrorist groups the world over to have access to material which will make bombs of a devastating size. Nuclear proliferation, something which the great nations a decade ago could have controlled had they not been stupid and greedy, is now beyond control and it may be only a matter of time before a terrorist group uses a nuclear device. The supply of arms-making equipment to Saddam Hussein by Western Europe and the failure in the Gulf War to curb his activities put the world at risk of biological attack by terrorist groups, especially by those who see self-sacrifice for the cause as the greatest good.

Less dramatic, but with the potential to make trouble for the insurance industry, is the growth of genetic engineering. The isolation of genes which are linked to certain physical diseases creates complex moral problems while the possibility of certain genetically engineered foods producing some untoward and serious effects in those who consume them is not far-fetched. After all, we have in this half-century seen a new disease come apparently out of nowhere and kill hundreds of thousands. Another concern develops from the way insurance has to date been largely an industry of the developed countries. What will happen once China and India join the club?

Still, we can take heart that the industry is trying to hedge its risks in the booming market of derivatives – or can we?

A Riskless Future?

It is fashionable to talk about the different kinds of bonds, equities, pensions and insurance available as financial 'products'. This word is used because, as a leading public relations manager said to me, 'People buy things. They don't buy concepts.'

The ethics of using such a word in this way are questionable because it gives a spurious reality to certain arrangements. I have bought several such 'products' but all I have to show for the money I've spent are some sheets of printed paper which I keep undisturbed in a box. These sheets of paper are certainly not products in the sense that my floor cleaner or car are products. Financial 'products' are imaginary. They are ideas which may or may not have some relationship with the natural world and the products which we can see, feel and use. We experience the natural world and such products in the here and now, whereas financial 'products' exist only in relation to the future. Yet the future has no reality. It is an idea in our heads. We believe that we have a future and we guess at what it might be, but we can only know what the future is when it becomes the present.

Step into a derivatives market and you enter a world of the imaginary, ideas about money and value in the future. Of course the floor of the London International Financial Futures and Options Exchange (LIFFE) looks real enough with its banks of computers and its pugnacious and noisy young men, but what is going on is a game of ideas.

Games are possible only when the group of people who want to play agree upon a set of ideas called 'the rules'. A game is distinct from other activities in that it always involves competition and an element of risk. Some games are more risky than others. The outcome can never be certain. Pleasure is optional. Some games are straightforwardly called games and other games masquerade as simple activities by calling themselves business, or marriage, or religion, or science, or art. There is no human activity which cannot be turned into a game.

Financial 'products' are games. Every so often someone thinks up a new game, called a new 'product'. However, most new 'products' are just a re-working or an extension of an old 'product'.

Derivatives are often spoken of as being new but in fact they have been around for a long time.

A derivative derives its meaning from something else. It's an idea developed from another idea, perhaps an idea closely related to the natural world and its products or perhaps an idea relating to a whole string of ideas. There is one kind of derivative we all use every day: money. Money derives its meaning from something else. The meaning that a derivative has always relates to the future. Its aim is to make something certain in the future for the purchaser of the derivative despite the fact that the future is always uncertain.

Derivatives have a long history. They actually predate stocks and bonds by several thousand years. Hammurabi, King of Babylonia in the eighteenth century BC, included in his Code a law allowing a grain merchant to make a binding agreement to borrow a fixed amount of gold to pay for the next harvest. If the price of the grain dropped he would make a profit when he repaid the loan and if it rose he would make a loss. The Greek philosopher Thales, born about 625 BC and regarded as the founder of science, studied the stars and the weather and developed a method for predicting the quality of the coming olive crop. Before anyone was aware that the next harvest would be exceptionally good he paid all the owners of the olive presses for the right to rent their presses during the harvest and he negotiated a rent. When the bumper crop came to be harvested Thales controlled all the presses, paid the owners the small rent he had negotiated and charged the olive growers what was for him a most profitable rate.

In the seventeenth century in Japan, a period of great unrest, the merchants worked out a way of protecting themselves against sudden fluctuations in the cost of rice. They would buy and sell rice for future delivery depending on what they as a group thought the price would be. In the same century but on the other side of the world the Dutch tulip bulb growers, recovering from the burst bubble of the tulip market known as tulip mania, developed a futures market. The opening of the Chicago Board of Trade in 1841 was yet another example of when 'merchants bought and sold the future for comfort in the present'.[92]

These historical examples are all tied very closely to the natural world and its products. The future they seek to control is not very far away and its outcome will be easily seen. The commodities futures markets are now huge and dependent on computers talking to one another to record the sale and arrange for the transaction to be carried out, but the rationale of their basic operations is as straightforward as that worked out by those merchants in Japan, Holland and Chicago. With the buying and selling of currencies and bonds the futures markets, where there is a promise to sell or buy at a future date, and the options markets, where there is an option to buy or sell at a future date, are not so straightforward and are dependent on some complex mathematics. Moreover, the language of these markets is obscure in the extreme. Paul Sheehan, writing about what he called 'the phantasmagoric world known as the derivatives market' which does not make a single tangible product but just money, listed 43 different kinds of markets and 61 different kinds of bonds. He calculated that in 1994 there were 47,000 different kinds of options.[93]

The derivatives markets exist in order to transfer risk. There's no escape from risk. There's only the freedom to choose which risk you want to take.

One way of dealing with risk when there is a great deal of money at stake is to buy into a hedge fund. The term comes from an American Securities law and in a strict sense means a fund which is able to trade in a wide range of financial 'products' but is exempt from registration under federal securities law. Because hedge funds are not likely to meet the requirements of the regulations in most countries, to protect investors these funds are set up either as private partnerships for those investing in them or they are based offshore where national regulations do not apply.

The term 'hedge' in 'hedge fund' is another example of how the financial world perverts language in order to bamboozle the public. (The financial world is not the only group of people to pervert language. Any person or group who is seeking power, wealth and prestige does so.) Anyone not intimately involved in the financial world recognizes the word 'hedge' in 'to hedge one's bets' as referring to laying off risk. Had I been in Australia for the Federal election of 1996 I might have taken a bet on Labor winning but also bought some shares in anticipation of a price rise with a Liberal victory. The idea is to take on two risks so that whichever fails the other is likely to win, cover the cost and may even give a profit.

However, hedge funds are not concerned with balancing risk but with making a profit. They assume risk by using the money put into them by their investors as well as using funds which were borrowed to increase the scale and risk of their activities in arbitrage strategies (taking advantage of small price differences in different markets) in derivatives. This is not hedging but speculation.

Not that the financial world is unanimous in regarding speculation as bad. The central banks might fear that operations of the hedge funds are adding to the volatility in world capital markets and so creating instability in banking which could lead to the collapse of one bank, triggering a domino effect on the other banks and bringing them all down. However, speculation can lead to profit and so it will always be popular.

What hedge funds have done to language is to blur the distinction between hedging bets and speculating. An essential part of business management is that of managing risk. A company which hung on to each risk its business created and did nothing to manage its financial risks would actually be speculating. As the cost of derivatives has decreased and the computer technology and expertise increased, more companies are using derivatives to manage their exposure to risk.

Alas, not entirely successfully. Between 1986 and 1995 some thirteen companies, local government agencies and banks, beginning with Hammersmith and Fulham local authority in London and ending with Barings Bank, ran up around $9 billion in losses by speculating in derivatives.

The problem, as it seems from my reading, was identified very early on, but in those thirteen cases and probably many others, it was not understood and resolved. It was that the top managers, the people who are ultimately responsible for managing their organization's risk, did not understand derivatives and so did not know what their so-called financial experts were doing.

> In early 1994 Thomas Riley, one of the supervisors of Robert Citron, the treasurer of Orange County (California) whose speculations ultimately bankrupted it (commented): 'This is a person who has gotten us millions of dollars. I don't know how the hell he does it, but it makes us all look good.' And how does Mr Riley look now?[94]

Orange County lost $1.7 billion.

As I read *Rogue Trader*,[95] Nick Leeson's account of how be brought down Barings Bank, I felt that I would not have trusted this young man to buy groceries for me. Not that he would have deliberately cheated me, but he would have carelessly got my order wrong and then spent the change on sweets for his mates. In his book Nick Leeson identifies the person who had hired him at Barings, but the blame should not be laid entirely at that man's door. All the senior managers who met Nick were in a position to assess his work. Were they such poor judges of character that they could not distinguish an immature, eager-to-please young man from one who can identify and assume the responsibilities of the job? Did the male managers see in Nick someone who was just like them when they were that age? Or was he seen as nothing but a working-class lad sufficiently intelligent to do the job but too stupid to know that he was being used?

Anyone who deals in derivatives, either directly or through an agent, needs to be a good judge of character. He should also know himself extremely well. The *Economist*, not a journal to promote the cause of self-understanding, said,

> The $64 trillion question, of course, is whether derivatives are safe. That comes down to three separate issues: how well the buyer understands what the derivative does; what the derivative is being used for; and what risks are inherent in the derivative itself. The first two questions are really about the qualities of the buyer rather than that of the product. Many so-called derivatives disasters are in fact speculative disasters that might just have easily happened if the investor had been punting in shares or equity.[96]

Situations change but certain problems remain the same. Here in the new world of derivatives we have the old problem of people who do not want to make the effort of understanding something which it is in their interest to understand. Of course thinking is the hardest work anyone can do, and many people try to avoid such hard work. But thinking is not as hard as many people believe it is. Faced with a new technology or a new procedure they feel overwhelmed by a chaos of detail. From an education which puts learning facts before gaining understanding of principles many people, who regard themselves as very well educated, fail to grasp that every technology, every procedure in whatever area of human activity, is based on a small set of principles which can be simply stated. It is not necessary to understand the detailed application of these principles in order to understand how this technology or procedure works.

However, it is not always in the interests of the experts in a particular field to reveal the set of simple ideas which govern a particular project. I belong to a profession which defends itself with a jargon in order to hide the fact that psychological principles are simple and obvious in the extreme. I've spent much of my working life listening to psychiatrists busy bamboozling their patients and the general public with nonsense far removed from real experience. Once you recognize jargon as jargon you can then learn how each piece of jargon can be translated back into ordinary, everyday language. Experts in the jargon might not want to help you lest they be revealed to be wearing the Emperor's new clothes, but you can persist, provided you have the self-confidence to ask in public what are apparently very naïve questions. If an expert cannot explain in ordinary language, he is either trying to mislead or he does not understand what he is talking about. But of course if you are a chief executive determined at all costs to hide your lack of self-confidence by maintaining your position of superiority you will have to continue in your state of ignorance.

A lack of transparency bedevils the use of derivatives. It is not just that people want to hide their ignorance or maintain their superior position. It is often the old deceit of not wanting others to know what profits you're making. Sometimes the people buying and selling derivatives don't know themselves what profits they are making.

Because so many people have not learned how to look for the

underlying principles in any activity they are often not aware of the principles or reasons which underlie their own actions. I shall talk about this at greater length in the next chapter, but here I shall note that many business people seem not to be clear whether they want to do business or to make money. Not being clear about this means that they are easily seduced into neglecting their work to make money. Alex Brummer saw this as pertaining to the directors of Barings.

> No doubt, as the experts keep telling us, the derivatives markets are wonderful places which have brought all kinds of real world trading efficiencies to financial markets, as they have to commodity markets. But there is strong evidence to suggest that the monster is out of control: making money from these extraordinary trading programmes has in some cases – including that of Barings – become totally divorced from the real-world activities on behalf of clients. Barings was not arbitraging in the Far Eastern markets to assist Inchcape or some other worthy client in the region: it was doing it for itself because it was an easier way of making money than, say, lending to medium-sized businesses in the UK. Why bother with relationship banking, when a 28-year-old dealer can bring in the profits at far less cost.[97]

Leaving aside the omni-present human stupidity and cupidity, derivatives will always be full of uncertainty. It is always likely that the value of the derivative will change and that it may not be a perfect match for whatever it is intended to hedge. Perhaps the greatest uncertainty lies in the way that derivatives have only a tenuous connection with the natural world and its products. In 1994 it was reported that, according to the World Bank, the volume of crude oil futures and options traded on the New York Mercantile Exchange amounted to 200 million barrels a day, or almost four times the amount of crude actually produced in the world.[98] Many of the people who are at what might be called the leading edge of derivatives are mathematicians, physicists and engineers, the kind of people who are happy to inhabit a world of theory but who in another age would have had to earn their living by actually being engaged in making real, not imaginary, products, an activity which would have served to keep them close to the natural world and the people who inhabit it.

The only way we can avoid being lost in our theories and led astray by our fears and desires is to recognize that, while all that we can know about the world is our ideas, we should strive to create ideas that reflect as accurately as possible what is going on. A major error is to think that our ideas are not ideas but reality.

The public meaning of money is a set of ideas which most of us hold. The world-wide financial and economic systems work as well as they do because the majority of us accept the current ideas which form the financial and economic systems.

It's a kind of faith, and, like the faithful of any belief system, we become fearful and angry when any of our number reject the faith. When in 1917 and again in 1949 first Russia and then China rejected the financial faith of capitalism, the horror this inspired in the remaining capitalist world arose not because these renegade countries were going to wage war against the rest of us (that fear came later) but because in rejecting the capitalist economy they showed that capitalism was a faith, a set of ideas, and not an absolute reality.

Had the faith which called itself communism proved to be successful and not been brought down by those most human of traits, stupidity and greed, the faith of capitalism could have been diminished if not destroyed simply because the communist faithful belittled and ignored it. This is what happened to the financial and economic systems developed by native people who were later invaded by capitalist conquerors. The English settlers in Australia didn't even *see* the finely tuned economic system developed by the aboriginals. They simply imposed their own set of ideas and the aboriginals, not understanding these ideas, could not adapt.

The set of ideas which is the financial and economic system requires group consensus and co-operation. Because we have to keep to the rules contained in these ideas we gain some security (though not as much as we want) and lose much of our freedom. However, much as we want the security of being a member of a group, we still hanker for our individual freedom and do what we can to get it.

Thus, while we share the public meaning of money, we also have the private meanings we each give to money. This does not necessarily increase our sense of security because our private meanings often run counter to our public ones.

4

The Private Meaning of Money

> Money is like a sixth sense without which you cannot make a complete use of the other five.
>
> W. Somerset Maugham

In all our thinking and talking we use metaphors and similes. One way or another we are saying that one thing is the same as something else or like something else. To know something we need to know what it's like. What is an option? It's like a promise. What is the GDP (Gross Domestic Product)? It's like the sum of everything you make. Often we no longer see the simile or metaphor contained in the words we use. Who, when talking about the economy, thinks of inflation as air being taken in and deflation as air being expelled?

Commonly used similes and metaphors lose their power to command our attention, with the result that we are often unaware that the metaphors used by another person might not be threadbare clichés but intimations of the person's own idiosyncratic view of the world. If a high-flying, hard-working investment banker says, 'People are trapped because they have built up their lifestyles to be equal to their salary and they can't get off the treadmill even if they want to,' it is highly likely that he has chosen, out of all the ones possible, the metaphors of 'being trapped' and 'on a treadmill' because they relate to how he sees his own situation. Perhaps he sees himself as being trapped and on a treadmill, or perhaps this is how he pictures the fate he dreads most and wishes to avoid.

Our own personal, idiosyncratic similes and metaphors have a force and an arresting charm that shared similes and metaphors, the common coin of language, never have. We usually experience our own idiosyncratic metaphors not just as words but as images. Indeed, some of our most powerful metaphors we might never put into words but simply see them in our mind's eye, hear them in our inner dialogue, and feel them wrench our gut, squeeze our lungs and press our body.

Often in my work I have asked people to make explicit their important private metaphors. With depressed people I ask, 'If you could paint a picture of what you're feeling, what sort of picture would you paint?', and 'If you could paint a picture of how you experience yourself in your very essence, what sort of picture would you paint?' The images described showed how each person was experiencing the imprisoning isolation which is the distinguishing feature of depression and how each person has turned against, denigrates and punishes himself. No two images are the same, thus reflecting the idiosyncratic nature of our experience, but all the images have the same meanings, the prison and the self-hatred of depression.

When I was researching for my book *Time on Our Side* I asked people to describe their image of themselves in relation to time. These images showed that we find the common clichés about time passing to be quite inadequate and instead we create our own vivid pictures which are intimately related to how we see our life. One friend, John, a very successful businessman, drew time as two parallel series of clocks and mountains with himself running along towards the clocks and the mountains. It might have been a picture of life as one damn thing after another, except for the fact that he drew himself as being bigger than the mountains. John knows how to solve problems and overcome obstacles.

Again in researching for this book I asked a wide range of people how they saw themselves in relation to money. The responses were so various that it is amazing that the public meaning of money functions as well as it does.

Physicists deal with the conundrum that sub-atomic particles can be pictured both as packets of energy or as continuous waves of energy. Such apparently disparate images are not as unusual as they are often taken to be. Should we picture money as being in discrete lumps or as a continuous flow? My friend Jane saw money as being discrete. She said, 'I'd be treading on it – tramping it under my feet. It would be crispy notes, not coins, and I'd be crunching them up with my feet like the leaves in autumn,' while my friend Ron saw it as a flow. He said, 'I don't see money as something that is ever anybody's. Money to me is like a toy we used to have here. You pour water into the toy and it goes round like a mill. Money to me is just like water in a mill. It really doesn't matter whose it is as long as you can be part of the flow. You can't do anything but be where money flows and to help channel where it is going. People think they have money but they don't. Money is just one part of life. Money is like water, just one of the things that makes other things.'

Money is both discrete lumps and a flow. It is also good and bad. The actor Peter Barkworth declared, 'Money should be fun,' while acknowledging his debt to Dodie Smith who thought that life should be fun – but note that 'should be'. Money isn't always fun, and the fun and the misery are intimately entwined, as the writer Douglas Kennedy described. 'I see money as the form of a large but tricky security blanket. Something which feels good to the touch and seems very comforting but occasionally you actually cut your hand on it. I hope I am smart enough to know that once you have that security blanket you are actually very vulnerable.'

Our vulnerability usually arises in our relationships with others. Alan Brien, writing in the *Spectator* thirty years ago said, 'It is money, not love, which has no objective existence. Money is mankind's way of refusing the human touch of flesh on flesh, of walling off your neighbour, of reducing people to things that can be entered in a ledger and costed on a balance sheet.' Our image of money can warn us of its dangers. Alan never troubles himself about money but he is passionate about not walling himself off from his neighbour.

Money is often seen as having a will of its own. A Palestinian financier said, 'Money is a coward. It will go only where there is security.'[1] In a workshop I ran I asked the people present to draw their image of themselves in relationship to money. Sheila drew money as a great big money bag tied securely at the top and with legs determinedly running away while she with arms outstretched chased after it, unable to arrest its progress. Adela drew herself climbing up a steep mountain while the money bird fluttered overhead and out of reach. 'Money,' said Adela, 'is freedom.'

Frank saw himself as being held captive by money, but he did not picture it as a trap or a treadmill. He drew money as a huge, black rectangular slab which towered over him. The slab was a magnet which held him fast in its power. Frank had a very well-paid, prestigious, highly-skilled job which gave him many rewards but which made it hard for him just to be himself and lead the life he wanted to lead. He wanted to break away but couldn't. Linda felt money as a force but in a different way. She said, 'I feel there's a hand in the middle of my back and it's pushing me along.'

As we all know, opposites attract and married couples can be pairs of very different people. My friend Tony described himself as 'a passionate, hot-blooded person', whereas his wife Helen is gentle, reserved, quiet and patient. When I got them to draw themselves in relation to money Tony drew himself in shorts and T-shirt, whizzing along on roller skates where the wheels were money. Helen drew herself sitting very still on a straight-backed chair. On her lap was a small, round object which she'd labelled 'handbag' and under her chair was a solid box which she'd labelled 'my own income, savings, etc.' In front of her, securely tied and apparently out of reach was a huge bag which she'd labelled 'the rest of the money in the world'.

Helen said, 'I was thinking over our discussion about money yesterday, about Tony's attitude to money. If I decided to spend half the money we have in our bank account on something, I don't know what, when I told Tony about it he'd say "Why didn't you spend more and get the best" or "If it was so good, why didn't you get two?" I knew when I married Tony that he had these big ideas and was over the top in some ways with generosity, but that was one of the things that I liked about him.'

Tony said, 'And has since tried to stamp out.'

There's the rub. Opposites attract, but their opposite points of view can so easily become opposing positions, especially where money is concerned.

We see money not just as good and bad but as real and unreal. Patrick had made a fortune in reinsurance, lost it, and made another. He said, 'I made about one hundred and fifty thousand dollars, and it was paid into my bank and it had the strange feeling of unreality about it. I would get my bank statement and it would show that my bank account had gone from 264 dollars to 150,000 and it was weird. I was rich but I did not actually feel that rich, I mean relatively speaking rich. But I didn't feel it because it was so unreal. I think you have to live with it for quite a while to get used to having money, or not having money. I mean, you can adjust to it. I have had underwriting losses well into six figures and I sort of look at it as being beyond my control, there is not much I can do about it. It's only money. But I would say that a better appreciation of life comes from not having money. You appreciate the things you cannot buy, that you can enjoy for nothing. Like a nice day or good friendship.'

Nick Leeson certainly saw money as being unreal.

> All the money we dealt with was unreal: abstract numbers which flashed across screens or jumped across the trading pit with a flurry of hands. Our clients made or lost thousands of pounds, we just made a commission. Some dealers in Japan did proprietary trading and risked Barings' own money, but not us in Singapore. We just arbitraged back to back with no risk or filled other people's orders. The real money was in our salaries and our bonuses, but even that was a bit artificial: it was all paid by telegraphic transfer, and since we lived off expense accounts, the numbers in our bank balances just rolled up. The real, real money was the $100 I bet Danny each day about where the market would close, or the cash we spent buying Kinder eggs to muck around with the plastic toys we found inside them . . .
>
> I could step forward and with just one wave of the hand buy or sell millions of pounds' worth of stuff. And it was just stuff: it wasn't bread or milk or something you could use if the world came to an end. My products were notionally called Japanese Government Bonds, or futures, or options, but nobody cared what the hell they were. They were just numbers to be bought and sold. It was like trading ether.[2]

Barings Bank might have lasted longer had Nick Leeson followed the policy towards money which George Kennedy, chairman of Sims, follows. He told me, 'When you're talking in amounts like telephone numbers it's easy to forget just how much is involved. It's easy to say, "I'll throw in another million." And then on Friday evening I'll go to do the weekend shopping and be shocked because something's gone up four pence in price. That's why when I'm talking in millions I try to think of the money as being my money. That keeps me in check.'

Thinking about vast sums of money as if it were your own might be a good way of keeping yourself in touch with the real world, but what happens when you start to think that the company money actually is your own?

A senior executive of a multinational told me about those top executives of large companies who regard company money as their own. He said that in the lowest rungs of the hierarchy executives are very careful to distinguish what is company property and what is their own – a company pencil from their own pencil – but the higher up the hierarchy the less distinction is made, until at the top the executive sees himself as having the right to everything the company owns. The company pays for everything – homes, holidays, cars, even cars for family members. Some of these executives, like the Queen, never carry money. In any situation requiring money – meals, drinks, taxis, tips – an accompanying subordinate pays. The subordinate should regard it as an honour to pay, but if he feels he needs to get the money back he can claim it on expenses – which the top executive signs. Yet that same executive will object most ferociously if a subordinate gets some kind of perk, no matter if it arises in the course of his company duties. A few top executives are highly obsessional about their own money and bring this obsessiveness to bear on the company's money. They continually worry about waste. Such obsessional executives are more likely to be found in smaller companies than in large international companies where, at the top, distinctions about who owns what are likely to be blurred.

We each have our own way of defining mine/not mine, and we each have our own way of defining enough money/not enough money, and rich/not rich.

The *Independent on Sunday* asked a number of people, 'How rich is rich? Of these, Ivan Massow, a financial adviser, replied, 'Rich is when you can live off the interest of your capital. To live comfortably, you'd need about £150,000 a year. So you'd be rich if £150,000 is the interest on your capital.' Quentin Crisp, well practised in living on very little, said, 'Everything is rich to me, I have nothing. I don't understand money. I'm happy as I am. If I had money I would be full of anxiety.' Richard Platts, a Lloyds Name, said, 'I think £50,000 would be a rich person's salary. I've never had an income approaching £60,000 or even half of that, yet before I lost everything I regarded myself to be relatively well off. Now, at 60, I've nothing except my £12,000 pension and I've just received a bill from Lloyds debt collectors demanding £800,000.' Hannah Moseley, unemployed, said, 'At the moment anyone who earns more than £7 an hour is rich. I consider really rich to be anyone who can do whatever they want to do and doesn't need to think about it.'[3]

Hunter Davies, interviewing David Hockney, wrote, 'He thinks that £1m for a Hockney is ridiculous. "Not that I've ever got that. Money doesn't mean that much to me. I've always felt rich. I do what I want to do, all day long. That's being rich." '[4]

I've never felt rich but I find that whenever I make a substantial purchase, no matter how carefully I've worked out that I can afford it, I take to catching buses where before I would take a taxi. If only I could be like Lady Colin Campbell who writes books about the Royal Family. When Lyn Barber interviewed her she asked whether she had ever been hard up. Lady Colin answered, 'Well, put it this way. There have been times when I've been *broke* but I've never been poor. Because I've always had *value*, even when I didn't have the readies.'[5]

Such a superior attitude is not appreciated by George Ball who used Channel 4 television to express his displeasure.

> There's a little group of words which gets my back up. You know the sort of thing – we recently had a politician saying quite flatly, 'Three million pounds is peanuts.' Then a lady, wanting funds for a pet Arts project asked for 'a *mere* £50,000'. Those are my hate-words – Only, Just, Mere, Peanuts. What they mean, of course, is that by comparison the money they seek is tiny. But, as

Shakespeare's Dogberry puts it, 'Comparisons are oderous.' They stink! But these words are used by responsible people speaking from national platforms. And how the words change when they step down from those public platforms. Every child has heard the shocked tones of parents: 'What! 35p for a comic? Never!'

Is this just nit-picking or does it really matter? I think it does and I'll give you two reasons why.

First, there is the effect in the average household where one man's 'only' is translated into another man's 'What!' 'Only £80' for a television licence is a huge sum when it amounts to more than a week's pension. The oddity in all this is that the politician pleading for £3 million as peanuts is also the parent shocked at the price of a comic. Not so odd: the only-just-mere-peanuts brigade is spending someone else's money. From Parliament down to the lowliest Parish Council they spend huge sums of OUR money. 'It is only £30,000,' they'll say. British Telecom will still try to justify (or onlyfy or merefy) the outlay of a million pounds on a new logo in similar terms. But £50,000, £3 million is a heck of a lot of money. What would you do with a mere £5,000?

Money is never, never only, or just or mere. Not your own money, that is.

Which brings me to the second reason why all this matters and that is the effect it has on the people who are spending OUR money; it changes their attitude. They quite forget that two or three of these 'insignificant' sums add up to a very large chunk indeed. And that spells trouble for you and me. For why? Because when we've finished paying for all these only and justs and meres we've got nothing left to buy a packet of peanuts.[6]

And then there's the phrase that Margaret Thatcher made famous, 'value for money'. Naim Attallah said, 'The richer the person is, the more he wants value for money.'[7] However, value for money doesn't mean the same for all of us. The mathematician John Allen Paulos told the following story.

I once wrote to a significant minority of the Forbes 400, a list of the four hundred richest Americans, asking for $25,000 in support of a project I was working on at the time. Since the average wealth of the people I contacted was approximately $400 million ($4 \times 10^8$, certainly a gargantuan number of dollars) and I was asking for only 1/16,000th of that wealth, I hoped that linear proportionality would hold, reasoning that if some stranger wrote me asking for support of a worthy project of his and asked me for $25, more than 1/16000th of my own net worth, I would probably comply with his request. Alas, though I received a number of kind responses, I didn't receive any money.[8]

One problem that we can all have with these private images, metaphors and similes is that they can just pop out at times when they should not. I attended the Extraordinary AGM of News International in March 1995. It proceeded like all those AGMs where everything has been decided in advance. However, when Gus Fischer, the chairman, was reading out the amendment on which we had to vote he said, 'revolution' instead of 'resolution'. When corrected he laughed and said, 'It's not a Freudian slip.' A week later News International announced that Gus had resigned. Roy Greenslade, writing in the *Guardian*, reported that, 'Fischer apparently told friends recently: "If Murdoch gives me another bollocking, I'm walking."'[9]

Security and Danger

All these different, idiosyncratic images do not arise as idle thoughts of no more than a momentary significance. Rather they come from the only possible source – our past experience – and they are selected from the wide variety of options our experience offers us because they represent something of great significance to us.

The concept 'our past experience' could be pictured in many different ways – perhaps as a well from which the person can draw, or as a supply of sustaining food. Scientific thought requires a picture, called a model or paradigm, which can be applied to all people and which allows for some kind of measurement and prediction. A model or paradigm should be able to encompass the relevant research findings to that date. When new research fails to fit the model, scientists should create a more appropriate model. Unfortunately, scientists, being human, often get attached to what they know and hate having to admit they were wrong, especially when prestige, power and money for research are involved. Battles between scientists are always along the lines of, 'My model is better than your model.'

The model I use for a person's past experience is remarkably simple, which means it fits easily with new research by cognitive psychologists and neurophysiologists. It is simply that of a structure, a kind of self-supporting scaffolding which at the same time is remarkably flexible. The structure is made up of every meaning the person has ever created. In it every part is connected in some way to every other part. This structure is the sum total of the person's attitudes, beliefs, opinions, conclusions, memories and images. Indeed, this structure is the person.

You don't *have* a structure of meaning. You *are* your structure of meaning.

Because no two people ever have exactly the same experience, no two structures can ever be exactly the same. Ever since in 1996 some scientists in Edinburgh managed to produce two sheep as clones, that is, having the same genes, there has been much ill-informed talk about cloning people, based on the idea that human clones would be identical persons. They would not. Human clones might be very similar to one another in appearance, but each would have had different experiences. Their meaning structures would be different. If carried to term by one mother they, like all identical twins, would have to jockey for position in the womb (one twin usually does better than the other) and they would be born one after the other. Were they carried by different mothers their experiences in the womb would differ even more. From about 18 weeks' gestation the developing brain becomes capable of generating meaning and so we are all born with a meaning structure in place and working. (Hence some of the images which inform your thinking go back to the days when you were a tiny baby.) Human clones would be very different people, seeing the world differently and interpreting what happens in their own individual ways.

You don't look out of your eyes and see reality exactly as it is, even though it seems as though you do. You/your meaning structure constructs a picture of reality. You have a choice. You can construct a highly fanciful picture of reality or you can try to make your picture as close to reality as possible. You observe carefully, you check, you compare notes with other people, you weigh the evidence. Or, at least, in some parts of your life you do. In other parts you operate on unthinking prejudice and in yet others on fantasy. You might in your work try to get as close to reality as possible, in politics and religion you operate on treasured prejudices, and you fantasize about your outstanding success in sex or sport when an honest look at yourself in the mirror would reveal these as outrageous fantasies never ever likely to be fulfilled. If you're lucky your meaning structure will be close to reality where it matters most.

If you're unlucky one day you will discover that there is a serious discrepancy between what you thought your life was and what it actually is. You have made a major error of judgement.

I think it highly likely that anyone who reads this book has lived long enough to have made a major error of judgement and so knows what a peculiarly horrible experience it is. However, I did find this not to be the case with Sir David Frost, the famous broadcaster who has had a very varied career. I met him on a train once where he interviewed me about my work. Perhaps he always interviews rather than converses, but in my case he made only one personal remark and that, in response to what I'd told him, was that he had never made a major error of judgement. He is indeed fortunate because major errors of judgement result in the most terrible fear.

Once you discover that you have made a major error, that you thought reality was such and such and now you find it is not, you begin to question every judgement you have ever made. If you were wrong in that you could be wrong in everything else. Such doubts soon lead you to feel that you are falling apart, shattering, crumbling, disappearing. Nothing is solid. There is no foothold, nothing firm to grasp. Utter, utter terror.

If, when this happens, you don't already understand that you are your meaning structure you can feel that you are going mad. Indeed, this experience and the desperate defences we can use to hold ourselves together when we feel ourselves falling apart comprise those behaviours which psychiatrists call mental illnesses.[10] If you do understand that you are your meaning structure, terrible though the experience is, you know that it is necessary and that you will pass through it. Your meaning structure, having discovered that it is out of sync with reality, has to change and so must break apart in order to reform.

Many people who've gone through such an experience talk of emerging as a stronger, wiser person. Certainly, there's nothing like the break-up of a marriage, the death of a loved child, or the loss of a fortune to change how we see ourselves and our world. Eddie Bell, the chairman of HarperCollins UK, told me, 'I look at people on their way up and they have one thing in common and that is that sooner or later they are going to stand on a banana skin. The measure of them at the end of the day is how they get up or if they get up and whether they learn from the experience of falling on their arse. We only learn from making serious errors of judgement and by God it's hard to take and it can live with you for ever. Some of the people I've met who went to public school seem to believe that they have never made a mistake in their life. I used to think I would love to be like that, I'd love to be able to shed all these inferiority complexes and all the ghosts that haunt me. But the older I am getting, and running a business like this, the more I realize that the mistakes I have made and the ghosts that haunt me actually are the most important parts of the ingredients to help me run this business. I never take anything for granted any longer. I don't take my family for granted and I did. I don't take my job for granted and I used to. And I don't believe I can walk on water. The only problem is that then there is a sense of vulnerability and a sense of dread which can haunt me.'

No one wants to go through such an experience, yet all the time we live with such a threat. Life is a chancy business, and there are always people who want to show us that we are wrong in our judgements. When other people press their ideas upon us we resist, lest by giving up our own ideas and accepting those of other people the integrity of our meaning structure becomes threatened. This is why advertising and public relations people and politicians find it so hard to achieve their aims. Moreover, competition, whatever form it takes, is always about protecting your own meaning structure by proving that someone else has got it wrong.

Competition is always about life and death – not necessarily the life and death of your physical body but the life and death of the person you know yourself to be, the life and death of your meaning structure. Your survival always has two parts. You survive as a body and as a person. You try to achieve both, but forced to choose you'll want to survive as a person. If we can't live our life as ourselves we'll die our death as ourselves. We'll kill ourselves or die a martyr's death.

We can, to some degree, come to terms with the idea of bodily death provided we can believe that some important part of us will continue. You might see the important part of yourself continuing after your death as the work you have done, or your children, or the memories your friends have of you, or you might see your soul or spirit continuing on in some form of afterlife or rebirth. But not surviving as a person means that you are nothing, you have no significance, no meaning, you vanish like a puff of smoke in the wind, unnoticed, unremembered. Our pride – or our meaning structure's instinct for survival – won't let us do that. We defend ourselves against anyone or anything which threatens our survival as a person.

So, when you observe the frantic activities on a trading floor, or the shenanigans of the participants in a hostile takeover, or the noise and bustle of a street market you are not just observing the functioning of world-wide trade but individual meaning structures busily expressing themselves and defending themselves.

We each express ourselves and defend ourselves in our own individual way, but these ways contain some meanings which others share.

Our language is inadequate in talking about what I want to talk about now, but if you want to understand yourself and others, if you want to understand fear, it is essential that you understand what follows here.

All the time you are experiencing a sense of being alive, of existing. Your sense of existence can be threatened with annihilation, not necessarily bodily death, but being wiped out, destroyed. You need to understand how you experience your sense of existence and see the threat of annihilation because this way of experiencing supplies the reasons why you do what you do. Every decision you make, from choosing a kind of toothpaste to committing yourself to a life's project develops from how you experience your sense of existence and see the threat of annihilation.

Let's take a simple example. You've noticed how some people who work at a desk create an unchanging scene of chaos while others are meticulously tidy. The fact that two people keep their desks tidy does not mean that they do so for the same reason. If I wanted to find out how these two people experience their sense of existence and see the threat of annihilation I would ask each of them a series of apparently simple questions. Let's call this pair Jack and Jill.

Jack might make some comment to me about the importance of keeping his desk tidy. I ask, 'Why is it important to you to keep your desk tidy?'

Jack says, 'If you make a mess it just spills over into other people's areas and they get really pissed off with you.'

'Why is it important to you that other people shouldn't get pissed off with you?'

'Well, it creates bad feeling. I like to get along with people.'

'Why is it important to you to get along with other people?'

'That's what life's about, isn't it, getting along with others, having good relationships.'

What Jack is talking about here is how he experiences his sense of existence. If I got him to expand upon having good relationships he would describe how he experiences his sense of existence as being in the relationships he has with other people. I could ask him what would happen to him if he was rejected and abandoned by every other person in the world, but this would be a very cruel question because I would be asking him to contemplate what he sees as the threat of annihilation. We could call Jack a People Person or an extravert, someone who is turned outwards to the world around him, which is where other people are.

Jill has very different reasons for keeping her desk tidy. She often shows she's annoyed when someone has left a mess of papers on her desk and she always spends time tidying her desk.

I ask, 'Why is it important to you to keep your desk tidy?'

'Because it's efficient. An untidy desk wastes time. I can't stand chaos.'

'Why is it important to you to be efficient?'

'Because that's how I achieve what I want to achieve.'

'Why is it important to you to achieve?'

'Isn't that what makes life worthwhile, having a sense of achievement?'

Here Jill is describing how she experiences her sense of existence. I don't have to ask her how she sees the threat of annihilation because she has already told me. It's the threat of overwhelming chaos. We could call Jill a What Have I Achieved Today Person or an introvert, someone who turns inwards in order to develop a sense of achievement, organization and control.

So Jack tidies his desk in order to maintain relationships and Jill tidies her desk to achieve and keep chaos at bay. These are the ultimate reasons why each of them do what they do.

Of course there are many extraverts who are ambitious and want to achieve, but this is not the ultimate reason for them. They want to achieve in order to maintain their relationships with other people.

The differences between people whose ultimate reason is maintaining relationships and those whose ultimate reason is a sense of organization and achievement are many and various and I have written about these at length in my other books.[11] I find that on the whole people whose ultimate reason is achievement and organization know that this is so without my telling them. After all, they are used to introspection. But people whose ultimate reason is maintaining relationships often don't know that this is their ultimate reason. They are action people, given to deeds, not soul-searching. They often get hung up on the idea that I am talking about types of people and do not take in that I am talking about reasons, why we do what we do. They will say to me, 'I think I'm a bit of both,' not seeing that reasons don't operate like that. Some of these people will say to me, 'I don't know why I do things,' and that is really very sad. If you don't know why you do things, who will?

Of course we all want to achieve and have good relationships, but there are many situations where we can't have both. If we don't know which is the more important to us we fail to recognize those situations which contain the greatest danger for us. What better example than Nick Leeson?

I have described how you can discover a person's ultimate reason by asking 'Why is that important to you?' but it isn't always necessary to go through such a procedure. We display our ultimate reasons in everything we say and do, so if you listen carefully to someone and watch what that person does over a period of time you can see a consistency in what the person does and in his choice of words and images. I watched the interview Nick Leeson did with David Frost, I read his book and newspaper interviews with his wife Lisa. I think it's fair to say that for Nick his ultimate reason was that of maintaining relationships with others.

Nick was a plasterer's son from Watford but his mother wanted him to achieve and to please her he was a good school pupil and got a job in a bank. Describing this part of his life he was at pains to stress that he was both a swot and one of the lads, and what comes through in his book is that being one of the lads is vital to him. Being liked was essential to his survival and, as such people usually are, he was very likeable. I've been told by someone who knew him in Singapore that Nick spent much of his social life with his mates and not with Lisa, but once he was threatened with the fate he feared most he clung to her more and more. This fate was that of being rejected and being left absolutely alone. Fleeing from Singapore after the collapse of Barings Bank he was arrested at Frankfurt airport and put in Höchst prison.

> I was now by myself and I had to learn to live with my own company in a tiny cell. I had never thought about how much space I liked to have around me before, but I'd been used to walking around the large SIMEX floor and having thousands of people all around me. I'd also never been out of reach of a telephone. And for the last two years I'd been living a life which was busy in itself and a double-life which was crammed full of deceit. I now had to focus on myself and the fact that my life was utterly empty . . . I repeatedly burst into tears and lay sobbing on my bed. I was so lonely and so frightened. I had no idea what was going on anymore . . . I couldn't get Lisa back. I couldn't speak to anybody on the telephone. I didn't have a television to watch. I was alone – in a white prison in silence – and I didn't know when it was going to stop.[12]

How did he get into this mess? The way extraverts so often do. They are good team people, but they can get into difficulties once they are promoted to positions of authority. It doesn't matter how nice and pleasant you are, if you're a boss you're always in danger of incurring someone's dislike. Wise extraverts recognize this danger and in positions of power they make sure they do not let their need to be liked interfere with the demands of the job. But Nick wasn't wise. He wasn't deliberately crooked either, but when he had to choose between having his staff and mates like him and being honest he chose being liked. Rather than sack George, a member of his staff, for making gross, expensive mistakes, Nick got drunk with him instead.

Introverts commit crimes too, but for very different reasons.

Introverts, each in their own way, want to have a sense of achievement. Just what this achievement might be and how it might come into being are part of the theories which each introvert develops. They are great people for developing theories. These theories might or might not bear some relation to the real world and they might or might not be capable of implementation, but they occupy much of the thinking of an introvert. Indeed, just devising a theory to account for something can give a sense of achievement. Quite often the introvert is keen to pass these theories on to others for the benefit of mankind. I'm an introvert and I not only devise theories about why we behave as we do but I pass these great ideas on for your benefit. However, I hope I have a sufficiently developed sense of the ridiculous not to suffer the delusions of grandeur to which so many introverts are prone.

One delusion of grandeur is that the introvert knows what is best for other people. Consequently they try to dominate people, interfere in their lives and, worst of all, become politicians. The other delusion is that the introvert is a special person, set aside from the laws and rules that govern ordinary people. Possessed of both delusions introverts can, given the opportunity, become power-crazed dictators and criminals. Ivan Boesky was one of these.

Ivan Boesky was one of the four men found guilty in 1987 of insider dealing on Wall Street. He was an extremely successful arbitrageur. Arbitraging, making a profit out of small price differences in different markets, had been a conservative, nearly risk-free process which gave small profits, but in the eighties, when there was a great increase in mergers and acquisitions of companies, the risks and the profits grew with the result that someone like Boesky could make a great deal of money.

From what is known of his early life it is clear that he wanted to achieve, though not in the traditional way of working hard at school. He did work hard, but at making money selling ice cream. At college he became passionately interested in wrestling, starving himself to achieve the right weight and following a punishing exercise regime. In later life images from wrestling informed his thought. He told a reporter from the *Atlantic Monthly* that, 'Wrestling and arbitrage are both solitary sports where you live and die by your deeds, and you do it very visibly.'[13]

Apart from wrestling Boesky appeared not to have achieved much by the time he was in his early twenties, but then he met Seema Silberstein who married him and persuaded her wealthy father to set him up in his own arbitrage business in 1975. By 1980 he owned an estate in Westchester, a Manhattan town house and an art collection. At his peak he 'controlled $3 billion worth of stock-purchasing power, enough to strike terror into almost any corporation with a single phone call.'[14] He always dressed in a black three-piece suit, even when he went to work in the office complex on his own estate. When someone asked him why he wore the same suit every day he said, 'I have enough decisions in my life already.'[15]

He must have devised some very effective theories about how the market operates in order to achieve such success. Alternatively, he might just have been lucky, but his behaviour does not suggest that he entertained this modest hypothesis. He not only believed that he was good, he also believed that he did not have to conform to the rules. He certainly did not conform to the rules of polite behaviour where his colleagues and staff were concerned. He wanted to control everything and other people had to conform. He did not waste time on being concerned about what human needs his staff might have. He barked orders and yelled at them. 'I'm the boss,' he said, 'I'm allowed to yell.'[16] No nonsense about needing to be liked was going to get in *his* way.

Neither did he see any necessity to conform to the rules that regulated the industry. He saw nothing wrong with providing suitcases full of banknotes to those who could supply the insider information he needed. Nor did he see anything wrong with praising greed. He told students at the University of California, 'Greed is all right, by the way. I want you to know that. I think greed is healthy. You can feel greedy and still feel good about yourself.' But also he wanted to pass on to the students the benefits of his wisdom. Before his lecture he told a reporter that he would tell the students that 'they must take the role that nobility played in ancient times, by becoming involved in the arts, politics, science and culture for the betterment of mankind.'[17]

At his trial his psychiatrist reported that Boesky 'has begun to recognize that he suffered from an abnormal and compulsive need to prove himself, to overcome some sense of inadequacy or inferiority which is rooted in his childhood. He was driven to work without any limit of time or effort. He sacrificed closeness with family and friends without realizing that it was happening.'[18]

The market offers great scope for rogues and criminals to pursue their interests. In terms of their meaning structure they are engaged in maintaining their meaning structure and warding off annihilation. However, it isn't necessary to be a rogue or criminal and be a player in the market in such a way in order to maintain meaning structure and ward off annihilation.

Design is a fiercely competitive market where Jane Priestman OBE is one of the leading players. She is an independent Design Management Consultant whose influence we enjoy every time we are in Terminal 4, Heathrow, Gatwick North Terminal, Stansted Airport, Liverpool Street Station and Waterloo International Terminal. Friends matter as much to her as they do to Nick Leeson, but she would never let the demands of friendship deflect her from what she knows is right. She scrupulously avoids using her influence to advance the careers of her sons, both of whom work in fields related to hers, though she is immensely supportive and proud of them. She is ambitious, but, as she said, it is 'ambition in its widest sense, not for oneself necessarily but for the worth of the contribution you can make.'

Everything she does, publicly and privately, she does with style. When I asked her to define style she said, 'It's the ability to include people and entertain them so that one's life is rich in all sorts of ways, not through money but through sharing. Style's a way of lifting the ordinary into something else. Life does not have to be ordinary. One daisy in a jam jar is as exciting as the most luscious lilies in a crystal vase to me. That's what I mean by specialness. If you can pick one daisy out of the garden and make it feel special. You can't buy style. It's a contribution to life which is special and that's without relying on anything like money or inheritance. Style is a leaning outwards rather than inwards. Some people contribute and some take. If I were in a wheelchair and couldn't make a contribution I think I would make the wheelchair look pretty good too. A stylish wheelchair.'

Isn't that a great way of defining your relationship to others?

In 1994 I sat on the veranda of what must be the most delightful house in Sydney. It looked north across Sydney Harbour to the dark green headland of Taronga Park. The view to the west encompassed the Opera House, the Harbour Bridge and beyond, and to the east the heads of the harbour which Captain Phillip in founding Sydney described as 'the finest harbour in the world', With me was the owner of the house, Kerry Manolas, whom I'd met through my son Edward, then Public Relations Manager for Jaguar in Australia. Kerry had lent his magnificent XJ220 to Jaguar for a number of promotions and charity events.

Edward had told me that whatever Kerry spent his money on it wasn't clothes. Kerry was dressed the way most middle-aged Australian men dress when they're at home – a well-worn polo shirt and trousers of indeterminate age – though few Australian men have achieved what Kerry has achieved.

Kerry described himself as 'a freelance business person. I am a person who needs to have a few challenges and have a bit of variety in the things I do.' He had begun his working life as a chemist in Darwin, but once his business was running well he began an interest in real estate at a time when Darwin was growing. He was in competition with some of the big players, but he succeeded immensely well. He said, 'I was always interested in property development. I would set myself a goal, perhaps a piece of property I'm going to do something with. I was in competition with people who had a great deal more resources and experience than myself, but I suppose I had certain things going for me. When you are young you are full of enthusiasm and you can sell things. If you have good ideas you can see opportunities and you can pull things together. It's like playing a game of chess.'

I asked him how he had developed his philosophy of life.

'Certain events affect your attitudes and I suppose twenty-odd years ago there were a couple of things that affected my outlook on life. One was my uncle who was one of the richest men in Australia. I remember him telling me that if he lived to be a hundred, and he must have been 59 at the time, he could not spend all the money that he had as hard as he tried. Three years later he was dead. His main enjoyment out of life was making money. A short time after that my mother died of leukaemia. She used to say to me, "Don't be like your uncle. There is more to life that just making money." At that particular point I decided there had to be a quality of life. One of the things that money does buy you is freedom. Mainly freedom to control your time because time is the thing that is irretrievable. Most things in life are replaceable. You can lose money and make money. Material things can be replaced and a lot of things that we do we can repeat, but when it comes to time, when that goes it's gone for ever. So I decided that once I was reasonably successful and reasonably comfortable I was going to do the things that I wanted to do and utilize my time as best as I could to give me the most out of life, the best quality that I could achieve in life. Making money, although it has always been important, has not been the most important thing. I prefer to have a more balanced life than to have just a life devoted to accumulating wealth.'

Despite his desire for a balanced life Kerry hadn't time for anything like a hobby. 'In 1979 my accountant was visiting Sydney from Darwin and he said to me, "Gee, you're boring. All you talk about is work. Why don't you get yourself a hobby? Buy yourself an old car." Just coincidentally I happened to be driving down William Street and there was a lovely old Bentley parked out in front of a dealers . . . In 1982 I started to get more adventurous and I started collecting early racing cars, or post-war racing cars and things like that. I became involved in the restoration of these cars and then about 1985 of course old cars and classic cars became really good investments as well. So what started as a hobby to get away from business ended up turning full circle and became a business again. But with all these things it is all timing. There is always a time for buying and a time for selling.

'I treated them like works of art, things that can't be reproduced again. I have always wanted to use them, either take them on car shows or car rallies or go racing with them or charity events. Using them was getting enjoyment from them. This is very, very important. It gives me a lot of pleasure to see how other people enjoy the cars. I am not a hoarder, I don't want to particularly own one thing for ever. I would rather have the experience of moving on and doing something else.'

I asked him why it was important to him to preserve things for posterity.

'I think these things have a certain significance and we are only temporary custodians for things in life. I am not an artist, I am not a good mechanic, but I can recreate things by bringing all the necessary elements together to restore something back to its former glory. That gives me a great deal of satisfaction. That is not just purely a monetary satisfaction, although in doing these things you also improve the value of the article. Cars can be considered to be works of art. Yes, I am a happy man, definitely, absolutely, because I am doing the things I want to do.'

So here we have someone who, like Ivan Boesky and other introverts, wants to have a sense of achievement, who develops theories and who wants to benefit mankind, but, unlike Boesky, in ways which can be called virtuous and life-enhancing.

Introverts and extraverts are drawn to one another because their attitudes and actions complement one another. Such partnerships in business and marriage can be highly successful. I talked to Elizabeth, a management consultant, and her husband Michael, a company director, about how they saw themselves.

What Elizabeth and Michael showed in what was a long conversation over a leisurely meal was that they each understood and accepted their partner's point of view. They were proud of each other and saw the other as providing what was missing in themselves. Together they made one unit.

Elizabeth said, 'I think I am extremely creative. Most days I think, "What am I going to do today?" and if I haven't done anything at the end of the day I do feel quite depressed really. I worry about things and can't sleep because I haven't exercised whatever powers I've got. I do like helping people, but in my heart of hearts I think being creative is more important. I am quite happy to spend three days by myself. I might get a bit lonely and I would like the odd phone call, but I find that more satisfying to me than three days when I couldn't create or had to spend time with other people all the time. I get really irritated by what I consider to be mindless socializing.'

Michael said, 'I think of myself as a bridge between creative people and the harsh realities of business. I'm like an interpreter between people who are artistic and people who profit from the art of others but at the same time invest in it. I am somebody in the middle trying to understand both. I am quite happy to be by myself for two or three days, but after two or three days I would want to be with somebody else. I don't think I am really creative anyway in the way that Elizabeth is. I do practical things and they tend to involve other people. I like to solve problems for other people, so people have to be there for them to be solved. On the other hand I am keen on sailing and I spend a lot of time on my boat by myself solving those problems – the practical minor engineering problems.'

A relationship between an extravert and introvert, whether in business, marriage or friendship, can work only if both share such tolerance and understanding. However, even in the best of relationships such contrasting experiences of the sense of existence and the threat of annihilation can lead to major disagreements. When an introvert and an extravert fall out over money, in whatever terms the argument is expressed, the introvert is saying, 'The money should be used for achievement,' and the extravert is saying, 'The money should be used to maintain relationships.'

When the argument is fierce, what one or both of the contestants see as the danger is the threat of annihilation. Often arguments seem to be extremely confusing, but all becomes clear when you can see how each contender is perceiving the threat. If you want to know why a person does what he does, you need to know how he experiences his sense of existence and sees the threat of annihilation. If you want to get a person to do what you want you need to know what frightens him the most, and that will be how he sees the threat to his sense of existence. Effective tyrants threaten extraverts with rejection and abandonment, and introverts with chaos and loss of control. Putting a person in complete isolation for an indefinite period makes both threats effective. Hence the use of isolation in prisons and concentration camps.

Just how it is that two groups of people have such profound differences in their experience of the sense of existence and consequently their priorities in making their decisions is not yet determined, but the lengthy research by Professor Hans Eysenck and his colleagues suggests that there are differences in the functioning of the neurological systems of extraverts and introverts. According to this research, the neurological systems of extraverts prefer an environment which offers much stimulation while those of introverts prefer a quieter environment. A preference is a meaning, so this seems to be the point of merger for the physiological and the psychological.

Whatever the differences in our physiology and our preferences, we are all in the business of maintaining our sense of existence.

A Secure Sense of Existence

In May 1994 and again in June 1995 I sat in the ornate dining room of a Wall Street hotel and talked for several hours with Terence who, at 38, was the chairman of an extremely successful trading investment house. I'd met him at his head office where certainly no money had been spent on anything but staff and computers. There weren't even enough chairs for everybody to sit down at once. Terence said, 'I have millions and millions of dollars and I still live as though I can't afford another pair of shoes.' He had thought a great deal about the meaning of money. One of the things he said to me was, 'What I have learned about money is that people have been taught to attach fear to it and at the same time they've been taught to attach value and worth and self-esteem to it.'

That is, money can maintain our sense of existence and it can threaten to annihilate it.

For many people just having money strengthens their sense of existence. I doubt if Terence keeps his money in piles of banknotes under his bed, unlike Rudolf Nureyev who, until he was persuaded that there were tax-free ways of banking money, used to keep it under the carpets in his home.[19] Terence does spend his money on his family and so, like the rest of us, he has possessions.

Isn't it curious that, while the number of objects we need for bodily survival is actually quite small, unless we are very poor or a member of a religious order which eschews possessions, we acquire many more objects than we need. We see this excess of objects as being necessary, and they are because they help us to gain a secure sense of existence. The rather unkind cartoon on the next page illustrates how.[20]

There's the introvert collecting things in order to have a sense of purpose and to keep things obsessively under control. There's the extravert seeking a sense of identity and friendships. Being stupid and needing something to talk to people about applies to us all.

People do acquire curious things. I heard a woman talking on Radio 4 about why she had tattoos on her body. She said, 'Whenever something important happens in my life I have a tattoo done to celebrate it. This one is in remembrance of my mother, and that one was for when I married. My first baby will be born soon and I'm trying to decide on a tattoo to celebrate.' Such acquisitions must have given her life a significance which it might not have otherwise had.

When we see our possessions as defining our self and giving our life its significance, if those possessions are then taken away from us we can feel quite unable to construct another definition of self to give our life significance. In such a situation we can feel that the only way to preserve our sense of existence is to die. When in June 1993 the Lloyds Names held a meeting in the Albert Hall to discuss

WHY people collect STUPID things

They're obsessive
THESE DON'T LOOK BALANCED! JUST TWO MORE TO MAKE THE SET!

They're stupid
WE JUST LIKE HEDGEHOGS!

Things give them security and an identity.
I MAY NOT BE MUCH BUT AT LEAST I'VE GOT MY TEAPOTS

Objects can become a centre-piece for conversation.

Friendships can be formed with like-minded people.

It gives them a sense of purpose, and they feel as important as they think their collections are.

a business plan which Lloyds had put forward they stood in silence for one minute for the thirty Names who had taken their lives over the past eighteen months.[21]

Just how much money and possessions we see ourselves as needing to maintain our sense of existence depends on how strong and enduring our sense of existence seems to us. Most of us are well practised in putting on a good front before colleagues and friends, but the number and types of our possessions and the care which we take of them can reveal vulnerabilities.

The fact that a person is highly successful in his field and receives universal acclaim does not necessarily mean that that person feels strong and enduring inside. Surely someone possessed of the vast, unique talents that Rudolf Nureyev had, someone who had achieved world-wide fame and acclaim, would not need possessions to bolster what he could not bolster for himself? Unlike most ballet dancers, however successful, Nureyev died possessed of a great fortune whose size in millions was hard to estimate because it included seven homes, an island and an impressive museum's worth of art. Before he defected to the West, as a dancer at the Kirov he was a highly privileged citizen of the USSR, someone who wanted for nothing. He chose the freedom of the West, but the uncertainty that went with that freedom must have frightened him greatly. Rather than accept that uncertainty he tried to make himself secure by acquisition. He made his money in two ways. First, he got the best in business advice and placed a high financial value on all his work. Second, when he dined out he never picked up the bill. Someone else always paid for him.[22]

The problem with seeking security through acquisitions is that other people can see what you've got. This invites thieves and burglars and dangerous envy. The American economist and social critic Thorstein Veblen, viewing the activities of the turn-of-the-century rich in America, coined the phrase 'conspicuous consumption' and argued that as people get richer what drives their behaviour is the attainment of 'the esteem and envy of fellow men'. This certainly is an accurate description of the behaviour of many people. If it ceased to be so the upper end of the motor trade, with its wildly expensive and exclusive cars, would collapse in an instant. But even if some people like to flaunt their possessions, most if not all of us are very secretive about money.

I found that the part of the research which involves talking to people was much more difficult for this book than it was for my book *Time on Our Side*. With that book all I had to do was to say I was researching about how we feel about time passing and growing older and without exception every person of whatever age talked immediately and at length about how they feared ageing. Asking people to talk about money produced very different responses. I saw bankers turn white when all I wanted was for them to tell me a little about their work. Part of the problem was that I am a psychologist and many people who ought to know better believe that anyone with 'psych' as the prefix to the name of their profession has the ability to peer inside their very soul and see what is hidden even from themselves. The other and larger part of the problem was that money as a subject for discussion is taboo. Ask about sex, no problem. Ask about money and you are asking to enter forbidden territory.

I mentioned this difficulty to a friend who works in a large publishing concern. She suddenly realized that while she knew all the scandal about the sexual activities of several of her senior colleagues, she had no idea what they earned. When I was talking to two old friends about another, we discovered that, while this mutual friend had never had any hesitation in talking to us about his sexual relations, none of us knew how he had afforded such a large, beautiful house. It gave us great pleasure to see him and his family enjoying such a house, but we each felt some degree of anxiety that he might have overreached himself with the purchase. We could express the first feeling to him but not the second.

Talking about money in public is seen by many people as embarrassing, even in bad taste. I was invited to lecture at a conference for new heads of preparatory schools and so was present when much of the discussion revolved around how to raise money to keep the school functioning. The new heads were urged to see their job as running a business, and so it was necessary for them to go out into the marketplace and sell. However, the organizer of the conference, a very senior figure in education, said, 'When I was a head I found money embarrassing.' One of the heads said, 'I'm bad at accounting.' Another said, 'Advertising is vulgar.'

The writer of a letter to the *Guardian* shared this view.

> I have just received notification that my old age pension, as a married woman, has risen to £37.36 per week – a princely increase of £1.28 – and that my husband's occupational pension has risen by 53p to £24.33 per week. (So far we have not received the good news of the rise in my husband's state pension of £63.72.)
>
> I swim three times a week for health reasons and this cost has just doubled from 50p to £1. What's more, the baths are no longer open at 7 AM, which means the lunch time swim will be filled with frustrated pensioners denied their early morning swim. This is not the fault of the local authority but the result of their helplessness in the face of the Government's insistence on cuts in their overall expenditure.
>
> This may not seem very important to most people, but in one's seventies, and enjoying good health so far, swimming is an imperative part of a healthy life-style which keeps us from cluttering up the NHS for arthritis cures.
>
> Unfortunately my blood pressure will be rising as I become increasingly bitter and angry at this government's total disregard for people on low incomes.
>
> The council tax is another £3.80 per week as we are lucky enough to live in a pleasant house in a lovely area but this, along with the impending increase in VAT on fuel and the lower interest rates on our life savings, is sufficient to lower our living standards quite considerably.
>
> As we can only afford your paper on Wednesdays and Fridays I will not even know whether or not you will publish this tirade. But if you do please withhold my name and address, as I would be too embarrassed at disclosing my financial state.[23]

Sometimes the need to know about money overrides what the person regards as good taste. When I was living in a house with a garden which once a month required the attention of a team of gardeners one of the neighbours, needing gardeners himself, approached me with, 'I hope you don't mind me asking, Dorothy, but what do you pay your gardeners?' Yet a year later when I had put my house up for sale he didn't hesitate to ask me without apology what price I'd put on it. In that little enclave all the houses were of the same vintage, the owners were houseproud, and so the monetary worth of each house was a strong point for competition.

The tradition maintained by men of keeping their wives under control by not letting them know how much they earned may have largely disappeared now that so many women work and enjoy greater financial equality with men, but couples can still be reluctant to talk about money. A study carried out by a research group, One Plus One, on how couples handled money reported that, 'Money seems unromantic, so people don't talk about it until something goes wrong or they haven't got any. There is also the feeling that talking about money goes against the trust and independence that are part of modern relationships.'[24]

When I talked to Ray Heath, *South China Morning Post* Business Editor, he told me that Hong Kong Chinese, but not Malaysians or Filipinos, will ask you in the first moments of the first conversation 'What is your salary?', 'How much rent do you pay?' and 'How much did you pay for whatever it is you've bought?' He said that he dealt with this invasion of his privacy with, 'We British don't talk about these things.' However, he doubted that the *Post* would carry something like the Forbes list of Hong Kong's richest men. These men wouldn't want their wealth to be known, even though they want to be seen as successful. P.E.H., who has lived in Hong Kong for a long time, told me that the Chinese will openly say what they have paid for something (truthfully or not) but never mention what they are paid. This is always due to their not wishing to lose face by admitting to a salary that does not carry the esteem they would like. However, they all want to find out what others earn. Civil servants know what their colleagues earn, as salaries relate to grades in the service, but what concerns them is the fair distribution of benefits like the square footage of an apartment. The size of an apartment is tied to position in the hierarchy. The Chinese, he said, admire the rich and despise the poor. If you are poor it's your fault.

Each profession has its rules about money and secrecy, though these rules can change over time. In the years I worked in the National Health Service all the clinical psychologists had jobs for life. We all knew what everyone earned because we all knew one another's grade and the money attached to that. With the advent of the National Health Trusts an increasing number of psychologists took jobs on short-term contracts. If asked what salary was attached to his or her contract the psychologist concerned was likely not to give a figure but to use the terminology of the business world: 'It's in the region of . . .' and indicate a figure.

Peter Barkworth felt that secrecy about money was necessary in the acting profession. He said, 'It is *de rigueur* with actors that we never talk about money at all. We are a feudal society. There are lords and ladies who earn enormous amounts and there are serfs who earn nothing and it is horribly, horribly old fashioned from that point of view. Even though in my lifetime Equity has gone on getting more powerful and more influential. The minimum fee varies for television, for filming and for theatre, and whether the theatre is in the West End, or the National or the RSC, or whether it's on tour, or whether it's provincial rep. There are so many categories you can't keep track. Actors think it is wrong to discuss money because there would be such friction in the air. For example, in the last play that I was in I had second billing, something which influences the amount of money one gets, even though I had the smallest part in it. I got what I often get in plays in the theatre and have got for some time, give or take, £2000 per week. I happened to find out that a very distinguished actor who was fourth billing was being paid less than half of what I was, so it is as well that we do not discuss it. I am told now that the person who was in first billing got an absurd amount of money, so I would have been cross if I had known that. It is all to do with demand. It is a matter of bringing money in. Star names bring people into the theatre, or make people watch television and so it is just like the film industry. Fortunes are made by the people at the top and hardly anything by the people at the bottom.'

As Peter went on he showed that he had great sympathy for those actors at the bottom. 'There are one or two people with whom I have talked money. I think a friend around a dinner table would be willing to swop, provided you offered first of all what you got, but it is terribly unusual. The only person I did it with seriously and at great length was the author of the first play I was in in London, Dodie Smith. She and I became really quite firm friends for the rest of her life. She was interested to talk about money, too, because she was by then a very rich woman and she remained a very rich woman. Her plays were so often performed and she wrote so many books, but she had known what it was like to be poor. When she left RADA she wanted to be an actress but she couldn't get a job so she worked at Heals. I found that I couldn't live in London on the £12 a week salary that I was given. I couldn't afford my digs, so Dodie gave me a magnificent gift of £20 and I swore to her that I would pay it back to her one day and I never did. But it was a shot in the arm, that £20. She always regarded money as fun. She tried to take every advantage she could to live very cheaply when she had no money. She chose a flat which was over a bakery because she wouldn't have to have any heating bills because the heat that rose from the ovens underneath her was enough to heat the flat. She managed to save up enough money by insisting for herself, and I tried to follow this, that she must save something out of every wage packet. I think her goal was £1 a week. Eventually, because she did this, she was able to have a little holiday. She went to Switzerland and got the idea for her first success which was *Autumn Crocus* and this just changed her life.

'I have had several times of being impoverished but they have been mercifully short. I started impoverished when I was a RADA student. Robert Shaw and I shared a flat on Regents Park Road looking out over Primrose Hill and it was three guineas per week. My allowance from my father was two pounds fifteen shillings a week. After I'd paid my share of the flat I had just under one pound five shillings left for everything else, mostly food and fares during the week. The flat didn't have a telephone, so we didn't have that bill and all bills like electricity and gas were included within the week's rent, but somehow Robert and I managed.'

I wonder how many struggling actors fail to get the kind of financial advice they need because their fellow actors are so secretive.

Professional writers worry about money but are careful in choosing whom they talk to. I met Douglas Kennedy after I'd read his entertaining book *Chasing Mammon*, where he had combined his passion for travel with his interest in money. He told me, 'I always live with the immense fear of not having money. I think most writers who have a third or fourth book out are doing reasonably well. They are building a reputation, but everyone wants the special sort of break, the phone call from New York or L.A., Spielberg wants your book – that sort of leap that will in some way or another end the worry. Yet I hope that I am smart enough to know that once you have that security blanket you are actually very vulnerable. I think you have to have a certain hunger to write and to keep writing, so a need for more financial security doesn't hurt.'

Secrecy, he said, was different with different people. 'There is one friend of mine who is a playwright and lives nearby and I would never tell her what I was making for a book. She would never reveal to me what she was making for her play. That's fine because she is just like that, she is by nature a private person and it doesn't affect our friendship in that way. Another friend of mine is a novelist and also does a lot of journalism and she asks straight out and I'm fine about that because she is interested. Writers have their own way of keeping score. All writers want their friends to do well, not too much better than them, but well. As a writer you're always in danger of thinking that because you've got a record advance for one book you're going to get record advances for every book. But it doesn't always work that way. Your next book could be rejected by the publishers. Pride goes before a fall sure enough.'

Here Douglas reminded me of what Patrick had said about making and losing money. If you have a fortune and you 'take your eye off it' you will lose it.

Many people realize this even though they don't have fortunes to preserve. My friend and colleague Kevin Sullivan, a much experienced family therapist, talked to me about how it is dangerous for a therapist to question how the responsible adults in a family earn their money. Query how a father chastises his children or makes sexual demands on his wife, fine, but ask why he must work so hard and the answer is in absolutes. It must be done and the subject must not be discussed.

Kevin said, 'When you're working with a family you can get them to look at what they are doing, the way they are treating their children and relationships and things like that, but then people will say, "Well, of course I can't do this or that because of the job." Because the job dictated this therefore this is an area which isn't open to discussion. You can't start arguing with them about "Do you really need as much money as you earn? Could you give up some of your time and spend more time with the children?" I was talking to a guy recently who came along – he and his wife were having troubles with their daughter – we talked about that and that was fine, and then we were talking about what the difficulties were and that was fine, and we were getting on and then it came around how much of the problem was dad, and dad was working fifteen hours a day, seven days a week. People were ringing him up in the middle of the night and things like that. He looked physically ill. He said, "It's just the work," and I said, "Well, can't you cut it down? It doesn't look to be doing you much good." He said, "Yes, but I've got to keep going at it." I said, "What if you just say that's it, forget it, I'm going somewhere else." He said, "I did that last year and they just put my pay up by 25 per cent and how do you walk away from that?" The position he was holding was that you cannot walk away from people throwing money at you even if it is going to kill you – which it looked like it was going to do to him.'

Kevin concluded that, 'It's not just money, it's about the sort of social and cultural expectations of money. They perceive themselves as particular people going in particular directions and the function of money is to help them go in those directions. To change their ideas about money would mean changing the whole structure of their ideas.'

Our ideas about money are thus central to our whole sense of identity, our sense of existence. But what a painful way to live life, seeing yourself as needing money, having to pay close attention to that money when you get it, yet at the same time feeling unable to talk to others about this important part of your life.

One of the questions I put to a wide range of people was, 'Why are we so secretive about money?' Not one person queried my assumption that we were secretive. Everyone knew it was a matter of shame, humiliation and envy.

Steve pointed out the danger in responding to the question, 'How much did you pay for – ?' 'People are always ready to tell you that you've paid too much and that they can get it cheaper elsewhere. You're left feeling a fool.'

Jane Priestman said, 'I've run huge departments where everyone is avid to know what everyone else is earning. I've had people working with me who were furious that somebody is earning £25 more than they are when they are doing the same sort of job, and it's only because they have been months apart in appointment or whatever it is. It's really ridiculous – absolutely ridiculous. I think we're secretive about money because it's always a measure of success. Some people feel it is very much more important than I do. I think I would feel a bit narked if somebody was doing the same job and earning more, but I don't think it would take over my life as it seems to take over some people's lives. In British Rail there were grades which the Director had to decide. That's why it got a bit secretive because it was entirely my decision to grade people within a scale up or down. Some stayed where they were and some went up if they really put in a lot of effort. It was a new system that was brought in and it worked quite well, I thought. It did mean that only the Director knew precisely what everybody was earning – that and the Personnel Department of course – and it was the Director who made the decision on the basis of the work of the people under the Director. So that power was suspect in a way or people felt it was.'

Lord Howie of Toon made the connection between money and sin and how we are very reluctant to be seen sinning. He said, 'Don't forget that Christ drove the moneylenders out of the Temple. There is the notion that money is rather sinful. Certainly money is totally associated with greed. People can easily become avaricious and want to accumulate money and hold it and not give it to people who deserve it. This seems very deep seated in the human psyche. Obviously greed and avarice are not desirable characteristics.'

He went on, 'Another side is that people are very unwilling to talk about money when later it turns out they have less than their neighbours have or their peers have, or less than they somehow appear to have. There is some shame in being poor or a certain shame in being hard up which would be a better phrase. Except the threadbare Duke. A threadbare Duke's all right because you know that his threadbareness is part of his characteristic eccentricity, but if you're threadbare because you could not afford a new suit – there's an element of social stigma attached to that.'

Shortly before I talked to my friend Tony about money the then Chancellor of the Exchequer had incurred some unfavourable publicity because it had been disclosed that the credit limit on his credit card was surprisingly low. I asked Tony whether he would be happy to have his Visa or Access account being made public.

He said, 'No I wouldn't. In fact, when I'm getting money out of a cash dispenser I can never bring myself to put the statement that comes with the money into the waste receptacle at the side of the machine even though it couldn't possibly be identified or traced to me. There is a lot of envy in the world – I think that this is a great taboo subject – but we have experienced it a lot because people think that I have a very cushy job and am paid a lot for doing what to them is a very easy job. I think we spend quite a lot of our time being fairly reclusive and low profile and not flaunting our money or whatever we have got. I would be very worried if it was made public – not that we have got that much money – if you looked in our bank accounts now we could probably lay hands on about two or three thousand pounds altogether. That's hardly a fortune, but people are very envious in an area like this. There are two worlds, really. There are the people with jobs like ours, but most of the people are on the dole.'

I asked Tony whether it was the danger of being envied which made people so secretive about money.

'Yes I think it is, and I think it is a thing that's been particularly developed over the last fifteen-odd years where there has been a growing disparity across the earnings range. Some people are doing very, very well and other people are really doing badly. There doesn't seem to be any kind of national average wage thing anymore. It's every man for himself. If anybody feels that they are doing all right there's an awful lot of people who would say, "I hate you because you have been luckier or more crafty than me and you are winning at this wretched game of life and money and I'm not. You are no better than me." I think people get embarrassed about this. I speak to patients and find that they are enduring financial hardships that would drive me up the wall. It's very difficult when someone is talking to me about their panic at the thought of such and such a bill or that they may lose their house, and I'm sitting there knowing that at the moment that definitely does not apply to me.'

I asked Tony whether those people who were not doing well also felt a sense of shame.

He said, 'Some are very ashamed but I think that a lot of people have gone through that and there is round here a sort of pessimism and a defeatism and a hatred of the system which makes them feel that they are not going to get a job and therefore let me get whatever I can. They say to themselves, "It's not that I'm hopeless. It's that the system has been rigged so that I am not going to be able to get a place on it." I would find it very painful to go down to the Social Security queue and endure the humiliation. There is no doubt that the DHSS interviewing techniques and activities now are becoming extremely abrasive and humiliating for those who have to claim unemployment. People have described it to me as being like interrogations, that nothing they say is believed, that people are sceptical about them, cynical and that they find that shameful – humiliating rather than shameful. I think the shame of being unemployed is diminished because there are just so many of us unemployed and there is a widespread recognition that it is nothing to do with whether you are a good worker or not. There have been some fantastic companies gone down the tubes – look at all the miners doubling their production and all that and they are all going to be on the dole. None of those guys has got to feel ashamed about anything. They have been defeated by an accounts sheet, by fuel purchasing policy of the government, not by laziness or ill-health. So I think the shame thing of it has gone.'

When I began talking to people about the meanings they gave to money I asked them to rate on a scale of 1 rising to 7 where they would place the importance of money in their lives. Everyone gave the same answer. Money was middling important. Relationships and health were far more important. I suspected that I was not always being told the complete truth, so I stopped asking this question. The connection between the amount of money and possessions we desired and what we actually did with regard to money and possessions was not that simple.

Kevin pointed out to me how, if he chose, he could earn much more money. 'I could do private evening work, or on Saturday mornings. I could do court reports and all sorts of things like that, but I don't choose to do those sort of things. Other things are more important – my family and finding out about the world because there's so much pleasure just in knowing. There are two separate issues, really. There is your relationship to material objects and your desire for objects, and your relationship to money both for those things and what it means in terms of security – how much there is behind you so that you can survive and have a good degree of independence.'

There is also the question, no matter what you want, of what you feel is the right way to behave. When I asked seven-year-old Billy how much money he would like to have he answered in an instant, 'All the money in the world.' Yet his father Tony told me that Billy was one of the few children he'd ever encountered who actually refuses to take his pocket money. He said, 'If I say to Billy, "Here's some money. Put it in your piggy bank," he says, "No thanks, Dad. I've got plenty and I really don't want any more."'

So I asked Billy, 'Do you think your father can't afford to give money to you?'

Billy replied, 'We might start to get poor and I will start to get rich.'

Tony: 'And that would not be very good?'

Billy: 'No.'

'Oh, I see,' said Tony. 'Well, that's very strange. I didn't know that was why.'

Such an understanding on Billy's part surprised me. I had found that many children and teenagers see their parents as possessing a bottomless pit of money and so they regard any scene that their parents might put on about waste and the cost of desirable objects and the wickedness of greed as evidence of their parents' madness. After all, most parents seem to possess a bottomless pit of concern for their children so why not a bottomless pit of money?

Billy reminded me of Marc, the son of my friends Helen and Galen who, now in his twenties, prefers a life of study and contemplation to one of making money. I've known Marc since he was Billy's age. On the one hand he consistently requires very little in the way of money and food, but on the other hand he collects a variety of objects to which he has a particular relationship, one which is like a friendship or a memento of a friendship. (I've slept in Marc's bedroom and have had time to look at his collection of interesting and beautiful things and to ponder their significance.) When a public relations firm, who were launching a particularly rich liqueur on to the market, asked me to write a piece about indulgence I set up a discussion with Helen, Galen, Marc and his sister Naomi. Helen, Galen and Naomi confessed to indulging in certain rich foods but not Marc. Our conversation went like this.

Me: Marc, what do you regard as an indulgence in your life?

Marc: I'm too much of a Spartan to indulge.

Helen: He is. That's the problem with Marc.

Galen: His indulgence is high-level asceticism.

Marc: I once bought myself a cartoon as a treat. What is an indulgence?

Helen: You're indulging yourself if you don't really need it for absolute necessity.

Marc: If things aren't necessary you don't bother. If it's an indulgence then it's a necessity. If I suddenly decide I need a bar of chocolate then it must be that I need a bar of chocolate. So it's not an indulgence.

Obviously Marc could do extremely well in the legal profession, but the riches he might earn there do not interest him. I guess he would say that he is rich in those possessions whose value we regard as non-negotiable, possessions which are pearls beyond price.

Everyone wants to enjoy those possessions whose value is non-negotiable – good relationships with others and the enjoyment of the beauty and wonder of the world, but all too often our view of money constrains us. There's an old adage: 'A man's soul is slightly smaller than his mortgage', and such a slightly smaller soul produces a certain meanness. When the merchant banker Robert Pasley-Tyler opened his exclusive club (only Americans with a net worth of $55 million need apply) he remarked, 'There is nothing more mean than a man down to his last $70 million.'[25] Prufrock, the diarist in the *Sunday Times*, reported that, 'The fundamentals of sound money are simple, as Milton Friedman, the arch-monetarist, demonstrated when he rang this office from America. He reversed the charges.'[26]

Meanness goes hand in hand with greed. These can be thought about in terms of hunger and in terms of entitlement.

The hunger for money and possessions which we can call greed is a feeling of emptiness which is a threat to the integrity of the sense of existence. Trying to get more and more money and possessions can be an attempt to fill the emptiness inside, while meanness, the refusal to part with money and possessions, can be a reluctance to part with anything which is seen as essential buttressing to the sense of existence.

However, much of the demand for money and possessions comes not so much from hunger as a sense of entitlement.

This sense of entitlement comes from the belief that there is a pre-ordained pattern to the world which ensures that certain things, certain rewards will be forthcoming to certain people. If you are one of those people you expect to receive your reward. When the rewards are not forthcoming you feel aggrieved and complain about injustice. Just how this group of people is defined and what the expected rewards are depends on who's doing the defining. Usually those certain people are self-defined.

Do you believe that there is a pre-ordained pattern to the world which means that you must receive certain rewards provided you meet certain standards?

Michael Lewis, writing about the financial world, described how that world's inhabitants view their entitlement.

> You can hear a lot of what has happened on Wall Street in those three words: YOU OWE ME. You can hear a chorus of twenty-five-year-olds complaining that their six-figure bonuses aren't big enough. You can hear bond salesmen building in their bigger-than-life fees. You can hear Bruce Wasserstein and Eric Gleacher baring their souls to Henry Kravis before the buyout of RJR Nabisco: 'Henry, we've been thinking about it, and we've decided we should be paid $50 million for this deal.' You can hear the voice of an entire culture based on entitlement.[27]

Lewis H. Lapham, writing about money and class in America, described what he called 'the equestrian class' into which he had been born.

> The immense prosperity accruing to the accounts of the United States after the victories of the Second World War produced a correspondingly immense crowd of newly enriched citizens. What was once a relatively small plutocracy, almost homespun in its pretension and amounting to no more than a few thousand semi-literate millionaires, has evolved into a large spawn of affluent mandarins – in government, the corporations, the professions and the media. If these people were counted as a simple percentage of the population they might be construed as a negligible minority, but the reach of their influence far exceeds both their numbers and their grasp. Whether new rich or old rich, Protestant or Jew, celebrity or anonym, they constitute the American equestrian classes that own the bulk of the nation's wealth, wield the instruments of power, write the newspapers and arrange the television schedules, perform the feats of higher shopping and personify the tenor of the age.[28]

Like the rich the world over, the equestrian class assume that being rich implies not just intelligence but virtue. As J. K. Galbraith commented, 'The most nearly invariant is that individuals and communities that are favored in their economic, social and political condition attribute social virtue and political durability to that which they themselves enjoy. That attribution, in turn, is made to apply even in the face of commanding evidence to the contrary.'[29]

For the equestrian class, to enjoy the pre-ordained rewards nothing has to be done except to be born into it.

> The accident of being born into the American equestrian class has obvious advantages, but it also has disadvantages that are not so obvious. Children encouraged to believe themselves either beautiful or rich assume that nothing further will be required of them, and they revert to the condition of aquatic plants drifting in the shadows. The lack of oxygen in the atmosphere makes them giddy with ruinous fantasy. Together with my classmates and peers, I was given to understand that it was sufficient accomplishment merely to have been born. Not that anybody ever said that

> precisely, but the assumption was plain enough, and I could confirm it by observing the mechanics of the local society. A man might become a drunkard, a concert pianist or an owner of companies, but none of these occupations would have an important bearing on his social rank. If he could pay the club dues, if he could present himself at dinner dressed in the correct clothes for whatever season of the year, if he could retain the minimum good sense necessary to stay out of jail, then he could command the homage of headwaiters. Headwaiters represented the world's opinion.[30]

However, Lapham saw that such a way of thinking was not confined to the equestrian class.

> Before I was twenty I thought the pathologies of wealth confined to relatively small numbers of people preserved in the aspic of a specific social class. By the time I was thirty I understood that much of what could be said of the children of the rich also could be said of the nation as a whole and about a society that comforts itself with dreams of power, innocence and grace.[31]

More recently Robert J. Samuelson took up the theme of entitlement.

> Call our era the Age of Entitlement. Stretching from the close of World War II to the mid-1990s, it is best defined by its soaring ambitions. We had a grand vision. We didn't merely expect things to get better. We expected all social problems to be solved. In our new society, most workers would have rising incomes and stable jobs. Business cycles would disappear. Poverty, racism and crime would recede. Compassionate government would protect the poor, old and unlucky. We expected almost limitless personal freedom and self-fulfilment. We not only expected these things. After a while we thought we were entitled to them as a matter of right.[32]

Such expectations have not been fulfilled. Samuelson believes that it is the task of American leaders to instil a sense of reality into the American people. However (and as I write the Republican Party is going through their primary selections preparatory for the Presidential election in November), American leaders seem somewhat devoid of a sense of reality themselves. All that seems real to them is getting themselves elected.

American leaders never make a public speech without peppering their discourse with references to 'America', 'the American people', 'the American dream' and 'God'. These are the basic concepts in the belief in the pre-ordained pattern that in America anyone who has a plan for success ('a dream') and who works hard to implement that plan will, as night follows day, be rewarded with success. In America all dreams come true.

Just how many Americans want to give up that fantasy, move their structure of meaning closer to the reality which shows that hard work does not always ensure success and that even when you get what you wanted you don't necessarily feel happy? How many Americans would want to be able just to laugh, as Europeans do, at George Bernard Shaw's famous dictum, 'There are two tragedies in life. One is not getting what you want. The other is getting it'? The success of the Disney empire in America suggests that the answer to these questions is, 'Very few.'

Not that Europeans and other non-Americans are immune to a sense of entitlement. Their history might show that the hard-working and the virtuous are not always rewarded, but they live in a society where religion, whichever it might be, teaches them that they live in a Just World where goodness is rewarded and badness is punished. If you believe this, and if you believe that you have always striven to be virtuous in whatever way you have defined virtue, when the rewards to which you believe you are entitled aren't forthcoming you can't help but feel aggrieved. No wonder the lads on the trading floor complain about their bonuses and the leaders of industry, all in their own light hard-working and virtuous, feel they are entitled to their huge salaries and perks. No wonder the unemployed suffer if what they see is not the random unfairness of the world but a world of glittering prizes from which they are excluded.

And if you do win a prize, you suffer the tragedy of getting what you wanted. Lapham pondered upon this.

> Nobody ever has enough. It is characteristic of the rich, whether the rich man or the rich nation, to think that they never have enough of anything. Not enough love, time, houses, tennis balls, orgasms, dinner invitations, designer clothes, nuclear weapons or appearances on *The Tonight Show* . . . There they sit, the wonders

> of the Western world, surrounded by all the toys available to the customer with a credit card, mourning the death of innocence, the limits of feminism and the death of bumblebees.
>
> Seeking the invisible through imagery of the visible, the American never can get quite all the way to the end of the American dream. Even if we achieve what the world is pleased to acknowledge as success, we discover that the seizing of it fails to satisfy the hunger of our spiritual expectation, which is why we so often feel oppressed by the vague melancholy that echoes like a sad blues through the back rooms of so many American stories.[33]

The source of this vague melancholy lies in our childhood. We entered the world full of unselfconscious self-confidence, curiosity, enthusiasm, and interest and delight in everything we encountered. We were untroubled by the belief that we needed to be good.

Our joy in being alive was soon taken from us. The adults around us deemed that we must fit in schedules of eating, sleeping, urinating and defecating which they devised, not us. (Recently I asked a proud uncle about the progress of his four-month-old nephew. He said that the little boy was being allowed his dummy only at night. 'Does he know when it's night?' I asked.)

These schedules are beyond our understanding, yet if we fail to conform to them unpleasant things can happen. We become confused, uncertain, and an emptiness, a darkness opens inside us. At the same time we are being offered things which we take to be compensation for the loss of the certitude and happiness we once enjoyed. 'Be good,' say our parents, 'and you'll be rewarded.'

We want to see a pattern in the chaos of events that is our life, and we seize on this pattern because it was simple and something we can learn to fulfil. We strive to fulfil the demands of virtue as it has been defined to us, and we come to believe that we are entitled to the rewards we've been promised. When the rewards do not materialize we feel aggrieved and when they do materialize we discover that they do not return us to our original state of certitude and happiness.

Money and possessions fail to assuage the pain of the loss of our initial certitude and happiness because we have invested them with a meaning they cannot bear. Every meaning is itself an expectation.

If we give money the meaning that it creates happiness, we expect that it will do so. If the meaning we create arises more from our fantasies than from our determination to create a meaning which as closely as possible resembles reality we can create for ourselves expectations which can never be fulfilled.

I've spent many hours listening to individuals who live in daily anguish, waiting for their mother to put aside her usual way of behaving and reveal herself as the all-perfect, all-loving mother the person longs for. The reality is that the mother is a meagre person, untouched by the generosity and compassion which are necessary elements of an unconditional love. She can no more produce unconditional love than she can win the Nobel Prize for physics or beat the market to make a fortune.

The expectation that money will fill the hole that childhood experience created in you or that possessions will shore up your shaky sense of existence is wildly wrong. It is based as much on a lack of understanding of yourself as it is an over-estimate of the powers of money and possessions. If we don't understand ourselves and if we don't try to set aside our fantasies in order to see life as it is, we cannot help but suffer.

Relationships, Childhood, Chance and Change

In trying to describe our structure of meaning and how we experience our sense of existence I am always in danger of giving the impression that all this goes on inside the person without reference to the world and the people in it. Of course this is not the case. Our survival depends on other people. Extraverts need other people to maintain their sense of existence. Introverts need other people to keep them aware of what goes on around them lest they withdraw into themselves and get lost in their theories.

However, other people are dangerous. They can challenge the meanings we have created or press their ideas on us and so threaten us. They can abandon us or create chaos in our lives. Other people can both maintain our sense of existence and threaten our survival. (Such people are usually our loved ones.)

Money is one of the media through which people interact. If you're alone on a desert island money is irrelevant. We use money to maintain and control our relationships.

Many of my friends now have children who have grown up. We often talk about what our children are doing. One friend remarked, 'The good thing about money is that it keeps you in touch with your children.' A common topic for our discussions is when is it appropriate to give our adult children financial help. The range of views on this is enormous.

My image of money, stemming from my childhood experience, is that it is in short supply and can easily disappear. It is only quite recently that I have enjoyed a surplus of money over what was needed for necessities, so I can easily envisage money disappearing not just from my life but from my son's, despite the fact that he provides extremely well for himself. It is as obvious to me as the sun rising in the east that whatever I die possessed of should go to my son. It came as a surprise to me that other people did not share my views.

One friend told me that she was very uncomfortable about her young son inheriting a large amount. 'Suppose he was a heroin addict or something like that!'

When the grandfather of two little children whom I love very much told me that he was not going to leave his money to his sons and did not want to spoil his grandchildren by leaving them money I hastened to assure him that these children could never be spoilt and that the money will be a necessity for them because free education is fast disappearing from the UK. However, when Terence talked about what he should leave his children I could only agree that money in millions was indeed a problem.

There's a saying, 'Clogs to clogs in three generations.' The first generation makes money, the second generation uses it, and the third generation loses it. There are countless stories of children who inherited vast wealth and who, even if they did not dissipate the fortune, lived empty, unhappy lives. Terence, the son of Irish immigrants to the USA, did not want this to happen to his children. He said, 'I view the world with a fundamental distrust, so I say, "I'm not going to let those bastards get my money, I'm going to give it to my kids." But if I think about it, I should give my money to people who really need it and provide my sons with an excellent thirst for life, a positive-based thirst for life.'

He explained how he saw the pattern of the lives of succeeding generations of immigrants and why he wanted something different for his sons. 'The immigrant is promised golden-paved streets and opportunity but what the first pioneer, the first member of the family finds is that it is a very, very tough, challenging existence that is fundamentally physically and psychologically debilitating. The vast majority of people who came over did so because they couldn't do well where they were. They were usually under-educated or under-prepared or under-skilled. The first immigrants form what I call the sacrificial generation. He has to work sometimes even today in inhuman conditions. So he really accelerates the physical death. He is easily taken advantage of because he doesn't speak the language and he doesn't understand the social mores and he doesn't understand just how the place works. He becomes psychologically threatened at every turn. Usually that person clings to some sort of escape. My grandfather drank a gallon of wine a day, for instance, and worked sixteen or seventeen hours a day. But the great lie is that he is told that he is doing something good. He is told, okay, we tricked you, it isn't really gold on the streets, but there is going to be gold on the streets for your son. So he says okay, my life is over anyway. The only thing that matters is my children. The father can't foster his child through any kind of educational process. The child of that generation is so close to his father's pain, but he does gain a little bit from the economic hard work. He usually winds up in some job, usually a union job or a city job. But he still does not have that breadth of education and creative nature that is needed eventually for freedom. It is the third generation now, the son of the City worker or this Union worker, has no chance of getting a true education because of the previous two generations, but usually he gets educated, and he usually now goes to a mid-level manager's job. It is usually his son who can get educated in a pressureless environment where he can maybe begin to develop a challenge or an approach to the idea of actualization, self actualizing.'

The problem for Terence is whether his children will interpret the education they receive in the way he does. The problem for all parents is that it is not what they do which determines their child's behaviour but how the child interprets what they do.

We might hope that in passing money on to our children we are doing something useful, but we can never be sure just how our children will interpret our gift. There can be nothing more destructive to family relationships than a parent's will. It can lay bare all the sibling rivalries, the feelings of entitlement and the proof of the nature of the parent's feeling for the child. Not all parents think as carefully about their children's future as Terence does.

Lewis L. Lapham, commenting that 'Among all the emotions, the rich have the least talent for love,' told what he called the saddest story, that of an acquaintance called Mills.

> (Mills) reached the age of thirty five before he found the courage to ask his father why his father had never loved him. Mills had been born to the privileges of wealth, but he had chosen to make his career as a professor of political theories of which his father disapproved. Mills put the question at a time when his father was senior partner in a New York investment bank, a director of corporations and a faithful servant of the plutocracy. He had deeded his fortune to the Smithsonian Institution – on the ground that an institution would be more respectful of it than his errant son and unkempt grandchildren – and his answer to his son's question was as quick and instinctive as the movement of an alarmed wolf. Mills told me the story several years later, but he could remember the expression on his father's face as vividly as if the conversation had taken place that same afternoon.
>
> 'That's not true,' his father had said. 'I've always been utterly honest with you. I've tried to deal with you exactly as I would deal with the Justice Department or the IRS.'
>
> Subject to the prejudices of his class, Mills's father over the years had been known to compare both the Justice Department and the IRS to marauding bands of the envious poor.[34]

(This is an example of how the similes and metaphors we use reveal our very private meanings.)

Just as a will can destroy family relationships so borrowing and lending can destroy friendships.

Kevin told me how they had 'lost friends who owe us quite a lot of money. We sold our car to a friend for £300 just before we set off on our world travels. She said she would send the money when she'd got it but she never did. You don't want to lose a friend over £300, but then again you can't also sort of be jolly and chatty and such when someone owes you £300. It feels embarrassing to say, "Just give us £10 per month." There is something embarrassing about contacting somebody if they owe you. It nearly broke our friendship.'

Peter Barkworth spoke of the delight there is in being generous in giving and generous in receiving. He said, 'I have a rule now that if I give money to people it is a gift, not a loan. It may on occasions be less than the person had perhaps asked for, although I find very rarely people ask for a specific amount. I can remember a time where I gave less because I said – it was a loan of thousands – and I said, "Frankly, I cannot give that because you cannot pay me back. So I will give you less but it is a gift."'

I asked, 'Did you discover subsequently that it altered the relationship?'

'That particular one finished it. I have not had a word since.'

My friend Anna Raeburn and I often talk about people and their problems because that's Anna's business as well as mine. She told me that she would never lend money because of problems with repaying, and then immediately went on to tell me of a successful interest-free loan she had made to a dear old friend who needed money to replace the taxi he drove. The banks in their ageist way wouldn't lend him any. With him she made very specific arrangements about the way the loan was to be repaid because she knew the pitfalls of having to pay back a loan.

She told me, 'I have been loaned money and felt so embarrassed about repaying it that I would never do it again if I could afford it. I could only pay it off in such small amounts, and then you start to think, "Well, they will never miss that so why am I bothering," and then you persuade yourself that you don't need to repay it at all. And it's because you can't write a cheque for £100 and say, "This is what you loaned me." Years ago I was very poor and in fact that was my first great lesson because the man who loaned me the money sat me down and said, "You are going to pay this back at £1 a week. Here's the card. You write the date, amount and sign." I did pay it all back. It was wonderful. But I didn't like it and would never do it again.'

But even giving has its pitfalls. Anna told me, 'When there is money in a relationship it is very often the vehicle of expression so that the other more human, kinder, nicer, more affectionate and infinitely cheaper gestures of affection are not there. I remember vividly a man who wrote to me who said I've given my wife everything she could possibly want and she's still unhappy. I wrote back and said maybe she would have liked to have chosen some of these things, maybe she didn't want what you gave her, maybe what she wanted to do was have a Saturday morning where she held your hand and went shopping for food rather than a new radio, new car, holiday, whatever.'

As an afterthought Anna said, 'Then, of course, there is the question about how much money and sex are intertwined in the British mind. I think it is quite considerable. Did you know that in the language of Victorian sexuality ejaculation was called spending? Not ejaculating was called saving. Virtue was saved.'

In this image it can be seen how money relationships and sexual relationships become entwined. Freud has shown how a small child who wants to retain his precious faeces might in later life seek to hold on to his money. Retaining faeces is one way in which a child can seek to maintain his sense of existence when it is threatened by the power his parents wield. But of course there are many more ways in which an adult's attitude to money can be linked to childhood experience.

People who deny that childhood experiences have any connection with adult life have forgotten what being a child is like. When you're a child a significant event occurs and it fills your whole horizon. There is nothing else you can see. It is on the widest screen. In childhood there are many events like this. But as you get older you rarely encounter events which take over totally your whole perception. Indeed, events appear smaller, surrounded by other events, ideas, attitudes. Only the most extraordinary, unbelievable events come in that all encompassing way.

As a child the meanings you create for these first time events become the basic assumptions on which all other later meanings depend. It should not be surprising that our early experiences with money still influence in later life our behaviour concerning money, even though our financial circumstances might be markedly different from those of our family when we were a child.

The life of Charles Dickens shows this clearly.

> The financial difficulties that plagued the Dickens family during Charles's youth had their beginnings in the first years of his childhood. The pleasures of conviviality were essential for John Dickens, but the family soon found that laughter was costly. The paterfamilias had little sense of the importance of adjusting his needs to his income. His wife either had not been taught economy or was a poor learner. The couple enjoyed dinners, parties, family gatherings, and assumed that their income would be sufficient sooner or later to redeem their current expenses.[35]

But such an assumption was soon proved wrong. John Dickens drifted further and further into debt. There was no net of Social Security to catch such a family. Charles's childhood became a nightmare.

> His need as a child to protect himself against diminishment, even annihilation, had its special points of location and expression. Reading was a way to augment the self with private protective treasure. Writing became a way to increase the self. Probably he heard family discussions, if not arguments, about money. Early acquainted with its value, he had little or none in his pocket. What he had, he protected. When a subscription was being raised for the mother of the dead infants, he was frightened that the little bit of pocket money he had might be pressured out of him. When he 'was earnestly exhorted to contribute,' he 'resolutely declined: therein disgusting the company, who gave me to understand that I must dismiss all expectations of going to Heaven.' At an early age he began to learn to say no, to exert his will to protect himself. The likelihood, though, of not going to a literal heaven had little terror for him. His family was not religious. Neither ritual nor theology had a place in its daily activities, except insofar as the public calendar mandated for people of such easygoing Anglicanism occasional attendance at church and the celebration of

> holidays. From an early age, hell was a place of the mind, an inner world of tensions, anxieties, and nightmares, the more terrifying because it could not be controlled.[36]

This hell remained with Dickens to the end of his life. Even in his last years when he was universally acclaimed as the great storyteller he worried about money, pushing himself despite illness to lecture in America and, with the help of his business manager, George Dolby, trying not to pay American income tax.

Dickens was not an exception, as Kit and Dorothy Welchman found when they ran a workshop on a subject rarely tackled by counsellors, money. They reported that,

> The next exercise provided an opportunity to explore some of these feelings and conflicts and their meaning and origin for each individual. Members were asked to think of three specific events connected with money in some way in as much detail as possible: who was there, what was said, how money was involved, what their feelings were. The events were to be selected from (a) their first decade of life, (b) their second decade, or (c) within the last year.
>
> Working with partners, each in turn recalled their three incidents, explored them with the partner's help and considered the question, 'What was the "message" or "messages" that they received from the two earlier experiences?' Finally they explored any connections between the messages and the recent experience.
>
> The group discussion conveyed some of the intensity of feeling of these experiences: fear, anger, bitterness, envy, the sadness of loss, the struggle with confusion, often in isolation, to gain some understanding or control over the world of power and possibility that money represented. As one put it, 'The subject of money can be loaded with feelings.'
>
> The messages themselves that were shared with the group involved trust: 'They let you down. They abuse your trust,'; value, 'My value is measured with money'; communication, 'Don't talk about money' and 'It's difficult to ask'; dependence and independence, 'Whatever you want you must get for yourself' and 'I mustn't be beholden to anyone else's sacrifices'. Characteristic of the messages is a quality of compulsiveness, of must and mustn't, and many are connected with a poor self-image, with power-

> lessness, 'Other people are in control', a resignation to a limitation of rights, 'I don't have a right to money' and of personal possibilities, 'Ball gowns are for other people.'
>
> The personal experiences encapsulated in these messages were explored with partners but were not available to the group or this article. It did seem, however, that for many the personal strategies which the messages suggest were still experienced as exerting powerful influence on the present.[37]

The messages we get in childhood can be from people other than our parents and can be very powerful, especially when they stand in contrast to the messages we get from our parents. This is what happened to Tony.

He said, 'When I was a little child somebody said something to me that was very important. My father never ever bought himself the best of anything. He always got about the second or third best thing on the grounds that you didn't pay so much. One of his friends turned up one day when I was only about Billy's age. He was an amateur photographer and he had this fantastic camera. My parents told me, this man is coming and he is a real connoisseur. Everything he does is very nice – his shoes, his clothing, his car – everything he gets is the best. I was quite interested in this camera. It had all kinds of automatic things. He said to me, "Anthony, whatever you get in the world, always get the very best that is made or that you can possibly buy. If you can't buy the best one, don't buy it. Always get the best." I don't know whether it was grandiose or not but I always take a great delight in things that I think are really good. I am never happy with something if I know there is a better one in terms of quality. I'm never happy about having something that I feel has been skimped or badly produced with an eye to price rather than to standard.'

What many of us do is to work out a combination of the views expressed by each of our parents. This is what Terence did.

'I grew up in an alcoholic household, with a very, very strong mother who made it very clear that if I was not worthy of the Presidency of the United States I was not worthy of her. My mother basically operates from a fundamental position that there is no joy in life and that life is totally fearful. That is the framework of her life. My father, on the other hand, is this unbelievably courageous, unconventional challenger of every system or institution that has ever been put before him. The rules do not apply to him and life is completely limitless and is fundamentally a party. My dad always was an excellent money-maker, tremendous money-maker. He just knew how to create money from nothing. I don't know how that comes about, but I think it is just a gift that some people have. My dad had the gift. He never valued money and he never lived in fear of it. He never lived in fear of anything, really, and so he would get the money and squander it. Drinking and gambling and throwing parties. At a young age he started to work in family restaurants and so he started to understand the fundamental dynamic of merchanting, which is basically: I am willing to put myself in the place of the provider of a transaction, be it over a piece of pizza or a bottle of soda. I will put myself in the position of responsibility to provide that. I will acquire it at a price and sell it for more. It is a fundamentally courageous position to be in and I saw that in my father at a very early age. My father with his fearlessness and his generosity has a very, very powerful spiritual aura, so at a very early age I was exposed to no fear about money.

'But I was also in a very, very penniless environment and as part of my sort of shameful environment I basically clung to whatever positive I could get out of anybody. The only person I could get anything positive out of was my father, who went to World War Two and fought through invasions and told me stories about the army and I viewed this man who had operated in businesses and made money and then squandered it. I didn't know why he squandered it, but I just knew that my father could make money and he served in the army. I also knew that I did very well in school and I always loved numbers and I was extremely mathematically comfortable. So when it came time for me to go to high school I went to an engineering high school. When it came time for me to go to college I applied and got accepted to go to one of the leading military academies. I got to the academy because I wanted to become the President of the United States. I didn't want to become a lieutenant at platoon level, I wanted to be the commander in chief. When I decided that I would need money to become the President I started to understand that there is a connection between money and politics. I decided that I would leave the army after five years and make a couple of million dollars and go back in the army or go into politics. I was twenty-six at the time. When I came out of the army and came to Wall Street I knew nothing about economics – I never took a course in economics in my life. I never took a course in finance in my life. But I fell basically in love with the challenge and the gains of Wall Street – of money. That has been so enjoyable to me on many levels, so enjoyable that I have abandoned the dream of becoming President.'

Terence had seen what his father did and wanted to do better, as his mother expected of him. Sometimes children want to do well in order to show their parents that they were wrong. When Angela Lambert was interviewing the highly successful blockbuster novelist Shirley Conran she asked her,

> 'You have enough money to stop working forever now. Why don't you?'
>
> She smiles. 'Because I'm a *writer*. And because it's a big responsibility, being a big earner. The publishers have a vested interest in you and they expect you to perform. In my teens, money was a dirty word. My parents would say, "You get everything paid for: what do you want *money* for? Be grateful for what you've got." But what women *experience* is that money can make unhappiness a great deal more endurable; 99.9 per cent of the goddam *globe* belongs to men. The importance of money is played down to women – but if it's so unimportant, why have the men got it all?[38]

Some children feel compelled to do the opposite of what their parents did. When the artist Pat McNeill wrote to me she said,

> My father and uncle were both bank managers and my mother worked in a bank too before I was born. In consequence I've always treated financial matters as grown-up stuff to be discussed "not in front of the Children" (me! – now aged 68). The barrier I encountered to planning sensibly about money is an immense ennui (masking a taboo, I think) whenever it needs to be seriously tackled. That said, I've always been solvent, own my house and car, but have remained more of a grasshopper than an ant as far as forward planning is concerned.

My friend Ian Stewart told me how money was of the utmost importance to his parents. His father was a bank clerk, the only one of his family not to go into the professions, so he struggled to send his children to private schools and into the professions. Ian's reaction to this intense importance given to money was to ignore it. 'I write cheques and I never fill in the cheque stubs.'

Children in the same family do not have the same experiences about money. When I talked with company manager Ray and his wife Julie, Ray said, 'For me to have enough money would be to be able to do the things that I want to do. But that's what I'm doing today, like for instance if Julie had to go back to Australia tonight I can go and get a ticket. I don't have to worry about where the money is coming from. I don't have an excess of money, I can't go out tomorrow and buy a thirty-foot boat, but my aspirations aren't that dramatically high. I am not really driven by money. My attitude is probably quite similar actually to my parents' attitude to money. They were comfortably off. As a child I don't ever remember having to worry about where money was going to come from for whatever reason. And even in my teen years I never really wanted for anything. I wouldn't say that I was spoiled, but by the same token I never really wanted for anything. Money was never an issue when I was growing up – lack of it or excess of it, it wasn't something that was discussed within the family. It wasn't because it was a taboo subject, it didn't seem to really mean that much. That's probably easy to say if you have enough money to do the things you want to do.'

Julie thought there was more to it than that. She said, 'Ray's the youngest in his family and from what Ray's older sister has told me it seems that she thought he was spoilt because he got things that they couldn't afford when she was little.'

Ray conceded this, 'Yes, then perhaps I was lucky. My sister definitely is motivated by wealth and acquisition. She now has several houses and she likes diamonds. She and her husband work very hard, but I think, rather than the work driving them, it is the financial rewards that are driving them.'

Sometimes the events that determine our views about money occur in our teens or early twenties. My neighbour at a lunch at the Savoy given by Australian Business in Europe was a businessman,

Stefan, who told me that he would never buy anything unless he already had in his bank account the money to cover the purchase. He had learned the hard way the necessity of doing this. At eighteen he had gone on holiday in Spain with a girlfriend whose father had interests in property development. On their return the father persuaded Stefan to invest in some property. Stefan said that he didn't have any money, whereupon the father advised him to borrow it, assuring him that he would have his money and more back within a year. So Stefan went to the bank, which he knew only because his father banked there, and, with no collateral and no actual support from his father, he borrowed £20,000.

He didn't get his money back in one year. It took five years of burgeoning interest rates, hard work and immense anxiety to get his money back with no profit other than a hard-earned experience which he uses in his present work in property development.

Even when our common sense tells us that we do not have to worry about money, we can still find a locus for the anxiety which we learned in our childhood to feel. Lord Howie of Toon told me, 'I was brought up in working-class circumstances where my parents were poor and we had a serious shortage of money. My mother used to say to my brother and me that she wondered how we would get to the end of the week. We did, but we were struggling up until we started working as professional people looking after ourselves after the war. So I'm very well aware of the restraints and constraints from the shortage of money. I don't really worry about money now except in one respect. I often worry that my children might not have enough money, that they might find themselves constrained in a manner with which I was once familiar and now only recollect.'

Thus the ways we think about money and the ways that we use it arise from many more sources than those of the simple rules of logic, that is, public, shared logic. Our individual meaning structures have their own private logic. Often that private logic is based on assumptions which are antithetical to public logic. This is especially so where the calculation of risk and probability are concerned.

In his study of the history of risk Peter L. Bernstein noted that

> The revolutionary idea that defines the boundary between modern times and the past is the mastery of risk: the notion that the future is more than the whim of the gods and that men and women are not passive before nature. Until human beings discovered a way across that boundary, the future was a mirror of the past or the murky domain of oracles and soothsayers who held a monopoly over knowledge of anticipated events.[39]

In theory the assessment of risk should have become easy now that computers can not only marshal vast amounts of information but also allow risk assessors to run simulations of 'what if?' situations, but in practice, especially in the financial world, the assessment of risk shows little improvement and catastrophes continue to occur. We continue to make the same mistakes over and over again.

> We display risk-aversion when we are offered a choice in one setting and then turn into risk-*seekers* when we are offered the same risk in a different setting. We tend to ignore the common components of a problem and concentrate on each part in isolation . . . We have trouble recognizing how much information is enough and how much is too much. We pay excessive attention to low probability events accompanied by high drama and overlook events which happen in routine fashion. We treat costs and uncompensated losses differently, even though their impact on wealth is identical. We start out with a purely rational decision about how to manage our risks and then extrapolate from what may be only a run of good luck.[40]

Camelot, the company which set up and runs the UK national lottery, is making millions out of the inability of most people to calculate and evaluate probabilities. The Conservative government was delighted with the success of the lottery. Such success was based on the fact that most of the population considered the one chance in 14 million of winning the lottery as good odds, even with the added uncertainty of how many people might share the win. The same government was hoist by its own petard when, through its own failure to deal with the problem, the news finally broke that British beef was tainted to an unknown degree by as yet unidentified agents which could create the fatal disease known as Creutzfeldt-

Jakob Disease. No matter how many politicians and government spokesmen might insist that there was only one chance in a million of contracting the disease, the public was unimpressed. If one in 14 million is good odds for winning the lottery, one in a million must be excellent odds for getting the disease.

The main difficulty people have in working out probabilities and risks is that they don't understand or will not accept the concept of chance, that things can happen without a pre-ordained cause. Instead, many people want to believe in some Grand Design of a universe where nothing happens unless it falls within and is directed by the Grand Design. Everything that happens has a significance because it is part of this Grand Design. Such a belief gives a sense of security (with the concurrent loss of freedom) and a sense of power gained from being able to contact and use the Grand Design. Believers often use the word 'chance' when they talk about the functioning of their Grand Design but it certainly isn't chance in the sense of random occurrence.

I have mentioned that gambling is very important to many Chinese people and how the number eight is considered to be lucky because the word for eight sounds like the word for wealth. Four is considered unlucky because the word for four sounds like the word for death. Scientific, rational thought requires us to understand that a similarity is not an identity. Powerful though our similes and metaphors might be, the fact that one thing is like another does not mean that they are the same. I guess if I pointed out to a Chinese believer that in English 'eight' does not sound like 'wealth' and 'four' like 'death' I would be told that, while English and other languages are no more than sets of sounds devised by inferior races, the Chinese language, in all its forms, comes from the Celestial forms which are Absolute Truth and Reality.

Thus the Chinese concept of luck and chance is different from mine. For me the world is in constant change and from time to time I encounter a chance set of circumstances which I interpret as being beneficial to me. That is what I call good luck. In Chinese thinking the world changes according to the Celestial plan. By reading the signs correctly a Chinese person can predict that good fortune is in the offing. Acting in a certain way, he can take advantage of this aspect of the unfolding of the plan. That for him is good luck.

To be correct in interpreting the plan gives a sense of power. This is important in societies where power is concentrated in the hands of a few and where criticizing their elders and betters simply is not done.

The Grand Design of the Just World as described by the Christian churches has become very popular in South Korea where Christians have grown in numbers from about 1.2 million in 1957 to some 14 million in 1994. The evangelical Protestant churches, which promise material rewards for faith in God, have done especially well there. It seems that many South Koreans have interpreted the rapid growth in the country's economy as proof that their prayers have been answered.[41] Alas, no country's economy burgeons for ever. What will these people do when the bad times come?

The fortunes of the economies of the USA, the UK and Australia do not lend themselves to the revelation of the beneficent hand of God, so many people turn to other sources which might reveal the secrets of the Grand Design. Tarot cards and the *I Ching* are popular, but not so popular as astrology. All popular magazines and all but the most discerning newspapers carry astrology columns whose vaguely worded advice is capable of any interpretation the reader might care to put on it.

It saddens me that so many otherwise intelligent and thoughtful people believe in astrology. If I query their beliefs, say, by pointing out that, though my sister and I were each born on the same date six years apart, we are very different people, I am met with the kind of hypothesis-saving, logic-fudging arguments of the kind used to such effect by Freud and Marx in their theories, which were so constructed as to account for everything. When a patient did not behave in the way his theory predicted, Freud said that the patient was exhibiting reaction formation. For Marx, whenever the ruling class failed to exploit the working class the ruling class was attempting to co-opt the working class. Apparently, in astrological terms, the reason my sister and I are so different is because we weren't born at exactly the same time!

Often a believer in astrology (usually someone claiming to be greatly impressed with my books) will ask me what my birth sign is and then nod sagely, remarking that I show the characteristics of that particular birth sign, whichever one I had named. I think that I should copy the logician Raymond Smullyan who says that the reason he doesn't believe in astrology is because he's a Gemini and Geminis never believe in astrology.[42]

This fantastic notion that planets millions of miles away from us determine our destiny may have been around for thousands of years, but that doesn't make it true. Human stupidity can be impregnable to reason. Sceptics like myself must have wondered why it was that the leading UK astrologer, Patric Walker, did not foresee the necessity of not eating chicken and eggs lest he die of salmonella poisoning – which he did – but doubtless astrologers neglect the portents of their own stars in the way that car mechanics neglect their own cars and bankers their own bank accounts.

Some astrologers offer advice on financial matters and some people take that advice. Robert Citron, treasurer of Orange County, California and author of that county's bankruptcy, consulted the 'spiritual medium' Jeannie Smith, who predicted that interest rates would rise but failed to tell him when they would be going down again.[43] The publisher's blurb for a book by another astrologer claimed that 'financial astrology is the only forecasting system which has shown itself consistently capable of accurately predicting the timing of growth and recession, the movements of the stock market and the changing fortunes of individual companies.'[44] If certain astrologers were able to predict the market, wouldn't it be likely that not only would these people now be extremely rich but they would be talked about with even more awe than George Soros, who is credited with moving the market? It seems that the money these astrologers have made comes not from the market but from their gullible clients.

The belief in some kind of Grand Design of the universe prevents people from being able to assess when an event happens by chance and thus the risk involved. Instead, all kinds of chance occurrences are interpreted as having a significance which in fact lies in the realm of fantasy rather than in the real world.

This inability to understand and assess chance is not confined to innumerate and scientifically illiterate people. (Scientific illiteracy abounds in the world of media punditry.) Psychiatrists, desperate to prove that biology alone determines our destiny, quote twin studies where identical twins are brought up apart and in later life show some similar behavioural characteristics. If, say, the twins are found to have chosen the same names for their offspring or if both the twins are unemployed, child-naming and unemployment are seen as having a genetic basis. No attempt is made to assess the probability that, given that the popularity of certain names varies from generation to generation, two children of the same age are likely to share the same name, or to assess the probability that a person of a certain age in a certain society would be unemployed.

Because people don't understand probability they rely on advisers who might understand probability no better than they or they fall victim to financial scams. John Allen Paulos has pointed out that,

> There's always enough random success to justify almost anything to someone who wants to believe ... The people who try their luck and don't fare well will generally be quiet about their experiences. But there'll always be some people who will do extremely well, and they will swear to the efficacy of whatever system they've used. Other people will soon follow suit, and a fad will be born and thrive for a while despite its baselessness.
>
> There is a strong general tendency to filter out the bad and the failed and to focus on the good and the successful. Casinos encourage this tendency by making sure that every quarter that's won in a slot machine causes lights to blink and makes its own little tinkle in the metal tray. Seeing all the lights and hearing all the tinkles, it's not hard to get the impression that everyone's winning. Losses or failures are silent. The same applies to well-publicized stock-market killings vs relatively invisible stock-market ruinations, and to the faith healer who takes credit for any accidental improvements but will deny responsibility if, for example, he ministers to a blind man who then becomes lame.[45]

In our private logic we might be very stupid, but such stupidity should not be incorrigible. We are not prisoners of a world where everything is created and maintained by divine decree, though many people think that they are. It is true that we did not create the conditions of our existence and that we have little control over them, but what we do control is how we interpret the conditions of our existence and everything that happens to us.

To create a better world, a society in which it would be a pleasure to live, we need to understand ourselves so we can choose those interpretations which would best serve our needs. Specifically we need to understand

* that we are always in the business of creating meaning and that what we know is the meaning we construct and not the world directly.
* that what matters most to us is to maintain our sense of existence and to ward off the threat of annihilation.
* as individuals, how we experience our sense of existence and see the threat of annihilation.
* how we use money and possessions to maintain our sense of existence and to ward off the threat of annihilation.
* what might be for us the optimum balance between freedom and security
* how we view the functioning of chance in our world.

Only when we have such an understanding of ourselves can we all appreciate and begin to create what might be a worthwhile, true value of money.

Is it possible to arrive at a true value for money? 'True' not in the sense of divinely decreed, an absolute value for ever and ever, but 'true' in the sense of what value we can give to money which would not constantly threaten our survival but rather secure the survival of both body and person, not for just a special group but for all of us, a value which would enable us to enrich our lives with all those aspects of non-negotiable wealth which cannot be reduced to mere amounts of money but which enable us to live full lives and become the most of what we could be.

I would like to think that the answer to my question could be yes.

5

The Value of Money

> You are free to do whatever you like. You need only face the consequences.
>
> Sheldon Kopp[1]

> The good society must distinguish between enrichment that is permissible and benign and that which is at social cost.
>
> J. K. Galbraith[2]

Would it be possible to arrive at a value for money about which we could all agree?

Any attempt would have to involve much more than agreeing to return to the gold standard, or tie all currencies to the dollar, or set a band within which all currencies could float. An attempt at an agreement would need to start with the question, 'What do we want money to do?' It is true that we want money to give us security while at the same time letting us have the freedom to do what we want, but this is an unrealistic expectation. Uncertainty is both an intrinsic part of freedom and an inescapable aspect of life.

However, it is possible to reduce uncertainty by being very clear about our ideas and the way we use them. We increase the uncertainty associated with money and its functions because, first, we don't understand that publicly we are dealing in ideas that may or may not relate directly to the real world, and, second, we do not make explicit to ourselves, much less to others, what our private ideas actually are.

Our ideas about money are not separate from what we do with it. We use money to buy and sell. We buy and sell things and ideas. Whenever we buy and sell, and whatever we buy and sell, we are making choices. Every purchase and every sale is a choice. There are always alternatives from which to choose. People sometimes argue that in certain situations they have no choice, but what in effect happens in those situations is that the person sees all alternatives except one as unacceptable. Most parents choose to buy food for their children because the alternatives of letting the children starve or being jailed for neglecting their children are unacceptable.

Whenever we make a choice about a sale or a purchase we have an aim in mind, that of maintaining our sense of existence and warding off the threat of annihilation. Parents buy food for their children in the hope of maintaining their relationship with their children and achieving their goals in raising a family, not having their children taken from them and not having their life's project collapse into chaos.

However, every choice we make has good implications and bad implications. In some choices the good outweighs the bad and in others the bad outweighs the good. In one family, even though the children complain of injustice because they are deprived of sweets and snacks, the parents buy wholesome food which ensures the children's health and growth. In another family the children feel loved and cosseted because the parents buy the food the children want to eat, but they do not thrive as well as they could.

Thus, to arrive at a true value for money we would need

* to find a value which gave an acceptable balance between security and freedom. For instance, having one currency for the whole world might give a high degree of security, but it would mean relinquishing the freedom to enjoy being patriotic. (Such a balance could not be acceptable until many individuals realized that they did not need to hold such valued ideas about nationality and patriotism in order to bolster their sense of existence.)
* to define those trades where good outcomes outweigh the bad so that those trades with a preponderance of bad outcomes

> can be eliminated. For instance, is it better to sell a developing country literacy skills rather than arms? (Selling literacy skills will be seen universally as being better than arms only when those people who trade in arms no longer need the money and power they get from this trade to maintain their sense of existence.)

Arriving at an agreed definition of 'value' and 'good and bad outcomes' will not be easy.

When she was prime minister Margaret Thatcher was always talking about 'value for money'. She said it in a way which implied that it was a fixed and explicit measure which we all recognized. We all knew whenever we contemplated a purchase whether the price charged was value for money. Everyone else would agree with our judgement because we could all measure every possible purchase against this objective standard. Tragically, many people believed her nonsense. They thought, 'I want value for money,' and, assuming correctly that everyone wants value for money, did not realize that no two people give 'value for money' the same meaning.

Ask anyone how they assess value for money and the answer will draw on how that person sees his past and future and how he experiences his sense of existence and sees the threat of annihilation.

At a workshop I gave in north London all the participants were asked, as is usual now, to fill in a questionnaire at the end of the session to evaluate its worth. As the participants had paid good money for this workshop they would be assessing it in terms of value for money. Just before we broke for lunch I asked them to scribble down the general principles they followed in deciding whether a purchase was value for money. Here are some of their replies.

'If I've enjoyed something – been stimulated. If I want something for myself/kids/house I will buy it and then feel guilty for spending too much. No logical feeling on value for money, i.e., will buy a punnet of strawberries off season and then refuse to buy a packet of crisps.'

'I ask myself if the product/or service met my demands and/or needs or if I felt at the end that something was lacking. If, perhaps, one or two of my demands were still outstanding this is OK, but any more than that leaves me feeling cheated.'

'Do I want it, how much do I want it, how happy will it make me feel, will it last, is it well made. I like special offers. I like to think I have got money off something, even if I know it is probably a marketing ploy.'

'I work out if something was value for money by the way I feel in relation to the energy I exchanged with a person(s). Was it a loving exchange, a positive exchange or was it a fearful and negative one? Even if it was negative, was I able to learn and grow from the exchange. I see money as a flow of energy in an exchange for goods and for service.'

'I support my three sons and myself on income support. If I think something might be extravagant I ask the boys if they think we need it. If they say no we go without.'

'Do I want it in my house? Can the children live without it?'

'Gut feeling. How close to pay day. What I feel I've gained.'

'Did I enjoy the events or the goods bought? If an event, do I feel enriched by the experience?'

'Can you buy an alternative cheaper? Is the alternative "better", i.e., appropriate to individual needs? Is the product of high standard? Is it a service giver, friendly, efficient?'

'Can it give hours of pleasure or years of wear or enhancement to self image?'

Many of the workshop members referred directly to what they regarded as value for money from the workshops. They spoke of understanding being 'worth its weight in gold', 'gave to the real me', 'if I've learnt something to feed my inside.' One said, 'Money spent on personal growth is always money well spent because it benefits, not only the person seeking help, but those he or she has contact with, i.e., family, friends, work colleagues.'

'Value for money' isn't like a tape measure which can be applied to a variety of objects. The cost of something always relates to the intrinsic value a person gives to the particular object offered for sale. All the workshop members valued something intangible as 'personal growth'. Many more people value something much more visible like a chosen career or something more tangible like cars, but even here there can be big differences in how people value such activities and objects.

When I was talking to an experienced public relations manager in the car industry about who is valued more, the person who produces real objects or the person who produces ideas, he said, 'It varies from country to country. In Germany engineers, people who produce things, are the absolute top of the pile – it's the sort of job that young people are desperate to get into – particularly in the car industry. In Britain it is the absolute opposite. The car industry is seen as not a very pleasant industry with unfortunate connotations and something that people don't want to get into. In Germany the car industry is seen as the heart of the renaissance of Germany after the war, whereas in Britain the car industry stands for the collapse of British industry after the war. In Britain there is only one car plant that is open for public tours and they only do about 50 people per month by appointment. It's Ford's Dagenham plant. Whereas in Germany every car plant is open to the public. Volkswagen alone puts half a million people through their tours every year – a huge difference. All the key factories in Germany now have display areas and museums attached to them for the public to come and inspect the products. In Britain there are people who aspire to go into banking and those areas of business, but there isn't the same aspiration in Germany. In the USA there has been a transition from one to the other. The USA always prided itself on its industry and now it's got more lawyers than it has engineers and people aspire to be lawyers not engineers.'

The answers to the question, 'How do you decide what is value for money?' are not only diverse but they refer to concepts which defy an objective definition.

Nevertheless, to arrive at a satisfactory value for money we need to decide what we can all accept as a satisfactory trade. But how shall we define 'satisfactory'?

To understand an idea it is always useful to look at its history.

Every species other than our own evolved a way of living and kept very much to that particular way throughout the total life span of that species. Crocodiles, who have been around for much longer than us, live very much the same sort of lives that they always have.

Changes in climate might necessitate some small adjustments. These might be changes in some habits or the gradual evolution of a different physical characteristic. Chimpanzees found that a stick could be as effective as their hands for digging out termites. Rabbits in very cold climates evolved white fur while those on the dry plains evolved brown.

Each species had its own economy which was simply that a certain amount of work had to be done in order to ensure survival. Only the climate and the birthrate changed the economy. In a bad year more work was required and in a bountiful year less. A bountiful year might produce more offspring than the following year could support, while a bad year or a sudden blight might reduce the number of adults. In both cases the adults would need to put more work into their economy or to stabilize their group's numbers by letting some of the young die.

These economies remained the same year after year, century after century. Dinosaurs appear to have lived much the same pattern of life for four million years. They don't seem to have been imbued with the notion that every generation ought to be more successful than the previous one. Rabbits appear to have spread across the world not by a curiosity to find what was over the far horizon but by an innate facility for effective reproduction.

Our earliest ancestors also had such stable economies. The toolmakers of two million years ago kept to the models they had designed and seem not to have needed to create a new model axe-head every spring.

Across the species our closest cousin is the chimpanzee, with whom we share a common ancestor. For several million years the brains of our hominid ancestors were the same size as those of the early chimpanzees, even though by three and a half million years ago our ancestors had left the trees and were walking upright. Some two and a half million years ago, when the ice ages began, the brains of our ancestors *homo erectus* grew larger, reaching our present size about 150,000 years ago. A mere 100,000 years ago *homo sapiens* appeared on the scene. 'At some point in the evolution of brains,' wrote Richard Dawkins, 'they acquired the ability to simulate models of the outside world. In its advanced forms we call this ability "imagination". It may be compared to the virtual reality software that runs on some computers . . . We know almost nothing of how language originated, since it started to fossilise only recently, in the form of writing."[3]

Along with the acquisition of language we developed the skills of agriculture and the arts – the beginning of what we call civilization. We did not simply develop these skills. We developed the ability to reflect on what we were doing. Our ancestors talked to one another and one day discovered that they could talk to themselves and, lo, consciousness was born. It might have been the other way around, but whatever, life was never the same again. Neither was the economy.

Fixed economies exist in unchanging environments, and in such consciousness is superfluous. Talking to one another can be no more than, 'Gimme that stone,' 'Find one yourself,' and all in an unchanging environment. But once there's consciousness there's imagination. We can imagine what isn't present. There's escape from the immediate environment into imaginary places with imaginary things, and some of these imaginary things can then be created at home. Now the bright young man needs a new model axe-head every year, and, in what is a moment in the history of the world, the axe-head itself evolves into a car and a machine gun.

In came consciousness and out went the fixed economy because consciousness always wants more. 'More' might be 'more more' or 'more different', but it is always 'more'.

I think that this is a good thing. Many people do not. They've been brought up to believe that wanting more is greedy, and greed is wicked. I think that the only way to give up being greedy is to die. While we're on this side of death we're greedy, even if it's only greedy to keep on breathing. The one criticism I have of greed is that most people are misguided in what they are greedy for. Why be greedy for money and possessions when as well you can be greedy for love, knowledge, experience and beauty in all their multifarious forms?

Consciousness says, 'More', and the economy changes. This is why we can never create a stable economy. However, we have the choice of creating a changing economy which harms us or of creating an economy which allows all of us to elaborate and implement our desire for more in ways which enhance our lives.

This is not just a matter of increasing the country's Gross National Product or Gross Domestic Product as they are measured by economists and politicians. The Gross Domestic Product is the money value, at market prices, of the goods and services produced in the country over a certain period of time. The Gross National Product includes all this plus income earned abroad. The calculation of these two indices excludes much of what occupies the time of a significant number of people and much of what people value. Housework and raising children are excluded, as is voluntary work. A garden or an allotment is a prized and productive possession for millions of people, but if you grow your own vegetables and flowers for your own use they are not included in the GDP, while if you sell the odd pound of tomatoes to the local greengrocer they are (or should be). Similarly, if you sell the picture or poem you have created you contribute to the GDP, but unsold creative products and the creative processes which enhance your life and the lives of those who know you make no contribution.

Another very creative aspect of our lives is also excluded – the black economy to which we all contribute when we need a tradesman in a hurry. (A cash only plumber I know reckons that no plumber ever need fear destitution because, no matter what the politics of the government, unlike all the other trades and professions, plumbers are always essential.) Professor Kent Matthews at Cardiff university has calculated that, taking into account the many ways in which people avoid declaring their full taxable income, the black economy is 12 per cent of the UK GDP. Though some analysts think he is placing the figure too high, others look at the amount of unexplained cash in the system and see it as the cause of the recent high level and erratic performance of the narrow money supply, one of the indices used by economists to measure the performance of the economy. Professor Matthews considers that about half the money in the black economy is spent in what might be called the criminal economy of drugs, prostitution, pornography and general criminal activity.[4]

A large and increasing GDP is considered by many to be proof not only that a country's economy is sound but that that country plays an important part on the world stage. 'Economic growth' is to international status as 'spiritual growth' is to sainthood. However, both kinds of growth can be dangerously skewed. Saints often love humanity but neglect the needs of individuals just as a country with a growing economy can be devoted to progress while its people suffer.

In calculating GDP vitally important intangibles like literacy and health are not included, although both contribute to the wealth of a country. What the research shows is that literacy and health do not relate directly to the wealth of a country but to how that wealth is distributed. The more evenly the wealth is distributed, the more literate and healthy the country is.[5]

Much political rhetoric is expended on the necessity of increasing GDP, rhetoric which is based on the assumption that an increase in GDP will not only increase the country's wealth but will increase the happiness of its inhabitants. Ever since the Second World War politicians in the developed world have been claiming significant increases in their country's GDP. Over that same time the suicide rate for young people, especially young men, has been climbing steadily. Will Hutton asked, 'If GDP rose by 3 per cent per annum over the next five years, while that of the suicide rate doubled, how much richer would Britain be at the end of that period?'[6]

The GNP and GDP take no account of what the country has lost. There is no measure of the cost of pollution or industrial damage like oil spills and asbestos, nor of the loss to the country of the skills and effort of the millions who are unemployed or working at jobs far below their ability.

It is now politically correct for governments and international organizations to talk positively about environmental issues, but actions to match the sentiments are restricted by the usual monetary considerations. However, sometimes they have to put their money where their mouth is and so it is to be welcomed that 'the World Bank has developed a "new wealth accounting system" including four kinds of assets as the real wealth of nations – natural capital, produced assets, human resources and social capital. The Clinton administration has published a measure of "green GDP", while the new "system of national accounts" developed by the OECD, EU, IMF and the World Bank has protocols for integrating social and environmental statistics into national accounts.'[7]

Other people who, if they had the money, would put it where their mouth is, are considering better ways of measuring wealth and the value of life. Brian Davey, social philosopher and development worker, wrote to me from Germany.

> Is it possible to think of forms of development where people's lives improve even though their money income may be stable or falling? If we switch to a quality of life paradigm – based on the quality of relationships and the ability to be creative in their environment – then of course we can. This then connects up with the sort of work we in Ecoworks have been doing and what I am trying to do here – improve people's opportunity for creative activity, including the improvement of the living environments and relationships – but outside the money economy.[8]

Very few people, if any at all, are able in the course of their lifetimes to develop and use all the talents with which they are born, but in economies where there is a modicum of free speech at least some people have the opportunity to become more than they are. Becoming more than you are isn't just a matter of becoming a brain surgeon or a concert pianist. It means retaining the curiosity about the world and the delight in living with which you were born as well as the confidence to use your natural talents. Many people lose all this because as small children they are punished for being curious ('Don't touch!'), restricted by rules and threats of punishment ('Sit down. Be quiet!'), and told that they have no talent ('You're stupid,' 'You can't draw,' 'You're tone deaf'). However, it is possible in adult life for us to regain our curiosity, delight and confidence. We do not have to be prisoners of our past.

GDP, GNP and 'value for money' are the kind of concept used by those people who, in the process of losing their curiosity and delight in the world and access to their talents, decide that the only measure of value is a monetary one. Such people have a much better chance of becoming rich than those people who believe that there are more valuable things in life than money.

We all live in groups and we all prefer to join a group whose members share our experiences and prejudices. So, quite naturally, the rich tend to live with the rich.

Perhaps the best thing about being rich is that it is easier to separate yourself from those people who are not members of your group. Why fly steerage when you could have your own Lear jet? Perhaps the worst thing about being rich is that those poorer than you envy your riches and want to take them from you. In a country where there is no great monetary difference between the rich and the poor the rich can move about freely. The greater the disparity, the more the rich must lock themselves away. Indeed, with the increasing disparity between the rich and the poor in the developed countries (in the undeveloped and developing countries it has always been huge), the rich increasingly live in more and more secure prisons. Luxurious prisons, certainly, but prisons nevertheless.

In such prisons the rich hope to keep themselves safe, not just from thieves and murderers, but from all the ills of the world. Money may not buy happiness, but at least you can be secure and healthily unhappy. In past centuries, on the whole, the rich were healthier and lived longer than the poor. True, rich women died in childbirth and rich people died of tuberculosis, but that was a woman's lot (doesn't the Bible say that women should bring their children forth in travail and suffering?) and wasn't it obvious that tuberculosis afflicted amongst the rich only the very sensitive and intelligent?

Such a degree of safety, whether from thieves and murderers or from disease and disaster, no longer applies. The rates of crime in rich areas may be lower than those in poor areas and the rich might score better than the poor on all measures of health and longevity, but there are now a multitude of dangers from which the rich can protect themselves no better than the poor.

Here is a summary of some of these current dangers.

1 Environment

* the hole in the ozone layer. Melanoma, the fatal form of skin cancer, is the one form of cancer which affects the rich more than the poor.

* earthquakes are expected in Tokyo and Los Angeles, but when?

As the fires following the Kobe earthquake showed, a lack of preparation for such a disaster causes even greater disasters.
* the North Pole is melting, causing profound changes in the world's climate. The scientific evidence for this includes the warming of the currents which flow up the Norwegian coast, something which can be measured by the radioactive pollution which comes from the Sellafield nuclear reactor.[9]
* environmental pollution. The earth is a unitary system, so pollution in one area affects other areas. Much of the vast industrial pollution of Eastern Europe and the old Soviet Union is moving westward. Most of the lethal man-made chemicals, now banned in Western industrial countries, have not disappeared but, as airborne pollutants, are now in the soil and ice of the Arctic Circle and carried by birds, animals and ocean currents.
* food comes only from the land and the sea. World fish catches are falling. Soil erosion world-wide means that topsoil is being lost at a far greater rate than the 500 years an inch of topsoil takes to form.

2 Terrorism

* terrorists aim to effect destruction in places that represent wealth and power. Hence the IRA bombs Canary Wharf and Harrods, not Job Centres.
* bomb designers are creating smaller though no less powerful bombs which are harder for security forces to detect.
* the arms trade and the multitude of conflicts in the Balkans, the Middle East and Africa ensure a steady supply of explosives, bomb-making equipment and weapons.
* in cities where the poor are very poor and the rich are very rich, the poor, seeing the State as the enemy, are at war with the city.
* as Johannesburg and Moscow have shown, no amount of high security enclaves and bodyguards can keep people safe.

3 Health

* asthma used to be a comparatively rare disease. Now it is common, equally prevalent amongst the rich and the poor, and linked to pollution.
* rich Victorians died of tuberculosis because it is a highly

infectious, droplet-borne disease. Now a drug-resistant form of the disease is spreading rapidly through the world and, according to the World Health Organization, killing more people than at any time in history.[10]

* the diseases of syphilis, cholera, diphtheria and polio, once thought to have been defeated, have now reappeared due to the breakdown of the economies in Eastern Europe and the old Soviet Union.
* now diseases like ebola and once rare diseases like Creutzfeldt-Jakob Disease are being shown to have crossed from one species to another.
* many strains of disease-carrying viruses and bacteria are now resistant to antibiotic drugs.
* a drug-resistant form of malaria is increasing and extending its geographical distribution with global warming.
* a new hepatitis virus, Hepatitis G, is now being carried by a million people in Britain and can be transmitted through blood transfusions and blood products. It is now thought that some 300,000 people are infected with Hepatitis C of whom 70,000 could develop cirrhosis or cancer of the liver. Dr Lesley Kay, consultant haematologist, said, 'New viruses will continue to appear while we have exotic holidays, foreign travel and sexual freedom. These viruses often exist in small human or animal populations for many years without spreading. Visitors travel to the region, contract the virus and take it back home. It enters the blood supply and is spread by that route or by sexual transmission.'[11]
* the potentially fatal diseases of salmonella and listeria remain a threat to anyone who eats eggs, chicken and soft cheeses.
* male fertility, as measured by sperm count and abnormality, is declining at a rate which threatens future generations. The decline might be linked to the increase in the amount of oestrogen used in many products entering the water system and the food chain.
* radiation does not decline as fast as governments would have us believe. Ten years after Chernobyl land as far away as Wales is still affected. Everyone in Europe lives within 500 miles of a nuclear reactor.

All of the above are dangers which affect the rich as much as the poor, but they are dangers which arise from or are intensified by the huge discrepancies between the haves and the have-nots. The drive to produce and consume has created industrial conditions which have led to extensive pollution affecting the whole planet. Large populations, usually of poor people, tend to live in places prone to earthquakes, floods, hurricanes, landslides and volcanic eruptions, thus turning each natural event into a major disaster with world-wide effects. Wars, conflicts and terrorism arise from one group of people regarding themselves as being deprived of something which is rightly theirs. Many of the current threats to health arise from pollution and poverty.

It should be clear to everyone, even to politicians, financiers and economists, that a solution to these problems can be found only if we organize our societies on a more equitable basis. In advocating this it is not necessary to seize the moral high ground of New Labour, Old Labour, socialism, communism or whatever, nor the moral high ground of humanistic altruism, Christian values or Islamic almsgiving and so on. As I see it, it is just a matter of wise but utter selfishness. I want to live a long and healthy life. Therefore it is in my interests to promote a form of society which enables me to do so.

Somehow we need to create a society where the differences between the rich and the poor are not so great that the poor rightly feel that they are demeaned and excluded from society, and where living conditions provide safety and health for all. A society based on the principle that everyone gets the same amount of money will never function properly, first, because some people, believing themselves to be more equal than others, will get for themselves more than others, and, second, such a distribution of money has not grown organically out of the work of the people in that society. Gifts are nice, but the lifeblood of society is trade.

Gifts and Trade

What is a gift?

Brian Davey told me, 'If I remember my economic history, trade first started as an exchange of gifts. This is a paradoxical concept as a gift is given as a gesture of good will without an expectation of anything in return. When something is expected in return it ceases to be a gift and becomes trade.'[12]

This, I thought, is yet another example of the simple-minded thinking typical of those economists Brian calls 'text book bog standard'. They had certainly not pondered the nature of gifts.

How often does one person give something to another person without expecting something in return? Not often. As the old Russian proverb goes, 'Only mousetraps have free cheese.' Or as we in the West say, 'There's no such thing as a free gift.' The only occasion when a person gives a free gift is when that person feels towards the recipient an emotion which I have described elsewhere, perhaps too romantically, as true love. True love says, 'I love you because you exist and I wish you well even though that "well" might not include me.' Not true love says, 'I love you therefore you must do what I want.'

Everyone is familiar with not true love. It's the one we usually get from our family and our lovers. They expect us to fulfil their expectations. If we are extremely lucky we might have one parent who gives us true love. More often we get true love from friends who enjoy our company and expect nothing from us. But, tragically, it's rare. Not true love is what we get – and give.

So, with the giving of gifts, more often than not we want something in return. Sometimes it's wanting the other person to think well of us. Hence the popularity of cards, Christmas and birthday presents and, in business, those corporate gifts, the size and value of which follow the biblical dictum, 'To him that hath shalt be given.' Sometimes we give gifts solely to make sure that the recipients remember that we exist. Here, again, corporate gifts figure largely. Sometimes it's not other people we want to think well of us but some unearthly power. So the churches receive their tithes and the Buddhist monks their breakfast.

Gifts are given in order to secure goodwill, and goodwill features on company balance sheets. With one exception, true love, gift-giving is trade.

In gift-giving as trade the giver and the recipient each invest the gift with a certain value. The two values are not likely to be the same. A successful gift/trade is one where both parties are satisfied. Such satisfaction or dissatisfaction can have many facets, few of which relate directly to a monetary value. My mother always disliked receiving gifts from people outside her immediate family (gifts from the family she regarded as her due) because she felt they placed her under an obligation. She would hasten to give a gift in return so as to remove the obligation. What she gave had little relevance for her provided it did not cost much and didn't look cheap. If ever you've been the recipient of a gift from someone who never considers what you might actually like, you'll know that mixture of feelings, puzzlement, amazement and hurt.

Much of what passes as gift-giving is actually barter. Children understand this very well and are prepared to barter good behaviour for presents. Barter has a long history. The way of life called hunter-gatherer has a much longer history than that of agriculture and industry. Hunter-gatherers, as we see from those existing today, bartered within the tribe and between tribes.

Although money came into use centuries ago, until fairly recently it was used by only a few people – those in power and the merchants. Most people bartered their services for protection by their overlord, either by working for him directly or by giving him and the Church part of what they grew in their peasant holdings. As J. K. Galbraith remarked, 'What was important once again was the intrusion of ethics on economics – the fairness or justice of the relationship between master and slave, lord and serf, landlord and share-cropper.'[13]

Ethics are often talked about in business and financial circles as an optional add-on. There seems to be little recognition that it is the warp and woof of our lives. Every judgement we make is an ethical judgement. Is this good or bad for me? Is this fair and just for me? Once we know what is good, fair and just for ourselves we can generalize this to others, but we first decide what is good, fair and just for ourselves because our evaluations of these impinge immediately on how we experience our sense of existence and see the threat of annihilation.

Whether we are bartering or buying and selling we are engaged in maintaining our sense of existence and warding off the threat of annihilation. This came out very clearly in some of the conversations I had with people about money.

My friend Paul, a marvellous extravert, is passionate about trading. Whenever I mention to him that I'm thinking of buying or selling something he gives me advice, some of which is excellent and some a bit closer to the wind than I would dare. He said, 'I love challenges and discussion and negotiation. I was doing deals in some capacity every day of every week. Contriving situations to find out information which would be useful for getting this business or whatever that might be. I used to thrive off that, so therefore – as the saying went at the time – I love it when a plan comes together. That was the kick, that was the high, the adrenalin buzz, whatever. I was mixing with people similar to me, so every day was a challenge. The actual amount of money I earned mattered to a degree, but it didn't matter as much as actually doing a deal, beating your opponent, finding out something that he didn't know, or protecting your corner, defending yourself, or sometimes putting myself in a weaker position to see if I had the strength to get out of it. It is all very strange, but it is all part of making life exciting. The one element that I would consider a weakness in that environment was that I did lack a certain killer instinct in the end and the politics used to appal me. Untalented, less able people could get into positions preferable to my own, because that's me being silly not shutting up when I should have done or whatever. But sometimes when I should have stuck the knife in, to use a phrase, I didn't because it just didn't feel right and somebody could get hurt by this.'

When I was talking to Elizabeth and Michael they told me how much they enjoyed the whole business of trade.

Elizabeth said, 'It is a way of communication, isn't it? I'll give you something, you give me money for it, and we both derive some sort of satisfaction from this. I would like to sell lots more products. I would like to make lots of different products, books and pictures and anti-stress therapy for working people, things like that and sell them. It would be really nice.'

Michael said, 'I do like piles of things, neat piles of things and then they get sold. The part of my work I like the most is concerts and ticket selling, people coming in and the whole thing of having done it properly. If you do it properly they do sell. It's lovely. You know the tickets have been on sale for six weeks and they gradually sell, and if the place holds 3,000 seats and five days before the concert you have sold 2,300 seats and the next day it's 2,440. There is the orderliness about it I think as much as anything else. Also when we went to Turkey on holiday there was so much trade going on there that, although it was a poor country, you felt it was sort of a vital country and a good country and a civilized one. Our rich friend bought a lot of carpets. We bought a couple of cheap ones and he bought three expensive ones. It was a lovely experience. It was a great retail experience. We were all getting something out of it. The most important thing is that people like the thing they are selling. When I bought some walking boots in Wales I went into a shop, a small retailer. They had a range and I was asking the difference and he wouldn't let me buy the most expensive pair. He said these are just as good, but these are from the eastern bloc, so they want the currency, so it's cheaper and, you know, but if you look at the soles on this one. It was such a fantastic experience that when I got back to where we were staying I said to Elizabeth, you must go and buy some walking shoes. He would probably be horrified if you told him he was a good salesman because he would think that that was not a very good thing to be. He was a man genuinely interested in what he sold and interested in people.'

The success of car boot sales is a measure of how much people generally enjoy trade. When I interviewed Kevin and Hilary I discovered that they had a passion for car boot sales and secondhand shops. They never bought new if they could buy secondhand. Hilary said, 'I find a certain amount of pleasure in being able to use something that somebody else didn't want. When I finish with my things I send them back to the junk shop so it's being much more part of the cycle that I feel. I put some things in a rubbish bin at Sainsbury's recently and ended up bringing a box full of odd things home because somebody had thrown away glasses and kids' toys and all sorts of things which I could take to a charity shop to sell. I'm the sort of person who always looks in skips – I'm a forager.'

When I asked her why preserving and recyling were important to her she explained that she saw herself and her family and everything in the world as part of an endless cycle. Car boot sales linked her to eternity.

Terence said, 'It's what you do from second to second, instant to instant, that has to connect to your soul, to your core, that is going to make you wealthy, truly wealthy. If what you do just results in you making money it is not going to promote health and wealth in your spiritual body.'

What these people are saying is that trade is good when it connects to something inside the individual, something which all people can share. If every time we traded this happened our world would be a very different place. Alas, there seems to be bad trades as well as good.

The words 'good' and 'bad' have many connotations. What Paul, Elizabeth, Michael, Hilary and Terence are saying is that 'good' in connection with trade means wholesome, healthy, life-enhancing and life-affirming, and that 'bad' is unwholesome, unhealthy, life-diminishing and life-denying. This is a meaning with which I agree, but I am aware that many people would add to such a meaning some mention of God. I am not sure what God's views are on trade. (Saint Thomas Aquinas did warn that charging an unfair price would bring punishment in the afterlife.) I would prefer to use words which relate solely to human actions and judgements. Many of the actions which get labelled as bad or evil I see as stupid, a failure to understand consequences, whereas intelligent actions imply an accurate awareness of consequences. Accordingly, I shall talk about intelligent trades and stupid trades.

It is amazing and tragic that so many people don't understand about consequences. I've had fathers say to me after discovering their young son's misdemeanour, 'I gave him a good hiding and that's the end of it.' What nonsense. Children have memories and at some later time they respond in some way to their father's violence. John Major was fond of saying of some unfortunate event that the matter was closed and he had 'drawn a line under it'. King Canute knew that he could not stop the tide but John Major seemed not to know that the consequences of our actions roll on forever, whether we discuss the matter or not. Moreover, consequences do not unfold in a neat linear fashion from A to B to C. They go in every direction and reach some far-flung and very unexpected places.

The perpetrators of stupid trades do not understand consequences. For some such people the consequences include arrest and imprisonment or receiving the fatal bullet. In photographs of these extreme moments their faces often bear the look of surprise and puzzlement. How could this have happened? It was not in their plan. Others, having managed to keep on the right side of the law, are affronted when confronted with consequences deleterious to others. 'I haven't done anything wrong,' they say. 'Don't blame me.' Harming others was not a consequence they considered important.

To take account of the consequences of our actions, including those in trading, we need to be aware that

* consequences spread in every direction. Chaos theorists illustrate this by talking about the legendary butterfly which flutters its wings in Rio and changes the weather in Chicago.
* consequences are always different from what we expect. Who would have expected that those workman's trousers called jeans would become the most popular garment ever made?
* consequences affect our whole life span and are never a matter of a few days, weeks or months. Ask anyone over forty to identify the event which determined the course of their life and they are likely to talk about a choice they made in their early teens or twenties.

Intelligent trades are those which maintain our life and in some way enhance it. Stupid trades might make someone some money which that person can use to maintain his life, but not only do they fail to enhance people's lives, they also degrade them. There are people who make a great deal of money out of selling arms or drugs, but to do so and not be overwhelmed by guilt for what they have done to others they have to destroy that part of themselves which makes them human, that special kind of imagination called empathy.

To treat other people as objects to be used and abused, we first distance ourselves from our own pain and thus treat ourselves as objects. Common examples of this are the schoolboy who prides himself on not showing any emotion when he is beaten by his teachers, and the man who says, 'As a boy I was beaten by my father and it never did me any harm.'

Since every trade has far-reaching consequences we are all affected by stupid trades.

Intelligent Trades and Stupid Trades

Here are some examples at their simplest.

A woman with a bundle of firewood meets a man who has a leg of lamb. They agree to barter the wood for the lamb. The woman goes home, cooks the lamb and feeds her family. Not only does the lamb stew ensure the physical survival of her family, the act of eating together strengthens family relationships. The man with the wood uses it to fire the oven where he bakes the beautiful and useful pots he has made out of the clay he has dug from the river bank.

This is an Intelligent Trade.

In contrast, consider the woman who has inherited a gun and the man who has a bag of gold. They barter their goods. The man takes the gun and shoots his neighbour whose religious beliefs he does not share. The neighbour's sons vow vengeance against him and his family. The woman, fearing robbers, buries her gold in the ground.

This is a Stupid Trade.

It would still have been a Stupid Trade if, instead of burying the gold, the woman had used it to buy herself a house, some clothes and an education for her children. The trade has diminished the quality of her life because it's no fun living in a place where people kill one another.

What is traded can be something which is essential to our lives or something which we feel adds something to our lives. Essential or additional, goods and services can be traded intelligently or stupidly.

Tragically, intelligent and stupid trades are now so entangled that a solution to our massive world-wide problems can be found only in a world-wide consensus which itself can come about only if we gain much greater understanding of ourselves and how we trade.

A great deal has been written about the world's burgeoning population, famine and food mountains, pollution and its horrors. Rather than repeat much of what has been said elsewhere, I simply want to look at some of these issues in terms of defining intelligent and stupid trades, and the difficulties in separating the two.

Air

Air is free, but stupid trades have left many parts of the world with air that, though it might be free, is lethal.

In the August of the very hot summer of 1995 the air quality in central London fell to dangerous levels. I was shopping in Oxford Street when I was overtaken by a tiredness very much greater than the tiredness which usually overtakes me when I'm shopping in Oxford Street (that tiredness is a combination of boredom and frustration). I suddenly realized that I was collapsing because my oxygen supply had so greatly diminished. I escaped from the situation as quickly as I could, but by using one of the things which was causing the problem, a vehicle with an internal combustion engine. This is the irony of our present predicament, that we are dependent upon the very things which are causing our suffering.

Food

Since food is so essential to life it would seem sensible for every food trade to be an intelligent trade. Alas, no.

When I set out to go shopping for food I always plan a healthy diet. I buy fruit and vegetables (which possibly contain pesticides), bread (which certainly contains preservatives), chicken and eggs (which perhaps contain salmonella), cheese (which perhaps contains listeria), beef and lamb (which are likely to contain hormones and possibly the mysterious prion that causes CJD). I can buy food labelled 'organic' or 'free range', but such labelling is not entirely reliable, and such food is considerably more expensive.

It has been calculated that, despite the burgeoning of the world's population, if food were properly farmed and distributed, there would be enough food for all, provided people are prepared to eat less meat. Famines are man made. Under British rule famine was a frequent occurrence somewhere in India. Since the establishment of self-government in 1948 there has been no famine in India.

India grows food to feed itself, unlike in other parts of the Third World where much of the food produced goes to feed the rich north. There, food collects in mountains and farmers are paid not to produce.

It would be possible to trade intelligently in food, but to do this would require world-wide co-operation and compromise. It is not just a matter of those in international agribusiness rethinking their priorities, but of ending the multitude of conflicts that destroy the land and its food producers, and of bringing the drugs trade under control.

Water

If there is a God he does seem to be more ironic than benevolent. When the Conservative government, pursuing its dogma of privatizing everything, decided to privatize the nation's water, the successful purchasers must have thought that they'd won the world's best lottery. Water falls from the sky, and Britain is always awash with rain. Well, at least until the privatization was complete. Then the rains stopped and across the country minds boggled. How could the reservoirs in North Yorkshire dry up? Yorkshire and rain go together like sun and shade.

As Yorkshire people queued for water from water tankers and across most of the rest of the country gardeners watched their gardens die, they could ponder the question of why the search for profit can produce a blindness to reality. The world's climate is changing. The changes might be no more than the extreme of a standard deviation from the norm which might last no more than twenty years, or the emergence of a new pattern, but whatever the cause, in relation to the world's climate, the past is no longer a good predictor of the future.

Unless we can come to see water as a resource which needs to be managed as a global concern and not as a local object to be bought and sold, conflicts will increasingly be wars over water. The long-drawn-out conflict between Israel and her neighbours might up till now have been largely a conflict between those with long and unforgiving memories, but those inhabitants of these countries who want peace will be drawn more and more into the conflict as it changes from one of who owns the land to one of who owns the water. There is a mass of evidence, if evidence were needed, to show that even the kindest, most caring, most intelligent people do not behave well when the basic necessities for living are in very short supply.

Clothing

Clothing is essential in more ways than protecting us from the elements. We use clothing to maintain our sense of existence and to ward off the threat of annihilation. We choose clothes which meet the approval of the people important to us (teenagers dress for each other, not for their parents) and which express our individuality (which can be, 'I am an individual who likes to be like everyone else'), and which keep us safe (if you're a trader at LIFFE don't wear anything which doesn't meet with the other traders' approval because they are experts in punishing those who don't conform to the group).

Our attitudes to clothing give many examples of how we turn an idea into what we regard as an absolute, unchangeable, unchallengeable truth. This is what groups of people do in order to show that they are different from and superior to everyone else. Whether it's the traders on the floor at LIFFE, or police on the beat, or royalty at Ascot, clothing defines who's in and who's out. This way of thinking enables the football industry to increase takings by each club making frequent changes to the team strip which their followers buy.

The aristocracy have always defined themselves by their clothes, and the middle classes, emerging later, did the same, but in past centuries the working class had to make do with cast-offs. The sewing machine and the increasing variety of textiles over the last hundred or so years meant that those of the working class whose earnings left them with some surplus could buy clothes new, thus creating a huge industry.

The products of this industry now spread around the world from one market to another. When I was in Harare my friends there took me to a huge outdoor market where on rows and rows of trestle tables were tangled piles of clothes. As I walked beside these tables I would not have been surprised to see there some old clothes of mine. In the home I grew up in nothing could be thrown out on the principle, as enunciated by my mother, 'You never know when you might need it.' During the war years when clothing was rationed my mother made and remade our clothes and taught me how to do the same. I know how to take two old dresses and turn them into one ghastly one. When I left home I took this habit of not discarding clothes with me. My wardrobes were full of stuff I would never wear. I was torn between a need for order and a fear of waste. Then I discovered Oxfam. What joy! I could discard without guilt. I traded old clothes for peace of mind.

What follows now is an example of how a seemingly intelligent trade can turn with a change of circumstances into a stupid one. So great is the volume of discarded clothes in the developed world that charities like Oxfam cannot sell or give to the needy at home all the clothes they collect. So they ship them out to Africa where they turn up at local markets and undercut the indigenous industry. Clothing manufacturers in Zimbabwe have to compete with what I have given away.

Shelter

If any measure is needed of how little we understand ourselves it can be found in architectural design. We build, or allow to be built, forms of shelter which provide no comfort or beauty for their inhabitants and can even degrade them.

I've spent years of my working life in psychiatric hospitals built in the nineteenth century and then called asylums. The horror these buildings inspired in me never diminished. The façade which these buildings presented to the outside world was one of solidity, worth, even opulence. Immediately behind the façade were grand public rooms, offices and special preserves like the doctors' dining room. In Lincolnshire, St John's Hospital, once the Bracebridge Asylum, had a ballroom with a wonderfully sprung floor to which I can attest. Up to 1939 the St John's ball was the social event of the Lincolnshire season.

Beyond the rooms which formed the façade were long, cold, echoing corridors, locked doors and huge, barn-like rooms which were called wards. There were some small rooms, some for nurses to enjoy privacy and their cup of tea, and others, totally barren and windowless, for those inmates who did not conform. Even the reforms of the seventies and eighties when a number of doors were unlocked and inmates provided with a bed and a bedside locker did not make these buildings any more fit for human habitation.

It was not just that these buildings were unsuitable but that they actually gave the inmates the opposite of what they needed. Madness is not the preserve of the few. Given the right circumstances we can all go mad. As I said to a young male journalist who wanted me to say that Princess Diana was fundamentally unstable while people like him were fundamentally sound, in the space of five minutes I can ask you certain questions and from your answers define the conditions under which you would go mad.

It's just a matter of discovering how the person experiences his sense of existence and sees the threat of annihilation. Psychiatrists have spent over a century trying to categorize the behaviours of people deemed to be mad, so far with very limited success, but have failed to notice that, whatever the behaviour, each person is trying to fight off the threat of annihilation and to maintain his sense of existence against the circumstances of his life which he sees as threatening to overwhelm him. In such a situation we all lose confidence in ourselves, turn against ourselves and hate ourselves.

How can we be helped? It should be obvious that what we need around us are people who treat us with respect and dignity and encourage us to get ourselves together again. Our surroundings should speak to us of respect, dignity, encouragement, and offer us the sense of worth which we are lacking – quite the opposite of a psychiatric asylum. The asylums may be closed now, but the lodging houses and the streets where many psychiatric patients now live, like the old asylums, offer nothing but degradation and despair.

Our homes, workplaces and public buildings should do more than just give us shelter. They should support and strengthen our sense of existence and not demean it or make us feel small and unimportant. Across the world when someone in power wants to keep his people in check he orders the building of huge structures which emphasize his power and the insignificance of others.

Buildings should allow us to explore and extend our sense of existence. They should not be like the kind of houses which were once so popular in Australia and many of which still exist today. In building their homes men would clear every scrap of bush, leaving not a shred behind to please the eye and cast a shade. In this devastation they would place a large box, devoid of any veranda or graceful window, and set it so as to absorb the full glare of the summer sun and to exclude any cooling breezes. Building such a home showed a manly disdain for weakness.

Of course these buildings which I deplore would be greatly prized by the millions of people who live in shanty towns around many big cities, or who live on the street with no chance of a home of any kind. Even if those of us who live in comfort feel no sympathy for shanty town dwellers and the homeless we should, if we are sensible, set about giving those people adequate accommodation and so secure our own better health and safety. It isn't just a matter of raising enough money to do so. Any successful re-housing programme has to begin with asking the people needing homes how they see the situation. Racist Australians give as proof of the utter fecklessness and uselessness of the aboriginals the fact that many of the homes built for them in the Northern Territory and Western Australia are soon left abandoned with the inhabitants returning to living in bark humpies. What these racists don't take into account is that in aboriginal tribal law a dwelling where someone has died has to be abandoned out of respect for the spirit of the person who has died. This belief is no more fanciful than the belief that the communion wafer turns to flesh and the wine to blood once they enter the communicant's mouth. Churches are built to accommodate this belief. Surely dwellings can be devised to accommodate the aboriginals' belief, especially as it is one with which many of us can sympathize. Grief is often felt more keenly when we are in the home where our loved one lived.

Leisure

In the fifties and sixties the pundits used to tell us of the glorious time ahead when computers and smart machines would take over all the drudgery of work. We would all work short hours in pleasant surroundings. Our only problem would be what to do with all our leisure time. We were advised to plan for the future by taking up hobbies and outdoor activities and extending our knowledge of the arts.

In a way the pundits were right. From the eighties onwards many millions of people the developed world over did have the problem of what to do with their leisure time. All their time was leisure, for they were unemployed. Those who were employed, in fear of losing their jobs, worked harder and for longer hours than did most people in the fifties and sixties.

Nevertheless, leisure has become big business and consequently conflicts about value often arise and stupid trades emerge.

The favourite leisure activity of many people, myself included, is *going out with friends for a meal*. There's nothing better than good food, good wine and good conversation. Where good food's concerned, if you're going to eat fish, the fresher it is the better. A freshly caught fish tastes infinitely better than one that's been caught, chilled or frozen, and transported hundreds of miles. In Hong Kong restaurateurs provide freshly caught fish for their customers by buying live fish and putting them in glass tanks in the restaurant. The diners have the fun of choosing their fish not from the menu but from the tank. For many people in Hong Kong this is the only way to eat fish.

These fish are caught by fishermen using cyanide which stuns the fish but does not kill them. The cyanide is destroying the magnificent coral reefs from Hong Kong to Papua New Guinea.

My dad, in a youth interrupted by the First World War, was a great footballer. When I was a child he used to take me to see *football* and tell me it was the greatest game because it combined physical skills and intelligence. Only the thickies played rugby. If he's still following the game on Heavenly Television he would agree with everything Hunter Davies, a life-long soccer fan, said in his television programme *J'Accuse Man UTD.*[14]

In an article accompanying the programme Hunter Davies wrote,

> Last season, Manchester United plc, our leading club, turned over around £44 million and made a profit of £11 million. So well done, Man U. In their annual report, the actual football successes – winning the Premier League and the FA Cup – were almost dismissed, meriting only a couple of sentences, while 24 pages were devoted to how marvellously they managed their finances and marketing. Merchandising their own brand name had earned them £14 million, an increase of 180 per cent on the previous year. More well dones . . .
>
> In just 20 years, money has taken over completely in football, dominating all decisions, corrupting and perverting traditional values. Manchester United, with its great history and inspiring legends, has grown cynical and arrogant in its mad pursuit of money, assuming that the feelings and loyalties of its hard-core fans hardly matter any more. They are in danger of cutting themselves off from their own roots and losing their soul . . .
>
> The enormous sums now sloshing around the elite clubs has had a corrupting effect throughout football. Bigger salaries have made players and managers just as greedy as the clubs. Managers on £250,000 a year are still willing to take bungs of £250,000. Players on half a million a year gamble for £1,000 a throw or spend £1,000 on cocaine . . .
>
> Football should not be run like a supermarket, or Alton Towers, a Take That concert or a raincoat factory. Football is not about profit and loss. It is about glory and excitement, about local identity and family history, about skills and talents, none of which can be computed on balance sheets. Football doesn't have a product. Every year United fans have their ashes scattered on the turf at Old Trafford. How often do you see that happening at Tescos?[15]

Big business has moved into *the arts*. A painting might be a work of art while the painter is painting it, but once it is offered for sale it becomes a commodity and subject to evaluations which often have more to do with fashionable taste than artistic worth.

Artistic worth, like beauty, is in the eye of the beholder. Great paintings, if unseen, add nothing to the quality of our lives. When I went to interview one of the leading economists in Australia I was taken to a floor high up in a tower block overlooking Sydney

Harbour and whisked along a corridor which was hung with what seemed to me to be magnificent modern paintings. I had no opportunity to study them or to find out about the painter. I hoped that the few people who had access to that floor took the time to absorb the paintings and did not ignore them, regarding them as no more than trophies demonstrating that organization's worth.

At least these paintings could be seen by a few people. In Switzerland there are large collections of art held in bonded warehouses. The owners do not wish to disclose the full extent of their wealth.

The art market provides extensive opportunities for tax avoidance. René Gimpel, of Gimpel Fils Gallery, London, in a lecture on art as a commodity, said, 'The art market in Europe is corrupt, self-serving and devoid of morals, but, unlike the Mafia, it does glitter.'[16]

The art market may glitter more than the Mafia, but it is not separate from it. The art market provides not just a haven for untaxed income but a resource for art theft which, in terms of international crime, is the third most lucrative activity, coming after drug smuggling and the arms trade. Indeed, it is an integral part of the trade in drugs and arms because it provides a bank for profits and a means whereby the money made illegally can be brought into the legal financial system, a process known as money laundering.

Gambling on the Stock Exchange is as exciting as betting on horses, as my friend Tim explained to me. He said, 'I think it is very important that you should gamble on shares, even though I lost quite a bit of money on Queens Moat Houses whose shares were suspended a few days ago. I think it's much more fun to gamble because it makes you more optimistic. It's chance. It's like horse racing, or gambling in any way, there's always a chance that something great could happen. So I think it's important to do that and not to have money just sitting around boringly in a building society and you know that in 40 years' time you will have got point eight per cent of interest and it will be just sitting there. Obviously I don't gamble vast amounts, but it just makes life more exciting.' For Tim there was also the thrill of rebelling against one element of his upbringing. He said, 'As a child I was taught to horde money and put it in piggy banks.'

The delight a child feels at being given money is diminished when the child is instructed to save it. Then it becomes something earned through good behaviour, and earned money is not a source of delight, as J. B. Priestley described.

> When we receive our wages, salaries or fees, we may be content, for this is what we have earned, but we are a long way from delight. It is the money that we have not earned, the windfall, the magical bonus, that starts us capering. Many sociologists, who understand everything except their fellow creatures, are bewildered and saddened by the ubiquitous passion among the mob for betting and gambling. But the more we standardise wages, hours and prices, the more we insist upon social security for everybody, the more we compel two and two to make four everywhere, the more people will take to greyhound tracks and the football pools. For it is when two and two miraculously make five that the heart leaps up at last. It is when money looks like manna that we truly delight in it.[17]

The view of money as manna becomes a way of life for many people, but more manna is collected by those who control gambling than by those who gamble.

Life in Australia for the early settlers was hard and generally dull. Gambling provided some excitement, especially when the government proscribed certain popular forms of gambling such as Two Up (betting on heads or tails on two pennies tossed from a flat piece of wood) and starting price betting on horse racing. As a child playing in the bush I knew that if I saw men gathering in a circle I should get right away lest I annoy the men who were on the lookout for the police. Although my mother forbade my father to gamble (a prohibition he did not take to heart) every Saturday afternoon our radio played nothing but racing reports. My memory of that time is of yellow sunshine, an inescapable droning voice and nothing to do – utter, utter boredom. No wonder I never gamble.

I must be un-Australian. As the *Australian Business Monthly* reported in 1994,

> Gambling is probably the fastest growing industry of any size in Australia and the trend looks likely to continue. Gambling turnover in the 1992 fiscal year was $31.2 billion, representing $21,400 for every adult Australian. Gambling 'expenditure' – the amount

lost by gamblers – was $5.25 billion. Most of that went to state governments as a semi-invisible tax.

Gambling statistics are somewhat unreliable because there can never be any certainty about how much is conducted illegally; but based on the known figures, Macquarie Bank recently calculated that legal gambling has grown at a rate of 14 per cent a year over the 20 years to 1992.[18]

Since that time a large number of casinos have opened and more electronic gaming machines have been introduced. For me playing poker machines has all the excitement of watching paint dry, but for many people it is a near full-time occupation.

In recognition, perhaps, that not everyone finds gambling exciting Las Vegas offers all kinds of excitement, some of it of the squeaky-clean Disneyland kind, some less so. I found the room prices in the hotels attached to the casinos remarkably good value, but the casinos themselves are prisons. There are no windows and no clocks in public places and the surveillance is total.

In the USA gambling was long confined very much to Las Vegas and Atlantic City, but many states in need of money changed their laws in order to allow gambling and to take much of the profits. In this they were following the example of those native Americans who had realized that their reservations were not covered by the gaming laws. Now 'of the 330 registered tribes in the United States, about 200 operate, or hope to operate, some form of gaming. They rake in $29 billion a year, of which $2.6 billion is profit.'[19]

So casinos were built and riverboats, once so famous for gambling, returned to the big rivers. However, while such places do increase tax revenues, there is no clear evidence that casinos and riverboats actually increase productivity. Rather, they shift productivity from one place to another. People who would have gone to the races and bet on horses are now more likely to go to casinos and riverboats (whose games require less mental effort than betting on horse races). People who would have eaten in restaurants in the town now eat at the casinos, and town restaurants suffer from a drop in trade.

What gamblers do do is pay more tax. As a non-gambler I should be pleased about this.

In the UK gambling has always been popular but linked to class.

The working class played bingo and filled in the pools. The aristocrats went to the casinos. (My friend Jeremy pointed out to me that what the British aristocracy know best is not trade or commerce but gambling.) Both classes went to the races, but in separate enclosures.

For the UK to remain a player in world markets it is vital that it export more than it imports. 'According to a study by KMPG, an accountancy company, two thirds of the trade in Britain's 119 casinos is done in London, and at least two thirds of London casino members come from abroad. Perhaps as much as 85% of the casinos' take is foreign money. Profits from non-Britons in 1993–94 amounted to £120m which, if generated by a single company, would place it among the country's top 100 exporters.'[20]

In 1996 the government proposed to remove many of the controls on gambling. The bingo industry was to be almost completely deregulated, Bookmakers would be allowed to advertise in newspapers, jackpot machines could pay out much bigger prizes and another thirteen towns were added to the list of 53 towns where casinos could be sited. These changes were put forward by the government in response to the complaints by various gambling entrepreneurs that their particular form of gambling was being disadvantaged by the success of the National Lottery which had begun in 1994.

'Lotteries,' ran a *Guardian* editorial, 'have a long history. Roman emperors used them to raise revenue and to finance building projects. Queen Elizabeth I started lotteries in Britain in 1569 since when they have had a chequered history partly because they were open to chicanery and partly because they were regarded by critics as a tax on the poor. Adam Smith dismissed them as a tax on foolishness and they were eventually abandoned in the nineteenth century though not before they had helped to finance a number of projects including the British Museum.'[21]

There were many objections to the lottery. Dan Atkinson listed them as,

> There is a moral dimension: the government taxes and regulates drinking and smoking, but has never felt obliged to set up the country's biggest distillery or cigarette plant. There is the economic dimension: thousands of jobs in the pools industry are at risk,

> because the pools (other than for the 5 per cent who actually use them to bet on soccer matches) are effectively a long-odds lucky number lottery. There is the public spending angle: how can ministers be prevented from letting lottery revenues take the strain during a period of cutbacks? If the lottery can be used to pay for arts funding, why not the health service? There is the regulatory angle: we have a strict Gaming Board and a strict vice squad. But the lottery regulator proposed in the legislation will inevitably be compromised by the fact that the lottery is a government enterprise. How healthy is it for the Government to be involved in vice?[22]

The government countered these criticisms by saying that money would be going to charity. The Jockey Club in Hong Kong provides handsomely for charities in Hong Kong. The UK government would do even better.

The government was relying on the innumeracy and the irrational hope of the general public, as Ian Stewart, Professor of Mathematics at the University of Warwick explained.

> My problem isn't about morality or ethics. I don't gamble, but I have good friends who do and I value their freedom to do so. My problem is that the Lottery is what is known in the trade as a 'sucker bet'. If a casino offered you comparable odds they'd be closed down – even if you take into account your contribution to charity, the arts, good causes, and the Tories' burgeoning war chest of pre-election tax cuts. The 'house take' on the Lottery – the amount creamed off the top by the government and by operating costs – is about half. In contrast, at roulette it is about three per cent. This means that for every £1 you bet on the Lottery, your average 'winnings' will be a loss of 50p. Roughly 10p of that goes to Camelot. In contrast, when you bet £1 on a roulette wheel, on average 3p goes to the casino (maybe 6p depending on local regulations) . . . Camelot's share is roughly as much as all the charities in Britain combined. Moreover, if you give money to a charity directly, you get to choose which one.[23]

'Irrational hope,' as Francis Wheen said, 'is the sibling of irrational fear: and where's the fun in that?'[24] There's plenty of fear in those who gamble.

There's the fear that the Just World might not be operating in your favour. You've worked hard, you've been good, but none of the rewards have come your way. Why not by gambling give the Just World a push along? Or perhaps you fear you don't deserve any reward but you decide to defy the powers that be and gamble in the hope that you will win. Will losing be your punishment?

Believers in the Just World might occasionally be tempted by gambling, but regular gamblers can have a deeper need and fear. Patrick Marber showed this in his play *Dealer's Choice*. In his review of the play Michael Billington wrote,

> As movies like *The Cincinnati Kid* long ago realised, any gambling story has a built-in suspense. But Marber's great gift is to use poker not as an end in itself but as a means of exploring character. On a general level, he subtly implies that these are all men who find it difficult to relate to women and who use poker as a sexual substitute.
>
> More particularly, he explores the nature of compulsion and suggests it is nothing to do with winning or losing: it gradually emerges that the most damaged member of the group is the strictest and most controlled, who uses this Sabbath ritual to fill up the cavernous emptiness of his life.[25]

Then there are the people who feel impelled to gamble every day and who spend every penny they have and more besides, irrespective of the shame and distress their behaviour causes others. Winning means no more to them than losing. To play is all. Gambling addicts are fighting the greatest fear of all, the threat of annihilation. Something is happening in their lives to which they respond with feelings of helplessness in the face of overwhelming odds. Whichever form of gambling they choose gives them the illusion that they have some power and control. The awareness that this is an illusion and that the threat is always there makes them go back and back to gambling. The kind of group support offered by organizations like Gamblers' Anonymous can provide the person with some defence against the fear, but the fear will not go until it is understood.

Education

Suppose you take a bucketful of marbles of many different colours and empty the bucket over a flat surface. When the marbles come to rest you will see in their scatter a number of different patterns according to the groupings of marbles of the same colour. Perhaps some of the groupings form patterns like letters of the alphabet. Can you assume that every person who might look at this scattering of coloured marbles will see the same patterns that you do?

I hope you've answered no. If you have colour vision, that is certain cones in the retina of your eye and certain connections between the retina and your brain, you will see patterns that won't be seen by people who are red-green colour blind or people who are quite colour blind. Such people will see patterns quite different from the ones you see. Moreover, seeing the marbles forming letters of the alphabet depends on which alphabet you've learned. Did you see A or Æ or Ω?

This simple example demonstrates that what we experience is a combination of what sensory equipment we have and what we have learned to experience. (We don't see and then interpret. Seeing and interpreting are one and the same process.)

It is remarkable and tragic how few people who would regard themselves as well educated understand this. Yet it is hardly surprising. It has never been in the interests of people in power, be they representatives of the State or of the Church, to let children grow up understanding that that we cannot help but have our own individual truths and that claims to be in possession of absolute truth which exists outside of human time and space are always fraudulent. It is not fraudulent to say, 'My experience tells me that there is a God who takes a personal interest in me,' but a statement of personal truth. It is not fraudulent to say, 'My experience tells me that there is a God who takes a personal interest in me and I hope that such a God does exist.' But to say, 'It is an absolute truth that there is a God who takes a personal interest in everyone' is to go beyond the realms of possible experience and into the realm of fantasy. Of course we are free to choose how much we wish to dwell in the realm of fantasy, but when we try to impose our fantasies in the guise of absolute truths on to other people, we become dangerous to the life and liberty of other people, as our history shows only too well.

Many people when presented with this understanding of themselves and what is truth reject it, because they feel it imposes on them too much responsibility and uncertainty. If the truths we live by are those we have constructed by ourselves we have no one to blame other than ourselves when things go wrong. One cannot luxuriate in being angry with God for failing to live up to one's expectations. Moreover, if the body of knowledge that has been put together over the centuries is a collection of approximations rather than certainties, there is nothing rock solid and sure in our universe. It's no wonder that so many people reject science because science says that all we have are theories, all measurements are approximate, and the task of science is not to discover facts but with each scientific discovery to ask better questions.

Fortunately there are people who have the courage and maturity to take responsibility for themselves and to live with uncertainty. Such people see the role of education as enabling children to explore and to think and to realize their own truths. For them the word 'education' is appropriate because its roots in Latin speak of 'leading out into the light'. This way of understanding the process of education is based on a model of the human being as in essence good, that there is something in a child which is good and which can be brought out given the right circumstances. Given the wrong circumstances the goodness is lost and the child behaves in ways considered bad.

Alas, not everyone uses this model of a human being. Many people regard children as inherently bad – born in sin, as the Christian Church teaches. (Of recent years many of the Christian churches have tried to hide this basic tenet of Christianity by placing emphasis on God's love and forgiveness, but the model of the human being as basically good is a heresy, as church history shows.[26] The fundamentalist churches make quite clear the inherent badness which can be overcome only by being saved.) If the child is born basically bad then what the child needs to receive is not a leading out but a restraining and moulding. Indeed, the most commonly used Russian word for education, 'obrazovanyi', has its root in 'obraz' meaning shape, form, appearance.[27]

Arguments about education usually turn on these two different models of the human being. Governments who want to coerce their people into obedience use the moulding model – as seen in the

Conservative government's emphasis on national syllabuses and examinations, and a memorizing of 'facts' rather than on discovery. (Guess who would decide what was a fact.) This kind of education might keep the general populace obedient and conforming, but whenever the government wants people to think for themselves – as in assessing just how dangerous it is to eat British beef – many people have neither the intellectual tools nor the inclination to think something through. Moreover, having given those in power over them the right to think for them, these people are dismayed and extremely angry when they find they have been let down.

Ever since the Second World War people who think about the future of our species have been saying that to survive we have to think globally, not in terms of our own national groups. However, having been educated under a system which does not let people understand how we each have our own individual truths and which insists that what the State and Church teach are absolute truths (different absolute truths for each state and each church), most people are not equipped to understand, much less accept, the meanings which we must construct if we are to plan our future in global terms.

Thus far I have been talking about areas of trade which are intrinsically intelligent trades because their aim is to meet essential needs and to enhance our lives. Unfortunately, in certain circumstances such potentially intelligent trades become stupid trades.

There is one area of trade which sets out to meet a profound and universal need but, since the need is not understood and the trade offers such potential for profit, just about all of it forms stupid trades. This is the trade in the mind-altering substances of alcohol, nicotine and drugs.

Alcohol, Nicotine and Drugs

Living as we do for ever trying to make sense of a reality which we can never know directly means that we are always uncertain, even when we claim that we are not, and uncertainty creates anxiety. Being anxious means being in a state of alertness, wariness and fear, states which involve certain bodily changes in heart rate and adrenalin production, all of which after a time produce weariness if not exhaustion. Even when we would describe our life as secure and happy we still experience some degree of basic uncertainty and anxiety with their resultant tension and tiredness. Most people would not describe their lives as unfailingly happy and secure.

In addition to this basic anxiety there is the effort to hold ourselves together as a person when for much of the time we are being assailed by people and events which threaten our structure of meaning which is our self. Simple things, like feeling tired or unwell as you get out of bed in the morning, the sight of your early morning face in the mirror, having your privacy in the bathroom threatened by a loved one banging on the door and telling you to hurry up. Any event which you respond to with irritation or anger is an event which you have interpreted as in some way threatening to you/your meaning structure. (Anger is a response to feeling afraid.) Then there are the major threats which can occur where you see one of your projects failing or your imminent rejection by people important to you. As well, there can be ongoing but imperfectly denied threats such as when you suspect that you do not possess the talents needed for success, or that in truth your parents never loved and wanted you. In the face of all these threats you have to make it through the day. No wonder you find yourself needing something to bolster your resolve and/or help you relax.

When living becomes too much we seek relief, and this relief usually comes from ingesting some substance. We learned how ingesting something could relieve tension when we were first born, and we go on doing this for the rest of our lives. We discover that ingestion can also take place by breathing in or injecting a substance directly into our veins. Whichever, we all take something to inspire us with joy or to find peace after the storm. Some of us do it occasionally, some every day.

Each of us has a favourite substance which we use for bolstering our resolve or finding relief. My mother thought that anyone who drank or smoked was the equivalent of a mass murderer, but it would have been a foolhardy person who stood between her and her cup of tea.

Back in the days when we were all hunter-gatherers someone

must have noticed that certain berries or grains left in a pot would ferment and produce a liquor which, when drunk, produced a feeling of happiness and release, or that certain leaves when chewed or burnt and the smoke inhaled did the same. The sickness and dangerous behaviour which followed ingesting too much must also have been noticed. If only then we had recognized the importance and the dangers of these substances and devised some sensible rules about their use.

Instead, world-wide, there is a failure by governments to recognize that there is a common element in *all* the substances used, that is, the potential to meet the universal need for relief of tension. These substances are divided into legal and illegal for reasons that arise out of history, not science. As a result no adequate measures have ever been taken to limit the deleterious effects which each of these substances has. The effects of this failure are enormous.

> One in five of all hospital beds in the UK are occupied by people with alcohol-related conditions. One in two people attending accident and emergency departments are there as a result of something to do with alcohol or drugs. The police and the Samaritans estimate that alcohol is the major scourge of our social fabric, although drugs are now progressively taking over that unenviable position. Each day in the UK one person dies of Aids, five people die of the effects of illegal drugs, 100 people die of the effects of alcohol and 300 die of the effects of nicotine. Yet expenditure on obvious clinical disasters, like Aids and Creutzfeldt-Jakob Disease, is vast, while a frequently unrecognised killer in our midst, addiction, is largely ignored, misunderstood and even, to some extent, encouraged. The production, distribution and supply of mood-altering substances of one kind or another are amongst our major industries.[28]

Over the last four decades the word 'drug' has come very much into popular use and is applied both to substances which are deemed wicked and substances which are deemed good, even saintly. These saintly drugs are the source of much profit and much pain.

We ingest certain drugs not to ease tension and anxiety but to end physical pain and to mend our bodies. The international market in these pharmaceutical drugs alone is enormous. Many of them would be unnecessary were we to organize our lives better. The *Financial Times* reported that in 1995 'the fastest growing sector was respiratory drugs, which include asthma inhalers, where sales of $11.5 bn were 14 per cent higher than a year ago in constant currency terms.'[29] The increase in the occurrence of asthma parallels the increase in pollution.

In ten major countries sales of pharmaceutical drugs grew by 8 per cent in 1995 to $114bn. This world-wide commodity market is exceeded only by the market in objects for killing people. The pharmaceutical drugs market, especially in the USA, is increasingly dependent on the market's third most popular group of drugs, those for the central nervous system. These drugs are substances which alter how we think and feel. Thus it is not in the interest of the drug companies for us to arrive at an understanding of ourselves in terms of how we create meaning and think, feel and act. These drug companies want us to believe that our behaviour is a result of biochemical changes which themselves result from the action of our genes.

This explanation suits those people who do not want to take responsibility for what they do. They say, 'It's not my fault I'm miserable,' and take a Prozac. Rather than face the questions about the purpose and meaning of their life which are the questions to which depression can be a response[30] many people prefer to collude with psychiatrists in regarding depression as an illness which can be managed by taking anti-depressant drugs. These drugs have been around for three decades now, and the long-term outcome for those people given the traditional treatment of drugs and electro-convulsive therapy (ECT) is now known. Joseph Mendels, Medical Director of the Philadelphia Medical Institute, reported, 'There is now clear evidence that, for a substantial number of the millions of people who suffer from major depressive disorder, the condition is often chronic or recurrent. Many of our patients require long-term maintenance treatment.'[31]

The central nervous system drugs which are most widely used are the group of drugs known as the major tranquillizers. Discovered in the fifties, these drugs were found to be effective in quietening those people who were tortured by recurrent ideas which can be called delusions and hallucinations. The use of these drugs is no longer confined to patients who are diagnosed as being psychotic. Any person given a large enough dose of these drugs becomes sluggish, even comatose. Hence their widespread use in any institution where the people in charge wish to keep their inmates quiet – prisons, children's homes, old people's homes, homes for the mentally handicapped. We now have a world-wide iatrogenic disease called tardive dyskenesia, a degenerative, incurable brain disorder caused by the use of these drugs.[32] The symptoms of this disease have been described as 'muscular spasms of face, neck, shoulders and body; facial distortions and grimacing; unusual eye movements when eyeballs become fixed in one position. Lip smacking, chewing movements, puffing of cheeks, darting tongue movements, uncontrolled movements of arms and legs. Restlessness, inability to sit or stand still, pacing up and down. Difficulty speaking or swallowing, loss of balance, mask-like face, muscle spasms, stiffness of arms and legs, trembling and shaking.'[33]

Whenever estimates are given of the numbers of people damaged by taking drugs the number damaged by the major tranquillizers is not included. In the USA campaigners against the use of the major tranquillizers like Dr Peter Breggin are ignored and despised by the medical profession and persecuted by the National Alliance for the Mentally Ill, an association of those parents who want their troublesome children who are psychiatric patients to be kept quiet. The Alliance believes that all mental illnesses have a biological cause and that parents are never responsible in any way for their children's distress. In the UK psychiatrists privately admit that what Peter Breggin says is right, but they then shrug and say, 'What else can we do?' There are alternatives but such methods in the short term, though not in the long term, are much more expensive than drugs.

Governments look at drugs not in terms of what would be best for us but in terms of money – what is the cheapest way of dealing with any problems and what money can be made. There is ample evidence which shows that the rate of alcoholism in a country correlates directly with the price of alcohol.[34] In terms of real wages, the cheaper the alcohol the higher the rates of alcoholism. The cure is simple. Make alcohol a luxury. However, this would reduce the excise revenues, thus leaving the government to choose between raising taxes or borrowing more, the kind of measures which can lead to loss of office.

Tobacco is another fine source of government revenue. Back in the sixties when the first reports of the connection between smoking and cancer were becoming public, governments were as reluctant as the tobacco manufacturers to admit the link. It was not just that nicotine contained carcinogenic substances. There was also the issue of addiction.

Of recent years the word 'addiction' has become extremely popular in the USA as a fatuous explanation of why a person does something over and over again. In addition to alcoholics and drug addicts there were shopping addicts and chocolate addicts. The actor Michael Douglas excused his philandering on the grounds that he was a sex addict. This use of the word not only provides a convenient excuse for those people who do not want to take responsibility for their behaviour, but it prevents a clear understanding of how our body can adapt to the ingestion of substances which give a sense of relaxation so that ceasing to ingest these substances causes considerable distress.

Much is said of the dangerously addictive properties of drugs like cannabis, heroin and cocaine, but the drug which is hardest to give up is nicotine. Nowadays no one in the developed countries could be unaware of the dangers of smoking, but these are long-term dangers, and the pleasure and relief given by nicotine is immediate. Moreover, smokers give to their cigarettes qualities which make them harder to give up. Whenever a possession becomes important to us we give that possession certain human qualities. Ask any confirmed smoker, 'If your cigarettes were a person, what sort of person would it be?' The answer is likely to be, 'My cigarette is the perfect partner,' or, 'My cigarettes are my best mates. They never let me down.' Thus government health campaigns to warn people of the dangers of smoking are always doomed to failure.

Even if a health department did create a campaign which took sensible account of the meanings smokers give to their cigarettes the tobacco companies are too great a force in the market to let any campaign succeed. When in the eighties there were sufficiently large numbers of men concerned about their health to give up smoking, the tobacco companies began targeting young women, assuring them that by smoking they would become sophisticated, self-confident and sexually attractive. Schoolgirls and young professional and business women, not caring that before killing you smoking ruins your complexion, responded. Young men and women often find the idea of death attractive. It's the *idea* of death, not death itself. They think that if they're happy and easy-going no one will notice them, but if they're suffering in a distinctive way – smoking a cigarette in an anguished manner can convey such suffering without having to explain – then people will notice and admire them. As we get older and death becomes real we're likely to abandon such a stupid idea, especially when we've witnessed people we love dying lingering deaths.

Then the companies started moving into other countries. Philip Morris bought a majority stake in a Ukrainian cigarette factory, built a leaf-processing plant in Malaysia and began manufacturing in Vietnam, while RJR Nabisco moved into Poland and Romania. BAT went into China and Hong Kong. Asia's millions provided an endless source of new addicts, so much so that smuggling cigarettes from the US to Asia became a major business. Even though the big tobacco companies lost money when they lost the cigarettes, smuggling provided opportunities for brand loyalties to develop. If your mates are Marlboro cigarettes, you always smoke Marlboro. Meanwhile the American tobacco companies became the biggest corporate sponsor of the 1996 Republican presidential convention while resisting legal attempts by lung cancer victims to sue them for causing this dread disease. As the lawyers for the tobacco companies constantly reiterated, it never crossed the company directors' minds that cigarettes could do anyone harm. How could they possibly have known that nicotine was addictive?

The separation of drugs into legal and illegal has made sensible discussion about drugs impossible. We are constantly being told that any use of illegal drugs leads inevitably to addiction. When the US forces in Vietnam were found to be using the readily available drugs widespread addiction was predicted. Yet, on returning to the

USA, most of these veterans gave up using drugs and got on with their lives. Drug-taking always relates to the situation which the person is in.

Nevertheless, any kind word said about cannabis produces a hysterical reaction from those who regard themselves as the experts on morality. To approach the subject in terms of scientific inquiry is anathema to them. They say that they want to protect society from the dangers of drugs, but they are, in effect, preventing this because they refuse to allow the discussion which has to take place if we are to arrive at a more sensible way of dealing with drugs.

Fortunately the morality police don't read my books, devoted as these books are to gaining clarity of understanding. So I can say, without fear of being overwhelmed by a torrent of ignorant abuse, that the history of cannabis is long and over the last three decades it has been subjected to much scientific research. All of this shows that, compared to alcohol and nicotine, it is remarkably safe. I first encountered cannabis at the end of the sixties when, as a postgraduate student, I went to parties which divided into the drinkers and the smokers. All the drinkers, of which I was one, behaved as badly as I had always known them to do, while the smokers were sweetly quiet and meditative. The greatest danger these cannabis users faced was being driven home from parties by drinkers confidently declaring, 'I always drive better when I'm drunk.' Nowadays, a number of my friends and acquaintances use cannabis to keep chronic anxiety under control, and they fare much better than those people who use alcohol and nicotine for the same purpose. The refusal of the UK government to let cannabis be used in the control of chronic physical pain is simply cruel.

Surely any sensible government would regulate the sale of cannabis and profit from a substantial excise duty? But there is a problem about this, as Noam Chomsky pointed out.

> One might ask why tobacco is legal and marijuana is not. A possible answer is suggested by the nature of the crop. Marijuana can be grown almost anywhere, with little difficulty. It might not be easily marketable by major corporations. Tobacco is quite another story.[35]

Cannabis users seek tranquillity, but heroin and cocaine users, along with the users of manufactured drugs like Ecstasy, love the intensity of feeling these drugs initially give. There is also the sense of doing something wicked. Bringing children up to believe that they are intrinsically bad and have to work hard to be good means that these children learn to divide every activity into good and bad, virtuous and wicked. Some children simply feel guilty when they commit what they feel is a sin, but others in secret rebellion against those in power over them mix guilt with delight. When a group of drugs which indeed are dangerous are labelled as wicked they become enticing to those who want to rebel against authority. Wise parents who want to deflect their teenage offspring from pursuing certain activities praise these activities in terms of being 'educational' and 'character building', and then rest assured that their offspring will find better things to do. It would be stretching the language too far to refer to the use of this group of drugs as 'educational' and 'character building' (although being a participant in the drug scene seems to be an essential chapter in the life of a Hollywood star, just as being a drunk was an essential for being a great American writer) but labelling them as 'stupid' rather than 'wicked' would have a greater deterrent effect. Wicked people can be thought glamorous and significant, stupid people never.

However, a change of definition won't solve the problem, because the trade in illegal drugs is now as important in the world market as is the trade in currencies. Indeed, the two markets are as one.

Neither can the drug trade be separated from the future of the developing world.

There was a time, before Europeans set out to trade world-wide and to build empires, when much of the rest of the world lived in some degree of economic self-sufficiency as farmers, choosing what animals to herd and crops to grow, subject only to the vagaries of the climate and the whims of their rulers. When the Europeans invaded they disrupted these patterns and forced the people they had conquered to farm and live in ways which met European needs and ambitions. When I was a child at school we were taught how the British nobly sacrificed themselves to establish the British Empire and bring virtue, law and happiness to the ignorant natives. We were not told about events like the Opium War with China, fought not to protect the Chinese from the evils of opium, but to force China to open its doors, in the name of free trade, to opium from British India. Nor were we taught how the British, and Germans, Dutch, Spanish, Portuguese, French and Belgians and Americans, seized vast acreages of good land to establish plantations of rubber, coffee, tea, sugar and tobacco.

The terrible poverty in the Third World comes, in part, from the fact that farmers are producing crops for the rich countries, not for themselves. Very little of the coffee or tea grown in the Third World is consumed there, and very little of the profits from that coffee and tea go back to the grower.

Such a method of production makes the grower very vulnerable to changes in fashion. When Zimbabwe's tobacco farmers became worried about the anti-smoking trend in the USA and Western Europe they started to grow another crop, roses, which, when picked as buds and chilled, can be flown to Europe and sold in the flower markets. Such a change was possible only because the growers had the resources to raise the capital needed. But what if roses cease to be Europe's favourite flower? Will the Zimbabweans take to eating roses?

It is not that tobacco is the most lucrative crop that the farmers could grow. The Panos Institute reported that 'although in 1992 the poorer nations exported 15 per cent more of the habit forming weed, they actually earned less – US $2,794m as against $2,951m in 1991. Food is a better bet, says Panos: in 1993 in Harare, maize earned 2.53 Zimbabwe dollars a kilo, whereas tobacco earned 1.62 dollars. Another smoker's cost: to cure 1kg of tobacco in Uganda, you need 7.8kg of wood.'[36]

Meanwhile, the farmers in Peru, Bolivia and Colombia were adding to their coca crops the opium poppy, which had become the staple crop for many farmers in the Golden Triangle where the borders of Burma, Laos and Thailand meet. In 1989 President George Bush singled out cocaine as 'our most serious problem' and declared war on drugs. He offered Peru, Bolivia and Colombia $2 billion in aid to fight the drug traffickers and to encourage farmers to return to growing food. This war was not waged against one very important participant in the drug trade, the CIA, which has been instrumental in setting up and maintaining the trade since the Second World War. It is now well known how the moral crusader Oliver North was given the task of setting up a supply line with General Noriega in Panama to bring arms to Costa Rica and drugs to the USA.[37] Noam Chomsky explained:

> There are good reasons why the CIA and drugs are so closely linked. Clandestine terror requires hidden funds, and the criminal elements to whom the intelligence agencies turn naturally expect a quid pro quo. Drugs are the obvious answer. Washington's long-term involvement in the drug racket is part and parcel of its international operations, notably during the Reagan–Bush administrations.[38]

Not surprisingly the drug war has been lost. All it achieved was to spread the production of drugs further into South America. The profits from this drug trade are vast. They have brought about an explosion in the industry of money laundering and they have changed the whole region.

> In one form or another, consequences of the drug business can be seen not just in the Andean countries but all over the region. Profits are laundered from Argentina to Mexico. Pass a new hotel in this capital or that, and you will be told it was built with drugs money. Venture into the *favelas* of Rio de Janeiro and you will discover that drug traffickers are providing rudimentary social services that the state disdains. Drive through Santa Cruz in Bolivia and see the spanking new buildings, partly financed by the cocaine that now is consumed by the smart set in their four-wheel-drives.
>
> In the Andes, chewing coca leaves is an age-old habit. But nowadays drug production means hard core drug consumption on a wider scale, and among many more people in many more countries. So long as it is illicit, it also means corrupt police, politicians, judges; and it means violence. The one certainty about illegal drugs is that in due course they bring bloodshed.[39]

In 1994 a BBC television series called *Dirty Money* described how 'sophisticated criminals have become masters of global finance. What is increasingly concerning governments is that a global financial system is developing which defies regulation, creating a world of electronic transfers and off-shore havens that benefits, not just trade, but those who wish to hide and move dirty money.'[40]

The drug cartels with profits of some $7 billion organize their trade like a multinational corporation with vice-presidents for finance, trade and production. It doesn't matter to them when shipments of drugs are intercepted by Customs. They can afford to lose half their shipments and still make a profit. Their problem is how to turn the huge volume of cash the trade generates into a form which allows them to evade the law and move the money to more friendly environments.

These friendly environments are private banks like those in Switzerland which will not disclose any information about their customers, and places which provide offshore banking. 'Off shore financial centres have expanded with the freedom to move money anywhere in the world, a key element in a global financial system that investigators are finding harder to police. The scale of what has happened can be judged by one statistic, over sixty per cent of the world's money now resides offshore. Caribbean sandbars and coral islands have become major financial centres. What they are selling is secrecy and an absence of regulation. Their defenders see them as essential to the global economy, their critics see them as places of hot money, undermining the fight against financial crime and fraud.'[41]

Ever since money came into being much of it has been moving around the world and evading government regulations and taxes. The Chinese call it *fei ch'ien*, flying money. Where family connections are spread around the globe, someone can deposit some money at a Hong Kong gold shop and be given a card to present to a money-changer in San Francisco who will provide a suitable sum. Another paperless banking system is that of *hawalah*, a system used by Indians world-wide, some to send money home and others to make transactions arising from various business ventures, including bribery, drug dealing, crime and terrorism.

Money laundering is the process whereby money which has been made in ways which the owners of the money wish to keep secret changes its form so that it can enter the legitimate financial market.

Drug traffickers aren't the only ones who want to launder their ill-gotten gains. Not everyone feels that it is their duty as a citizen to pay tax. The Italian designer Aldo Gucci washed more than $11 million through a number of shell companies and stashed it in Hong Kong rather than pay tax on it. People who've made money through insider dealing on the stocks and bond markets need to put their profits somewhere. Most, it seems, do better than Dennis Levine, the investment banker who used non-public information to deal in these markets, making a profit of some $13 million. Becoming greedy, he left a trail which investigators could follow, but many other insider dealers have not been so stupid.

Certain multinational corporations have been known to launder money in order to evade taxes, or defraud their shareholders, or get around currency regulations, or to bribe prospective clients. Sometimes governments find money laundering useful as a way of pursuing their foreign policies. In the Iran–Contra scandal this was one part of the complex story which President Reagan couldn't possibly remember. Outstanding characters like Ferdinand and Imelda Marcos in the Philippines, General Noriega in Panama and Erich Honecker in East Germany made a major contribution to money laundering.

Money laundering has been estimated to be the world's third largest business. However, most of the dirty money working its way through the world financial system comes from the illicit drugs trade. When Jeffrey Robinson published his book on money laundering, *The Laundrymen*,[42] the dust cover was decorated with a dollar bill captioned, 'This real dollar has been used in a drugs deal. It contains minute traces of cocaine.' He explained, 'Because drug trafficking through Western Europe and North America has reached such a crisis point, random forensic testing in America revels that practically every US dollar in circulation – including the *genuine* dollar bill on this cover – bears minute traces of cocaine. In other words, practically every US dollar in circulation has at some point been used in a drug deal.'

There are many ways, which Jeffrey Robinson describes, which allow drug dealers to get their money into the banking system under the guise of coming from a trade which accepts cash – pizza places, the antiques and art market, video rentals – and which rely on banking staff not being suspicious. Commercial banks have been making huge reductions in their staff numbers. Experienced staff have gone and those left have little time to ponder the source of their clients' money. New methods for getting dirty money into the system to clean it arise as trade changes. There is now a huge market in counterfeit goods passing themselves off as expensive name brands, and counterfeiters and those in need of money laundering can do business. The possibilities for unregulated business on the Internet could turn it into the Wild West of the next century.

At an international conference on money laundering held in Lisbon in 1996 the delegates were told that the US government was planning to declare war on money launderers by investigating any transaction, even money moving en route from one country to another, if it appeared suspicious. However, laws to enable such investigations could well run counter to the deregulation of the financial markets regarded by many as necessary to allow markets to flourish. This is yet again an example of the impossibility of being secure and free.

In the meanwhile there is our current situation, summed up by Jeffrey Robinson as, 'The Third World is filled with people who can't see how putting an end to drug trafficking is in their interest, while the industrial west is filled with well-meaning souls who don't have the slightest clue of what life is like in the rest of the world.'[43]

The problems that all the tension-relieving substances have produced are not going to be solved by wars on drugs and money laundering or by moral crusades. A solution needs to begin with a recognition of the universal need for the relief of tension and of the function these substances, be they cream cakes or heroin, play in our lives. Only by understanding what we are doing can we find ways of changing.

There are three areas of trade which are intrinsically stupid trades. They can assist in the physical survival of some people and some of those who profit from these trades use their profits to improve their own lives, but it is intrinsic to these trades that they diminish and destroy those who trade in them or get caught up in the process. These trades are prostitution and pornography, slavery, and the arms trade.

Prostitution and Pornography

In prostitution and pornography those who sell are trading what is sold not as people in their own right but as objects to be used and abused. Even when a woman acting on her own behalf and not at the behest of a pimp offers sex for payment she is treating part of herself – her body – as an object from which she has separated herself. The people/objects which are sold in prostitution and pornography are always the weak, helpless and poor members of society – women, children and powerless men.

When economic power is held by men women have to sell themselves, in either prostitution or marriage, in order to survive and to support their children. In times of war and civil turmoil prostitution becomes for many women the only means of survival and the only hope of betterment. The break-up of the Soviet Union left many women without economic power. Many of them made their way, or were taken, to the brothels of Western Europe or else lined the roads leading to the West and sold themselves to visitors from the West.

Prostitution and pornography are big business. Accurate figures are hard to come by because much of the business is not recorded in a country's tax records, and the business can spring up and disappear according to changes in local conditions. Emma Daly in 1995 reported in Zagreb that since Unprofor, the United Nations peace-keeping force, arrived some 15 stripclubs-cum-brothels had opened in Zagreb, 'keeping up the UN's reputation for boosting the sex industry – and fear of Aids spreading – wherever task forces are sent.' One bordello owner told her, 'I spent 33,000 Deutschmarks (£14,000) to start this place: I made it into the black in 23 days.'[44]

The sex industry in the Far East is vast and now part of the tourist industry. Many of the prostitutes in Pakistan, India and the Far East are children, sold into prostitution by their parents. As the *Economist* reported,

> Lurking in one of the Internet's sleazier corners, the World Sex

> Guide is excited but nervous about Cambodia. 'If you're looking for an adventure, Cambodia's IT right now,' it enthuses, before appending, without comment, a press report that in Phnom Penh, 'a six-year-old is available for $3.'[45]

Throughout human history children and young people have been used in prostitution. The history of childhood is the history of cruelty where adults use children as objects to meet their perverse needs.[46] Apart from the occasional tribe deep in the Amazon jungle who are reported to be unfailingly kind to their children, all societies treat their children not as persons in their own right but as objects to be used to meet the adults' needs. This can range from using a child for sex to wanting your child to fulfil your ambitions and being a credit to you.

If our society really cared about children they would be brought up by adults who saw them as persons to be cared for, not as objects to be used. One of the results of such an upbringing would be that there'd be no market for prostitution and pornography. Children would not grow to adulthood filled with the kind of uncomprehending misery for which they seek relief in perverse sexual practices. There'd be no British cabinet minister wanting to be spanked, and no US president believing that to ward off terrible dangers like a bad headache he had to have a woman at least every three days.

The uncomplicated, straightforward purpose of our sexual behaviour is to strengthen and deepen our relationships. When we engage in sexual behaviour which does not have this aim we are trying to use sex to express or achieve something which in itself has nothing to do with sex.

Some couples, so I am told, use pornography in order to make their love-making more exciting. This implies that their love-making has lost its zest and interest, which means that their relationship has changed. The appropriate response to a changed relationship might be to find other partners or, if the couple still value one another's company, to take up gardening or hang gliding instead of sex. In using pornography the couple are not rekindling an old passion but each creating a private fantasy and using the other person as an object to enact it. Using another person as an object never creates a relationship and always destroys what relationship there might have been.

Using pornography as an aid to masturbation is at best sad (not being able to think up an exciting sexual fantasy is really pathetic) and at worst dangerous to those people (women, children, youths, animals) who are represented in the pornography. Being used as an object means being put in someone else's power, and that power can be used to destroy.

To call pornography 'adult' is to pervert language by calling something the opposite of what it is. Pornography is un-adult. Not childish, because children have a straightforward view of sex until corrupted by adults – usually the adults who, in teaching them to be good, teach them that sex is dirty and sinful. Un-adult means never having made it to adulthood but instead being left in a limbo, excluded from both childhood's hope and enthusiasm and adulthood's mature satisfaction.

How many pornographers use pornography? If they didn't, how could they know what would sell?

Prostitution and pornography offer endless scope for self-delusion.

One delusion held by many men and often repeated in cinema and on television is that of the happy, heart-of-gold prostitute. Certainly there are women who, having discovered how hard it is to leave a life of prostitution, decide to make the best of it, but no woman would choose prostitution if economic security and a satisfactory position in society were also available. Some women who hate themselves might choose prostitution as a punishment for their wickedness, but this is not an argument for prostitution, rather an argument for better care of those suffering distress.

Prostitution is a power relationship. Those who buy have power over those who sell. (Even the man who comes wanting the woman to beat him has the power of the buyer over the seller.) A sexual relationship which strengthens and deepens a personal relationship is not a power relationship but a mutual relationship between two equals. In such a relationship there is an opening to one another and a joining together which is not just of bodies but as persons. In power relationships bodies act and the persons remain separate.

The person with power uses another body as an object while the person attached to that body remains separate.

Whenever we treat another person as an object we diminish our ability to make a very important distinction between objects and beings who feel and think. To make this distinction we have to exercise the ability to make that leap of imagination called empathy. We can't literally get inside another person's private world of meaning, but we can imagine what it would be like. As with all our abilities, if we don't use it we lose it. Learn a foreign language or how to play champion squash and if you then fail to use these abilities they vanish. Not being able to speak a foreign language or to win at squash does not diminish you as a person, but not being able to exercise empathy does. Empathy is made up of two parts, an ability to reflect upon others and an ability to reflect upon oneself. It is this power of self-reflection, not only to think but to think about what we are thinking, that is the only quality which marks us out as being different from and perhaps superior to other animals and to objects. When we treat other people as objects we diminish ourselves.

The powerless person who is being used in sex detaches her/his person from her/his body and treats this body as an object. This is a way of protecting the person. It is a defence mechanism which we all have available. It's an excellent way of coping with physical pain, especially when the pain is of relatively short duration, as in the dentist's chair. However, a frequent or long-term use of this defence has two profoundly deleterious effects – an increasing inability to make relatively accurate assessments of reality and a dwindling self-confidence which leads to self-hatred.

Arguments against prostitution and pornography are usually presented not in terms of how these trades diminish all who take part in them but in moral terms. The phrase 'family values' is often used as the standard of morality which is required. Politicians are particularly attached to family values. However, as Linda Grant has noted, 'If one wants the measure of a government's commitment to family values, one will find it in the wages on which they expect the poor to bring up their children.'[47] Any society which has a flourishing trade in prostitution and pornography has a government uncommitted to family values. An honest government would talk about prostitution and pornography not in terms of family values but in terms of the lack of economic security.

Slavery

As long as there are people so deficient in understanding of themselves that they can regard whole sections of the population as objects which they can use there will be poverty and slavery. Slavery arises out of conquests and poverty. It has by no means vanished from the world. Slavery is flourishing in the Sudan after years of civil war, and in India and Pakistan where poor farmers heavily in debt to their landlord become his bonded slaves. The debt and the slavery are passed down from one generation to the next. These families have the barest necessities for living and work in vile and degrading conditions. In 1992 the Pakistan government under Benazir Bhutto passed an act prohibiting forced, unpaid labour and forbidding landlords from lending money to villagers. In 1996 the organization Anti-Slavery International issued a report saying that little had been done to implement the law. Unsurprisingly, the Bhutto government rejected this criticism and claimed that much had been done.[40] In China people convicted of crime are compelled to work as forced labour, and in Burma the military junta uses much of the workforce as slave labour. When these countries calculate their GDP the work of the slaves is not likely to be included.

The profits from slavery are hard to estimate. They are not declared to the revenue authorities and indeed many slave owners deny that their labourers are slaves. Not included also are the profits from the selling of young girls, a trade based in Pakistan and serving the male population of the Arab world. It is based on a belief which is held by many men world-wide, that women and girls are not human but merely objects which can labour, incubate a child, and be fucked, abused and killed. Such a belief allows fathers to sell their unwanted daughters to the middlemen who take them to places where the markets in these girls are held. There they are sold to rich men who use them as extra wives, or as concubines and domestic slaves.

Boys when they are babies and toddlers think that women are

wonderful. They look at their mothers in wondering admiration and love. They know she is not a toy or a piece of furniture. How does a young boy turn into a man who buys and sells women?

The answer lies in what happens to a boy when the men in his family deem he is no longer a baby. He is taken from his mother and the other womenfolk into the company of men. He has to please the men because they hold the power, so he copies their ideas and practices. At the same time he blames his mother for deserting him. He deals with the pain of his loss by denying that women are human, and by using women as the objects of his revenge against his mother. In doing so he becomes less of the person he might have been.

A society in which the men live separately from the women and have their strongest relationships with other men, and in which the women are subjected to the power of the men is a society which has not recognized the mutual dependence of men and women, not just in matters of procreation but in the contrasting but complementary approaches by men and women to every aspect of life. Such complementary contrasts create the balance which is necessary in our society where extremes of attitudes always lead to disaster. A society without such a balance is always much less than it might have been.

The Arms Trade

The arms trade is the largest commodity trade in the world. What is traded can do only two things. It can kill or it can rust. It produces nothing which can sustain or enhance our lives.

A relatively small number of people profit greatly from this trade. Millions are injured by it. Millions are killed or wounded. Millions have their homes, lands and lives devastated by it. Millions live in ill-health, poverty and ignorance because their leaders buy arms rather than food, shelter, medicine and education.

Some people argue that each country must have arms to defend itself against other countries, thus ignoring the fact that wars do not produce peace. One army conquering another army always produces further wars. Only talking together and agreeing on common aims and compromises produce peace. However, politicians the world over have talked of peace, but have never given the UN the help it needed for it to work as it was intended to ensure peace.

Some people argue that the arms trade 'makes work'. Politicians, however much they say they are devoted to peace, will strive to keep armaments factories functioning in their constituencies, lest a closure loses them votes. Much as people need jobs, there cannot be much honest, clear-sighted satisfaction in knowing that what you are producing will kill and rust and nothing else.

It is a common human characteristic that whenever we are engaged in some activity of which we are ashamed, or know that we ought to be ashamed, we present ourselves to the world as being purer than pure, engaged in a task which can only benefit mankind. Prostitutes offer their clients 'relief'. The chairman of British Aerospace, Bob Bauman, in the 1996 company report, assured shareholders,

> While the priority for your Company has been to improve its performance we have not overlooked our responsibilities to other members of the British Aerospace family. Your Company has examined its role in corporate governance and continues to comply with the Code of Best Practice of the Cadbury Report on the financial aspects of corporate governance. We also are meeting the requirements of the Greenbury Committee in publishing a report about the remuneration and compensation of directors and senior executives.
>
> Our suppliers are an important part of the British Aerospace team and we have increased our efforts to ensure that we are working effectively with them. Finally, we want to make sure that we are good citizens in the communities in which we operate and are working to ensure that we fulfil these obligations.[49]

Again in the report the Chief Executive Dick Evans writes about noble aspirations. 'The process of cultural improvement rather than revolutionary change will harness the energies and involvement of all our people, building on our strengths, addressing our weaknesses and securing our long term future.'[50] British Aerospace takes care of others. 'During 1995 the Group made donations in the UK for charitable purposes amounting to £625,000 (1994 £913,000). No contributions for political purposes were made.'[51]

If British Aerospace did contribute to Conservative Party funds it would be giving back some of the money the government had already given it.

British Aerospace has two principal activities, called in the report 'Defence' and 'Commercial Aerospace'. There is also a property development subsidiary called Arlington and the UK's fourth digital mobile telephone network called Orange. Dick Evans wrote, 'Defence continues to be the main source of the company's profitability.'[52]

The Conservative government always made much of the success of the British arms trade – sorry, defence industry – which made a major contribution to exports, thus allowing the government to boast of a favourable balance of trade. In 1995 the World Development Movement, which specializes in studying Third World poverty, issued a report called *Gunrunners' Gold* which showed that at least a fifth of the total value of British arms exports, about £384 million a year, are paid for by the taxpayer and not by foreign governments buying the weapons; that for the preceding five years the Export Credits Guarantee Department met the bill for unpaid arms sales; and that in promoting sales the government spent over ten times more on arms sales than on civil exports.[53] It was not only the government which liked to invest in the arms trade. As the Campaign Against the Arms Trade showed in its search of the Share Registers 1993–4, millions of pounds donated by the public to health charities, hospices and hospitals were being invested by these organizations in firms which contributed to the arms trade.[54] While an increasing number of people were trying to make sure that the money they were putting into pension funds, bonds and unit trusts were not being invested in the arms trade, many organizations devoted to maintaining life were investing in death.

For those people who appreciate irony the arms trade provides an endless source. Volumes could be written about it on this theme alone.

Martin Woollacott, himself no mean ironist, spoke of 'the tyranny of trade' when noting that 'the past 25 years have demonstrated that the maintenance of an advanced military-industrial-intellectual complex is becoming more and more difficult. Fewer and fewer countries can keep up anything like the whole range of advanced industry, weapon production, and the research centres to support them.' As a result 'even the Unites States, the solitary country still able to maintain a full military-industrial base, is having difficulties, with President Clinton ringing up Gulf monarchs to sell tanks personally . . . China saw off President Clinton's attempt to make trade conditional on human-rights "advances" in his first year in office. Now the President signs an order permitting the sale of satellite technology to China on the same day that Chinese exports of nuclear materials to Pakistan are revealed.'[55]

The arms trade is now too complex and involves too many players for any one person or government to change the rules, much less abolish it. When the Falklands war broke out in 1982 the cartoonist Gibbon published a cartoon which applies to every conflict (see over).[56]

In this cartoon only the figures at the back of the group, Reagan, Brezhnev and the Warsaw Pact, are no longer here. Replacing them with the current president of the USA and the leaders of the countries in the European Union would make the cartoon totally relevant to present conditions. The little mice are still dying, women and children suffering, and death wondering what it's all about. Why kill when death will come inevitably in its own good time?

Apologists for the arms trade might argue that what the trade actually sells is insurance, weapons as a defence against what might happen. It is a very expensive form of insurance, costing the purchaser and the provider dear. The main competitors in the arms trade, the USA, China, the UK, France, Germany and Italy, all want to increase their GNP by selling more products than just arms to countries in the Middle and Far East and Africa, yet because the governments of these countries spend so much on buying arms they cannot raise the standard of living of their people so that they can afford to buy the goods which the arms trading countries want to sell them.

Under the present political system in those countries which like to think of themselves as democracies, a politician, in order to succeed, must be able to hold two opposing ideas at one and the same time – what George Orwell called 'double-think'. Thus John Major as prime minister could be appalled when a lone gunman

QUIET!
FALKLANDS EXPERIMENT
NATO
THIRD
WORLD
WARSAW PACT
DEFENCE STRATEGY
ORDERS
ARMS DEALERS
ARMS INDUSTRY
SCIENCE
TECHNOLOGY
Gibbard

killed sixteen children in Dunblane, Scotland, and another lone gunman killed thirty-four in Port Arthur, Australia. In the same period of time as these killings occurred John Major refused to stop the production of land mines. He agreed to get rid of old stocks of mines, but he reserved the right for the UK arms industry to continue developing the so-called smart mines.

As a result of the many conflicts in the post-war world, some 120 million mines are currently laid in 62 countries. Someone, somewhere is killed or injured every two minutes. In Cambodia alone there are 30,000 amputees as a result of mines. It costs $3 to make a mine, $1,000 to dismantle it. The estimate of time for clearing just one country, Afghanistan, at current rates is 4,000 years.[57] Despite all this the Foreign Office minister David Davis informed parliament that while 'the UK will actively work towards a total, world-wide ban on anti-personnel mines . . . We shall also pursue procurement plans to replace our existing mines with self-destructing ones.'[58]

Doesn't that 'self-destructing mine' sound great? Can't you just imagine the little mine sitting there in the ground and thinking, 'That's not the enemy coming towards me. It's a child. I shall self-destruct'?

The proposed new mines won't work like that. They will simply have a battery with a limited life span. Once the battery is flat, so the theory goes, the mine cannot be activated. In the conflict in Bosnia the opposing sides made little attempt to keep complete and correct records of where they laid mines, or where they did the records were lost. Vast areas of land are now unusable. How likely is it that in future conflicts records will be kept not only of where the mines are laid but when they would be likely to be no longer active? All that the development of self-destructive mines will achieve will be the development of further mines.

In its 1995 survey of defence technology the *Economist* described

> the smart minefield, in which the mines tell each other what is going on and are able to jump up and explode above the tanks passing through . . . Such mines are known as brilliant pebbles; they were thought up by Mr Canavan, Lowell Wood and Edward Teller, the latter pair at the Lawrence Livermore Laboratory in California. The brilliant pebbles would be small rockets a metre

> or so long, with lots of computing power and good sensors on the front end; thousands would swarm around the earth in low orbits . . . To disable it means engaging each pebble on its own terms. Although, at present, no brilliant pebbles are being built, the idea of low-orbit swarms is gaining ground among both civilian and military satellite makers.[59]

In the debate about land mines the Foreign Office minister David Davis argued, 'We do not believe that it would be right to deny other responsible countries the right to have land mines too.'[60]

Now here's an interesting use of 'responsible'. As I understand it, a person behaving responsibly is taking care not to harm or infringe the rights of other people. Can this be said of the governments of Saudi Arabia, Indonesia and Nigeria, all welcome purchasers of the products of the UK arms industry? Does David Davis's use of the word 'responsible' include the lack of human rights in Saudi Arabia, the deaths of some 200,000 people in East Timor at the hands of the Indonesian army, and the murder of Ken Saro-Wiwa and other opponents of the Nigerian regime?

In the arguments presented for the necessity of having an arms industry the word 'defence' takes on a somewhat extended meaning. Defence of one's country against its enemies is considered to be right and proper, even noble, but what are the connotations of 'defence' when the arms are used by the purchaser against its own people? How can a country call itself democratic when it sells arms to a regime which uses these arms to repress its people?

It is not just tanks and guns that repressive regimes use against their people. They also use the weapons of torture which are manufactured and sold by the arms industry. 'The Federation of American Scientists, using the US Freedom of Information Act, found that between 1991 and 1993 14 licences valued at $5 million were issued for exports to Saudi Arabia under Department of Commerce category OA84C, covering "thumb cuffs, thumbscrews, leg irons, shackles and handcuffs; specially designed instruments of torture; strait-jackets, plastic handcuffs." A further 14 licences valued at $5.4 million were allowed for a category including "stun guns, shock batons, electric cattle prods".'[61]

These instruments are displayed and orders taken at arms fairs like COPEX, the Covert Operations and Procurement Exhibitions, held annually in the USA and the UK. One of the most popular instruments is the electro-shock baton, a penis-shaped metallic object which can deliver shocks of up to 150,000 volts and cause severe pain but leave no marks. They are used to rape women, for anal rape of both sexes, and to be placed on testicles and in mouths, ears and eyes. The television series *The Torture Trail* has reported on the investment of the UK arms industry, including British Aerospace, in this trade.[62] It is common for apologists for the arms industry to refer to this part of the industry as producing 'non-lethal' weapons.

The amount of money involved in the arms industry is hard to comprehend. In 1994 Nato's military spending was $464 billion.[63] The USA spends about $265 billion annually.[64] 'Defence spending by Japan and Asia's six newly industrialised countries (Indonesia, Malaysia, South Korea, Taiwan, Singapore and Thailand) grew from $49 billion in 1985 to about $85 billion in 1993. At the end of 1995, the figure exceeded $130 billion.'[65] Such figures do not include secret trades with armies involved in conflicts where sanctions against arms sales have been imposed by the USA or the EU, or secret sales to international drug dealers.

Efforts to get agreement on the Nuclear Test Ban Treaty, if eventually successful, will not mean that the nuclear war industry will shut down. In the USA the Department of Energy will continue 'stockpile stewardship' at a cost of £2 billion a year while another £700 million will be invested in the Livermore Laboratory's National Ignition Facility, on 200 lasers that can focus on heavy hydrogen and produce temperatures comparable to that in a fusion bomb. The French have a similar programme costing £1.3 billion a year. In the UK the Ministry of Defence will not disclose the size of its current budget but it is probably about £800 million a year.[66]

World-wide military spending amounts to $800 billion a year. In 1994 Unicef, the United Nations department concerned with the care of children, issued a report on the effects that wars and conflicts had had on children around the globe. It had been found that over the past decade 2 million children have died, 4 to 5 million have been left disabled, 5 million become refugees, and 12 million made homeless. All that Unicef required to help these children was a mere $34 billion. The report commented, 'The very young are paying the highest price of all, because they are paying with their one chance to grow normally in mind and body.'[67]

The arms trade has a long history. The historian Bernard Lewis wrote,

> The trade in weapons, unlike that in slaves, exhibits uninterrupted growth. Even before the Crusades, passages occur in Arabic texts praising the high quality of Frankish and other European swords. By the time of the Crusades, this had become an important export commodity which helped to redress the otherwise unfavourable balance of trade between Europe and the lands of Islam. The export of arms to the Muslims, even more than the export of Christian slaves, aroused the ire of the ecclesiastical and, sometimes, the royal authorities, but to little effect.[68]

Important though the trade in arms was, it was not until this century that it became the biggest of the commodity markets. The story of the rise of the arms trade in this century is told by Anthony Sampson in his book *The Arms Bazaar*.[69] Central to this process was Robert McNamara who, in running the Pentagon under President Kennedy, applied to arms sales the same methods he had used as president of the Ford Motor Company. 'An arms sale office was established under Henry Kuss, in the Pentagon's department of International Security Affairs, with a de facto mandate to promote American arms sales . . . Within a few years Kuss's operation could boast that it was selling $2 billion worth of US arms on average per year.'[70]

The future looks bleak, not for the arms trade profiteers but for the rest of us. The threat of nuclear war has not gone away. Many countries now have the technology and the technicians to make nuclear warheads. A major war seems unlikely, but what seems to be inevitable is a continuation of old conflicts and the creation of new ones in the Middle East and the Third World. Conflict is likely over oil in those countries around the Caspian Sea, while the peace in Bosnia is fragile. Conflict too is likely in those big cities where the disparity between the rich and poor is great. Adherents of those religions which claim the virtues of peace and forgiveness seem unlikely to end their religious wars.

In 1994 Saferworld, an independent foreign affairs think tank, set up an international inquiry into the true cost of conflict in terms of a cost benefit analysis. They looked at the costs and the benefits to all the participants in seven conflicts, East Timor, Iraq, Kashmir, Mozambique, Peru, Sudan and the former Yugoslavia, including the UK, the European Union and that group of countries often called 'the West'. They found that:

> the message of the seven conflict studies is unequivocal. The impact of conflict on human lives, economic development and the environment is devastating. While there will always be those who benefit from conflict, the studies demonstrate that these gains are short-term and partial, and are outweighed by the wider, long term costs of war. Quite apart from the costs to those directly involved, the costs to Western industrial nations are substantial.[71]

The outcome of the arms trade is always poverty and suffering. All who participate in it, even if they survive and are rich, are greatly harmed by it. Practise double-think and you become even more stupid than you already are. Become an arms salesman or a soldier and a necessary part of your training and practice of your job will be to lose your humanity. You learn how to see people as objects in order to kill them, and you become an object to yourself.

Is it possible for all this to change, or is war and conflict an inevitable part of our lives?

Certainly war and conflict are inevitable for as long as we go on bringing up our children and organizing our societies as we do. I have set out the reasons for this inevitability in my book *Living with the Bomb: Can we Live without Enemies?*[72] But the argument in its simplest form goes as follows:

The way we are constructed physiologically means that the only way we can perceive/interpret anything is when that thing exists in contrast to something else. We know light only because there is dark, life only because there is death, friends only because there are foes. Thus we define our groups in terms of those people who are excluded from our groups. We each belong to many groups, but the group we identify with we define as good. Our enemies are bad. 'Good' we define as clean, unselfish, unaggressive and honest. 'Bad' we define as dirty (hence 'ethnic cleansing'), selfish, aggressive and dishonest.

We bring up our children by teaching them that as they are they are unacceptable and have to work hard to be good. They are dirty (hence toilet training), selfish, aggressive and dishonest. (Children are taught that they mustn't lie to adults, no matter what the consequences of telling the truth. The child who takes this teaching to heart must of necessity become very obedient.) The more the adults bringing up children demand total obedience, and punish infringements of the rules severely the more the children need to project their feelings of badness and unacceptability on to those people the adults have told them are their group's enemies. Thus the children can give themselves courage by thinking, 'I might be bad but I'm not as wicked as those Arabs/Jews/Serbs/Protestants/Catholics/blacks/whites.'

In the early eighties when the threat of nuclear war was at its height I attended a number of conferences where those men who were making their name as being tremendously well-informed about the dangers of a nuclear war showed remarkably little interest in the question of whether having enemies was an inevitable and unchangeable feature of our species. At one such conference I asked Joseph Rotblatt and Carl Sagan one question, 'Is having enemies an unchangeable part of human nature?' Joseph Rotblatt answered immediately, Carl Sagan only after I had cornered him and demanded an answer. Both said, 'Yes.'

Anthony Sampson warned that, 'No politician can altogether afford to ignore the atavistic appeal of arms to the male psyche. The word weapon was up till the fourteenth century synonymous with penis; the missiles and machine guns, and the sexy roar of the Tigers, still hold their phallic spell whether in Iran or Los Angeles.'[73] However, he does not seem to think that all men are inevitably drawn to arms and war. He concluded his book with, 'The more the public is informed and involved, the more prospect there will be of achieving a saner world.'[74] Alas, there are none so deaf as those who don't want to hear. Perhaps some men do carry a gene which leads inexorably to their involvement in conflict, or perhaps it is simply a matter that some men are so totally identified with the aggressive possibilities of their most precious possession, their penis, that they are unable to understand anything that falls outside that little world.

If this is the case, rather than let these men go on and on ruining the lives of the rest of us, why don't we have international rules for war which ensure that they can have their wars and the arms trade its profits, but the rest of us aren't harmed in any way. I suggest the following rules:

1 Those people who declare war have to *lead* the fighting. No armchair warriors. Not just glamorous jobs like flying fighter planes, but with the Kalashnikov at the ready, fighting from street to street, going on dawn patrols through the jungle, driving a tank over a minefield, being in the trenches as the bombs rain down.

2 Have specially designated places where wars are to be fought. Vast areas of land all around the world are already controlled by the military for their war games. Each government could set some land aside especially for war, or several countries could co-operate in establishing their war zone.

3 Only those people who want to take part in the war do so. If you say you don't want to be involved, then you aren't.

4 There would be lots of dressing up and marching around, perhaps a parade like the Olympics opening ceremony before the war starts, thus meeting the participants' need for public display and adulation.

5 There would be an upper limit to the amount of money that can be spent on a war. Governments would build this cost into their budget. To keep the Public Borrowing Rate down the Chancellor could decide that we can't afford a war this year.

6 There would special access for the media to cover the war. Given the success of the programme *The Gladiators*, war on television would be a money-spinner, perhaps more popular than football.

Or would it?

If everyone saw that the arms trade does nothing but enable the playing of the most deadly game, war, would we decide that this game wasn't worth its cost? Could we ever be so sensible?

The Outcome of Stupid Trades

Stupid trades mean the loss of what makes life worth living. Not everyone suffers the same degree of loss, but we are all losers. The loss is never simply in pecuniary terms. In fact it is possible to make great financial gains yet lose a significant part of what makes a person human.

Whatever the loss, we all feel the effects because everything in this world is connected to everything else. For instance, an arms trader or tobacco manufacturer uses some of his profits to support someone who owes him a favour to run for office. Thus we can all suffer from bad government. Or a small farmer, displaced and impoverished by war, drifts to a shanty town and becomes a successful burglar and pickpocket. We all suffer from crime.

A world where everyone tried to trade intelligently would not be a world where everyone had the same income, simply because people vary so much in the meaning and value they place on money and goods. There'll always be people who love trading and people who have better things to do than go shopping. However, there would not be such a huge gap between the rich and the poor as exists at present. Indeed, the extensive poverty which exists today is the outcome of stupid trades along with what might be called the popular habits of greed, cruelty and power-seeking.

Actually, there's no such thing as poverty. All we can see is people living in ways which we call poor. 'Poverty' is an abstract noun, a tool for thinking. I describe poverty as being 'extensive', when what I mean is that there are a great many people who own very little and therefore can be described as 'poor'. I not only use this abstract noun as if it referred to a thing but I have views about it. I think there is too much poverty. Not everyone would agree with me. Some people see poverty as being inevitable, like rain.

The trouble with using abstract nouns is that they provide a means of getting further and further away from reality. If we talk about people, some of whom are rich and some poor, we stay closer to what is actually happening.

When the International Bank for Reconstruction and Development, known as the World Bank, was set up in 1944 it aimed to help the undeveloped and developing countries. However, a failure to observe what was going on in these countries led to billions of dollars being wasted. Bank officials, knowing that in the West the man in the family was usually the breadwinner, organized schemes in Africa where aid was given to village men. The officials failed to note that it was the women who did the work. They raised the crops and sold the produce in the markets while the men did important things like talking, fighting, playing and carrying out rituals. Similarly, in an effort to limit the burgeoning population of the Third World money was poured into birth control schemes, but with little effect. Gradually the realization dawned that birth control didn't operate in isolation. It related directly to how well the women were educated.

> Women account for 70% of the world's poor and nearly 70% of all illiterates: in no country, not even in top-notch Scandinavia, do women fare as well as men. But when girls go to school the knock-on effects in terms of lower fertility, healthier children and longer lives are striking.
>
> Mortality among Indian babies of mothers with primary education is half that of those born to uneducated women. A literate mother is better equipped to understand hygiene; literate women can be trained as midwives and rural health workers, which is crucial to public health. A shortage of such women is one reason why many Muslim countries, even rich oil states, have surprisingly low social-development indicators. Buddhist societies on the whole do better. Buddha encouraged women to seek enlightenment, and thus girls have long attended school at much the same rates as boys; better health is a natural consequence.[75]

The fact that, if we care to look, we can easily see that the conditions of our lives arise out of what we have done has never prevented anyone from claiming that people are poor because nature made them that way. In the nineteenth century Herbert Spencer gained enormous fame with his theory of Social Darwinism, where the rich were rich because, by natural selection, they were the fittest, and the poor should not be helped because that would interfere with nature. Although its adherents use the jargon of science, Social Darwinism, whether applied to economic inequality or racial differences, is utterly without a scientific basis, but it remains popular because it gives the more fortunate members of society a reason, however spurious, for neglecting and rejecting those less fortunate than themselves.

Social Darwinism is lurking in the background every time a politician claims that being poor isn't really a problem. Peter Lilley as Social Security Secretary stated that the government would not be taking part in the 1996 International Year for the Eradication of Poverty, even though as a signatory of the UN's Copenhagen Declaration it committed itself to setting targets to reduce inequality. In justifying this he said that there was no poverty in the UK. How could anyone say they were poor when they had clean water and adequate food? Some of these self-styled poor had a car, a video and a telephone. They couldn't possibly be poor with such possessions.

Yet at the same time the Child Poverty Action Group published a survey which showed that in the UK one child in three was growing up in a poor family with consequent deleterious effects on health, education and life span.

I suppose a benchmark measure of poverty could be devised. If you're starving, living on the streets, and possess nothing but a few rags to cover your nakedness, you're poor. Many millions match this description. But if you're on the other side of this, if you're living on the streets but you've got a set of clothes and you get fed, you're not poor. Try telling that to Britain's homeless!

Actually, you're poor if you think you're poor. I grew up in a home which had electric light, a gas cooker, an ice chest and a radio. No refrigerator or telephone, and if we wanted a hot bath we had to boil the water in the copper in the laundry and carry it in buckets to the bathroom. Most people in Australia lived in much the same way, so we didn't regard ourselves as poor. However, nowadays, if

I were forced through lack of money to live in the same way I would regard myself as being poor. I would know I was poor because I know about being not poor.

If everyone is poor, no one is poor. We know poverty only because there is wealth. The greater the disparity between wealth and poverty, the greater the consciousness the poor have of being poor.

It's not just a matter of knowing, 'I am poor.' It's a matter of knowing how you feel about being poor. Do you tell yourself that it is your fate and destiny to be poor? It is a matter of karma, or God's will, or Allah's wisdom. Many people see their poverty like this. Some might sink into despair, but most accept their religious leaders' teaching and put their hope in the promise of rewards after death for leading a good life. Such an interpretation of poverty might help some people to survive the daily vicissitudes of their life, but it militates against change, which is what is wanted by those who benefit from economic inequality and the distribution of power. Jesus might have taught that we are all equal, but woe betide any of his followers who try to put this teaching into practice.

Or do you tell yourself that it is bad luck and the selfishness of others which has brought you to this state? You might then decide that you deserve no better and sink into despair. Or you might burn with resentment and seek change and revenge. Now you have made yourself a dangerous person, and those who benefit from your poverty will seek to destroy you.

The poor in early nineteenth-century Britain who chose to interpret their poverty in this way were treated with great brutality by the government of the day. Many were killed, imprisoned or transported to the colonies. The rich fought against giving up one iota of their wealth, but fortunately for this country there were a tiny handful of the rich who knew that it was better to give a little and retain most rather than refuse to give any and lose all. Reform, not revolution was the slogan of the day. The best Will Hutton could hope for in the changes he proposes is some small reforms. Demand more, and it'll be the gallows or the convict hulk for him (or their latter-day equivalents).

Meanwhile, in those countries where the leaders want to preserve the status quo, the arms trade makes sure that the poor who want to improve their lot will receive nothing more than torture and execution.

The poor who do not reject their state but wait instead to be reborn as a rich man, or to receive the rewards of Heaven or Paradise, do not strive to find ways of bettering their lives and thus adding to the quality of life not merely of their country but of the whole world. Those who do protest are likely to be punished in ways which put the rest of us in danger. An army which has learned to be cruel to its country's poor will be even more cruel to other people when circumstances permit. In the old Yugoslavia Tito's army oppressed potential dissidents, out of which practices came the savageries of the conflict in Bosnia. In Ruanda the Hutus oppressed the Tutsis, and the massacres of 1995 followed. A significant number of tourists visiting Egypt have discovered that possessing a foreign passport is no protection against bombs and bullets. While there are armies and police who know how to be cruel no one is safe.

Thus it is in our own selfish interests to find ways of reducing the disparity between the rich and the poor. It is also in our own selfish interest to reduce unemployment.

Life is full of relationships between certain conditions which are not problems to be solved but paradoxes requiring the maintenance of an optimum balance. Freedom and security is one such relationship, unemployment and inflation another. When there is full employment people have money to spend and, with money chasing goods, prices rise. The Thatcher government reduced inflation by depriving many people of the money to buy goods. Inflation was seen as the great bogeyman, but now some economists are wondering whether the price of low inflation, high unemployment is too great a price to pay.

It would be quite wrong to say that unemployment is solely the result of stupid trades. As Samuel Brittan pointed out,

> A complete theory of unemployment would have to be a theory of the simultaneous determination of all the key prices – of goods and capital as well as labour – in an imperfectly clearing national and international economy. Needless to say, I cannot provide such a theory. Nor is there any widely accepted and illuminating theory

available from economists, but only a menu of incomplete individual models.[76]

However, as trade creates employment and employment trade, and as being employed is not just a matter of earning a living but having a place in society, any trade or organization of trade which does not take account of our need to earn our living and have a place in society can be said to fall into the category of a stupid trade.

It was only at the beginning of this century that the word 'unemployment' came into use as a reference to a social or economic problem which was now being recognized. In previous centuries anyone who could not or would not work was referred to as a pauper, a vagrant, a vagabond, an idle person, someone who was out of work. These words laid the blame clearly on the person, never on the system. However, the economic depressions of the 1890s and 1930s showed that workers could not always be blamed for factories closing and share prices dropping. The number of people unemployed became an important economic indicator, and as such the government of the day had to use it to prove that the government's policies were working.

One would think there'd be no difficulty in counting how many people were unemployed. Just shout, 'Hands up those who want a job,' and count the show of hands. But no. The government, so as to look good and pay out as little in unemployment benefit as possible, would, metaphorically speaking, tie some people's hands down or suffer functional blindness when counting. In the UK no attempt was made to count those people working part-time who wanted full-time work or those people who held jobs far below the skills they possessed.

When unemployment is discussed it is usually with reference to inflation as opposed to price stability and economic growth. Inflation is seen as bad, price stability and economic growth as good. Some commentators see unemployment as essential in maintaining price stability and growth. Some do not. Samuel Brittan wrote,

> One of the main reasons I took up the study of economic problems was indignation at the absurdity of unsatisfied wants side by side with idle hands, willing to work, which I believed existed before

> the Second World War. This feeling persists. While both price stability and high employment are, in the last resort, means to human contentment and not ends, I still attach more value to avoiding the waste of large scale unemployment than I do to price stability as a proximate objective. I also attach more value to growth than to price stability, provided that it is growth in the output of goods and services (including leisure and amenities) that people want, rather than in the products that some political leader, technologist or industrialist has decided are good for us.[77]

Here Samuel Brittan is putting price stability last in the hierarchy of values, a heretical view in the eyes of the Thatcher and Major governments for whom keeping inflation down was the be-all and end-all. Yet, while an individual might say, 'I'd rather be employed with inflation than be unemployed without inflation,' the three concepts, unemployment, price stability and economic growth are, in society, inextricably entwined. The theory espoused by the Conservative government (an incomplete theory, as Samuel Brittan pointed out) was that a high degree of unemployment kept wages, and therefore inflation, down. But in that case unemployed people and people on low wages could not spend in the way that encourages economic growth.

In defining unemployment as 'necessary' supporters of this economic theory were careful to exclude two of the connotations common to 'necessary', 'sacrifice' and 'evil'. Those who were unemployed felt that they were being sacrificed and that it was evil. Many people say they do not live to work, yet even they would admit that it is work which gives them the feeling that they are part of society. Without work they would be nothing but flotsam on the stream of life.

Adam Smith in the opening words of his *Wealth of Nations* said that it was not gold or silver which measure a nation's wealth but 'the annual labour of every nation'. Indeed it is not just a matter of what is the product of the work but what the work means to the person performing it. There are many vile jobs, but if the person carrying out such a job feels that the product is worthwhile, then the job itself is not degrading, though the conditions of its performance may be so.

When we say that something is degrading we are saying that it is an insult, something which diminishes a person. Being unemployed diminishes a person.

Paul had been a successful advertising executive, then along came the recession and the job vanished. He applied for other jobs, and others, and others and so on. Six years later he was one of the long-term unemployed. In a letter to me he said,

> Simplistically put, those that have money merely worry about losing it or not having enough, but those that don't have money understand its real value and meaning.
>
> May I suggest that for a period of one month whilst carrying out your research, you try a little experiment. This should offer you a real insight as to how we feel about money. Attempt, literally if you are able, but at least 'emotionally' to live on £44 per week, which is the current allowance for a single person (of my age) receiving income support. Then note the compromises you will have to make and what now becomes a luxury; your daily meal, being able to pay your heating bill.
>
> The MP for Cheam, one Lady Olga Maitland, while extolling the benefit system on a London radio station, was challenged to live on income support for one week. To which she 'felt obliged' to do and has since attempted to make political gain from such a stunt to the point that one should aspire to such an existence!!! Only those who have 'lived on' such a sum month in and month out and its resulting despair should be listened to.
>
> It is only when you don't quite literally have enough money that you truly understand its value and importance. It is an understanding that YOU NEVER WANT TO FIND OUT. Because it means that you have to DIE. Not physically of course, although sadly that does happen (not having checked I would estimate that it plays a large part in suicides) but spiritually. And there's no more appalling way to go than that.
>
> The money that I have performs one simple function – it keeps me alive – I eat, I sleep, I have a roof over my head, and I pay my heating bill. My lack of money that I have precludes me from actually living. I perform my primary functions – I stay alive.

Later Paul told me how devastated he was when he applied for a cleaning job (he was a big, athletic man) and was rejected. He'd thought, 'My God, I'm not even qualified to clean a floor.'

If there were no work which needed doing then there might be some sense in paying someone to be idle. One of the fallacies which underlies many debates about unemployment is that there is a fixed amount of work to be done and therefore a fixed number of jobs. Economists call this the 'lump of labour' fallacy, and point out how the number of jobs has expanded.

Work isn't in the same category of meaning as is the water supply, the amount of which depends on the size of the rainfall. How much work there is depends on what activities we choose to call work. Many of us spend our days engaged in activities we call work but which mean so much to us that we'd go on doing these things even if we won the lottery. (I would go on writing but I'd give up doing housework.) These activities entertain us, they give us companionship and a feeling that our life has significance.

We not only designate some activities as being work but we divide work into essential and non-essential. I have met many women who know beyond a shadow of a doubt that there is a Heavenly Housekeeping Book which lays down immutable rules such as that sheets must be ironed and windows washed. Yet I have discovered that it is possible to live with unpressed sheets and unwashed windows.

Certain jobs disappear and others are created because we change our ideas or find other ways of expressing and meeting our needs. In the UK in past centuries every parish had its vicar, but, as people changed their ideas about religion, jobs for vicars became much fewer. In the eighteenth and nineteenth centuries London had hundreds of boys employed in carrying messages. Now, even though the telephone, the fax and the Post Office are ubiquitous, the army of boys is still there but equipped with bikes and helmets.

We designate certain activities as work not merely because through work we earn our living. Work gives us a place in society. It should not be beyond the wit of our leaders to organize society so that everyone has the opportunity to spend at least part of their adult lives in an activity which gave each person a sense of belonging and contributing to society.

There is much talk of job creation and training, but the current dogma is that only the private sector can create jobs. If the private sector chooses not to, what is the point of training? Why be a computer programmer when there are no computers to programme? There is a great deal of work which could be done in areas which would provide a benefit to us all but where the scope for profits is limited or long term. Two such are in basic science and community care.

In every discussion about the destruction of the rain forests someone will talk about the disappearance of unknown amounts of insect and plant species, and how insects are indispensable to the food chain, and plants the source of medicines. Much of the identification and classification of insects, plants and animals that is currently used is based on the work done in the eighteenth and nineteenth centuries by underemployed vicars and spinsters with minimal scientific training. This work needs to be continued and developed.

The level of culture in a nation is not just a matter of education and a devotion to the arts. It is also a matter of how well that nation looks after those citizens who cannot look after themselves. Good care (as distinct from much of what passes for care) needs high numbers of well-trained staff. An autistic child, a lonely, frail old man, needs at least one person to be a steadfast, reliable and skilled friend.

The development of this kind of work needs a partnership between government, business and the professions. It requires not merely expertise and money but imagination, something which is in remarkably short supply, particularly among our politicians.

When Margaret Thatcher was prime minister she was always telling us how the country's economy should be run like a household economy. Yet her government and her successor's government never seemed to do what most of us do in trying to see the overall pattern in what we spend and what we earn. In the long run, is it better to buy expensive shoes infrequently or cheap ones frequently? First class train travel is expensive, but if I travel first class I get more work done than if I travel in crowded standard class. The balances we try to make in our budgets might not always be cost effective (some expensive shoes can be really bad buys), but at least we have a sense of handling our money in ways which meet those values we want to give to money. Yet I get the impression that cabinet ministers and Treasury officials never seem to look at the economy as a whole, except in terms of arriving at a figure for GDP or the inflation rate.

This comes out clearly whenever there's talk of how it doesn't matter if manufacturing industry declines, there'll be growth in the service sector.

Workers in the service sector don't make things. They do things for people. If you're a street sweeper or a brain surgeon you're in the service sector. Growth in the service sector, it is often said, could mop up unemployment.

Or could it? Hamish McRae cast a sceptical eye on this. For growth in the service industries to improve the economy it must produce efficiency.

> Being efficient at running service industries is not just a question of doing jobs as well as possible; it also involves not needing to do jobs at all – not needing to spend resources on police or security guards because the streets are safe without them; not needing to spend money on divorce lawyers because people stay married to each other; not needing to spend so much on health care because people lead healthy lives; not needing to spend money on unemployment benefit because a combination of cultural values and education levels enables economies to operate with low unemployment rates.[78]

High unemployment prevents the service sector from being efficient. A study by the Employment Policy Institute in 1995 showed how closely the increase in crime from 1970 to 1993 correlated with the increase in unemployment.[79] Remember the old adage, 'The devil finds mischief for idle hands to do'? When one or both partners in a marriage become unemployed the marriage is often put under great strain and ends in divorce. The 1996 edition of *Social Trends*, published by the Central Statistical Office, showed that neurotic disorders and depression are much higher for unemployed people than for those in work, and that death rates are higher for the unemployed.[80]

The hard fact may be that if our economic life is based on the market place there will always be a certain amount of unemployment. Much nonsense has been written about NAIRU, the Non-Accelerating Inflation Rate of Unemployment, often referred to as 'the natural rate of unemployment', as if there is a level of unemployment which is natural, just as there is a natural rate of death. In the long run we are all dead, as Maynard Keynes so sagely remarked. In the end, some of us are unemployed.

Unemployment isn't a natural fact of life but an outcome of our activities. Samuel Brittan described unemployment as being a reserve or margin, much like the stocks of materials held by a factory as a buffer against changes in conditions. He considered a 5 per cent rate a possible benchmark against which fluctuations could be measured. In the UK this would be the equivalent to 1.3 million people. Samuel Brittan recognized that unemployed workers would suffer hardship and suggested two remedies. 'Just as modern methods of stock control have enabled economics to operate with lower levels of inventories, so they ought to be able to operate with lower labour reserves. The second remedy is to have a labour market where most of the unemployed are short-term, spending a few weeks between jobs rather than languishing for years on the dole.'[81]

In this case unemployment could be organized so that we could come to view it, not as a bad outcome in the lottery of life, but as a civic duty. It could be organized like National Service or jury duty, and when it was your turn, instead of feeling an outcast from society, you could loll around at home and feel the warm glow of virtue.

The Value of Money

We are free to create whatever values we want for money, but whatever values we choose certain consequences follow. We can anticipate the consequences of the decisions we could make and decide whether the consequences were what we wanted, or we can make decisions solely in response to our immediate needs and then plunge blindly on being constantly surprised by the consequences of our decisions.

Making decisions solely in response to immediate need (which is usually the need to protect our structure of meaning from threat) always leads to some kind of disaster. There are many kinds of disaster which could follow, but in this chapter I have concentrated on pointing to the disaster of losing something of what you might have been, a loss of that awareness and sensitivity to what is happening to you and in the world around you. Speaking as someone who has lived long enough to see the outcome of many people's lives, I can say that what matters most in life is this awareness and sensitivity.

It is this awareness and sensitivity which enables us to have sustaining relationships with other people, without which we die of a profound loneliness which is far more than not having many friends when you need them, a complete estrangement from close human contact. It is this awareness and sensitivity which makes life interesting, without which we die of boredom.

The world is full of people who are dying of such loneliness and boredom. Many of these people have power and wealth, but gained from stupid trades where they treated other people as objects, and thus became objects to themselves.

Money has a meaning only when it is being used in trade, so the value of money is really the value of what is being traded and its consequences. Trades take place in the market, an entity which exists more in our heads than in the real world.

How does the market affect the value of money and trade, and who are the people who know about the market? What has the market to do with morality?

6

The Market and Its Experts

> Everything is for sale, even friendship.
>
> Ferengi Rule of Acquisition No. 121

> The justification for profit is profit.
>
> Ferengi Rule of Acquisition No. 202

The Ferengi have a very simple view of the market. They buy, sell, and let no person or scruple stand in the way of their making a profit. The Ferengi are amongst us, and they always have been. These Ferengis don't spend much time bothering their pretty heads with theories about the market, unlike the economists since Adam Smith who have woven endless theories about how the market operates. This was a fairly harmless occupation until politicians started to use the economists' theories – or at least their own version of the economists' theories – as a platform for their own political ambitions.

When Margaret Thatcher began using her version of Milton Friedman's monetarist theory as the basis of her political programme the word 'market' without the prefix 'super' or 'street' entered our common discourse. Suddenly 'the market' was almost as common in conversations among the British as is 'God' in conversations among Americans.

Indeed, the market's praises were sung with a religious intensity, and it took on a Godlike quality. 'The market,' said Margaret Thatcher, 'is always right. You can't buck the market.'

The market is omniscient, omnipotent and infallible. Its judgements are always entirely correct, lawful and moral. It punishes those who do not heed its power.

This, of course, is the free market, unfettered by the laws which foolish governments create in order to hinder its progress. All right-thinking people believe in the free market in the way that all right-thinking Americans believe in God. Simon Hoggart described one of these right-thinking people, Peter Lilley, a cabinet minister in John Major's Conservative government:

> He is one of the leading free marketeers in the Cabinet . . . He believes that the beneficent hand of the market can soothe all pains and remove all ailments. It maketh the poor wealthy, the hungry sated, and the shoeless shod. It can probably cure warts.
>
> Mr Lilley detests big government and has a deep suspicion of bureaucracy. He makes Adam Smith look like a Marxist, Milton Friedman like Maynard Keynes.[1]

If you asked Peter Lilley, 'Where is the market?' he might say that it was, like God, invisible, but everywhere men and women gather together to buy and sell. Or perhaps he might have the good sense to say, 'It's nowhere. It's an idea in our heads.'

Like all abstract nouns, 'the market' is a tool for thinking. Turning an abstract noun into a thing to be worshipped is as sensible as worshipping a washing machine.

Tools, depending on the situation, can be useful or useless. A washing machine is useful if you want some clean clothes but not if you want to cook dinner. 'The market' is a useful tool in giving a brief exposition, as in saying, 'the commodity market' instead of listing all the people who buy and sell various commodities and all the activities and records that this buying and selling requires. If we talk about patterns of human activities, 'the market' delineates certain activities, such as selling rather than sleeping. 'The market' is not a useful tool if we want to talk about the existence of black holes in the universe or the process whereby we create a poem.

The market is not an entity which would go on functioning after the last human being had left the planet. The market is not a sentient, infallible being. The market is right only in the sense that at a particular moment the price for a particular item is such and such. We might wish it were otherwise or feel it ought to be otherwise, but that is irrelevant. The price simply is.

Prices are what they are at a particular moment, but time passes and prices change. Some people prefer prices to remain the same, and other people want them to change. Price stability is important if you're manufacturing something you want to sell. You need to be able to predict the future of your enterprise, so you need to know the future costs of the raw materials you use, the costs of the manufacturing process and the wages of those you employ. But if all these prices remain the same, the traders in currencies and in futures and options would starve. Fortunately for them, prices rarely stay the same for long, and money can be made when the market moves. The trick is to know when the market is about to move.

Predicting the Market

According to conventional economic theory, the market is efficient. Eddie George, Governor of the Bank of England, said, 'I have a firm belief in markets. I don't believe they are always perfect, but by and large, if they get it wrong, they put it right faster than administration or bureaucrats could.'[2]

As well as being efficient, the market is considered to be random. Prices reflect all available information about the future. Buyers and sellers efficiently absorb the information they need, make predictions on the basis of their past experience (the more mature the market, the more efficient it is) and buy and sell in a variety of ways which, if plotted on a graph, would produce a random scatter. However, when something unpredictable happens, buyers and sellers get frightened and all run in one direction, thus producing a regularity in the market. When an electricity company warns of widespread blackouts the price of candles goes up. A speculator who predicted this course of events could buy up all the available candles and later sell them at his own price, thus making a tidy profit.

However, some people believe that the market is not a sea of uncertainty in which some patterns can from time to time be seen, but instead emanates from some Grand Design where nothing happens by chance. To be rich all you have to do is to find the Grand Design. Every financial journal carries advertisements for systems which will reveal this. The question to be asked is, 'Is the person selling the system very, very rich?' I asked a buyer for Dillons bookshops if Napoleon Hill, author of *Think and Grow Rich*,[3] is wealthy. She said, 'He is from the sale of his books.' The circus proprietor Phineas Taylor Barnum knew that human credulity knows no limits. He said, 'There's a sucker born every minute.'

Is the market random or non-random? The answer is not either/or but both.

Much of the market is random. Participants change their minds, often for no better reason than that they read some astrological prediction or had a argument with their wife. Participants make mistakes. They get their figures wrong when they speak to their stockbroker or tap certain numbers into their computer. Most of all, every participant in the market has his/her own way of interpreting and predicting the dealings of the market. Sometimes the predictions are right and sometimes they are wrong, but, right or wrong, they affect the market. Nowadays information flows around the world extremely fast. *Bloomberg's Business News* gets news to subscribers in 'real time', that is, within seconds of it happening. According to the *Economist*, 'One firm recently spent $35m on a supercomputer to gain a two-second advantage in arbitraging stock futures in Tokyo.'[4] The recipients of such news have little time to think about their response, and so mistakes are made. Some people get their responses right but for the wrong reasons, and so their subsequent responses can be in error.

While groups of people from time to time might interpret the market in more or less the same way (for instance, by following the principle of buying cheap and selling dear), individuals differ greatly in what they see as the purpose of their trading and on how they assess risks, as Jack Schwager demonstrated in his studies of the Market Wizards, the men and women who are very successful traders. Moreover, non-human factors like the climate, earthquakes, tornadoes and tidal waves do not lend themselves to the detailed predictability which would be required if the market were non-random.

However, within the great mass of activity which forms the market certain parts have a very simple, predictable structure. For instance, floods which destroy the soya bean crop are usually followed by a rise in soya bean prices. Other more complex parts of the market can have a fairly predictable structure. A decision by the men of the Bundesbank to change interest rates sets in train series of events, the outcomes of some of which might be predicted. In addition there are the patterns which arise by chance but which have outcomes which might allow the formation of a prediction.

Waves appear in the market like the waves that result from the random movements of the ocean. These waves can be bull and bear markets, long periods in which prices rise followed by long periods in which they fall. Or they can be sudden bursts of activity which can disappear as quickly as they appear. Those of us who spend time watching the ocean can easily discern the first faint swelling which will grow into a mountainous line, then sharpen, curve and break. Those of us who surf can tell whether an approaching wave will bear us smoothly to the shore or tumble us over and over and dump us on the shore. We can tell too whether the smooth water between the waves contains an undercurrent that will drag the unwary swimmer further out to sea. Similarly, market watchers can discern the random movements in the market which now and then form a moving pattern which has a predictable course and which ends like an ocean wave dissolving into unpredictable swirls of market movements. Such patterns in markets, like patterns in waves, cannot be lifted out of their context. They are no more than a momentary part of the whole.

Some of the patterns we see are simple relationships where the more there is of one the more there will be of another. The more water you pour into a glass the higher the level rises. Such relationships are called linear relationships and can be represented by a straight line on a graph. Linear relationships abound in theoretical physics and mathematics, in economics and in the minds of the simple-minded. Politicians like to blame their opposing political party for all the ills of their country. However, in real life simple linear relationships are comparatively rare.

More frequently very simple events can give rise to enormous consequences. On 9 January 1991 the then US Secretary of State James Baker only had to say one word to set in train a vast array of events. That day he met the Iraqi ambassador in an effort to avert war. Later, making a statement to the waiting media, he began, 'Regrettably . . .' 'Traders didn't wait to hear the second word and a wave of selling hit the stock and bond markets.'[5] In 1996, when Wall Street share prices had climbed to record levels, Alan Greenspan, Chairman of the US Federal Reserve Bank, brought them tumbling down simply by inserting into an otherwise very boring speech the question, 'How do we know when irrational exuberance has unduly escalated asset values, which then become subject to unexpected and prolonged contractions?'[6]

Such arrays of events do not always display themselves in ways which fit the mathematical models used in science, psychology and economics, so for many years scientists, psychologists and economists ignored such events. Then in the early seventies a few intrepid scientists and mathematicians, aided by their computers, began exploring large chaotic systems. They found some surprising patterns. Out of this early work has come the science of chaos, which is a science of the nature of global systems, 'a science of process rather than state, of becoming rather than being'.[7]

Professor Paul Ormerod, chairman of the organization Post-orthodox Economics, said, 'The single most important scientific advance of the latter decades of the twentieth century has been the perception that the world is fundamentally non-linear.'[8]

It has been found that predictable patterns can arise out of the extremes of chaos. Such patterns in the market are like the patterns in nature which scientists like Ilya Prigogine[9] call *dissipative structures*. These are structures which arise in far-from-equilibrium conditions when disorder transforms into order. Dissipative structures can be very different from the original equilibrium. This process has been observed in liquids which, when heated, convert into a convection current and the molecules suddenly form themselves into hexagonal cells. It has also been observed when, in far-from-equilibrium states, certain molecules organize themselves into a regular colour-changing pattern. Analogous dissipative structures are likely to emerge after some major event destabilizes the market, such as would happen after a huge earthquake in Tokyo or a domino collapse of international banks following a derivatives disaster.

Predictability in the market appears as patterns which can be observed. Sometimes we can simply see a pattern and sometimes we can extract a pattern by using mathematics to derive a formula. (All formulae are patterns.)

However, all that glisters is not gold. Not all the patterns we can see relate in a useful way to the activities of the market. This problem arises because we are far too adept at seeing patterns. All we ever do is see patterns. Sometimes these patterns relate to the world around us and sometimes they don't. We see patterns when we look at the world around us and patterns when we daydream or close our eyes and go to sleep.

Even when we look at patterns in the world around us we cannot always be sure that they tell us anything useful about the world. If you're enjoying one of those hot lasagnes that British Rail catering sells and the train suddenly halts, throwing the lasagne over your white shirt, the fact that the brown and yellow stain resembles a rose in bloom does not assure you that it will disappear in the wash. In contrast, the pale yellow smudge left on the bottom sheet when you lift your two-year-old out of his cot does predict that his nappy needs changing.

Moreover, there are patterns which some people see as revealing predictability while others do not. Some people believe that the pattern of the planets determines human behaviour and some do not. Often we resist the idea that other people see patterns which are different from the ones we see, and sometimes other people can persuade us to change what we see. Jack Schwager, from his talk with one of the few highly successful women traders, Linda Bradford Raschke, changed one of the patterns he saw. He wrote,

> Occasionally, an interview provokes me to reassess my view of reality. I have long assumed that markets might be predictable over the long-term but that short-term price movements are largely random. Raschke holds exactly the opposite point of view. She believes that in the markets, much as in weather forecasting, short-term predictions can be quite accurate but long-term forecasting is a virtual impossibility. With her ability to see patterns

> that others don't, she has been able to trade short-term price swings with a consistency that would defy the laws of probability, if indeed there were no patterns in these movements. Raschke has made me a believer. Clearly, there are predictable movements in price even over periods as short as a few days or a single day.[10]

A comparable problem in everyday physics would be to predict the minute by minute temperature of a cooling cup of initially hot coffee. Predicting the long-term temperature of the coffee is simple. It will reach the same temperature as its surroundings.

Believing that a certain pattern exists increases significantly the likelihood of seeing it. If you hadn't believed it you wouldn't have seen it. Believing that a pattern exists can prevent us from acting in ways which lie outside the predicted pattern. Researchers into the outcome of the serious illnesses of five different types of cancer, heart disease, diabetes, peptic ulcer, pneumonia, bronchitis and cirrhosis of the liver found that

> A strong belief in Chinese horoscopes can significantly affect lifespans. While not endorsing the accuracy of Chinese astrology, the researchers say that their findings provide yet more evidence, as seen in cancer patients, of how ill people with a positive outlook tend to do well and those with negative views badly.
>
> Professor David Phillips and colleagues, from the departments of sociology and mathematics at the University of California, San Diego, compared the deaths of 28,169 adult Chinese-Americans with the deaths of 412,632 white Americans. They state in the *Lancet*: 'Chinese Americans, but not whites, die significantly earlier than normal – 1.3 to 4.9 years – if they have a combination of disease and a birth year which Chinese astrology and medicine consider ill-fated. The more strongly a group is attached to Chinese traditions, the more years of life are lost' . . . The researchers add: 'Patients with an ill-fated combination of birth year and disease may refuse to change unhealthy habits because they believe their deaths are inevitable, and thereby reduce their longevity.'[11]

Believing that a juxtaposition of planets predicts that you will lose money in the market can lead to you responding with a 'What's the use?' when you see an opportunity to avoid a loss. The belief that you are doomed to failure can prevent you from even seeing opportunities for success.

Even when we can feel sure that the pattern we see does actually exist in external reality, its mere existence does not mean that the parts of the pattern relate together in any useful way. For instance, most of us have observed over the past few years that there has been an increasing number of starving people in Africa and that world-wide there has been an increasing number of portable phones. Does this mean that starvation in Africa causes portable phones? Or that portable phones cause starvation? Since everything that exists is connected to everything else it is often possible to trace connections between one event and another through a set of common causes. Portable phones and famine in Africa are each outcomes of the wealth created in the developed world. However, there is not a direct causal link between portable phones and famine in Africa. Banning portable phones will not end the famine in Africa, and encouraging Africans to starve will not boost the market in portable phones.

Monroe Trout, an outstanding public money manager, when asked by Jack Schwager how he could distinguish between patterns that reflect real inefficiencies in the market and those that are merely coincidental, said, 'A pattern has to make sense. For example, if I find that the price change of the British pound forty days ago is statistically significant in predicting today's price in the S & P [Standard and Poor, a New York share index], I wouldn't put any faith in it. Why would the British pound price forty days ago affect the S & P? So we toss out a lot of these types of patterns even if they have a high percentage of success.'[12] As statisticians always say, a correlation is not a cause.

Thus it is that when we search the market for predictable patterns we need to establish that the patterns we see do not exist just in our mind's eye and that even when a pattern does exist in the market it does reflect some useful and predictable part of that market.

Moreover, we need to be aware that as soon as we act to make use of a pattern we change the pattern. Buying or selling just £500-worth of shares changes the market because every sale and purchase is part of the whole. Big players in the market don't even have to act to change the market. When the word went out that George Soros was interested in investing in real estate or Sir James Goldsmith was considering his position on gold, the market changed.

In the manufacturing area of the market, where real things are bought and sold, much thought and effort goes into the creation of new things and the improvement of the old. The design of these things is enormously important because it is design which creates beauty and efficiency, or, in many cases, does not. Designers are passionately interested in the future. What objects will people want and what will they regard as beautiful and efficient? Some designers make the future their area of expertise. However, only those designers in academia are likely to be in the business of predicting that in 2020 people will want such and such objects designed in such and such ways, and then waiting to 2020 to see if they are right. Most designers want to sell their predictions to the manufacturers who will develop their productions along the lines the designers predict will be popular. However, these actions of the designers and the manufacturers and their multitudinous effects create a different future from the one originally predicted. The success of a product is very much a matter of timing. If the product appears too soon, possible purchasers don't see the point of it, and if it appears too late the need has already been filled in some way. Futurologists need to be lucky.

People have been predicting the market ever since markets began. To do this well requires a good memory and computational skills. Computers have good memories and excellent computational skills, so they now play an enormous part in predicting the market. However, many people who don't understand computers believe that computers can make discoveries which humans could never make even if they could do a trillion of sums in half a second, and there are many computer experts who, for their own benefit, are happy to let people think this. Some computer experts know quite well that, no matter how large, fast and sophisticated computers may become, they can never overcome their inherent limitations, but there are some, particularly among those Artificial Intelligence experts who seek publicity, who seem really to believe that computers have, or will have, the capacity to be more intelligent than humans.

I encountered my first computer, a cumbersome creature that chomped numbers, in 1968 at Sheffield University. A computer expert said to me then, 'If you put garbage in you get garbage out.' That truth has never changed. No matter how huge the memory of a computer, no matter how hard it can work and what variety of exercises it can perfect, a computer can never do more than its software allows. Who writes the software? A human being. Who decides what data should be used on the software? A human being. Who types in the data? A human being. If they put rubbish in they get rubbish out.

Computers are good at doing sums and so they lend themselves readily to the quantitative analysis of the market – buying and selling and the degree of change in prices called volatility. They are not good at handling the fundamental analysis of the market which entails studies of political and economic changes and the theories of political and economic change which different people hold. However, technical analysis can cover a long time span and thus reflect in part economic and political changes. Al Weiss who, according to Jack Schwager, 'may well have the single best long-term track record for a commodity trading adviser'[13] developed long-term chart analysis, even going as far back as the 1840s in his study of the grain markets. He said, 'One of the keys to long-term chart analysis is realizing that markets behave differently in different economic cycles. Recognizing these repeating and shifting long-term patterns requires lots of history. Identifying where you are in an economic cycle – say, an inflationary phase versus a deflationary phase – is critical to interpreting the chart patterns evolving at that time.'

Even though Al Weiss's day-to-day work depended on computers he did not see computers as the source of special knowledge. He said, 'The essential element is that the markets are ultimately based on human psychology, and by charting the markets you're merely converting human psychology into graphic representations. I believe that the human mind is more powerful than any computer in analysing the implications of these price graphs.'[14]

Computers are good at doing statistics, but statistics follow the same rule as computers. If you put rubbish in you get rubbish out. Whether you work out a probability in your head or on your computer, the value of your result does depend on the accuracy of your arithmetic, but even more on the value of the data you have collected and the suitability of the statistical measure you have chosen to use. You then have to decide how you are going to interpret the probability measure which your statistics have provided. Probability is not a fact of nature but an opinion, and even when a number of people hold the same opinion that opinion can be wrong. 'Our innate desire for meaning and pattern,' wrote John Allen Paulos, 'can lead us astray if we don't remind ourselves of the ubiquity of coincidence, an ubiquity which is the consequence of our tendency to filter out the banal and impersonal.'[15]

It isn't necessary to understand the complex sums used in statistics to understand what statistics do. Statistics are simply a collection of methods for comparing one part of the world with another. We are doing this all the time.

All statistics, from the simplest to the most complex, are based on assumptions about the nature of the world. If these assumptions are wrong then the results which the statistics give are wrong.

Throughout human history a popular assumption about our world was that in essence it contained perfect symmetries. Anyone who dared to suggest that the world was not composed of ideal symmetries was severely punished.

Ptolemy, the most famous astronomer and geographer of the ancient world, described the Earth as the centre of the universe with the sun and the planets moving in perfect circles around the Earth, and later the Church agreed that this must be because God was perfect and so must be all His creations. When Copernicus realized that his study of the movements of the planets showed that not only was the Earth not the centre of the universe but that the planets moved in ellipses, not perfect circles, he feared to let his discoveries be known because the Church would punish him for his heresy.

Not only the planets but man himself was the subject of that perfect symmetry. The Church taught that even though man was tainted by original sin he held a central place in the Chain of Being, a line of God's creations from the smallest of inanimate objects to the throne of God. Man was at the nodal point, the junction of matter and spirit. Below him were the birds and the beasts and inanimate matter, while symmetrically above him was the line of seraphim, angels and archangels. Darwin's crime was that he threatened to destroy this perfect symmetry.

We may have discarded Ptolemy's cosmology and the Chain of Being, but we can still be seduced by the desire for perfect symmetry. Hence the statisticians' fascination with the concepts of the Normal Distribution and the Normal Curve. Measure the height of a thousand people and you'll find a few very short people, a few very tall people and most people around the middle of the two extremes. However, the occurrences of many phenomena are not distributed in this way.

William Eckhardt, a mathematician who became a most successful trader, said, 'Most classical applications of statistics are based on the key assumption that the data distribution is normal, or some other known form. Classical statistics work well and allow you to draw precise conclusions if you're correct in your assumption of the data distribution. However, if your distribution assumptions are even a little bit off, the error is enough to derail the delicate statistical indicators.'[16]

Symmetries in nature can appear to us as both comforting and magical. Markets are not immune to magical thinking. Monroe Trout described how

> Markets almost always get to the round number. Therefore the best place to get in is before that number is reached and play what I call the 'magnet effect'. For example, I might buy the stock index markets when the Dow is at 2,950, looking for it to go to 3,000. When the market gets close to 3,000, things get more difficult. When that happens, I like to have everybody in the trading room get on the phone with a different broker and listen to the noise level on the floor. How excited does it sound down there? What size trades are hitting the market? If it doesn't sound loud and order sizes are small, then I'll start dumping our position because the market is probably going to fall off. On the other hand, if it sounds crazy and there are large orders being transacted, I'll tend to hold the position.[17]

Markets get to a round number because we count in tens and give every number which ends on 0 a special, magical significance.

If we counted in sevens we'd give each multiple of seven a special, magical significance. Whenever we designate a certain number as the marker for a set of numbers, each time we're counting we get a sense of closure when we reach a multiple of that number. However, this sense of closure is entirely our construction and without parallel in reality where everything is connected to everything else.

> Things flow smoothly into nonthings. The atoms in our finger tips swirl into atoms in the air. There are finger atoms and non-finger atoms. And there are the atoms in between, the atoms to some degree both finger atoms and air atoms and to some degree neither. A rose is a rose is a nonrose when its molecules change. The finger shades into the hand, the hand shades into the wrist, the wrist into the arm. Earth's atmosphere shades into space. The mountain crumbles into a hill and in time into a plain. The growing human embryo passes into a living human being and a living brain decays into death. We can put black and white labels on these things. But the labels will change from accurate to inaccurate as the things change.[18]

That was written by Bart Kosko, one of the pioneering exponents of fuzzy logic, a way of looking at the world which recognizes both the way everything is connected to everything else and how we think in terms of 'almost', 'not quite', 'just about'. Eastern philosophers in the tradition of the Buddha and Lao Tzu, have always recognized the seamlessness of the world on to which we impose our meanings, or fictions as they are called in Buddhism. In the West philosophy and science has always been dominated by Aristotle's binary logic of A and not-A. It's either raining or it's not raining. You're either buying or selling. Fuzzy logic deals with the states in between A and not-A, from fine to cloudy to a few drops to a sprinkle to a shower to rain, from 'This might be a good time to buy', to 'Possibly not', to 'I'd better sell'.

Most computers operate on a binary system of 0 and 1, but now fuzzy logic systems have been created where, instead of a simple open or closed switching state, there is a system which could be open, slightly open, half open, nearly closed and closed. These fuzzy logic systems have many practical applications, as in that most wonderful car to drive, the Audi.

> Ask any keen driver if he wants automatic transmission and he'll probably tell you he prefers to change his own gears, thank you. Conventional automatics have a reputation for killing a car's performance and frequently being in the wrong ratio at the wrong time. All Audi automatics, however, now have computer controls smart enough to detect each driver's individual style and choose a shifting pattern from a bank of built-in programmes. Audi calls its system, introduced in 1992, a dynamic shift programme – DSP for short.[19]

A series of fuzzy logic arguments can be put together to form what is called an expert system. Audi engineers built up their system by gathering data from the driving style of different drivers (we each have our own individual style), the various driving conditions, and the spontaneous engine functions.

Similar expert systems have been created where experts in the market have tried to describe their processes of thought in such a way that their statements can be codified in either binary logic or fuzzy logic.

That fuzzy logic does play a part in successful trading or money management is an idea that has only recently been accepted. A financial consultant told me that when he was first studying for his professional qualifications he was given to believe that there was one right solution for each financial problem with which he was presented. This caused him enormous anxiety because he could never be sure that the solution he was presenting to his client was the one and only correct one. He later found when he attended advanced courses for financial consultants that the concept of the one right solution had disappeared and that the received wisdom was that every problem can generate a multitude of possible solutions.

Buddy Cicchino described to me how he had found the fuzzy logic of Lao Tzu invaluable in his trading in futures and options. 'I learned to remain flexible and not to be frightened of being weak, because out of weakness comes strength. Markets change so dramatically that if you approach the market with the same attitude or the same strategy every time, you will lose money.'

These expert systems are often referred to as AI, artificial intelligence. They have been used for everything from evaluating mortgage applications to predicting currency fluctuations, but developing an expert system for money managers who have to make choices in different financial markets has proved to be very difficult.

In 1993 Pareto Partners, a firm of fund managers, formed a venture with the research laboratory of G. M. Hughes Electronics, a giant defence group which was looking for new markets. They decided to use a 'knowledge acquisition kit' which Hughes had developed 'for mapping how military commanders make their decisions. The parallels between war and investing are uncanny. As Mr Liesching, research director of Pareto, puts it: "Both have lots of data and poor signal-to-noise ratio; both require quick decisions based on robust models of what's going on; and both punish wrong decisions with loss." '[20]

The subject whose knowledge and expertise was to be acquired for the expert system was Christine Downton, a central banker and money manager. It wasn't a matter of putting some electrodes to her head and transferring her knowledge to a computer, as some science fiction stories would have us believe. She had to make explicit what is usually implicit – the thought processes by which we make a decision. Decision-making is always a mixture of public and private logic. When that part of British Rail called Railtrack was put up for sale in May 1996, people bidding for shares had not only considered that mathematics of possible profit and loss but issues of value and trust, which are matters which can never be decided by public logic alone. Did they believe what the politicians were telling them? Did they believe that the directors of Railtrack would look after the shareholders' interests? When someone says, 'I knew intuitively . . .' that person is saying in effect, 'My private logic tells me . . .'

The *Economist* commented, 'Of course, in one sense AI will put Miss Downton and her ilk out of a job. But in a deeper sense, it frees experts to think harder about the rules and knowledge they have given up. Moreover, because economic relationships are dynamic, there is a constant need to monitor and update the rules which govern the AI system. As always, the hardest bit about making a machine think is working out what human thought consists of.'[21]

I doubt if Christine Downton and her ilk will ever be out of a job. No matter what expert systems, fractals and chaos theory, neural networks, fuzzy logic, genetic algorithms and data visualizations might be developed, life and the market will always be different from what we expect. In predicting the unpredictable you can sometimes get lucky.

A Free Market?

Participants in the market want the freedom to trade as best suits them and the security of maintaining and elaborating what privileges they enjoy. Hence free marketeers like protective trade laws when it's their privileges and advantages that are being protected. The fact that freedom and security exist in inverse proportions doesn't stop them from trying to have their cake and eat it because, while they might say they want a free market, they don't want a free-for-all. Thus a free market needs to operate within a set of rules which all participants agree to follow.

Democratically elected governments, like monarchs and dictators, want the security of knowing that they will continue in power along with the freedom to do what they want. Thus governments are always prepared to interfere with the market in order to keep themselves in power.

Some kinds of government interference have little effect on the market. In the early months of 1995 the US dollar dropped in value against the German mark and the Japanese yen to a level which the US government found unacceptable, so the chairman of the Federal Reserve, Alan Greenspan, and Bob Rubin, Treasury Secretary, got together with the Bundesbank to talk up the dollar. This kind of activity market members unkindly call 'a dead-cat bounce'. You can make a dead cat bounce once, but it won't keep on bouncing. The market might respond once, as it did on this occasion, but, as soon as it was clear that really nothing had changed, the dollar subsided to the level the market thought it should have.

The US government here was sharing what Paul Tudor Jones, described by Jack Schwager as a master of aggressive trading, saw as the most prominent fallacy in the public's perception about markets, namely, 'that markets can be manipulated, that there is some group on Wall Street that controls price action in the markets. I can go into any market and create a stir for a day or two, maybe even a week. If I go into a market just at the right moment, by giving it a little gas on the upside, I can create the illusion of a bull market. But, unless the market is really sound, the second I stop buying, the price is going to come right down. You can open up the most beautiful Saks Fifth Avenue in Anchorage, Alaska, with the most wonderful summer menswear department, but unless somebody wants to buy the clothes, you will go broke.'[22]

Governments can pass laws which limit the freedom of the markets. Of course, one person's freedom is another person's insecurity. The General Agreement on Tariffs and Trade (GATT '94) gives opportunity for free trade between all countries who are signatories to GATT, but threatens the livelihood of those who have been benefiting from laws which had been protecting their trade from outside competition. Governments can create forums where disputes between those who benefit and those who don't can be addressed, such as the by-product of GATT, the World Trade Organization (WTO) for all countries who are signatories to WTO, but even forums like these can be seen as both liberating and imprisoning. American rice growers supported by government subsidies can sell their crop in South East Asia more cheaply than the local growers. One person's freedom can be another person's prison.

Adam Smith taught that self-interest tempered by competition in a free market would bring prosperity. Such a view threatened those who enjoyed inherited wealth and royal monopolies. So in the early nineteenth century the battle to repeal the Corn Laws which protected English landowners was bitter. Subsequently the governments of the UK and the USA showed some favour to the idea of free trade, but money and finance were constrained until the ideas of Milton Friedman began to influence a generation of politicians. He won a Nobel Prize for economics 'despite, not because of, the theories that ushered in the era of the vigilantes (the banks, investment banks, hedge funds, and other private financial institutions that judge governments and punish them financially). In writings as passionate as an anarchist's bomb, he equated capitalism with democracy, and economic choice with freedom of speech.'[23]

It might be said that the time had come for Milton Friedman's ideas, but that saying always carries the implication that the idea is a truth, and truth, as they say, will out. Truth doesn't, you know. Lies will hold the stage for as long as enough people benefit from them.

For an idea to be accepted by a large group of people it doesn't need to have any relation to reality. What it needs to contain are a set of meanings which are already held by a large group of people, put together in a framework which is sufficiently novel to be exciting but not so novel as to be frightening. Politicians don't like democracy (if they did they wouldn't have these power machines called political parties) and they don't like freedom of speech (see their complaints about the media, even though the media's freedom of speech is limited by the media-owning moguls), but they do like the *ideas* of democracy and freedom of speech. Unfortunately, power-mad politicians turn ideas into ideologies, that is, they turn perspectives on reality into absolute truths.

Once politicians are gripped by an ideology they start proclaiming that it will solve all problems and produce universal happiness. But of course it won't. No set of ideas, no matter how well conceived and grounded in reality, will do that, for the simple reason that every idea and every action has good implications and bad implications, good and bad consequences. There are always winners and losers. The deregulation of the currency and financial markets showed this clearly.

The currency and the financial markets were regulated by governments, partly for their own interests, such as raising taxes and keeping themselves in power, and partly because there always needs to be, more or less, an isometric relationship between the amount of money in circulation in an economy and the value of the assets of that economy. Too little money in circulation inhibits trade and too much can lead to inflation. The same principle applies to individuals seeking loans. In theory no bank should lend me more money than my assets are worth.

Such financial stringency very much disappeared when the financial and currency markets were deregulated. It became much easier for individuals to borrow money, especially if they wanted to borrow a lot of money. If I ask the bank to lend me £10,000 there'll be all sorts of ums and ahs and forms to fill in and a probable refusal, but if I ask the bank to lend me a million and Terence, a mover and shaker in the world of finance, puts in a good word for me, I could be lucky. If Terence says he has confidence in me, and if the bank has confidence in Terence, the bank then has confidence in me. If the City, the Bank of England and the financial markets have confidence in the bank, the bankers can feel confident in lending me money.

Thus I could acquire sufficient money, far in excess of what my assets are worth, to enter the financial and currency markets. Provided I had steady nerves, adequate knowledge of the markets, enormous good luck and sufficient profits to service my debt, I could be an effective player in the game.

If all these conditions pertained, all I would have to do is keep on playing. I can't leave the market until I've made enough money to pay back the debt plus interest, otherwise I'll lose everything I have, and if I want something to show for all my hard work, I shall have to keep on playing.

I would be playing with hundreds of thousands of individuals and institutions, many of whom have arrived with money far in excess of the value of their assets. It's the sort of game where to be admitted you have to bring your own ball. The players spend their time throwing and catching the balls. It might seem that the aim of the game is for players to acquire as many balls as possible, but it is not. The aim of the game is to keep on playing. The balls must be kept in the air because if the players stop playing or if a large enough number of them decide to take their balls and go home, the whole edifice of the international currency and financial markets will come tumbling down because the balls that are being kept in the air are not just lumps of money but also money's anti-matter, debt. As Adam Mars Jones said, in his review of Lisa Jardine's study of the amassing of artistic treasures in the Renaissance, 'If to some extent the history of culture is the history of money, then *Worldly Goods*[24] makes it very clear that the history of money is essentially the history of debt.'[25]

In 1993 the foreign exchange markets were sending a tidal wave of money around the world which was twenty times greater than the volume of trade it was supposed to be financing.[26] By now the figure is probably much higher. Some of this difference can be accounted for in terms of borrowings in excess of assets, and some in terms of the laundering of dirty money arising from theft, bribery, extortion, insider dealing, embezzlement, tax avoidance and illegal drugs and arms, but just what these proportions are no one can tell. In their study of the Bank of Credit and Commerce James Ring Adams and Douglas Frantz said,

> No one knows how much money is being laundered around the world. A 1989 report by the U.S. State Department estimated that drug profits in the United States were $110 billion a year. Others have put the figure as low as $10 billion. A report in 1990 by seven leading industrial nations said drug dealers in the United States and Europe earn $232,115 a minute. Some of the smartest minds in law enforcement, people such as Treasury Department financial crimes expert Brian Bruth, believe there is no way to come up with an accurate measure of the underground money market. Yet it is known that untold billions of that money move through CHIPS, quickly and anonymously.[27]

CHIPS is the New York Clearing House Interbank Payment System, and 95 per cent of the world's US dollar transactions between banks flow through its computers. It works like this:

> A bank in Spain is instructed by a customer to transfer $1 million to an account at a bank in Panama. The Spanish bank transmits electronic instructions to its correspondent bank in New York, where a computer operator enters the transaction into the CHIPS computer through a secure link over private telephone lines. The CHIPS computer authenticates the transaction codes and automatically deducts $1 million from the Spanish bank's account and adds it to the account of the bank in Panama. It also sends a message notifying the Panamanian bank of the transaction. At the end of the day, the transaction is included in summary reports of all the day's transactions, showing which banks owe money and which have money due.
>
> This happens in a matter of seconds 150,000 times each business day at CHIPS and involves banks in almost every country in the world. In processing a transaction, the CHIPS computer knows

> and records only four scant pieces of information: the account number of the sender, the identity of the sending bank, the identity of the receiving bank, and the number of the receiving account. Often there are no names for account holders. When one or both of the banks involved is situated in a country with strict secrecy laws, anonymity is guaranteed.[28]

Any attempt by a government to regulate the money market would send the money fleeing from that country. The huge volume of transactions that go through the US and UK financial markets make a major contribution to the US and UK economies and balances of trade. The financial markets in other countries compete keenly to increase their volume of trade, and often their governments give their markets direct support. It is highly unlikely the governments would combine to regulate the markets, but, if they did, the regulations they devised would have to take account of the dirty money washing through the system. Either the proceeds of crime would have to be publicly accepted as legitimate or the proceeds and the criminals who acquired these proceeds would have to be excluded from the markets and dealt with. However, if there were a concerted effort by the governments of all countries to set up a system for regulating the money markets, these efforts, by excluding many of the players, could well bring the whole edifice down, thus disrupting the world's economy to an unforeseeable extent. So it is likely that as long as the money market enjoys the freedom it has, dishonest players will flourish.

Not that the stock market in the US is a stranger to crime. There 'for nearly two centuries, the stock exchanges had been neat little cartels, undisturbed by outside forces, conferring wealth and a comfortable if somewhat dubious status on their members.'[29] In his study of money and class in America Lewis L. Lapham argued that 'to the extent that money becomes synonymous with freedom, Americans learn to think of it as a preliminary to the fact of existence. It is no wonder that we so seldom question the means of obtaining money.'[30] He went on:

> The routine thievery in Wall Street shouldn't need much annotation. Despite the occasional and much advertised instances of financiers found guilty of 'insider trading' (most notoriously the

> fine of $100 million imposed on the arbitrageur Ivan Boesky), the money earned from privileged information continues to feed and clothe a sizable population of well-dressed embezzlers. Experienced traders on the floor of the New York Stock Exchange say that they can see mergers and takeovers reflected on the ticker tape several hours, sometimes several days, before the public announcement. The Securities and Exchange Commission in March 1987 published a study of 172 tender offers brought to the markets between 1981 and 1985; in every instance abnormal rises in stock prices (of between 39 and 50 percent) occurred three weeks before the bid was announced.[31]

How free can a market be if the participants, or a significant number of them, cannot be trusted to behave honestly?

In more measured terms the *Economist* in 1995 surveyed the changes brought to Wall Street by the deregulation of the financial markets in the eighties.

> These days it is hard to describe 'Wall Street' as anything other than an idea, or a set of activities. For one thing, the physical concentration of intermediaries around the narrow Manhattan road stretching from Trinity Church to Water Street and beyond is much less marked than it was 20 years ago, when the tag neatly captured the geography of America's dominant financial marketplace. Today's financial giants, and particularly the small firms which trade in niches in the market, are spread all around lower Manhattan and beyond. Some eschew New York altogether, preferring cheaper New Jersey or the gentler-paced Connecticut . . .
>
> H. L. Mencken, a journalist, once described Wall Street as a 'thoroughfare that begins in a graveyard and ends in a river'. Plenty of observers thinks that this remains apt. After a decade of greed and glory, today's top managers meekly put the emphasis on ethics and responsibilities to customers. The Street's long history of mis-selling and misrepresentation suggests that today's desired qualities are honoured in the breach as they are in the observance. But even if securities firms do betray their own language at times, they are at least talking sense. They have realised that their business can no longer be run as a giant screen behind which customers are ripped off. After all, they look after other people's money.[32]

If only the directors of Barings Bank had remembered that!

The City of London is geographically quite clearly delineated, 779 acres bounded by ancient monuments and police barriers to deter terrorists. It is on the site of the Roman settlement Londinium which became a mediaeval town, a safe port and a home for merchants. It is curious that a city which owes its existence to the fact that people wanted to trade goods which they had created – real objects being bought and sold – has become a centre where ideas (notional money) are traded – or speculated or gambled – in the pursuit of profit. (Victor Sperandeo, a market wizard, made the distinction that, 'Gambling involves taking a risk when the odds are against you . . . Successful speculation implies taking risks when the odds are in your favour.'[33])

This progress, if progress it is, came from two ideas which were successful because from them flowed wealth and status. These are the ideas that a gentleman does not engage in trade, and that the task and the pastime of aristocrats is to gamble.

The transition from trading goods to trading money was slow, and there are many in the city today who would argue that they are intimately connected to the reality of trade in goods. A test to see if they actually are would be to see if they would have their portrait painted in the style favoured by eighteenth-century merchants. In such portraits the sitter is surrounded by the tools of his trade – account books, ledgers, gold and coins. These objects were both a sign of the sitter's pride in his work and a warning about the transience of life. By the nineteenth century such paintings of merchants are very rare. Instead, the sitter is accompanied only by the accoutrements of a gentleman – elegant clothes and furnishing suggesting fine inherited possessions. (No gentleman ever has to buy furniture. He inherits it from his family.)

The idea that a gentleman does not engage in trade is still alive and well. Publishing was seen as a gentleman's profession, trade is not. There still are English publishers who publish books but don't sell them. Unfortunately for their authors, their books rarely make it to the bookshop shelves and the public has few ways of discovering these books' existence. A book might be a wondrous creation while you're in the process of creating it, but once it is complete it becomes a product which needs to be sold.

Because engaging in trade was considered a mark of inferiority, engineering, so basic to manufacturing, has never enjoyed the same status in the UK as do the other professions. Anthony Sampson, in his study of Britain published in 1992, quotes Sir Monty Finniston, an outspoken Scots-Jewish metallurgist: 'In Germany or America engineers are regarded as right at the top, next door to doctors; but here we find that engineers are rated below male models.' Yet, as Christopher Lewinton, the chairman of Tube Investments said, 'Unless you make something and sell it, no wealth has been created.'[34]

When successful merchants, having made their money, wanted to become gentlemen, and gentlemen wanted money but not to have to work for it, there was a meeting of minds which created a financial centre uninterested in manufacture. Many enterprises, respectable and dubious, were glad to have a lord or duke on their board of directors, and many lords and dukes were glad to accept a director's fee. This respectability of the City made it an ideal place to launder dirty money. Many a Russian grown rich since the end of the USSR has cause to be grateful for the veil of respectability the City has been able to draw over the proceeds of his nefarious dealings back home. Indeed the City has always been useful to people whose affairs might not withstand an inspection in the clear light of day.

In the eighteenth and nineteenth century Britain changed from an agriculture based economy to one based on manufacturing. The money that made this change possible did not come from the City, its members lacking as they did an interest in manufacture. The Industrial Revolution was funded partly by the slave trade, which was based in Bristol and Liverpool, and partly by the manufacturers' own money and what they could raise from family and friends or borrow from overseas banks.

The City had other fish to fry. The stock exchange in the eighteenth century was chiefly engaged in raising money for the government to fight a series of very expensive wars. These wars were chiefly about extending Britain's influence and security and securing trade routes, but also about the notions of fame and glory which were used to delude people into thinking that dying for your country was infinitely better than making something which gave sustenance and pleasure.

In the nineteenth century the City very much concentrated on financing world trade, that is, lending money overseas. Of course this meant that, when these overseas sources were threatened, something had to be done to save them. Hence the Boer War in South Africa, which was about the control of the goldfields, a war whose cruel consequences are still being felt today. Needless to say, these wars were conducted behind a screen of patriotic fervour, and none were more patriotic than the gentlemen of the City. How different the UK's economic history would have been had such patriotism included practical co-operation with manufacturers!

The conditions of life place great restraints on us. You can't turn the clock back, or be in two places at once, and if you don't die young you grow old and die. However, the restraints which limit us the most are those we create for ourselves when we invent an idea and then regard this construction as an absolute law or an absolute truth which must never be broken or denied. The idea that the class into which you were born must preclude you from gaining knowledge which is grounded in reality is just plain silly. It's very easy to create theories about other people's work, but if you don't actually experience what goes on in such work your theories are very likely to be totally wrong.

I was working in the National Health Service when, in the eighties, the Conservative government decided to abandon the idea that this organization provided a service to the public and replaced it with the idea that it ran a business. In came a flock of managers convinced that they knew all they needed to know about what health care professionals did. They set about re-organizing without actually finding out what it was that we did. The pain, confusion, frustration, anger and misunderstandings that followed were immense. Fortunately, there were some managers whose modesty matched their good sense. They took the time to learn about how the service actually functioned, not just about the explicit rules and organization but about the implicit rules and organization. Only then could there be efficient, productive co-operation between service providers and service managers.

There is no practical reason why the trade in those ideas we call money should be divorced from the activities of making and selling objects which sustain and enhance our lives. There is no reason why the profits from the money market can't be invested in industry, except the reasons of desiring a quick profit and being unable to tolerate the uncertainty involved in the long-term investments which industry needs if it is to flourish. The inability of many of the players in the City to tolerate the uncertainty engendered by change was shown in the hiring in 1993 and firing in 1996 of Michael Lawrence as Chief Executive of the Stock Exchange. All he wanted to do was to improve the efficiency of the stock market by changing the method of trading shares. 'Mr Lawrence's supporters,' reported the *Financial Times*, 'say his dismissal is a symptom of market makers responding to a reduction of their power. "They love the old system and they want nothing to threaten it. If they are allowed to win, it will throttle change," says one.'[35]

A desire for a quick reward and an inability to tolerate uncertainty are evidence of immaturity. A mature person sees change as opportunity and can exercise patience in the pursuit of enlightened self interest. Of course, any apologist for the City can advance excellent economic reasons why the City should do what it does, but how much are these sound economic reasons and how much are they an example of that most readily available defence we can all use when we are terrified, the defence of intellectualization?

This is one reason why we should always be wary of experts.

The Experts

The ancient Chinese philosopher Chung Tzu was somewhat sceptical of experts.

> If an expert does not have some problem to vex him, he is unhappy!
> If a philosopher's teaching is never attacked, he pines away!
> If critics have no one on whom to exercise their spite, they are unhappy.
> All such men are prisoners in the world of objects.

> He who wants followers, seeks political power.
> He who wants reputation, holds an office . . .
> Where would a gardener be if there were no more weeds?
> What would becomes of business without a market of fools?[36]

We all like to be an expert on something. Being an expert does wonders for our self-confidence. But we need to remember how limited and partial our expertise can be. Scientists, when they talk about an area of scientific expertise, usually hedge their statements with 'possibly', 'perhaps' and 'approximately'. Because they deal with the world of objects, be they as large as the universe or as small as a particle, and the world of objects is something we can never know directly but only through our constructions about it, scientists are well aware (or should be) that everything they know is an approximation, and that the world of objects is likely to let them know if their approximations are markedly wrong. Their experiments won't turn out the way they expect.

Others of us are experts about what people do, and this is quite different from studying the world of objects. People do what they do, not because their actions are the outcome of some physical changes which can be expressed in the form of a scientific law, but because they have interpreted a situation in a particular way. It is not what happens to us which determines what we do but how we interpret what has happened to us. No two people interpret a situation in exactly the same way.

The market is an arena where untold billions of interpretations are enacted. The experts on the market are engaged in trying to guess what these interpretations are and whether these interpretations will form some kind of predictable pattern. The experts' interpretations of other people's interpretations form theories which are expressed in the language of an area of expertise which the expert has learned to use. Thus economists use the language of economics, politicians the language of politics, managers the language of business, and traders the language of trading.

Traders

Traders, in one form or another, have been around for many years, but most UK residents weren't very aware of them until 16 September 1992, when the currency market traders forced the Conservative government to admit defeat and take the UK out of the European Exchange Rate Mechanism.

On that particular night I ate my dinner in my hotel room so I could see the drama as it unfolded on television. All the preceding week we had been treated to sights of John Major standing firm (shades of Dunkirk and Winston Churchill), shoulder to shoulder with his Chancellor, Norman Lamont. However, on that night John Major disappeared into the safety of 10 Downing Street, while poor Norman had to run the gauntlet of reporters and television cameras as he scurried between Downing Street and the Treasury.

Interspersed with these unedifying sights of the Chancellor in flight were pictures of young men, in front of computers, phones clamped to their ears, yelling and shouting in a frenzy.

It was the frenzy of sharks circling their prey. To stay in the ERM the pound had to maintain a certain price, but the traders had decided that the pound was overvalued. The markets were selling pounds and the prices was dropping. The only buyer was the Treasury. After years of telling us that the UK couldn't afford a good health service or good education for our children, the Treasury was hurling money into the markets in amounts which took our breath away. The then shadow chancellor, Gordon Brown, later said that the Labour Party's City advisers had calculated that the defence of the pound cost the Treasury between £1.3 and £1.7 billion. John Major insisted that the amount could not be calculated.[37]

Whatever the amount the Treasury, and thereby the country, had lost, everyone was now aware of these traders who wielded more power than the government and were motivated by nothing but a desire for profits. Denis Healey, no doubt glad that when he'd been chancellor he hadn't become their prey, called them 'a mafia of gilded young lemmings'.[38] David Austin drew them in their favourite haunt, a wine bar.[39]

We were learning all about their champagne tastes and huge salaries and bonuses. The media were hard at work explaining them to us. We saw them at the computers and in funny jackets on the trading floor. We became even more keenly aware that they'd had a great time during the boom years of the eighties, that it was a man's world where women were given a bad time, that they had to make split-second decisions, lived with high tension, and that they soon became too old and slow and had to retire. Our hearts did not bleed for them.

Other people outside the UK were kinder. Gregory J. Millman, in *Around the World on a Trillion Dollars a Day*, described how, 'Like bounty hunters in the Old West, the traders enforce the economic law, not for love of law, but for profit. They have only one goal – making money . . . For better or worse, since the collapse of the Bretton Woods international monetary order, traders provide the only financial discipline the world knows. They are financial vigilantes. Because governments could not provide financial law and order, traders took the law into their own hands. They sell protection at a price . . . [They are] the vandals, the agents of creative destruction. They have mastered the science of risk, won the power, survived the disasters, and now they rule, in their inconstant and relative way, all of the world's wealth.'[40]

New though traders might be, some ideas reinvent themselves forever, and what is more durable than the male idea of war? Every army has its officers, men who have status, knowledge, power, prestige and the best equipment, and the footsloggers who have hardship, dirt, and the opportunity for that kind of glory which makes a man a real man. In such a tradition, amongst the traders are the footsloggers who'll be footslogging all their life, footsloggers who graduate to being officers, officers who are prepared to run the risk of the footsloggers' derision to do what the footsloggers do, and officers who stay behind the lines and plan the strategies. If Sharpe, the fictional hero of the Duke of Wellington's army, were alive today, he'd have started his career on the floor of LIFFE.

The lads on the trading floor are rough, tough and merciless to those they define as outsiders or the enemy. 'They are amazingly quick with figures,' Buddy told me, 'but they can't deal with abstract ideas beyond the figures.' This would prevent them from moving into what Buddy does, trading in futures and options, a task which requires the ability to think abstractly about a number of variables.

The trading floor, like much of the rest of the City, is a male province, and, as usually happens when men get together in groups, women become the enemy. Any woman who ventures near or on to the trading floor takes a great risk. When in 1994 a woman broker charged her former employer with sexual harassment, Buddy remarked, 'After three years of trading on the floors in London and New York I think that the idea of identifying sexual harassment is like finding salt in the water in the Pacific.'

When I showed Buddy this diagram of a currency dealer's head[41] he said, 'What's missing is an area for foul behaviour.'

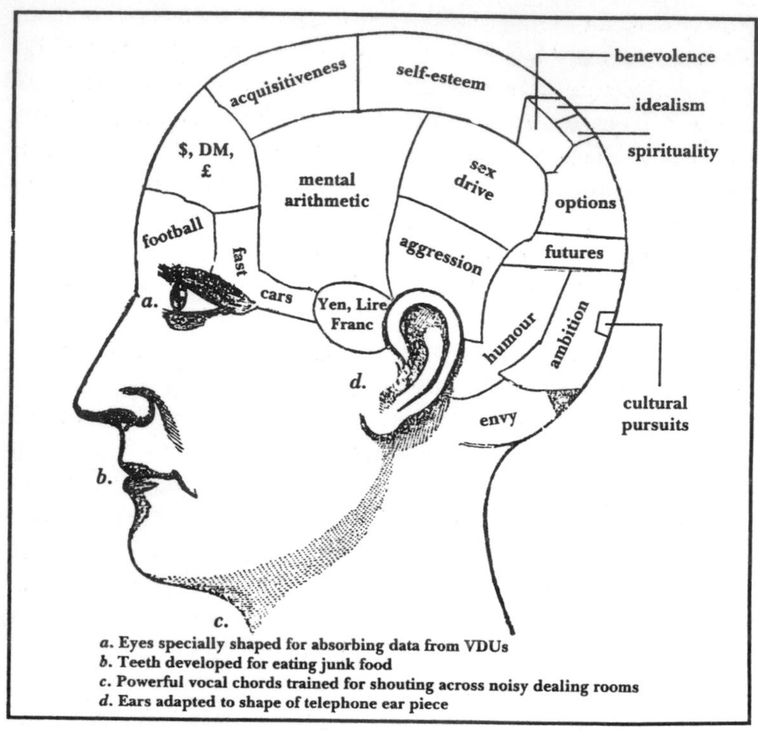

a. Eyes specially shaped for absorbing data from VDUs
b. Teeth developed for eating junk food
c. Powerful vocal chords trained for shouting across noisy dealing rooms
d. Ears adapted to shape of telephone ear piece

Buddy had taken me on a tour of LIFFE, but too quickly for me to appreciate its subtle nuances. In gratitude for all his help I gave him a book of Tony Harrison's poems which, so I told him, he might enjoy dipping into when he was at work and the floor was quiet.

He thought that was a great idea. 'If you do anything even slightly intellectual it is received with complete disregard and a procedure to discourage the activity. It would be mostly verbal, likely to be some repetitious remark that would be repeated to the end of the day. Sometimes when people make a mistake the repetitious behaviour goes on for weeks. There was a guy on the floor who wears a trading mnemonic JAC and last August he made the mistake of making an offhand remark in the pit that he thought he was a very good broker. He was tagged immediately as Jac the Star Trader, and every time Jac comes into the pit people stop what they're doing and clap and scream for Jac. People would actually leave the pit and allow him to stand there in isolation because he was so much better than them. They would worship him, and they made large yellow stars that said Jac the Star Trader and they'd wave them. Then someone went out and bought him a trophy and presented it to him at lunch.

'There's a real herd mentality in the way people dress. The exchange has a relatively strict dress code, but it is nothing to that enforced by people in the pit. You'd never ever wear a bow tie to the floor for fear that people would sing the circus song to you all day long. You'd never wear brown shoes, or brown trousers, you'd never wear a bad shirt/tie combination because people would call you "Goodfellas" all day long. People don't want to step out of the herd. If someone does seem to have stepped out they put cardboard things on that person, a hat on their head or a shark fin on their back and then get them to believe that it's really somebody else that's got something on them. That's when the hilarity really begins. They try to distract the person and get him to believe that someone else has something stuck on them. The worst thing you can do is to point out to the person that they've been decorated with the cardboard because then you become the target of the attack because you are considered a grass and people will make snake hissing sounds at you for the remainder of the day. If somebody speaks in a funny way everybody imitates the way he speaks. When I was trading in New York there was a trader with a deep, gravelly voice and when he came on the floor everyone talked in a deep, gravelly voice. The clerks take a lot of flack. A favourite trick is to get the clerk to step into the pit where they're not allowed to be and all the others get around him and won't let him out.'

Officials get a bad time too. 'There are electronic signals to delineate different trading periods. Then a horn was introduced to mark each fifteen-minute period. For the first week or so the traders would start to stamp their feet, clap their hands, then go dead silent just before the horn. On the last one on the Friday there was confetti thrown everywhere. On the Monday morning there was a message on the message board saying that anyone who cheers will be fined, so on the very first horn everybody booed. There are fines for bad language and for fights. These are usually just one punch sort of thing. There's about one fight a month. The worst thing you can do is to get drawn into a verbal confrontation because it will go on endlessly. At present they're into football kicking. Someone makes a ball and they try to kick it out of the pit. As soon as an official confiscates it another is made. This only happens when the market is slow. When the market's busy there's no time for that. The smell of the pit is unbelievable. There's one guy in the options pit who can clear the pit. It's so foul you could not believe it. Then it's "Who farted? What died?" The farting isn't aggressive but a complete disregard for others. In the afternoon there's an awful smell of beer and cigarettes.'

This behaviour has a purpose. 'In the way you trade, if you are outside the little core group of people, it's harder to do the business. It's a matter of who plays around and jokes together in the pit. People are included or excluded according to whether they've chummed up with others. It's a high stress environment. There are periods when you're euphoric and periods when you're battered.'

I asked Buddy about the background of these traders. He said, 'The average age would be twenty-five. You have to be eighteen to trade. The age range would be twenty to thirty-five. A lot are school leavers with an O level or GCSE. I don't know anybody in my pit with a university education. The people are bright but have not had the education. Most are unbelievably quick with figures. They get the job by being brought in by somebody – a brother or a friend. There are large sums of money being dealt with, so you need someone you know.'

There is the occasional touch of humanity. 'If someone had a tragedy there'd be a display of support on the floor. They stopped the Exchange as a mark of respect for those killed in the Dunblane shooting. There wasn't a sound and afterwards I could see people had been affected by it. They took up a large collection. Otherwise personal lives don't come into the pit very much, though it might if you'd started to date someone or gone home with a woman. That would be commented on.'

The behaviour in the pit is not unlike the behaviour of young men in army barracks and undergoing training. It's about reducing tension, dealing with fear and forging alliances.

In the past all the financial and commodity markets had a trading floor, but the advances in world-wide communications and the advent of computers brought great changes. Markets were receiving an increasing amount of information and computers could collate and present that information more efficiently than could a person with pen and paper. Earlier this century in the New York Stock Exchange clerks recorded prices with white chalk on blackboards for the brokers to read. Now Dow Jones Industrial Averages are updated every second on computers. The currency markets now require footsloggers with an education, and so many university graduates familiar with computers, quick with figures and able to work in noise and tension became currency traders.

Trading, whether in currency, commodities, or futures and options, requires more than following the rule, 'Buy cheap and sell dear.' How do you know what is going to become dear? What is needed is some way of turning the vast array of today's prices into some form which will predict tomorrow's prices. For decades investment managers and analysts have been studying company balance sheets in the hope of finding useful predictors, but to no great avail. Analysts and investment managers have never found an effective way of beating the market. Now the hope of doing this is seen to lie in the market figures themselves.

Which group of people understands figures? Mathematicians. So the big banks and investment houses went looking for mathematicians. They found them in university ivory towers, or launching satellites, or creating guidance systems for smart bombs. They became that branch of traders called 'rocket scientists'.

The only way we human beings can understand anything is to look at something and decide that it looks like something else. Earlier in this chapter when I wanted to convey to you, the reader, something of my understanding of how traders operated, I likened them to an army. Similarly, when mathematicians and physicists started to examine market prices, they sought an understanding which was not in the prices themselves but in something which physicists and mathematicians study, the movement of particles.

Particles move in a seemingly random fashion, but there may be an underlying pattern, hence the analogy to prices.

Much of the theory which has provided a basis for the trade in derivatives is that created by Fischer Black, a mathematician and physicist, who likened the changes in prices (called volatility) to the movement of pollen grains when they are suspended in water. This is called the Brownian motion after the Scottish botanist Robert Brown who discovered it in 1827. His French contemporary Joseph Fourier, a mathematician, developed a form of calculus for the analysis of events which have many causes, called stochastic calculus. With his colleague Myron Scholes, Fischer Black devised a theory of volatility which underpins the Black-Scholes pricing model. Many of the complex formulas for valuing options are derived from this model. In the USA options had been banned in 1933 but the Black-Scholes model, developed in the seventies and showing the potential of options for limiting risk, was instrumental in influencing the US Commodity Futures Trading Commission to allow options to be traded again.[42] Fischer Black became a partner in the investment bank Goldman Sachs.

However, it was known that theory had gaps which could lead to an underestimate of risk. More recently, Christian Walter, an actuary working in Paris, read an account of the work being done by a group of French physicists led by Jean-Philippe Bouchard on the movement of molecules of detergent, and was struck by the similarity between these movements and that of prices. Out of this has come the Bouchard-Sornette theory, which uses some research from pure mathematics and seems to have a particular relevance for emerging markets as compared to established markets.

All this seems to be a world away from the inanities and obscenities of the trading floor, but the footsloggers and the rocket scientists are all part of an enormous and powerful whole. Consider the question which the *Guardian* asked in 1993: 'Question: What is the difference between Tanzania and Goldman Sachs? Answer: One is an African country which makes $2.2 billion a year and shares it among 25 million people. The other is an investment bank that makes $2.6 billion and shares most of it between 161 people.'[43]

There was a time when many people believed that if the government managed the country's economy well, and the bosses and workers were honest and did their best, there would be a stable currency and people would be able to plan for the future. Manufacturers would know what prices they would be paying for raw materials, and workers would have secure pensions. Such a way of living is no longer possible. Currency prices are determined by traders, and manufacturers have to do the best they can to protect themselves from changes. A government might raise interest rates to encourage saving, or lower them to encourage house buyers, but traders turn changes in interest rates to their advantage. In the 1970s American products sold fairly cheaply and well all round the world. 'In the early 1980s, as American interest rates rose, traders poured massive amounts of capital into the American markets, bidding up the price of the dollar. Because the dollar became more expensive, American tractors, cars, machine tools, and many other products became most expensive too. Journalists coined the term "Rust Bowl" to describe the effect on once thriving American manufacturing centres.'[44]

These financial vigilantes, like the Ferengi of *Star Trek*, seem to be motivated solely by the desire for profit, a state of mind inimical to introspection. Yet curiously, of recent years many of these traders have begun a search for self-knowledge with a degree of passion and modesty greater than that possessed by many psychologists and psychiatrists whose professions should be devoted to self-knowledge. What accounts for the difference is that in psychology and psychiatry self-knowledge brings no increase in earnings, whereas amongst many traders there is the belief that it leads to higher profits.

Self-knowledge might be their last hope of finding a foolproof way of predicting the market. Analyses of company balance sheets do not yield reliable predictions, and charting prices has limited applications. The theories of Black-Scholes and Bouchard-Sornette did not produce immediate, reliable results. So now the question being asked is, 'Is predicting the market a matter of studying price changes or is it a matter of studying how a trader trades?'

Is the trader part of the problem? If so, he must be part of the solution.

This had always been Terence's view. 'How you bid,' he said, 'is a mirror of you.' When a young trader joined Terence's organization Terence always told him, 'Trading is the oldest and most basic dynamic through which money is created and transferred. Trading is not about the technical systems. Strategic trading systems, computer trading systems, these are all clerical tools which you use, but what you do is based on what you already know about yourself and your soul. Trading is really an intro-psychological exercise because all of these various tools result in a decision, a financial decision.'

Terence stressed finance because 'the best money makers are those people who know that they love money. They love the way it feels, they love the way it looks. They have enormous respect for how it is created and how it is put through the system.'

Ed Seykota, a market wizard, identified a winning trader as someone who loves to trade and wants to win. When Jack Schwager queried this, 'Don't all traders want to win?' Ed explained:

> Win or lose, everybody gets what they want out of the market. Some people seem to like to lose, so they win by losing money. I know one trader who seems to get in near the start of every substantial bull market and works his $10 thousand up to about a quarter of a million in a couple of months. Then he changes his personality and loses it all back again. This process repeats like clockwork. Once I traded with him, but got out when his personality changed. I doubled my money, while he was wiped out as usual. I told him what he was doing, and even paid him a management fee. He just couldn't help himself. I don't think he can do it any differently. He wouldn't want to. He gets a lot of excitement, he gets to be a martyr, he gets sympathy from his friends, and he gets to be the centre of attention. Also, possibly, he may be more comfortable relating to people if he is on their financial plane. On some level, I think, he is getting what he really wants.[45]

Martyrdom is a very popular game and can be played in every walk of life. I've had the opportunity to talk to many martyrs – wives and mothers, men who, as one of them said, always manage 'to snatch failure out of the jaws of success'.[46] These are all people who would rather be good than happy. They feel that they are, in essence, so bad and unacceptable that they do not deserve to win. Being successful they find frightening because they have been given something they don't deserve, and they should be punished for their hubris. If they fear other people's envy, and feel close to other people only when other people comfort them, they refuse to be separated from their suffering.

Another group of people who have not put happiness as their top priority are those who would rather be right than happy. Bill Lipschutz warned traders to avoid the temptation of wanting to be completely right.[47] Wanting to be right arises from a fundamental insecurity about one's worth and ability to make sense of what is happening. People who value and accept themselves have a far higher tolerance of uncertainty than those who don't. Wanting to be right and wanting to be seen as right always leads to disaster because life always turns out to be different from what we expect, and reality never conforms to our wishes.

Having published two books about his interviews with successful market traders Jack Schwager concluded,

> 'We has met the enemy, and it is us.'
>
> The famous quote from Walt Kelly's cartoon strip, 'Pogo', would provide as fitting a one-line summation of the art of trading as any. Time and time again, those whom I interviewed for this book and its predecessor stressed the absolute critical role of psychological elements in trading success. When asked to explain what was important to success, the Market Wizards never talked about indicators or techniques, but rather about such things as discipline, emotional control, patience, and mental attitude towards losing. The message is clear: The key to winning in the markets is internal, not external.[48]

Gil Blake pointed out that, 'Trading puts pressure on weaker human traits and seems to seek out each individual's Achilles heel.'[49] This is because, as Victor Sperandeo said, 'There is no other profession where you have to admit you were wrong . . . In trading you can't hide your failures. Your equity provides a daily reflection of your performance. The trader who tries to blame his failures on external events will never learn from his mistakes. For a trader, rationalization is a guaranteed road to ultimate failure.'[50]

What a trader needs is courage. There's an old Wall Street saying, 'Scared money never wins.' Bill Lipschutz, having listed intelligence and extreme commitment as essential to a trader, went on to speak about courage. 'It's not enough to simply have the insight to see something apart from the rest of the crowd, you also need to have the courage to act on it and to stay with it. It's very difficult to be different from the rest of the crowd the majority of the time, which by definition is what you're doing if you're a successful trader.'[51]

Of course it is much more difficult for an extravert, someone who experiences their sense of existence in relation to other people, to be different from the crowd than for an introvert, whose sense of existence is maintained by a sense of achievement and being in control. The introvert's Achilles heel is the fear of chaos. Every trader ought to be clear about which he fears the most, being abandoned and rejected or being overwhelmed by chaos.

James B. Rogers Jr talked about a rare quality, common sense. 'Good investing is really just common sense. But it is astonishing how few people have common sense – how many people can look at the exact same scenario, the exact same facts and not see what is going to happen. Ninety per cent of them will focus on the same thing, but the good investor – or trader to use your term – will see something else. The ability to get away from conventional wisdom is not very common.'[52]

It is not just a matter of having sufficient intelligence. It's a particular kind of mind, according to Gil Blake. 'A critical ingredient is a maverick mind. It's also important to have a blend between an artistic side and a scientific side. You need the artistic side to imagine, discover, and create trading strategies. You need the scientific side to translate those ideas into firm trading rules and to execute those rules.'[53]

There is also the matter of being able to deal with pain. William Eckhardt, talking about those who survive as traders and those who don't, said, 'The people who survive avoid snowball scenarios in which bad trades cause them to become emotionally destabilized and make more bad trades. They are also able to feel the pain of losing. If you don't feel the pain of loss, then you're in the same position of those unfortunate people who have no pain sensors. If they leave their hand on a hot stove it will burn off. There's no way to survive in this world without pain. Similarly, if the losses don't hurt, your financial survival is tenuous. I know a few multimillionaires who started trading with inherited wealth. In each case they lost it all because they didn't feel the pain when they were losing. In those formative first few years of trading, they felt they could afford to lose.'[54]

William Eckhardt also stressed the addictive dangers of trading. 'When behavioural psychologists have compared the relative addictiveness of various reinforcement schedules, they found that random reinforcement – positive and negative dispensed randomly (for example, the rat doesn't know whether it will get pleasure or pain when it hits the bar) – is the most addictive alternative of all, more addictive than positive reinforcement only. Intermittent reinforcement describes the experience of the compulsive gambler as well as the futures trader. The difference is that, just perhaps, the trader can make money. However, as with most of the "affective" aspects of commodity trading, its addictiveness constantly threatens ruin. Addictiveness is the reason why so many players who make fortunes leave the game broke.'[55]

Intermittent or partial reinforcement works when we allow hope to triumph over experience. Many people remain tied to someone who hurts them because they cannot give up the hope that one day the cruel person will give them limitless, unconditional love. The chances of this happening are likely to be the same as the chances of the market giving a trader limitless, unconditional success, but many people prefer to hope and suffer than give up hope and be happy.

In all, it comes down to a matter of understanding yourself. Randy McKay spoke of how important this is in terms of selecting the right way to trade. 'It is remarkably common for traders to adopt methods entirely unsuited to their personalities. There are traders who are good at system development but end up consistently overriding and interfering with their own systems, with disastrous results. There are traders who are naturally inclined toward developing long-term strategies but end up trading short term because of impatience or a compulsion to "do something". There are naturally born floor traders who abandon their area of expertise and become mediocre portfolio managers. And there are the theoretically oriented individuals who develop intricate, low-risk arbitrage strategies but then decide to become position traders – an approach that may require a degree of risk acceptance far beyond their comfort levels in order to be applied successfully.'[56]

Know yourself and accept yourself seems to be the formula for a successful trader. Mark Douglas, once a successful commodities broker and now head of Trading Behavior Dynamics, Inc., wrote *The Disciplined Trader*, 'a comprehensive guide to understanding the psychology of self-discipline and personal transformation needed to become a successful stock or futures trader.'[57]

He emphasized self-knowledge, self-acceptance and self-discipline in a context very similar to that in which I work.

> The meaning that you place on any particular price change is the result of your beliefs. As a trader you constantly have to define what is high and what is low relative to your beliefs about the future. That is the only way you can make money: buy low and sell it back at a higher price (in the future) or sell high and buy it back at a lower price (in the future). As long as prices continue to move, that movement will create opportunities to buy low and sell high or sell high and buy low, and these opportunities are available for all traders. *You create the game in your own mind based on your beliefs, intents, perceptions, and rules.* It is your own unique perspective and no one else's and the secret is, you can do and choose how you perceive events. Even if you are not aware of exactly how to control and change your perception to make other choices available to yourself, you are still choosing, even if it is out of ignorance.[58]

However, what Mark Douglas is promising is far in excess of anything I would promise. In his final note he says, 'The more positive you feel about yourself, the more abundance that will naturally flow your way as a by-product of those positive feelings. So, in essence, to give yourself more money as a trader you need to identify, change or decharge anything in your mental environment that doesn't contribute to the highest degree of self-valuation that is possible.'[59]

What Mark Douglas is stating here is a reworking of the belief that we live in a Just World where goodness is rewarded and badness punished. Here he defines 'good' as 'feeling positive about yourself'. Feel positive about yourself and success as a trader will follow as night the day.

Alas, this is not so. Certainly feeling positive about yourself is likely to make you a better trader. When we don't value and accept ourselves we spend most of our time thinking about ourselves – 'I'm useless', 'Will that person like me?', 'Have I done that properly?' When we do value and accept ourselves we don't have to spend time and energy absorbed in ourselves and instead we can look outwards and learn more about what is going on around us.

Moreover, when we don't value and accept ourselves we are always frightened of other people in case they see how bad and unacceptable we are and reject us. Thus we never get to know and understand other people. When we do value and accept ourselves we are not frightened of other people. We get to know them and, unless they are absorbed in disliking themselves, they get to like us.

When we don't value and accept ourselves we are so absorbed in ourselves that we fail to notice much of what is going on around us. We are not interested in anything that happens that does not have us as its centre of interest. When we do value and accept ourselves we find the world interesting, even those parts of it where we play no part. Thus we acquire information and experience which can be very useful to us.

However, feeling positive about yourself isn't going to stop the European Union from getting its act together and forming a single currency, thus throwing thousands of currency traders out of work. It isn't going to stop another Nick Leeson toppling another bank. It isn't going to stop the Tokyo earthquake, or the next war in the Middle East. Feeling positive about yourself doesn't have some magical control over the market.

Feeling positive about yourself will give you courage when things go against you, but if you believe that because you're positive about yourself you must be successful you have written yourself a recipe for disaster. When things go against you, you either blame yourself for the disaster ('If I'd been really good this wouldn't have happened') or you blame others (people, the government, God) for denying you your just deserts. You can choose between being depressed or being paranoid, or you can enjoy the delights of both.

All valuing and accepting yourself does is that it enables you to live comfortably with yourself and other people. Is that way of living advantageous to trading?

Economists

Once when I was in Sydney I spent an afternoon with Edna Carew, an extremely knowledgeable financial journalist who watches the shenanigans of the financial world with a sharp eye and writes about them with a dry wit. In her book *The Language of Money* she defined economists:

> Various definitions of economists have been advanced. They have been described at times in terms of grey suits and grey minds. Another suggestion is that an economist is 'someone who can draw a mathematically precise line from an unwarranted assumption to an incomprehensible conclusion'. Cynics have proposed 'soothsayer' or 'witchdoctor'.
>
> For centuries many economists have created and enveloped themselves in a mystique marked by a proliferation of models, theories and jargon which explain some of the facts of life; in this process, they have tended to align themselves with schools of thought, many of whom disagree, often bitterly, about causes and effects.[60]

(The more that is known about a subject, the less the controversy about it.)

In her definition of economics Edna Carew said, 'It is often described by those who have studied it as commonsense, but for the uninitiated it is crammed with jargon and shrouded in mystique. Just as you think you have come to grips with economics, an economist will change the answers to the question.'[61]

The problem is that, when a group of people with academic qualifications get together and call themselves something ending in 'ist' and claim that their common pursuit is science, they lead other people to expect that their pronouncements will have the accuracy and predictive power of the science of physics. But of course their pronouncements do not have these qualities, because observing the behaviour of matter, which is what physicists do, is very different from observing the behaviour of people, which is what economists, sociologists, psychiatrists and psychologists do. People behave in many and various ways, while matter in its different forms has a limited range of behaviour. When matter is behaving it is not considering various options and deciding on one. It behaves in accordance with the conditions pertaining to the situation of which it is part. The behaviour of people is not a response to the conditions pertaining to their situation, but to how they have interpreted these conditions. These interpretations arise from the hopes, fears, attitudes, prejudices, beliefs, needs and wishes each person has brought to the situation.

Real scientists (the ones who study matter) are usually very modest. When questioned about their work they define very carefully the limited area of their expertise. There are a few power-mad and/or publicity-seeking scientists who claim to know the mind of God (such a claim sells books), but on the whole scientists don't claim that they can explain absolutely everything. Whereas economists, sociologists, psychiatrists and psychologists do. They mightn't be too hot on nuclear physics but on what really matters – what people do and the future of the world – they are the experts. Ask them anything and they'll have an answer.

They can give you the big picture and the little picture. Sociologists look at huge groups and at small groups, psychiatrists look at national groups and huge groups of people called schizophrenics and depressives and individual people (patients), and psychologists divide their subject into social psychology and individual psychology. Economists have macro-economics and micro-economics.

Paul Ormerod, an economist and successful businessman, has let his side down badly by writing *The Death of Economics* where he is highly critical of what economists do. He wrote,

> The ability of orthodox economics to understand the workings of the economy at the overall level – the macro-level in the technical sense – is manifestly weak (some would say entirely non-existent). This is not to say that the subject is a completely empty box. At the detailed level – the micro-level – economics might be able to

> offer certain insights. In terms of understanding the impact of various taxes and subsidies, designed to deter or encourage the consumption of particular goods or services, a combination of theory and applied work can sometimes be useful. It is when economics strays from the particular into the general that its weaknesses are exposed more ruthlessly.[62]

The function of science is to explain and to predict. Anything that happens can be explained in an infinite number of ways. One way of deciding whether one explanation is better than another is to see how accurate a prediction can be derived from each explanation. Given A, B and C, will X then follow? Scientists know that they are getting close to reality when their experiments turn out in the way they predict. In economics it isn't easy to set up experiments where the experimenter determines the starting conditions of the experiment, but economists believe that they can identify the relevant conditions (called variables), measure them, and, on the basis of their theory, or model as they like to call it, predict what will happen.

If economists are good at predicting what will happen, why aren't they all billionaires?

Perhaps they are too selfless to use their knowledge for their own private gain. In which case they would want to benefit others, and what could be more beneficial than the economists at the Treasury helping the Chancellor and the government to do their very best for the country?

When Denis Healey was Chancellor in 1974 the Treasury forecast for the public sector borrowing requirement was £4 billion too low. In 1976 it was £2 billion too high. In a BBC Radio 4 programme called *Economics Is Bunk*, Lord Healey said that as Chancellor,

> You cannot rely on any of the statistics you get. If I'd had accurate figures, for example, for our balance of payments and our fiscal deficit in 1976, I would never have had to go to the IMF. Even now, even in the hard headed city offices where clever young men who got first class degrees in economics and mathematics are supposed at least to tell you what'll happen in the next twelve months, nobody foresaw the fall of the dollar in this year or the collapse in the bond markets. And this is because the academics

> and the economists, who are supposed to study how the economy works, have simply not caught up with these colossal changes, I mean a world in which a thousand billion dollars a day can go three times around the world in microseconds and ninety eight per cent of those flows are purely speculative. Two per cent of those flows would finance the whole of the world trade in both goods and services.[63]

Economics has been an academic subject for long enough for there to be an orthodoxy about what should be studied. Many of the people who criticize economists point out that by concentrating on things which can be measured economists do not pay attention to much of what is important in life. The Uruguayan poet and historian Eduardo Galeano in his poem 'The Right to Dream' said that in the future,

> Economists will not confuse the standard of living with the level of consumption, nor the quality of life with the quantity of things.[64]

Even when things might be measured they are often ignored because to study them might be embarrassing, dangerous or distasteful. How many economists would want first-hand experience of drug dealers, slave owners, pornographers, pimps or those shady entrepreneurs in the arms trade? But surely these activities play a part in the economy in some way? How can bribery be fitted into a model of supply and demand? A survey by the *Far Eastern Economic Review* found that 'nearly one in three respondents would pay a bribe rather than lose a deal. The least likely to offer a bribe were Australian, 17 per cent of those surveyed, and Hong Kong Chinese (21 per cent). But the survey found that more than half of Indonesians who had responded would resort to a bribe, with 47 per cent of Thais saying payment would be made in preference to losing a sale.'[65] How much does bribery contribute to Thailand's economic growth?

At least some economists, mostly Italian, have looked at the problem of organized crime, but were then met with the economist's usual problem of what model would be appropriate to use. Should the Mafia be considered a family firm producing goods and services, or a form of government which organizes and enforces agreements?[66]

Even when economists have decided what variables should go into their model they then have to work out ways of measuring them. Measurements need to be very accurate because in complex, non-linear models a small error in measurement can produce wildly wrong results. Paul Ormerod pointed out that 'unlike many measurements in the physical sciences, there is no unique way of measuring either the size of an economy at a particular point in time, or its growth over time.'[67]

It might be possible to find a readily available but sensitive measure which is intrinsic to what is being examined. The *Economist* uses the Big Mac index as 'a light-hearted guide to whether currencies are under- or over-valued. It is based on the theory of purchasing power parity – the notion that a dollar should buy the same amount in all currencies.'[68]

Big Macs are universal and so are politics, but how can political factors, which undoubtedly affect the economy, be measured? It isn't just a matter, say, of getting measures on a scale for democracy but of determining the interaction between the politics of a particular government and the attitudes of those it governs. The model of highly authoritarian rule in Singapore which has played a big part in that country's prosperity could hardly be successfully applied in Australia where the natives like to conform to the rule of not conforming, no matter what economic miracle it might bring.

Despite such difficulties, having determined the variables and the way they are to be measured, economists apply their models and come up with forecasts. The results can hardly be said to inspire confidence.

In 1993 the United Nations released their *Trade and Development Report* which

> demonstrates that the heavyweights in the forecasting business – the Organization for Economic Co-operation and Development (OECD), the International Monetary Fund (IMF) and the UN's own conference on Trade and Development (UNCTAD) – have between them hardly scored a direct hit in picking economic growth over the past half-decade . . . The forecasting bodies have consistently missed major economic turning points, especially in the era of financial deregulation. The report notes the forecasters

> failed to pick the significance of big changes in debt, saving and consumption patterns caused by interest-rate volatility – in short, the bust of the late 1980s . . .
>
> The UN report admits that forecasting models tend to rely on inertia and cannot really cope with a climate of rapid change. 'It is at such times that an experienced forecaster has to make an unusually important act of judgement by modifying the model to take account of the effects of the new behaviour, even though there is at first very little quantitative evidence of the magnitude of the effects,' the report says. 'If the record of forecasting is to be improved, it will require not only technical advances in modelling and learning from previous mistakes, but also the experienced intuition that is the privilege of only a small number of experts.'[69]

In May, 1993 Christopher Huhne of the *Independent on Sunday*, announcing the results of his Golden Guru Awards, noted that since he first gave the award in 1986 the number of forecasters had jumped from 12 to 43. What Christopher Huhne called 'the mainstream forecasters' and the Treasury did badly. The two forecasters he singled out for commendation, Patrick Minford of Liverpool University and Wynne Godley of Cambridge, were economists who are 'never afraid to stand outside the pack'. However, forecasters can be right for the wrong reasons.

> Prof Godley's forecasts of high unemployment in the early eighties were right not because output fell by as much as he predicted but because productivity rose by more. In the winning forecast, Prof Minford predicted that output would drop despite a rise in consumer spending of 1.5 per cent in real terms, because investment would drop. In fact, consumer spending was flat and investment fell.
>
> Given the need for forecasting in policy and planning, there is another worrying factor. Someone always produces a good forecast, but it is rarely the same person as before. Even those who are above average are prone to serious lapses. It seems there is still nothing so uncertain as the future.[70]

In 1993 Paul Ormerod noted that 'economic forecasts are the subject of open derision. Throughout the Western world, their accuracy is appalling. Within the past twelve months alone, as this book is being written, forecasters have failed to predict the Japanese recession, the strength of the American recovery, the depth of the collapse in the German economy, and the turmoil in the European ERM.'[71]

Forecasting the economy is a game anyone can play. In 1995 the *Economist*, well able to take a long-term view, published its results of a study begun in 1984 when they 'sent a questionnaire to four ex-finance ministers in OECD economies, four chairmen of multinational firms, four students at Oxford University and four London dustmen. They were each asked to predict economic prospects over the next decade. Final figures for 1994 now allow us to pick the winners.' These were the company chairmen and the dustmen. The *Economist* concluded that 'the contents of dustbins could well be a useful leading economic indicator.'[72]

The Treasury had its 'seven wise men' to advise it, so in 1993 the *Guardian* brought together its seven wise women economists who were also prepared to advise the Treasury. However, the wise women decided to eschew forecasting and instead to identify those questions which needed to be addressed over the next twelve months, questions like 'What form of society do we want?' and 'Should the aim of government policy be to promote growth or should a wider definition of living standards be used?'[73] No doubt the wise women would agree with Samuel Brittan's observation in his review of *The Death of Inflation* by Roger Bootle that 'In truth we just do not have the knowledge to predict historical trends and are never likely to have it.'[74]

(*The Death of Inflation* is the kind of catchy title that publishers like, but it is a nonsense. Inflation is an idea, and ideas don't die. They might become unpopular or be confined to a small group of people, but they can always be rediscovered, smartened up and put into service again. Taking into account J. K. Galbraith's observation that 'the financial memory should be assumed to last, at a maximum, no more than twenty years',[75] I am prepared to predict that, if inflation remains low for long enough for the memory of the high inflation years to fade, someone will be advocating the benefits of inflation.)

Despite all these criticisms, economists do fill an important role which has existed ever since human beings first got together in groups under a leader. Every leader needs a soothsayer. Fashions change in how a soothsayer should conduct himself and frame his utterances. Cynics may have laughed when it was revealed that Nancy Reagan consulted an astrologer and then advised Ronald about his conduct of the country's affairs, but astrologers who specialize in financial and business advice say that they are successful both in their predictions and in what they earn. However, businessmen who want to appear hard-headed can't afford to be seen dabbling in magic, and so in the seventies and eighties it became increasingly fashionable for the soothsayer to be an economist. John Shepperd, chief economist at Yamaichi International in London, said, 'The explosion in the number of economists working in the City suggests that we do add value somewhere along the line. It should be said that many clients will not take seriously the house that does not have an economist.'[76]

As soothsayers have always known, the problem is that when you say your sooth, how do you get people to take any notice? Sir Bryan Hopkin, chief economic adviser to the Wilson government, commented, 'Wynne (Godley) has quite a high opinion of his ability to make advice, but has not been as successful in selling his ideas as Keynes was. Keynes was silver-tongued, Wynne is not. He is not very good at understanding what makes other people think as they do.'[77]

If you can't persuade people to take your advice perhaps you should sell it. One of the arguments used by advocates for private practice in medicine and psychotherapy is that people take more notice of the advice they've paid for than of that they get free. Many of the economists in Australia who had worked in the federal public service in the sixties and seventies set up their own private consultancies in the eighties. Three of these firms became what the *Australian Business Monthly* called 'a powerful new force in Canberra – a kind of government in exile'.[78]

However, to adapt George Bernard Shaw, there's only one thing worse than not having your advice taken and that's having it taken. The *Economist*, springing to the defence of economists and contrasting the great influence of the profession with the derision it attracts, said, 'The chief explanation for the contradictory standing of economics is that although it is economists who produce economic ideas, it is other people who use them. And abuse them.'[79] The abusers are usually politicians.

The abuses much favoured by politicians were listed by the *Economist* as: a one-sided coin, shoot the messenger, and allergy to change. Typically, politicians are unable to understand that every event has good consequences and bad consequences. They claim responsibility for the good consequences and blame their opponents or the economists for the bad. Members of the government, rather than question their own policies, will blame speculators who benefit from changes in the value of the currency. Rather than do the hard work of re-thinking certain issues when conditions change, people, not merely politicians, will lay blame, ignore the evidence and produce illogical arguments.

Like economists, psychologists have often had cause to regret not keeping their ideas to themselves. For instance, I might be asked to explain why certain boys who have been sexually abused in adult life become abusers themselves. My explanation would concern the way in which we can deal with pain by separating ourselves from it, becoming indifferent to it, losing the ability to empathize with other people's pain, and trying to master the memory of a traumatic event by re-enacting it in the role of the victor, not the victim. However, there are many people, politicians, tabloid newspaper editors and guardians of the nation's morals, who cannot distinguish an explanation from an excuse, and I am criticized for excusing the behaviour of a child molester and murderer. Yet had I given an explanation as to how cancer develops, no one would accuse me of being an advocate for cancer.

The histories of economics and of psychology have striking similarities. Both academic disciplines devoted years of effort to proving that they were sciences. They wanted to discover laws which would rank beside the laws of physics, a desire which showed how little they understood their subject-matter. They wanted to reveal the meaning that they believed was hidden in the world. They didn't want to recognize that what they were doing was creating their own meaning as a way of understanding what they had observed.

When I've been teaching clergy and lay members of the Church about depression and fear I have found that a religious upbringing can often impede an understanding of how each of us lives in a world of meaning which we have created. The Church's teaching that when God created the world he filled it with meaning for us to discover has made it difficult for some people, especially those who take their theology seriously, to see that all we can ever know are the meanings we create, and that the meanings we create need to have a relationship to the reality of which we are part but which we can never experience directly.

Thus mathematics is a set of meanings created by mathematicians. Some of these meanings relate reasonably accurately to reality, which is lucky for us otherwise our buildings would fall down and our boats sink. We could argue that mathematics is a set of meanings which are contained in the world and which we can discover, a kind of universal truth existing outside human time and space, but we cannot be sure of this until we discover other sentient creatures from other parts of the universe very different from our own. If they have arrived at the same set of mathematical meanings as we have, then the likelihood of a universal, immanent mathematics is increased, but it is also likely that they, having had a different history from ours, would have arrived at a different way of accounting for the pattern events they observe, especially if their sensory equipment proves to be very different from ours. On this planet there are big differences in sensory equipment among the different species, so it is quite likely that species from other parts of the universe will differ from us, perhaps in ways which we cannot even imagine. Paul Robertson, leader of the Medici String Quartet, in his television series *Music and the Mind*, said,

> In other species, there seems to be no distinction between music and 'language'. For instance, I do not believe we shall ever understand the 'musical language' of whales and dolphins, because their brains are probably expressing their consciousness directly as music, rather than translating experience into an abstract system like human language. We are not equipped to comprehend such outpourings and could certainly never do so in words.[80]

Central to Paul Ormerod's criticism of economics is the way an intellectual orthodoxy has emerged where 'the subject is not taught as a learning to think about how the world *might* operate, but as a set of discovered truths as to how the world *does* operate.'[81] That is, the orthodox economists claim to be revealing immanent, universal truths. When God created the world he built in the law, as stated by Will Hutton, 'Price stability is the absolute precondition for economic good.'[82]

In science, where it is non-sentient matter that is being studied, certain laws can be shown to work time and time again. Build a ship according to a well-tried formula and it will float. But in economics and psychology exceptions can be found to every rule. Low inflation does not always lead to growth in the economy. Not all sexually abused children become adult abusers. Moreover, in economics and psychology theories aren't abandoned because they have been proved wrong. There is simply a change in fashion. Freud's theories used to be all the rage while Jung's were seen as the product of an unworldly nutter. Now Freud is deplored or ignored while Jung is all the rage, especially with those people who talk reverently of 'spirituality' and 'transpersonal'. Maynard Keynes went out of fashion and Milton Friedman became the rage, but now Keynes's theories are increasingly being mentioned, and with some admiration. Economists who talk about the relationship between inflation and growth are not revealing immanent truths but giving guidance which is in some cases wise.

One Japanese economist recognizes that there is a fashion in economic theories. Takamitsu Sawa wrote, 'The prevailing economic theory is the other side of the coin to a country's normative values.' Thus, 'modern economic thought does not represent a steady advance towards a perfect understanding of immutable economic phenomena, but instead is an ideological product of the Western industrial world in a particular phase of its historical development.'[83]

Anyone claiming access to a universal truth is making a bid for power. If I know a universal truth, I am more powerful than you. Moreover, I can claim that knowing a universal truth puts me in touch with even greater powers. Priests, claiming access to universal truths and therefore to God, claim more power than mere mortals. Economists, claiming access to a universal truth, might have access to even greater powers, especially if the economist's particular universal truth gives comfort to those in power. J. K. Galbraith warned, 'If an economist gets too much applause from the affluent, you should always be suspicious. The rich in all countries combine a fairly acute self-interest with an ever-present feeling of anxiety and guilt. Anyone who relieves that anxiety and guilt is assured of applause, and seeking that applause, not the truth, easily becomes a habit.'[84]

Claiming access to universal truth also means that the claimant can ignore the personal meanings that individuals create. This economists and psychologists have done for decades. The most damning thing which could be said about a psychologist's work was that it was subjective. Despite the fact that the physicists, whom economists and psychologists wanted to emulate, had known since 1927 when Werner Heisenberg established his Uncertainty Principle that the experimenter is always part of the experiment, economists and psychologists insisted that they took an objective stance and neither their attitudes nor the perceptions of them by those experimented upon played any part in the outcome of the experiment.

Thus economists saw nothing amiss in the way they separated the economy from social relations, as if we conduct our trades separately from our conduct of relationships. Psychologists balanced such an approach by steadfastly refusing to admit that money played a part in people's lives. How pure-minded such economists must have been, never to have noticed that markets, from street markets to stock exchanges, are rife with prejudices, and how insensitive they must have been not to have noticed that many of us like to create a friendship with those with whom we trade.

'Insensitive' is the key word. Objective psychologists and economists who studied an economy unsullied by human relationships were men who saw emotion as weakness and who took pride in their ability to separate emotion from reason, making emotion subservient to reason.

Believing that emotion can be separated from reason is a delusion. Emotion is a meaning. Feeling angry is an interpretation. If you interpret a situation in such a way that you feel angry, telling yourself that you don't feel angry is simply lying to yourself, something that always leads to disaster.

Nevertheless, economists who prided themselves on their rational control of emotion were following an old masculine tradition as exemplified by the founder of the *Economist*, James Wilson, who wrote, 'There is no inconsiderable school of talkers and writers nowadays who seem to forget that reason is given to us to sit in judgement over the dictates of our feelings, and that it is not her part to play the advocate in support of every impulse which laudable affections may arouse in us.'[85]

One of the disasters which can arise from lying to yourself about the emotions you feel is an inability to understand why people do what they do. As the Irish suffered and died in the famine of 1845–9 James Wilson could not understand why the Irish peasantry did not behave as a sensible Scottish businessman would in such a situation. The Irish, he believed, should be self-reliant. Sending them food would discourage them from being self-reliant. So the Irish died in great numbers and James Wilson made a lasting contribution to the Troubles.

A refusal to understand that we see the world only from our own standpoint has led to theories about the world and the people in it from which all sense of personal experience has been removed. Psychologists have developed models of the person where we are nothing but puppets manipulated by the strings of behaviourist stimulus-response, or of genes, or of unconscious drives. Economists, wrote Paul Ormerod, 'see the world as a machine. A very complicated one, but nevertheless a machine, whose workings can be understood by putting together carefully and meticulously its component parts. The behaviour of the system as a whole can be deduced from a simple aggregation of these components. A lever pulled in a certain part of the machine with a certain strength will have regular and predictable outcomes elsewhere in the machine.'[86]

Models of any set of phenomena have by necessity to leave out parts of the phenomena. Anyone who finds personal meanings disturbing is likely not only to leave such things out of the model but to be unaware of why he is excluding this particular aspect. Then there are those beliefs we hold thinking that they are rational beliefs, but which in fact have developed out of childhood experience. The Keynes 'paradox of thrift' might well have developed as a reaction to the 'waste not, want not' Victorian values of his family. Added to all this is our universal predilection for ignoring events which run counter to our theories.

No wonder our models can bear so little relationship to what actually happens, and no wonder an introductory textbook on economics can begin with 'Nearly all governments, whatever their ideology, are committed to programmes designed to promote the growth of living standards and a more even distribution of wealth both nationally and globally.'[87] On what planet do these economists live? Not the one I live on.

Still, an assumption of the altruism and wisdom of those who gain political power is no further from reality than the assumptions of the Rational Man and the static model of competitive equilibrium. There can be no equilibriums in a universe where everything is changing all the time, and the Rational Man does not represent all the people who take part in the market.

Alfred Marshall, the great Victorian economist, said that economics was about '"man in the ordinary business of life", not about all aspects of human behaviour, but about man as buyer and seller, producer and consumer, saver and investor, employer and worker.'[88] He seems not to have noticed that women, even in Victorian times, filled all of these roles. Such blindness still exists. Consumer research shows that in households it is the woman rather than the man who decides which car will be purchased, yet the men in the car industry, seeing it as a male province, aim their advertising at men, not women. (Audi-Volkswagen is a notable exception.) Much that economists write about poverty fails to note that most of the world's poor are women.

Economics has always been a masculine profession. It is only recently that women have been joining it in increasing numbers. Many of these are highly critical of traditional ideas. Diana Strassman saw that the assumptions on which these ideas are based 'may be typical of the perceived experiences of adult, white, male, middle-class American economists, but they fail to capture economic reality for many others. Economic theory's conception of selfhood and individual agency is located in Western cultural traditions as well as being distinctly androcentric. Economic man is the Western romantic hero, a transcendent individual able to make choices and attain goals.'[89]

The romantic notion underlying the major part of the work done by psychologists (and psychiatrists as well) is that of the wise observer, superior to the person being studied, who knows more about the person than the person can ever know about himself. This way of viewing themselves prevented such psychologists from realizing that the behaviour of the people being studied depended on their interpretations of the behaviour of the psychologist. Freud did take some account of his patients' interpretations of him. He called these 'projections' and claimed to show how they were wrong while his interpretations of the patient were right.

Economists have always been aware that buyers and sellers are busy interpreting the behaviour of one another, but have assumed that such interpretations followed the rules of public logic in the pursuit of self-interest, and that their effects were limited. In a perfectly competitive market a firm could ignore the effects its behaviour had on other firms. Yet in the real world rival firms watch one another closely and plan their strategies accordingly.

In 1994 three economists, John Harsanyi, John Nash and Reinhard Selten, shared the Nobel Prize for economics for their work in game theory. They developed mathematical models to explain the process by which competitors compete, compromise and decide. Though the mathematics are complex, the theory suggests many practical applications, and it does recognize that the market is one big game.

The Nobel Prize committee seem to be rewarding those economists who are as much concerned with real life as with theory. In 1992 Gary Becker, professor of economics and sociology at Chicago University, was awarded the prize for his work in extending economic theory into matters like racial discrimination, marriage, fertility, education and crime. In 1995 Robert Lucas of Chicago University won the prize for developing the theory of 'rational expectations' which 'argues that people learn to anticipate government policy changes and act accordingly; since macro-economic fine-tuning requires that governments be able to fool people, this implies that it is usually futile.'[90] Economists who believe that governments can fool people so efficiently obviously haven't come across Abe

Lincoln's advice that 'you can fool some of the people all of the time, and all of the people for some of the time, but you can't fool all the people all the time.'

Rational Man might be disappearing, but the word 'rational' is still very much around. It is used to mean that people are guided by self-interest and that they are consistent in their choices. Yet people often act in ways which do not seem in their interest. Many people go on smoking despite their knowledge of its dangers, while others are prepared to die for a cause. We can be consistent in our choices in one situation but not in another. A few economists have realized that their judgements about why people do what they do might be improved by drawing on the work in cognitive psychology.

This involves actually asking people about the meanings they have created. Doing so isn't simple.

First, there's the language problem. Even though two people speak the same language, the meanings each gives to the words used can be very different because the words have different connotations for different people. Do you link 'saving money' with 'wise', or 'foolish', or 'boring'? Standardized questionnaires where the interviewer cannot ask supplementary questions like, 'Would I be right in thinking that what you mean is . . . ?' always lead to results skewed in directions unknown to the researcher.

Second, there's the problem of trust. Can the interviewee trust the researcher not to respond in ways which hurt the interviewee? If not, answers will 'fake good'.

Third, how much does the interviewee lie to himself, denying certain fears and feelings?

Fourth, does the model of the person which the researcher uses have a close relationship to actual people?

Commentators on the market are always talking about how fear drives the market, but the notion of self-interest, even if it is extended to take in ideas of altruism, does not identify what we see as our greatest self-interest.

We need to survive both as a body and as a person. We want to survive as both, but surviving as a person is always more important to us than surviving as a body. Whenever we behave in ways which to the outside observer seem to be irrational and inconsistent we are defending our sense of being a person. The logic we use to do this is the private logic of our meaning structure, not the public logic of rationality. Any theory which sets out to explain and predict the behaviour of people in the market place needs to take account of the functioning of private logic in the defence of the person.

Politicians

Over the years I was researching this book I asked a wide variety of people , 'Do you think politicians understand business?' Opinions ranged in tone from the kind to the damning, but the consensus was that they didn't. Margaret Thatcher agreed. On a Radio 4 *Today* programme in 1993 she told her interviewer, Brian Redhead, 'Politicians know nothing about business so they shouldn't be running businesses.'[91] She was justifying her party's policy of selling all the state-owned industries – what Harold MacMillan called 'the family silver'. But if politicians don't understand business, how can they possibly know how to run the country's affairs in such a way that industry flourishes?

One businessman who had been very much involved in the Labour Party told me, 'If you think the Tory Party is the party of business, you would find that business people generally prefer the Tories to be in power, not because they understand business, but because they usually keep corporation tax down.' Low corporation tax means higher profits. Members of the Tory Party would argue that higher profits lead to more investment, which leads to economic growth and a fall in unemployment. Would that were universally so! Alas, many company directors and shareholders take their profits and run!

However, keeping corporation tax down is one way of winning votes, and this, my informants assured me, was far more important to politicians than meeting the needs of industry. One senior manager in a multinational said, 'Politicians are too busy trying to justify their own existence.' The founder of a very successful private company in Australia said, 'If you're in government you make a decision, and if you're in the opposition you reject that decision, no matter how great the idea might be. Politicians aren't doing the best for the country. They're doing the best for their party.'

Politicians work on a very short time scale – the space of time between now and the next election. For the British government the longest time scale they work on is five years; for the president of the USA it's four years; and for the Australian Federal government it's three. George Kennedy, Chairman of Sims, Smiths Industries Medical Systems, told me how, when the medical schools in British universities were known the world over as the best, overseas students flocked to Britain to train. There they learned their skills using Sims instruments, and so when they went back home they continued to use Sims instruments, and the company's overseas trade flourished. Then in 1993 the Conservative government, thinking only in the short term and keen to raise money, increased substantially the fees paid by overseas students.

I met George shortly after he had returned from a government trade mission to the Far East. He described how, in the hospitals he visited, nearly all the consultants had trained in Britain but the junior doctors had trained in America or Japan. In the long term the government's policy would have the effect of reducing overseas trade and thus government revenue.

Eddie Bell, Chairman of HarperCollins UK, told me that 'very few politicians seem to have a grasp of business.' At the time we talked a Labour Party victory at the 1997 election was predicted. Eddie deplored the way the Labour leadership were so vague about their policies. He said, 'I don't believe that Tony Blair understands business. We need a government, we need a leader of a government, who understands the business impact of the policies the government is to follow. If there are no policies, or if it's difficult to find out what the policies are, making it impossible for businesses to plan their future, then one has to conclude that there is not a great understanding of the business impact.'

Politicians understand very well the impact their policies have on their supporters. In the USA both the Republican and Democratic parties are closely linked with big business and derive much of their money from these sources. There politics is a game only the wealthy can play. It's still possible to go from log cabin to White House, but only if you gather money and wealthy friends along the way.

Such money gathering almost inevitably involves an American politician in corruption, as Martin Woollacott described:

> Corruption is a shadowy but constant presence in American politics. Always there are allegations, always there are investigations, only rarely are there any formal conclusions, legal punishments, or effective reforms. Yet the never-ending drama can also deliver victory to those who claim to be the scourges of corruption, or who successfully paint their opponents in those dark colours.
>
> The paradoxical result is that corruption is a vote-winner in the United States in two quite different ways. Corruption and the practices approaching corruption, rake in the money without which campaigning would be impossible, while the promise to end corruption or the successful pinning of corruption allegations on an opponent can swing a political contest. Politicians shimmy along a tightrope, precariously balanced between the enticing possibility of exposing the irregularities of their opponents or of having their own sins revealed.[92]

Wealthy friends might make demands on an aspiring politician, but there are also the demands made by the vociferous religious community. Every American politician must claim a belief in God, and demonstrate this with frequent references to the Deity. To do otherwise would be political death. Whatever their views on policy, every politician must take account of the views of the religious groups, no matter how intolerant and undemocratic these views might be. It is ironic that in the USA, where the Bill of Rights, framed by men well mindful of the dangers of religious persecution, separates Church from State, religion has such power, while in the UK, where the Head of State is also the Head of the Church of England and Anglican bishops sit in the House of Lords, any cleric who publicly criticizes the government is condemned by the government for meddling in politics. However, British clerics do not pursue their political aims with the ruthlessness of the American Christian Coalition who 'so free with funding allegations against the Democrats, themselves built a highly effective cash machine which scooped in money from the tobacco and gun lobbies, amongst others, and evaded funding limits by various subterfuges, such as claiming that spending was for state rather than federal political purposes.'[93]

Politicians often talk of being in partnership with whatever group it suits them to be seen in partnership with, but few politicians who get into power seem to be able to act upon an understanding that politics and the economy are parts of an indivisible whole, and that if the demands of one become paramount over the demands of the other disaster follows. A market place without law is savagery. An economy subjugated to political ideology destroys people.

Such disasters might be that of the tragedy of those countries which espoused Communism, or that of mad cows and Creutzfeldt-Jakob Disease. In 1979 the Royal Commission on Environmental Pollution warned of the dangers of animal waste being included in animal feed. The report said, 'The major problem encountered in this recycling process [involving animal waste] is the risk of transmitting disease-bearing pathogens to stock and thence to humans.' In 1980 ministers preferred to take account of 'the current economic climate', which meant taking account of the government's ideology of the free market. The agro-chemical companies saw this as an opportunity too good to miss, and what followed might be regarded as an example of the savagery of a market untrammelled by law.[94]

It is only quite recently that politicians have been expected to appear to have some knowledge of economics. Along with psycho-babble there is now economist-babble arising, like psycho-babble, from hidden shallows. All that a politician in the government needs to know about economics is that anything that goes wrong at home is the fault of the world economy, which lies outside the government's power, and anything that goes right has been achieved by the government. All that an opposition politician needs to know is that anything that goes right at home is the result of the world economy and anything that goes wrong is the fault of the government.

Columnists in the business pages of the national papers seem to have little faith in politicians' understanding of economics. Christopher Huhne remarked, 'It sometimes seems that the book British politicians have taken most to heart is Darrell Huff's *How to Lie with Statistics*.'[95] I certainly won't believe that politicians understand economics (or science for that matter) until I hear a politician praising or condemning some statistical result and giving the standard error of that particular statistic so as to show its significance in terms of the probability of its occurrence.

One politician who did try to understand the economy was Paul Keating. Edna Carew in her biography of him wrote,

> Keating's interest in finance was developing through the 1970s though he is remembered at that time as being no more financially or economically literate than anyone else in the Whitlam government. 'He was as ignorant [about economics] as the rest of us, and that was pretty bloody ignorant,' says Jim McClelland, a minister in the Whitlam government. But Keating was dedicated to self-improvement – at home he was reading the economic texts of Adam Smith and Paul Samuelson, in Canberra he would haunt the office of the *Australian Financial Review*, absorbing information on how the economy ticked.[96]

In the first long conversation I had with Eddie Bell he was quite critical of Paul Keating, but by the time we met again he had been talking with him and revised his opinion. He said, 'I discovered that this was a guy who had a vision of Australia within the world, certainly within the business world. I found he did have a fairly clear vision of Australia as a trading nation within Asia, not only in terms of what Australia produced and where it could sell, but also Australia as a market place for Asia. He understood the growth that was taking place in Singapore and Malaysia and places like that, and he felt that Australia should be able to enjoy the same level of growth. I was left with the feeling that this was somebody who had much more of a grasp of business than he had been portrayed in the British media.'

Politicians are always talking about the future, but if, like Paul Keating, they want to concentrate on the future and the predilection of their public is the past, they can, like him, lose their popularity. On a flight from Sydney to Los Angeles I talked to an Australian businessman. He thought that the Keating government was reasonably knowledgeable about the needs of business. However, he thought that what held Australian business back was the conservatism of Australian businessmen. Unlike their American and British counterparts they did not see new ideas and new business practices as a challenge but as a nuisance.

The security of the past is all very nice, but the market and the economy are all about the future. To think and work in these terms requires a high tolerance of uncertainty and considerable knowledge and expertise. It's no wonder so many politicians turn their minds to simpler diversions. Such diversions, they hope, will also divert the public and prevent them from noticing what actually is going on in the business of government.

In 1994, when the Labor Party formed the Federal government in Australia, the *Australian Business Monthly* interviewed Don Mercer, managing director of the ANZ Bank, who believed that the Federal government had allowed itself to be diverted from what was important, economic recovery from recession. He said, 'This government has several economic issues to address, but these are not getting anywhere near the attention they merit. I am talking about market de-regulation which hasn't happened, taxation reform which hasn't happened, superannuation and the redirection of financial flows in the economy. These are massively important issues. But in Canberra no one wants to know. What *are* they doing down there? They're re-designing the flag, they're pushing a republic, they're lumbering us with Mabo [a legal ruling on aboriginal land rights, an issue which provokes strong feelings amongst most Australians]. None of those things come close to the real issues that should be commanding attention. What Canberra has to understand is that what business wants is outcomes, not ideologies!'[97]

Eddie Bell saw British politicians behaving in the same way. He said, 'Politicians think Europe is a key issue and the truth is the key issues are – Will there be a health service? Will I manage to get a pension? Can I get my kids educated to put them out in the world with any good chance? What's happening to the fabric of the country, the family? Law and order – will I be living in a house that will have barbed wire around it and bars on the windows? Politicians seem to be besotted with Europe and are ignoring the real concerns of the people.' The British politicians who are besotted with Europe are those who look to the past, not the future. They think that this is what the British people want. While there are some people who look back to some mythical golden age, most see Britain's place as part of Europe as so obvious as to be boring, while the issues Eddie listed are keenly felt.

Diverting the public from what is actually going on has always been part of the politicians' stock in trade. The Roman emperors used bread and circuses. The Conservative government in 1996 was using the National Lottery and hatred of the Germans because they wouldn't eat British beef. When George Walden, Conservative MP for Buckingham, announced that he was leaving politics at the next election he said in his resignation letter,

> Our politics seems to be increasingly about the management of illusions, and I possess no talent for soothing and sweet-talking the public like infants. If we have so little faith in the intelligence of the electorate I can see few reasons for being in politics, other than to keep things as they are, or to dance like a fly in the beam of public attention.[98]

However, diversions work only if the politicians have gauged correctly just what the public is prepared to be diverted by. Since what entrances us most is what speaks directly to our private logic, they need to have a good understanding of what might be common elements in the private logics of the public.

Politicians often boast how well they understand their constituents. Yet the policies they adopt show how little they do understand. For instance, those politicians who want to be seen as 'strong on law and order' claim that the public wants to see criminals punished, and so prisons continue to be run with the emphasis on punishment rather than reform. Certain politicians talk about reform as being 'soft on criminals', which only serves to show that such politicians have never sought any form of self-knowledge. Being in a prison regime devoted to punishment is a harsh and often cruel experience, but being forced to look at yourself and take responsibility for what you have done creates that terrifying uncertainty from which most people flee. Yet until you face that uncertainty – the shattering of essential parts of your meaning structure – you cannot change.

Politicians who espouse punishment, not reform, are people who have constructed a shell of denials and pretences in which to hide, and who fear self-knowledge for it would shatter the shell and leave them exposed and naked. So concerned are they with self-preservation they fail to understand that, while seeing a criminal get his just deserts might give some satisfaction, what most people want is a society without crime. Knowledge of how to help people who break the law to change their ways is extremely limited. Crime will always be a solution for many people as long as there is inequality, poverty and unemployment, and it will not diminish in any significant way until there are a sufficient number of politicians who are unafraid of self-knowledge and all that implies.

One reason why some people do not want to understand how we create our own individual worlds is that it brings them face to face with our essential aloneness. But if we don't understand this, we don't realize how important it is to share experiences with other people.

In past decades many politicians could claim to have shared the work experience of their constituents. Now, concluded Peter Riddell in his study of the House of Commons,

> the British parliament, and hence the government, is increasingly dominated by career politicians – by men, and a few women, who have dedicated most of their adult lives to entering the Commons, staying there and advancing to become ministers or spokesmen. The conclusion of this book is unmistakable: the balance has shifted to the full-time politician.[99]

Many of these career politicians see law as a suitable stepping-stone to a career in politics. Eddie Bell did not agree. He said, 'I think it takes a particular brain to be a lawyer, and at the end of the day there's a rule book, there's a precedent, there's always something you can look back on. You can't do that in business. It doesn't work like that. While there's no doubt that the legal brain is a very sharp brain, it's a brain that's been developed out of a set of rule books. The business brain is a very sharp brain, but there are either no rules or the rules change as you go along.'

He felt that there were far more appropriate ways of preparing for a political life. 'I certainly would like to see more and more people coming into Parliament after they've had some sort of business grounding, though I still believe if some of them had an idea of what it was like to live in a council house, or work in the Social Services in some of the more difficult areas of the country, that would also be a help.'

I think Judge Stephen Tumin, the scourge of the UK prison service, has the right idea. At a conference of the National Association of Prison Visitors a speaker commented on how good the Spanish jails were. 'Yes,' mused Judge Tumin, 'I have a conviction that to have a good prison system you have to put your political leaders in jail at some stage.'[100]

However, career politicians or not, there is one aspect of life which politicians now share with the rest of the workforce. Those of us who are lucky enough to have jobs have to work very hard, so now politicians work very hard, or at least look as if they are doing so. Despite the wear and tear of hard work, it does have one great advantage. Even if you produce nothing of value, you are virtuous.

If hard work is virtuous and Satan finds mischief for idle hands to do, wouldn't a government concerned with morality develop policies aimed at keeping people usefully, even if not gainfully, employed?

Whenever a politician talks about morality listeners should remember what Ralph Waldo Emerson said: 'The louder he talked of his honour, the faster we counted the spoons.' Whichever aspect of morality a politician chooses to emphasize might just be the current party line, but I am often reminded of some research I did into which of the virtues individuals saw as the most important. Whichever it was – truth, courage, honesty, love, generosity and so on – that was the one where the individual had the greatest difficulty. This came to mind when I saw the slogan of the Australian Democrats at the 1996 general election, 'Keep the Bastards Honest'.

It is a tradition for Australians to distrust their politicians. In the USA, according to Lewis L. Lapham, it is a tradition for politics to operate like the market.

> The politicians dress up the deals in the language of the law or policy, but they're in the business of brokering the tax revenue. What keeps them in office is not their talent for oratory but their skill at redistributing the national income in a way that rewards

> their constituents, clients, patrons and friends. They trade in every known commodity – school lunches, tax exemptions, water and mineral rights, aluminium siding, farm subsidies, pension benefits, weapons contracts and prison uniforms – and they know that the simple act of writing a single sentence into a trade or housing bill can result in the making of fortunes. They work the levers of government like gamblers pulling slot machines.[101]

It is easy for those who merely observe politicians to make damning judgements of them. Occasionally politicians themselves make judgements from the standpoint of direct knowledge. In an interview with the *Observer* Alan Clark, who was junior Minister at the Department of Employment for three years during the Thatcher administration, 'said that his party has held power for three-quarters of the past 70 years through a mixture of "greed and fear" – "the greed of wanting power and the fear of losing it."'[102]

Such greed and fear can be seen operating in the Conservative Party's reluctance to disclose who makes contributions to the party and how much. In the USA candidates are required to disclose any contribution over $200. In the House of Commons members are now required to list their interests outside the House. A study of these interests in 1994 distinguished 'two main attitudes. Some MPs were puritans, broadly opposed to making money by serving outside interests. Others were entrepreneurs, seeing it as part of an MP's prerogative as well as a contribution to the public weal. Predictably, the puritans are overwhelmingly Labour and the entrepreneurs overwhelmingly Tory.'[103]

'My theory,' wrote Simon Hoggart, 'is that some politicians regard bungs and a spot of bonking as their perks, rather like the bonuses for Barings directors – to be protected at all costs, in spite of the catastrophes caused by their own incompetence.'[104] Such bonuses are more likely to be available to politicians in government than in opposition. Being in power is the real test of a politician's honesty.

I guess that some politicians would enjoy the pleasures of immorality no matter what trade they followed, but for others who would not dream of taking a bribe or indulging in insider trading, much less adultery, the actual organization of the democratic system forces politicians, honest and dishonest, to lie.

When I started politician watching many years ago it was easy to tell whether a politician was Labour or Conservative (in Australia, Labor or Liberal). The clothes, the voice, the mannerisms distinguished the two groups. Although the extremes of each group still feature in parliament, most of the members, men and women, are now indistinguishable. So are the policies. Yet they are required by the system to be adversaries. Whatever the party in power, the other must oppose. The fact that the position most in accord with reality is somewhere in between is deemed inadmissible, as is admitting that your opponent is right. Thus politicians constantly have to refute truths and support lies. This leaves them with two choices. They can lie and know that they are lying, or they can lie to themselves and tell themselves that they are truthful. Both activities are highly damaging.

What damage is done from lying and knowing you are lying depends on whether the person holds concepts about the necessity of being good. If the person does believe in the necessity of being good, unless he can persuade himself of the utter nobility of the party's cause, he suffers the tortures of guilt. Guilt and self-hatred lead to depression. Rates of depression among politicians aren't particularly high, so it seems that not many politicians fall into this category.

A person who is untroubled by the necessity of being good can lie quite cheerfully. However, the problem for the congenital liar is that he is certain that everyone else is a liar, too, and so he becomes suspicious of everyone. Paranoia is rife amongst politicians, as it is among lawyers.

Those people who lie to themselves and tell themselves they are truthful prevent themselves from thinking clearly and from being aware of the consequences of their actions. They damage their intellect and their sensitivity to others. Or, as Eddie Bell said of all politicians, 'You could hit them with a shovel and they'd still keep walking and talking.'

Managers and Directors

Adam Smith did not think highly of merchants and managers. Of the former he said, 'People of the same trade seldom meet together, even for merriment and diversion, but the conversation ends in a conspiracy against the public, or in some contrivance to raise prices,'[105] and of the latter, 'Being managers of other people's money than of their own, it cannot well be expected, that they should watch over it with the same anxious vigilance with which the partners in a private copartnery frequently watch over their own.'[106]

Besides watching over money, managers watch over people. How well do they do that?

Managers, with or without anxious vigilance, became inevitable as, with the Industrial Revolution, the size of firms grew, making it impossible for partners or family members to supervise every part of the firm. In the USA from the 1870s factories used continuous-process machinery which allowed Henry Ford to develop the assembly line and mass production. The goal was increased productivity, and out of this came a set of concepts and practices which became known as management. Management was not simply part of what went on in factories. It became a subject for intellectual study and institutions of higher education set up management courses, the aim of which was to turn management into a profession alongside medicine and law. First there were degrees in management and then the graduate business schools. The MBA had arrived.

A perusal of the advertisements in business magazines and newspapers for business courses would give the impression that the MBA is now a world-wide phenomenon, but it is not. Germany and Japan did not develop such business schools. 'The Japanese firm hires people right out of school, trains all of them in various jobs through a carefully worked out system of job rotation, supplementing this on-the-job training with short in-firm or extra-mural courses. German firms hire functional specialists but do not consider management itself a specialty. In neither country are there MBAs to claim privileged "management" capability. Everybody in the firm learns about management, beginning at the bottom with a broom, and then, based on performance at the job, moves up.'[107]

During and after the Second World War American management techniques greatly impressed the British and French. The London Business School and the Manchester Business School were set up using the structures of American business schools. In France businessmen, industrialists, bureaucrats and academics combined to set up the National Management Education Foundation and sent graduates to train in the USA.

'Productivity, the gospel Americans convincingly preached,' wrote Robert Lock, 'presupposes the existence of a new middle class of managerial functionaries to fill the leadership space – trained in modern management methods, dedicated to the cult of work, competence and efficiency . . . This new managerial class believed and believes that the creatures of their management brought about the world's postwar economic successes.'[108] Such a view ignores the economic success of Germany and Japan and the large number of highly successful entrepreneurs who were quite untrained in management techniques.

Robert Locke contends that over the years American management has turned into 'managerialism', a change which parallels the change from 'the military way' to 'militarism'. Here he is drawing on the work of historian Alfred Vagts who said that militarism

> presents a vast array of customs, interests, prestige, actions and thoughts associated with armies and wars and yet transcending true military purposes. Indeed, militarism is so constituted that it may hamper and defeat the purposes of the military way. Its influence is unlimited in scope. It may permeate all society and become dominant over all industry and arts . . . Militarism displays the qualities of caste and cult, authority and belief.[109]

American management, says Robert Locke, shows all these characteristics. As a result American managerialism does not achieve what American management set out to do.

Militarism needed military academies, and managerialism needed business schools. Neither type of institution is noted for its espousal of democracy. The workforce, like ordinary soldiers, are seen as a problem to be managed, not as partners in the enterprise. Such a hierarchical structure could not produce the Japanese concept of

Total Quality Manufacturing with its sharing of ideas, multiple-skilling, job rotation and continuous interaction among all managers and employees. Nor could it, by imposing rules and sanctions from above, build up the trust between management and employees necessary for a successful enterprise.

Robert Locke concluded,

> American managerialism has created a myth about itself, that it knows what is best for the firm. It might know best how to maximize profits in the short run for the stock holders, but no evidence exists that American management knows how to look after the well-being or long-term interests of a firm . . . Unless some restraint is put upon American management, it will simply pursue high profits through low-wage strategies, refuse to invest sufficiently in the skills and talents of its people, and go off-shore.[110]

Each country which adopted American management ideas and methods added to them in its own national style. In the UK most managers come from that well-established group, the white, middle-class male. The debate is over how many of these white, middle-class males are part of the old boys' network, membership of which is obtained by attending one of the well-known public schools.

In 1991 Richard Thomson of the *Independent on Sunday* studied what he called 'the 10 most powerful men in England . . . they are the senior exectives of the 10 largest investment institutions, responsible for deciding how £100bn of funds under their management should be invested in the stock market . . . Most are in their forties or early fifties. They have spent their lives in the fund management industry after making their way through grammar school and university.'[111]

In 1992 David Bowen, also of the *Independent on Sunday*, reported the paper's study of 'the backgrounds of 97 senior partners or chief executives of the top City firms: 10 went to Eton, nine to Winchester and 37 to other public schools . . . (After that) if they went anywhere it was to Oxbridge: only 12 of the 52 graduates of British universities went to a redbrick.' Also examined were 'the pasts of top industrialists: the FT-SE 100 chief executives and chairmen and, separately, more than 3,000 directors of medium-to-large companies listed in

Who's Who in Industry (less than 2 per cent of whom are women).' This showed that 'the FT-SE 100 is run by public-school old boys just as much as the City is, although the spread of schools is much broader . . . Business schools had a much greater impact among the upper echelons of industry than the city. Not a single City boss has an MBA, while 12 FT-SE top executives do. Of the 2,249 industrial directors who name their university in *Who's Who in Industry*, 100 went to business school: 44 to Harvard.'[112]

Yet a year later the *Financial Times*, under the headline 'Old boy network loses hold on the boardroom', reported a study by Professor Leslie Hannah of the London School of Economics showing that over half of the chairmen of the top 50 UK companies were educated at state schools. Professor Hannah claimed that 'It seems not only has there been a revolution at the top in the boardroom, but that revolution is firmly rooted in evolutionary cultural and educational change.'[113] This seems to me to be just another version of the argument I've been listening to for nearly thirty years, where someone British tries to prove to me that Britain is now a classless society. Does British society have classes? Does the Australian bush have flies?

The following year some diligent financial journalist on the *Guardian* drew a black and white four by four chequerboard, labelled each square with the name of a major company, and on them plotted the names of ten company directors who held two, three or four directorships in these companies. This exercise was to show how 'more than a third of Britain's company boardrooms are "connected" through a web of directorships involving some of the country's best known captains of industry.'[114]

A much larger diagram showing the interconnections of 49 non-executive directors and 63 major companies is given in Bob Garratt's 1996 study of directors called *The Fish Rots from the Head*.[115] Another study by Richard Thomson showed how, while most of the workforce has to retire at sixty-five, company directors can go on forever.[116] For some of these directors it seems essential to go on working because it is their work which gives them a sense of identity, while for others, particularly the non-executive directors, attending board meetings is a congenial hobby that fills in time. Quoting

Sunbridge Park Corporate Research, Bob Garratt showed that between 64 and 80 per cent of board members were over fifty. The percentage of women members ranged between 0 and 8.[117]

Being a non-executive director shouldn't be a hobby. If non-executive directors did their job properly, which is to audit the work of the executives and look after shareholders' interests, the company Queens Moat would not have gone to the wall in 1993. This happened despite the 1992 recommendations by the committee under Sir Adrian Cadbury in its Code of Best Practice for British Industry. They recommended that non-executive directors be genuinely independent so that they can carefully audit the work of executive directors. One of their tasks would be to fix the pay of directors.

I wish that when I was working in the National Health Service it was some of these non-executive directors who had fixed my pay. There'd have been no cheese-paring rises of a few per cent, but whacking great rises and magnificent perks. My psychologist colleagues, now on fixed term contracts, would really appreciate a director's roll-over contract where a four-year contract, say, is always four years away from expiry. On such a contract if you do decide to leave you get paid at least half of what you would have earned on your current contract. And then there are the perks – a large pension and a satisfactory portion of share options.

Apologists for a system where the members reward one another very generously argue that directors work hard and earn their money. Yet research shows little relationship between directors' pay and company performance. A study by CM Financial Analysis showed that between 1991 and 1994 'nearly one-third of Britain's biggest companies have given their top directors pay rises which outstrip the rate of return to shareholders . . . At Barclays, for example, the remuneration of the highest paid director rose by 243 per cent while total returns to shareholders grew just 39 per cent.'[118] No such rises were given to employees. Any increases in wage rates were at or below the low rate of inflation. In the USA in the seventies chief executives of large corporations were paid 35 times the wage of the average worker. In the nineties they earned 130 times more.[119]

Company directors who reward one another so generously show

that they are quite out of touch with their employees. When Ricardo Semler in Brazil set out to turn his family business Semco into one where the virtues preached by management gurus of democracy, empowerment and mutual trust were actually practised he knew that whatever he paid himself would have to be seen as appropriate by the firm's employees.[120] In my thick file of newspaper cuttings about rises in directors' pay between 1991 and 1996 I could find no report of an employee saying that such rises were fair and well merited.

The reporting of financial and business matters does not always make a clear distinction between managers and directors, yet, as Bob Garratt's work shows, for the successful performance of a company such a distinction must be made.

> There is a vast difference between 'directing' and 'managing' an organization. Managing is literally, given its Latin root, a hands-on activity thriving on crises and action. On the operations side of an organization it is a crucial role. Directing is different. Directing is essentially an intellectual activity. It is about showing the way ahead, giving leadership. It is thoughtful and reflective and requires the acquisition by each director of a portfolio of completely different *thinking* skills.[121]

In his study of companies in the UK, the USA, Japan, Germany, France, Hong Kong, Australia and New Zealand, Bob Garratt found that, with some notable exceptions, directors 'have not been through the training, induction or inclusion processes necessary in order to make the transition from managers to direction-givers.'[122] What is needed is for the organization to become a learning organization with a board of directors, not at its head, but at its heart. This can only happen when directors recognize that to become a director is not a matter of joining a cosy club but a matter of entering a profession for which training is required. Only then 'in the balancing of shareholder and stakeholder demands the Anglo-Saxon mindset of business as a "finite game" – win or lose, based on the short-term, bottom-line driven results – will itself evolve towards the idea of business as an "infinite game", of continuous learning from success and failure over the long term.'[123]

Democracy has never been a feature in firms in the UK, USA and Australia. Trade unions in the USA fought many valiant battles in the nineteenth and early twentieth centuries but they never became a significant force. Ask any New Yorker where Union Square got its name and the answer is likely to be the union of the States and not, correctly, trade unions. The American union, the AFL-CIO, is trying to increase membership of unions but where labour is required to be flexible, that is, easily sacked, many people feel that, while they have the right to vote, they don't have the right to join a trade union.

In the UK trade unions lost much of their power under the Thatcher government. Since 1980 some six million people no longer belong to a union. In Australia businessmen still complain that unions have too much power. In each country, because trade unions have always had to fight for workers' rights, the relationships that developed between managers and workers were usually adversarial, which is in essence undemocratic and bereft of trust.

The history of the Industrial Revolution shows that industrialists saw their employees as no more valuable than their machinery and often a good deal less. Very belatedly managers have discovered that employees are people. As Eddie Bell observed, 'I haven't met a business man or woman yet who doesn't say that our greatest asset is our people, and then when businesses run into problems the first asset to go is your greatest asset.' Businesses which stripped themselves of their so-called finest asset in the eighties and early nineties were supposed to become leaner and fitter, but by 1996 the word being used was 'anorexic'.

Then Stephen Roach, the American economist who made 'downsizing' (sacking) fashionable recanted his gospel. 'If all you do is cut,' he said, 'you will eventually be left with nothing.' Which, as Francis Wheen observed, is something any trainee hairdresser could have told him. 'If management gurus genuinely satisfied their customers' demands, they'd be out of a job – which is why they have to keep changing their product. Having made his fortune from his "downsizing" method, Stephen Roach can now expect to earn it all over again by telling companies how to cope with the malign consequences of heeding his earlier advice. One can almost hear the boardroom conversation. "But Steve, we fired all our workers, just like you told us, and now we have an empty factory. What can we do?" "Uh, rehire them." "Gee, thanks. Do you take American Express?"'[124]

If there is reincarnation I bet Phineas Taylor Barnum has come back as a management guru. The credulity, unworldliness and gullibility of many managers astounds me. They pay vast amounts of money to be told what their common sense and general education should have told them, or to be asked to believe the unbelievable, which is what they are willing to do. Other managers are highly sceptical of gurus and management consultants, but often they go along with the whole charade because they deem it politic to do so.

A management consultant who frames his message with 'Here are some ideas which you might find useful, but remember that all ideas have good and bad implications' is honest. The ones who say, 'Here is the solution to all your problems' is a charlatan.

Not content with simply teaching management methods, some gurus preach that a major personality change in each of the staff will lead to corporate success. Whatever the technique used, it is a confidence trick because it promises the impossible. Such gurus adapt the ideas of psychotherapy to suit their purposes. These ideas get their validity from the basic premise of psychotherapy which is that people can change. Psychotherapy properly practised is simply going on a journey of self-discovery. Where the journey will end neither the traveller nor the psychotherapist knows.

I have watched many people take that journey and I can say that they all became very different from what they were and they lived their lives very differently. They changed jobs, changed partners and changed their priorities. Much of what was once important to them ceased to be so. Life still presented them with difficulties, but they'd learned how to take life easy in the sense that they became more skilled in identifying where reality might be made to conform to their wishes and where it would not. They knew that in time everything passes. Such an attitude is not necessarily conducive to devoting yourself to your company and its profits.

There are gurus who don't practise psychotherapy properly. They use the methods derived from the brain-washing methods of the

Chinese in the Korean War. Research by the American psychiatrist Robert Lifton and others showed that weak, gullible and immature soldiers were easily converted to Communism, while older men with well-worked-out philosophies of life remained convinced of the rightness of their own views.

Any guru who uses methods which involve disorientating and humiliating participants is using the methods derived from brain washing. These are exercises in power manipulation, not enlightenment. What manager would want his weakest employees to become even less capable of thinking and his strongest even more entrenched in their views? Only a manager who didn't understand people.

Accountants

If there is one group of market experts who want to be seen as practical, down-to-earth people it's accountants. They count what they can see. If they can't see it, they can't count it.

When the National Health Service was being changed into a business I, like many other psychologists, had enormous difficulty in getting accountants to understand what went on in psychotherapy. They could not frame sensible questions. They wanted to know what number of hours of therapy would produce Y amount of improvement. Public Relations managers have the same problem. They get asked what amount of expenditure produces Y amount of the 'warm fuzzies' that aid brand recognition.

Such an approach by accountants could lead a non-accountant to think that accountants need accurate figures relating to precise events to feed into the one, true accounting system which all accountants use.

How comforting it would be if everything in the market could be accounted for in this way. But, alas, it is not so. Accountants are merely human, and so they can devise an infinite number of systems whereby they can arrive at a bottom line which purports to show the profit or loss from a particular enterprise. True, Luca Pacioli founded accountancy and the double-entry book-keeping which accountants use when he published his *Summa de Arithmetica* in 1494, but within the general form of the balance sheet there can be found many ways of displaying or hiding certain information.

Accountancy schools teach their favourite methods and each country has some form of regulation of accountancy, so within a country there is some consistency of approach. However, between countries there are significant differences, and such differences can become issues of national pride. The Federal Accounting Standards Board in the USA has taken the stand that the American system is inherently the best, thus causing some pain to accountants unfortunate enough not to work in the USA.

Efforts are now being made to establish an accounting system recognized world-wide, but a number of present systems raise the question: how can investors invest wisely and analysts analyse wisely if they don't know how earnings and cash flow are calculated in each different market?

Whichever way accounts are done, there are always figures which do not relate to something which can actually be measured or counted. A company balance sheet can include a figure for 'goodwill'. This can be defined in two ways. It can be 'The value of a business to a purchaser over and above its net asset value.'[125] Or it can be 'An intangible asset. It is the good reputation enjoyed by a company, individual or product; the asset constituted by the tendency of the customers or clients of a business or professional practice to deal with that business or practice despite a change of personnel operating it – i.e, the attachment of existing customers.'[126] Even though the first definition does allow for a figure to be quoted, our reasons for being prepared to pay a certain amount for something can relate as much to our private logic as do our reasons for feeling warmly about a certain business. It's like putting a figure on how much somebody likes you. Can a Public Relations manager say, 'I've spent X amount on PR to create warm fuzzies and so increased the firm's goodwill by Y amount'?

Why not? It can be part of that artistic endeavour called financial engineering or creative accounting. As a company lawyer told me, 'There is an accountancy standards body, but in all the rules there are loopholes, and if you're paid enough money by a client to find a loophole eventually you'll find one.'

Every profession has its secrets. Usually the secret is that there is no secret, but in some professions the secret, if divulged, would threaten the profession's survival. Psychiatry's secret is that there is no satisfactory evidence to support the assumption on which psychiatry rests, that there is a physical cause of mental illness. Accountancy's secret is that there is no one true way of measuring profit and loss. Many psychiatrists have never forgiven their renegade colleagues R. D. Laing and Thomas Szasz for criticizing psychiatry, and many accountants might never forgive Terry Smith for revealing in 1992 in his book *Accounting for Growth*[128] how it was that apparently successful companies like Coloroll and Polly Peck could be making huge profits one week and go bust the next.

At that time Terry Smith was Head of UK Company Research with UBS Phillips and Drew. He was fired, and some of the companies whose accounting methods he analysed in his book first tried to stop its publication and then sued him. By then the Accounting Standards Board had moved to close the loopholes Terry Smith had identified. However, creativity, whether in the arts or in accounting, can never be completely stifled. In 1996 the second edition of *Accounting for Growth* was published. In this Terry Smith identified those parts of a company's accounts which investors should read most carefully.

The advice he had given in the first edition had not changed. In 1992 he wrote, 'Don't look at the profits, look at the cash. Cash is a fact. Profit is a guess.' In 1996, 'Cash is ultimately more important than profits. It pays the dividends and lack of cash is the reason businesses fail.' However, 'Cash flow needs as much thought and analysis as any other part of the accounts before it will yield its answers.'[129]

'The trouble with company accounts,' said the *Economist* in its survey of corporate management risk, 'far from being the authoritative documents they seem, are a curious cocktail of hard facts (many of them out of date) and subjective judgements – an ambiguity arising in part from the dual role of accounts as both a historical record of a firm's performance and a guide to its short-term prospects.'[130]

It is not just the figures in a company's accounts which can be ambiguous. Words can be very slippery. In comparing British Aerospace's company accounts for 1992 and 1993, Terry Smith noted that the income from sub-leases on certain aircraft 'was no longer "receivable" but just "expected"'. He asked, 'What are we to read into this change in wording? Frankly, I do not know. But "receivable" has a firmer feel than "expected". "Receivable" suggests that it at least refers to a sub lease which has been signed. Even then the lease income is not certain to be received – the lessee may go bust for example. But "expected" sounds like something much less definite. Does it indicate that BAe management had guesstimated the operating lease income from renewals after the existing operating leases, which are generally shorter than the head leases, expire? Once again, I don't know, but I feel that we need to know in order to reach an informed judgement on BAe's financial condition. After all this was not a trivial liability. The head lease liabilities were much larger than BAe's shareholder funds.'[131]

When a company's accounts are audited the auditor signs that 'the financial statements give a true and fair view of the state of affairs of the Company'. The auditor isn't saying, 'This is exactly how it is', but, 'This is how I think it is'. Or, as Sir David Tweedie, chairman of the Accounting Standards Board, said, 'Accounting is really all about judgement – truth and fairness is about judgement.'[132]

Judgement is always about morality.

7

Money and Morals

The invention
Of weights and measures
Makes robbery easier.
Signing contracts, setting seals,
Makes robbery more sure.
Teaching love and duty
Provides a fitting language
With which to prove that robbery
Is really for the general good.
A poor man must swing
For stealing a belt buckle
But if a rich man steals a whole state
He is acclaimed
As statesman of the year.

Chuang Tzu[1]

In the financial world there's no shortage of statesmen of the year. If there is one enduring, universal rule it's, 'In making money you can break the law and get away with it provided the sums of money involved are huge.' Steal a hundred dollars and you'll go to jail. Steal a hundred million and the worst that can happen to you is that you'll have to live in luxury in some foreign clime.

This is not just because if you're rich you can afford good lawyers. (Isn't it strange that in this context we say 'a good lawyer' when in fact we mean a wily, scheming, sailing-close-to-the-wind lawyer?) Stealing a hundred dollars is something you can do on your own. To steal a million you need help. Dishonesty on a massive scale involves many people, most if not all of whom like to think of themselves as honest and upright. They will use their power and influence to protect themselves, and thus you.

Why do people who pride themselves on being highly moral stray from their principles when money is in the offing? Because money means more – more choice, more freedom, more goodies. We want more partly because we are trying to fill the hole left in us by a childhood of inadequate love and concern, and partly because consciousness always wants more, be it more and more or more and different. There is also our fundamental insecurity of being a person always in danger of being overwhelmed by events in a world over which we have so little control. With money we can demand that the world be what we want it to be, and parts of the world will comply with our wishes. So Asil Nadir, who in 1990 faced a bankruptcy petition for £60 million and a set of criminal charges so long that it instantly found a place in the *Guinness Book of Records*,[2] suns himself on a terrace in Northern Cyprus, and Mrs Jones is banged up in Holloway because she can't pay her television licence.

To Jesus' question 'What profit a man if he gains the whole world and loses his soul?' the market offers a graded answer, as Michael Leunig showed (see over).[3]

Here Michael Leunig is illustrating both the callousness of the market and the fine distinctions we all make about the importance of money. This was a lesson I learned early in life.

My mother was a woman of absolute principles. She disapproved of the universe, and in it she particularly disapproved of gambling. Shortly after she married she discovered that my father had given his brother money to help him with a gambling debt. She threatened to end the marriage there and then. To make amends Dad offered that in future he would give Mother his unopened weekly wage packet. From then on she paid the bills and gave him a few shillings for his tobacco.

There was never much money in Dad's wage packet so luxuries were few and saved for special occasions. Mother had a habit of hiding special things away, sometimes in the oven of the fuel stove, which, once gas had been connected to the house, was rarely used. One evening Dad arrived home and found her beside herself with rage and tears, barely able to tell him how, because the weather had suddenly turned cold, she'd lit the stove and, alerted by a strange smell, found the remains of a very special pair of silk stockings.

Calming words from Dad had no effect. He reached into his pocket, took out a small wad of notes and offered them to her. She looked at the notes. They could have come from only one place, a bookmaker. Without a word she reached out and took the money.

Why does the chance of getting some money so often override the most dearly held principles? In my mother's case I know why. She was the fourth of six children in a family where blows and harsh words were plentiful and kisses rare, and so the hole inside her was as wide and deep as the Pacific. Relationships could never fill that hole because she hated herself and hated other people because she expected them to dislike her. So when she had a chance she turned to things to fill that hole. Alas, things can only fill holes in the space around us, never the holes inside us.

The fact that we go around with these holes inside us, some big, some small, but all of which give us a feeling of ache and emptiness, is not an excuse for being greedy or behaving dishonestly. That aching hole is simply one of the factors we need to take into account when we are choosing how we shall live our lives. We need to consider as well our responsibility to other people and the consequences near and far of our actions. Our actions are always a result of our choices, and we are not impelled to behave in any particular way except when we choose to see ourselves as being impelled to behave in a particular way. We always have a choice, and our choice is our responsibility. Those infamous men who have awarded themselves huge salaries or perks, or manipulated the market so as to cheat others and fill their own coffers, may or may not have had horrendous childhoods, but they have failed to consider their actions in terms of their responsibility to others and of the consequences of their actions. They have failed to behave in an ethical way.

Ethics has become a popular topic in many business schools in the UK, the USA and Australia. This sounds great, but ethics can be taught in two very different ways. It can be taught using the model of absolute values or, as some theologians and philosophers say, first principles, or it can be taught in terms of how we all have our own individual way of seeing things, so values are relative to individuals and the situations in which they find themselves. The first model has no grounding in science and the second has, but the first model is always popular because out of it can come an elite, the people who claim some special connection to some set of absolute values. The second model is the ultimate democracy. We all start at the same place, our unique perspective, and we have to argue and prove that our perspective is a better approximation of reality than that of anyone else. Users of the first model can always claim infallibility, while users of the second model always have to acknowledge doubt. American business schools must favour the first model, for out of them comes, as Robert Locke said, 'the self-serving elitist ideology of American managerialism".[4]

According to George Carey, the Archbishop of Canterbury, and other clerics, the people who hold the view that morality is relative to individuals and situations are responsible for the wickedness of the world. On BBC Radio 4 he gave this as the reason for the massacre by Thomas Hamilton of sixteen children and their teacher at Dunblane. There must be, he said, a return to absolute values. To which absolute value, I wondered, was he referring? Did he means an absolute value like 'All killing is wrong'? I waited for him to demand world-wide disarmament and to announce the withdrawal of all Anglican clergy from the armed forces. He did not. Did he mean killing children is wrong? I think killing children is wrong, but this is a relative value because you then have to decide at what age a person can be killed. When does a child cease to be a child? Is it all right to kill teenagers?

Paul Flynn, Member of Parliament for Newport West, has established that on the matter of killing people the Church of England keeps to relative values. First he asked Michael Alison, Second Church Estates Commissioner, representing the Church Commissioners, what new proposals the Commissioners had to improve the ethical content of their investment.

Michael Alison replied that the Commissioners' investments were always subject to ethical criteria and are continuously reviewed. Paul Flynn congratulated the commissioners on selling two million shares in BSkyB because of its investment in a pornographic channel. He then asked, 'When will the commissioners deal with their investment in another, more dangerous, obscenity – the international arms trade? It was reported recently that they had nearly 3 million shares in GEC. A quarter of that firm's production is for the arms trade and it is reported that the commissioners have discussed with it its exports to Indonesia and Nigeria. Did such a meeting take place and, if so, what was the outcome?'

Michael Alison replied, 'The Honourable Gentleman's question covers a wide spectrum. We are investors in GEC, whose armaments portfolio is held to be less than 30 per cent, which is the cut-off point for our ethical application. I remind the Honourable Gentleman that the five permanent members of the Security Council have reaffirmed, and continue to reaffirm, the inherent right to individual or collective self-defence that is recognized in Article 51 of the United Nations Charter, which implies that states have the right to acquire means of self-defence. Nevertheless, the Church of England does not invest in companies whose main business is armaments. It has to be less than 30 per cent.'

(In 1994 the Church Commissioners had 2,700,000 shares in GEC; their equity was valued at £1,772,000.)

Paul Flynn then issued a press release 'on behalf of the Archbishop of Canterbury':

> In its report today, the Archbishop of Canterbury's working party on Sin proposes a radical new approach to the whole question. In future, it suggests, Sin should be defined as 'immoral behaviour in which a person engages for not less than 30 per cent of the time.'
>
> Commenting favourably on the report, the Archbishop said, 'Our approach to sin has always been subject to ethical criteria and is continuously reviewed. We need a practical definition based on the realities of modern life, including the lives of members of the Royal Family and Conservative Members of Parliament. Nevertheless, the Church does not approve of those whose main business is sin. A cut-off point of 30 per cent is realistic.'[5]

Christians are not the only believers in absolute values which in practice become relative. The Taliban militia, fighting a holy war to establish the Islamic Republic of Afghanistan, applied their absolute laws in the areas that came under their control. Girls' schools were closed, women were confined to their homes, televisions smashed, law breakers had hands and feet cut off or were subjected to public hanging. The Taliban were also absolutely against the trade in heroin. But wars are expensive. As reported Maggie O'Kane in her article *God's Dealers*, 'God's soldiers – who swore to wipe out the poisoned poppy from the new Islam Republic of Afghanistan – have decided to use it to fund their crusade. The poppy harvest in Afghanistan this month will be the biggest in the country's history – enough to finance the Holy War by supplying more than half the world's heroin needs. God has been good.'[6]

Many people, distressed by the amount of suffering they see, want to believe that there exists some absolute truth concerning the rights, needs and feelings of all human beings and, once we are aware of this truth, it will reform us. Somehow, the scales will fall from our eyes, we shall see the truth and become good. Cruel people, greedy people, power-hungry people can all, if the conditions are right, be touched by this truth and so repent and reform.

Of course some such people do change. They go through experiences which lead them to look at themselves critically, they take responsibility for what they have done, they become wiser, happier, and nicer to other people. The first step in such a change is to stop lying to yourself. Unfortunately, for many people lying to yourself is established in childhood and becomes such an ingrained habit that the person is unaware of doing it. Sometimes therapy creates an awareness, but the person cannot change any more than confirmed smokers, though they know the dangers, can change. Lying to yourself, like smoking, brings immediate rewards. Nicotine brings relief of tension, and lying to yourself gives the illusion of self-confidence.

John, a thirty-eight-year-old paedophile, served an eighteen-month sentence during which he attended a therapy group and became aware of how he lied to himself. He 'believes fooling other people comes naturally to child abusers, because they spend so much time lying to themselves. "You have to be an accomplished liar; that goes with the territory. I would convince myself that I was different from the paedophiles I read about, and I would make people see me as John, the nice geezer. Some of these people found out in the most horrific way when I abused their children that I wasn't quite what they thought . . . No one can ever stand up and say I'm cured. There is no cure."'[7]

Studies of adults who become paedophiles show that in childhood they suffered much physical and sexual abuse. To survive they had to distance themselves from and deny their pain. Distancing and denying are ways of lying to yourself.

Another much more prevalent way of learning how to lie to yourself comes from being born to parents who believe themselves to be good parents because they are strict with their children and demand obedience. Such strictness, often accompanied by physical chastisement, places a child in a great dilemma. When his father beats him he feels anger to the point of hatred for the parent who inflicts the pain and for the other parent who fails to protect him from the pain. But these are the people on whom he depends. His own truth is, 'My bad parents are hurting me', but this truth leaves him alone and helpless. To protect himself he lies to himself and says, 'I am bad and am being justly punished by my good parents.' To protect his parents and see them as good he learns how to lie to himself, a skill which as a child he had to use constantly. Asil Nadir's biographer David Barchard recorded that,

> the Nadir children accepted their parents' constant discipline, and the corporal punishment that came with it, but they could see that they were treated more strictly than many of their friends. They belonged to a strongly patriarchal culture. There was no question of openly defying their parents or resisting their authority, although in childhood there were many occasions when they whispered their resentment at their harsh upbringing to each other in secret. There was nothing they could do to change it, and in time they would all accept the mould, more or less as their parents wanted.[8]

Lying is often necessary in order to survive as a body and as a person. However, when lying becomes a way of life we do severe damage to our ability to work out what is actually going on. The way we are constructed physiologically means that we can never be certain of what is going on around us. Throughout our lives the only thing about which we can be absolutely certain is what goes on inside us – our thoughts, feelings, images. But if we lie to ourselves we lose the only certainty we have.

If we tell ourselves lies like, 'I value the way my father beat me for my own good', 'I love my parents, I couldn't possibly get angry with them', 'I'm not jealous of my brother even though my mother preferred him to me', 'What's happening to me isn't happening to me', we can no longer carry out the one act which gives us a still, firm centre to a continuously changing universe. It's the act where, when we are not sure how to respond to a certain event, we pause, look inward and say to ourselves, 'How do I feel about this?' If you are not in the habit of lying to yourself, the answer which arises in you is a truth which forms a reliable basis on which to proceed. It might not be politic to tell others of this truth, and indeed in some situations you might deem it best not to act directly on this truth (like 'I'm bloody angry but if I let on it'll only make things worse'), but you know for certain where you are and then you can make your way in an uncertain world.

Lying to yourself means denying your own certain truth. You can perform the act of pausing and asking yourself how you feel, but you cannot be sure of the truth of the answer you receive. Is this what you really feel or is it what you think you ought to feel?

Lying to yourself often involves the necessity of lying to other people. The Nadir children might have whispered to one another, commenting unfavourably about their parents, but if their father Irfan or their formidable mother Safiye demanded to know what they were saying they would lie for fear of being punished further. Children of strict parents have to learn to lie in order to survive their childhood. They discover that they can use this skill on other people. So it is no wonder that Asil Nadir could woo and charm people who could help him on his path to success, and no wonder he could later protest his innocence with such sincerity.

David Barchard called Asil 'an indomitable spirit'. Asil had another reason for feeling confident. Irfan repeatedly told his children that God forgives sinners who work very hard. Asil Nadir always worked very hard, so God will forgive him even if his creditors don't.

To draw comfort from the idea that God always forgives sinners who work very hard you always have to refrain from asking awkward questions like, 'Didn't Hitler and Stalin work very hard? Should God forgive them?' Believing that values are relative to individuals and situations always requires much thought and questioning. If it is wrong to steal a million from a company, is it also wrong to steal small quantities of that company's stationery? A personnel manager of a large company in the UK told me how she had done some research on the quantity of stationery lost when employees think along the lines of 'I need a new hole punch at home, so I'll take this one and order another through stationery.' The total value of the stuff taken made it a very major crime. A hotel manager in Australia told me that pilfering is chronic in the hotel business. Staff think that, because they're not stealing money, taking soap, shampoo and toilet paper isn't stealing. Such activities can arise from having a relativist view with very relaxed definitions of right and wrong, or an absolutist view and be well practised in fudging.

By fudging I mean, in thinking something through, not proceeding carefully, step by step, with much checking against reality, but instead making big leaps in argument, changing the meanings of the words used from one statement to another and ignoring inconvenient facts, to arrive at a conclusion which benefits the fudger in some way.

In my childhood home Dad often talked about the iniquities of the rich industrialists and, although not a believer, would quote with great satisfaction Jesus' teaching that 'It is easier for a camel to go through a needle's eye, than for a rich man to enter the kingdom of God.' Mother insisted that I attend Presbyterian Church and Sunday School, and so there I became aware of the art of fudging. In one Sunday School lesson my teacher, whose reason to protect the rich was beyond my ken, explained that Jesus wasn't actually talking about a sewing needle. She told us how in Jesus' time each city was surrounded by a wall whose gates were locked at sunset. However, a small gate called a Needle's Eye was kept open for latecomers. It would be a tight fit for a camel laden with goods to get through this gate, but with a push and a shove it would. No doubt all those industrialists who were making huge fortunes out of the war and so incensing my father got the right push and shove and are now ensconced in heaven.

To be able to fudge you have to be able to think two opposing things at one and the same time and not notice the incongruity. Whenever we think something through without resorting to fudging and we feel reasonably sure of our arguments we can listen to our critics without getting frightened by their arguments, but consider them carefully, perhaps refuting them, perhaps amending our own arguments to take account of certain points. Whenever we use fudging we see our critics as being dangerous and evil. We seek to silence them. We might try to do this by repeating our arguments more and more loudly, brooking no interruption while slandering our critics. As individuals we can get very angry and abusive with anyone who criticizes us, or we can try to make the person feel guilty by showing that we are deeply hurt by their criticisms, or we can sulk, punishing our critics by shutting them out of our lives. At a political level we can charge our critics with blasphemy or crimes against the state. We have to silence them at all cost because they are threatening to make us see the lies we are telling ourselves. A good measure of how much a person is resorting to fudging is how angrily he responds to criticism and what he does to silence his critics.

One of the problems of believing in absolute values is that such values tend to come in sets where one value doesn't fit logically with another. Both Calvinists and Muslims are presented with the absolutes that all events are determined by the will of God and that people are responsible for what they do. Thus God determined that Asil Nadir should use some very creative accounting, but that poor Asil was responsible for what he did and should get clobbered, if not by a God who forgives sinners, by a Serious Fraud Office which does not.

Another problematic set of absolute beliefs is that of the Just World.

Many religious faiths have at their centre one God, the Creator, who is omni-present and all-knowing. So far, so straightforward. The problem arises with his benevolence and power. Take these statements:

> God is all good.
> God is all powerful.
> Suffering exists.

As many philosophers have pointed out, if two of these statements are true the other statement is false. No doubt we'd all agree that suffering exists, so is God all good or all powerful?

From the stories in the Old Testament it would be possible to make a case for God being all powerful but not good, but it would be very scary to have a God like that, a sort of Saddam Hussein God. A God who is benevolent but incompetent and absentminded is quite heart-warming, but you couldn't rely on him. At present there's a fashion for tender-hearted clerics who want a benevolentGod to talk about God sharing our suffering. This might comfort some people, but what would we think of a father who sympathized with his children's suffering but did nothing to protect them?

Religious leaders don't confront this dilemma. They fudge it. Of course we all fudge when we're thinking. We're all capable of holding two opposing ideas at one and the same time and often we're far too lazy to think something through. Thinking clearly is the hardest work of all. However, we cannot enact two opposing ideas simultaneously. We can pretend, conceal, deny, but we cannot, say, simultaneously gamble and refrain from gambling, be honest and dishonest with regard to a certain event, or simultaneously present one argument and its opposite. Of course, many people do try to get away with fudging and, because their audience is unskilled in identifying fudges or too docile or frightened to charge them with hypocrisy, they get away with it. But in the end someone suffers. In personal relationships, in religion, politics, economics and all aspects of our lives, fudging leads to disaster.

You don't have to have had a religious education in order to know how to fudge, but it certainly helps. Fudging in religious arguments is a skill that's been developed over many centuries. Sometimes the fudge is complex, with words changing meaning from one use to another and gaps in the argument being pasted over. Sometimes the fudge is simple. The leaders say, 'God is mysterious. We cannot understand his ways. You must have faith.'

Those people who believe that to be good they must have faith but who have failed to learn how to lie to themselves make their lives a misery as they berate themselves for their lack of faith. In the course of my work I have met many such people – kind, truthful, loving, honest – suffering the tortures of the prison of depression, hating themselves, feeling themselves to be shut out from God's love because they doubt when they should have faith.

Other religious followers shut off their ability for critical thinking and tell themselves that they must do what their leaders advise. They must be as docile, obedient children who never question their elders. They find security in obedience and tradition. Anyone who tried to make the kinds of changes advocated by Will Hutton and Hamish McRae would meet tremendous resistance from such people. Any moral change which economists and others might advocate asks us to reconsider the answer we gave to the question we had asked ourselves, 'How shall I live my life?' Deciding to become docile and obedient to leaders, whether religious or political, means giving the leaders the right to answer this question. People who have done this find thinking for themselves far too frightening.

Not all religions postulate a single God, but all religions postulate that we live in a Just World where goodness is rewarded and badness punished. Religions differ on definitions of goodness and badness, rewards and punishments, but they agree that we live under a Grand Design where justice reigns supreme. The belief in the Just World gives a wonderful sense of security. Be good and nothing bad can happen to you. You are also spared the pain of pity, for when you see a disaster occurring to other people you know that they are getting their just deserts. Aren't we always being told that people are unemployed because they are lazy and feckless? It becomes a bit tricky when the victims are children and presumably haven't lived long enough to deserve such a punishment. But then these children might have some kind of inherent wickedness. It could be because we were born in sin, as the Christian Church teaches, or it could be one of those genes that American scientists keep finding. It could be that aggression gene that unemployed black men have, or it could be that homelessness gene found in people sleeping rough, or the depression gene so prevalent among the poor.

The problem with believing in a Just World arises when the disaster occurs to you. You ask, 'Why did this happen to me?' You can't explain it as happening by chance because in the Just World nothing happens by chance. You can only say, 'It was my fault,' or 'It was someone else's fault.' People who are well practised in guilt blame themselves and become depressed. People who are well practised in not assuming responsibility for their actions blame other people and become paranoid.

The prevalence of depression would suggest that many people choose the first alternative, but actually the majority of the believers in the Just World choose to blame others for their disaster. There are many people who would say that they are not at all religious, but they believe that somehow, in the end, it turns out that the good are rewarded and the bad punished. When believers in the Just World look about them they can hardly be impressed with the efficiency of the system. Indeed it would be easy to argue that actually the system works in the opposite way, that the good are punished and the bad rewarded!

Rather than abandon their belief in the Just World many people explain their failure to be rewarded for their goodness in terms of injustice and betrayal. This way of thinking underlies all racism. I often hear someone complaining, 'What's the council ever done for me? I've paid my rates and got nothing but those blacks, they've only got to step off the plane and the councils given them a flat.' The sub-text is, 'I've been good and I've never got my reward.'

Some people decide that if the Just World system has failed them they have the right to take what they should have been given. Many a solicitor who, after years of honest practice, helps himself to his clients' money, or an accountant, always scrupulously honest in his accounting, who fiddles the books to his own advantage, has in his own way of seeing it given himself the rewards he deserves.

When believers in the Just World do enjoy good fortune they are likely not to see themselves as simply being lucky but as receiving their rightful rewards. Some people born into the aristocracy consider themselves to be what the word aristocrat originally meant, 'the best', and they see their wealth and privileges as their just dues. To prise these privileges away from them Will Hutton would have to get them to confront their belief in the Just World and recognize it as false. Alas, the beliefs that are the hardest to relinquish are those that feed our vanity.

Whether we are rewarded or not, the belief in the Just World is important because it is a defence against one of the worst feelings we can have, the feeling that we are helpless and in the power of forces we cannot control. We will lie to ourselves and hold all kinds of irrational beliefs (like believing in astrology) rather than feel helpless.

As a species we're physically rather puny and we live on a planet and in a universe which are indifferent to our existence (although there are a number of scientists who would have us believe that this unimaginably vast and strange universe was created just so we could exist – which is a nice piece of conceit). No wonder our early ancestors dreamt of gods who might care for them and protect them from danger just as parents do for children. However, children who, as they get older, fail to develop the capacity to take responsibility for themselves never grow up, no matter how old they might become. Just as children will want to boss other children around while still being dependent on their parents, so there are many adults who are very ready to tell the rest of us what to do while being very dependent on parent surrogates. Many of these dependent children in adult bodies inhabit the very institutions which Will Hutton wants to change. These child-adults will resist any effort to get them to change by those reformers who see change in terms of people taking responsibility for themselves. Yet this is the only kind of change that can produce worthwhile results. Change through coercion is never real change, only actions driven by fear.

In recent years religious groups have espoused environmental or anti-war causes and religious leaders have stressed the importance of cherishing God's gift to us, the planet. However, the thrust of the religious argument is always to the future. If you're good you'll get rewarded. That doesn't necessarily mean that you'll get your rewards in this world. If you've been a good Christian you'll have stored up treasures in heaven and if you're a good Hindu you could be reborn as a rich man.

The promised perfection of heaven has always been a bother to me. It also increasingly annoys me that I have, at the very outside, twenty years to go and, if death is the end of my identity, I'm not going to know how all the news stories I follow will turn out. I'm not going to be here in 2020 to see if Hamish McRae got it right. On the other hand, how can I be sure that heaven takes the *Economist* and the *Guardian*?

Believing that death is the end is, as many religious people have told me, very scary, but believing in an afterlife creates other troubling dilemmas. In the afterlife, are you still able to see what's happening on earth? Do you remember your past life? Each of these questions can be answered yes or no and combined with each other to form four outcomes. Which of these do you prefer? Note that to understand morality we have to be able to remember the past.

	Remember the past	Don't remember the past
Can't see the world	Anxiety about what is happening in the world, especially to loved ones.	Don't know who you are. No understanding of morality
Can see the world	Can see your loved ones suffering but cannot help them.	Don't know who you are. Confused about what goes on in the world. No understanding of morality.

Thus in the afterlife if you remember your earthly life you continue to care about your children and your friends, and you go on caring, as we do, about your children's children, and your friends' children, and so on for eternity. You might be able to tell yourself that eventually they'll be in a happy afterlife too, but you either feel eternally anxious or you have to become indifferent to their current suffering and the suffering of those who do not qualify for eternal happiness. If you don't remember your past you cannot enjoy the satisfaction of being rewarded for your goodness, nor can you understand why some poor sods are being punished. Worse still, you've lost your identity, something you've fought against losing all your life. True, you might have merged into the cosmic whole, as Hinduism and Buddhism promise, but you won't know about this any more than those people who, on death, decompose into the particles that form the universe.

Whatever belief we choose to hold about death it will be like every belief we hold, having good implications and bad implications. We all hold metaphysical beliefs, that is, about the nature of death and the purpose of life. Choose to believe that life ends in death, and your purpose in life becomes to make this life satisfactory in whatever way you choose to define satisfactory. Choose to believe that death is a doorway to another life, and, assuming that the next life has the possibility of being better than this one, your purpose in life becomes to qualify for the better afterlife. Dither about choosing and you get double the bad implications as well as double the good.

Neither belief about the nature of death is more conducive than the other to leading a moral life. Many people who see life as the real thing, not a dress rehearsal, define a satisfactory life as one where they have done something to make the world a better place. Many villains believe that by working hard or saying enough prayers they'll win a place in heaven.

Believing that death is the end does help people to focus on the present. If you're one of those people who'd rather be good than happy you can skip the next few pages, but, if happiness appeals, read on.

The religious way of looking to the future is often accompanied by a profound distaste for the world and present time. If you adopt this way of thinking and feeling you prevent yourself from being happy. Make millions and you'll still be miserable. Happiness is something that can only be enjoyed in present time. You can gather around you all the treasures in the world but if you can't enjoy them in the present you can't enjoy them anywhere. A religious belief which focuses on the future and rejects the world precludes happiness.

To explain how this rejection of the world comes about I'd like you to remember an event in your life when you were in a particular place and something happened which led you to an intense disgust with yourself. It might be that you made a fool of yourself in front of people you wanted to impress, or you made a grave error of judgement, or you were betrayed or rejected by someone important to you or you suffered a terrible loss. Recall the dark turmoil of feelings inside you. Recall too the place where this happened. Do you feel the same about that place as you did before this event occurred? Very likely you don't. Before the event perhaps you had no particular feelings towards the place, perhaps you'd seen it as being delightful. After the event you saw the place differently. All the pleasure it gave you had drained away and instead it had taken on qualities which repelled and disgusted you. You hoped never to set foot there ever again. You might tell yourself this is irrational but you can't change how you feel.

Many people have this kind of experience in the first years of their life, but in a much more profound, all-absorbing way. The child has perhaps been punished severely, or abandoned, betrayed or humiliated by those who should have cared for him. Adults are very prone to place all the blame on the child when something goes wrong, and children are very prone to blame themselves for things that are not their fault, such as their parents separating or a parent dying. When this happens the child is suffused with dark feelings of self-disgust and self-hatred. These feelings spill over and in the child's eyes suffuse the world around him. He becomes as disgusted with the world as he is with himself.

You might not recall such an incident from childhood but you might have seen a child who has made a big mistake, or has been punished severely or humiliated, set about destroying his own beloved toys.

This experience takes away from the child something very precious with which he was born. Babies come into the world full of joy and interest in the world. They are curious about everything and everything has the potential for arousing joy. Everything for them happens in the present and so they can be very happy. Later in life they can be happy only if they have retained this joy and interest in the world around them and the capacity to live in the present and not be constantly thinking about the future and the past.

The child who has learned to feel disgust and hatred for himself and the world around him loses the ability to live in the present because the only way he can prevent himself from being overcome by despair is to give himself hope for the future. He tells himself stories of how in the future he will redeem himself in some way and thus be rewarded for his valour and goodness. You can probably remember some of the stories you told yourself about what you would do when you grew up. Just what you dreamed of doing depended on what rewards you saw were adequate recompense for what you had suffered. If at the same time you were having a religious education you were being told that the world and the flesh should be rejected. Only the spirit and the future after death should be cherished.

Perhaps, despite various childhood traumas, you retained your pleasure and interest in the world and ability to enjoy present time and you were untouched by religious teaching. Out of your childhood dreams you created your plan for life, and you set about achieving your goals. Perhaps you planned to be a successful concert pianist, or a parent, or a successful entrepreneur with a passion for great cars. One glorious day your audience rises in thunderous applause, or you hold your perfect new baby in your arms, or you take possession of the world's most expensive car. You are suffused with, nay you become an intense feeling of joy and delight. The past and the future vanish. You are happy.

But what of those people who, even if they achieve what they set out to do, still see the world as somehow tainted? When their moment of achievement comes any feeling of joy and delight is tempered with doubt, even certainty, that their achievement is not right. They think that they do not deserve the applause, that the baby is flawed, that owning the most expensive car in the world leaves them feeling flat. Money doesn't buy happiness so the Church teaches, but that's only when we despise the world and cannot live in the here and now.

The only way to hold religious beliefs and not have to resort to fudges and lying to yourself, all of which cripple your intellect and make you less than the person you are, is to hold the beliefs as hopes in a world where the future is uncertain rather than absolute truths in a world where the future is absolutely certain. If you simply hope that somehow, in the end, a beneficent God will make everything right, you won't ever commit a cruelty such as telling people who suffer, like the parents of the children massacred in Dunblane, that this tragedy was part of God's plan. If you simply hope that by living decently you'll achieve happiness and security you'll feel sad but not in danger of being annihilated when people betray you or rewards don't come, and you won't be so stupid as to think that being rich proves that you are good.

Simply hoping that your beliefs about life, death and the hereafter might be right and knowing that other people hold different beliefs means that you will never turn against the people who don't share your beliefs, hating them and trying to destroy them. You don't become a dangerous person.

Unfortunately the world is full of such dangerous people. They are sure that the values they hold are the absolute right ones. They take no account of the fact that when it comes to virtues and vices we each have our own ideas.

A Choice of Values

In some of the workshops I ran over a period of some fifteen years I used the following worksheet to create a discussion.

> Here is a list of virtues. Choose the one which for you is the most important and put a 1 beside it.
>
> Now choose the next most important and put a 2 beside it, and so on down to 10.
>
> | | |
> |---|---|
> | Concern for truth | Ambition |
> | Love | Generosity |
> | Team Spirit | Loyalty |
> | Perseverance | Courage |
> | Gratitude | Kindness |
>
> Now look again at the virtue you regard as the most important. Why is .... important to you?

I could have chosen other virtues for the list of ten, but the list itself was not of prime importance. I wanted to show, first, how much individuals differed in their priorities, and, second, that whatever choice was made, the first choice related directly both to how individuals experienced their sense of existence and how they had interpreted their past experience.

The answers to the question 'Why is (top priority) important to you?' showed how those people who experienced their sense of existence in relationship to other people (extraverts) tended to choose virtues which could relate to relationships, virtues like love, kindness, generosity, and those people who experienced their sense of existence in achievement, organization and control (introverts) tended to choose virtues which could relate to gaining these, such as concern for truth, courage and ambition. Why an extravert person chose love rather than generosity, or an introvert person truth rather than courage could relate to that person's past experience.

My choice was always courage, a choice I backed up with the argument that without courage none of the other virtues are possible. This might have sounded profound, but whatever profundities, wise or not, we approvingly utter, they have rarely come solely from our calm reflection. Mostly they come from hard experience.

My priority of courage came from my early experience of its opposite, fear. I was born into a family who didn't want me. Dad, as he later told me, had wanted a boy and so had to make a great and, I think, an eventually successful effort to love me. My sister never forgave me for being born, and on her sixth birthday, and she showed this constantly in all the delightful ways a big sister can. My mother, when alone with me and in a despairing rage, would beat me and say she was going to kill me and then kill herself. From what evidence I have I suspect that I survived babyhood by good luck and because a caring aunt and grandmother sometimes looked after me. In such circumstances it is essential to create the virtue of courage in order to overcome fear.

It is often said that the market operates on fear and greed. If this is so, it would be interesting to see how many players in the market would divide between those who choose courage and those who choose generosity, the first group having had childhoods where they were often frightened and the second childhoods where they were deprived not so much of things as of love.

Ask a Market Wizard what makes a good trader, or a manager a good manager, or a doctor a good doctor, and the answer you get is a list of virtues. When a group of people working together to achieve something agree upon a list of desirable virtues that list very easily turns into an ideology. The political philosopher Shirley Robin Letwin defined the ideology of Thatcherism as being 'the vigorous virtues' of the individual who is 'upright, self-sufficient, energetic, adventurous, independent-minded, loyal to friends, and robust against enemies'. She contrasted these virtues with the 'softer' virtues of 'kindness, humility, gentleness, sympathy, cheerfulness'.[9] Of course an upright, independent individual could also be kind, but in situations where the individual deemed there was a conflict between uprightness and kindness, kindness would be abandoned. A result of this priority of virtues was that, when Margaret Thatcher was showing how exceedingly kind she was, many of us were repelled by the hollowness of such a display.

The virtues which Margaret Thatcher admired and emulated suggest a childhood where much was demanded of her and little given. I could feel sorry for her, had she not tried to force her ideas upon us with the self-righteous cruelty of one who believes she knows best. As she showed in her 'this lady's not for turning' speech and in many other ways, Margaret Thatcher was one of those people who regard being true to her own ideas as being more important than being liked by other people. In contrast, her great mate Ronald Reagan spared no effort in getting everyone to like him but was indifferent to being consistent and accurate in what he said. An introvert and an extravert, they made a matched pair.

In general observation and in my clinical work I have often seen how married couples or couples living together are made up of an introvert and an extravert.[10] More recently I have found the same combination in business partnerships. These can be very successful when each person appreciates the other's talents, and both sets of talents form a complementary whole, but problems can arise when the partnership is faced with the following fairly common dilemma.

> Suppose you were faced with an inescapable situation where you can act only in one of two ways. If you act in one way people will like you but you won't respect yourself, and if you act in the other way people won't like you but you will respect yourself. Which will you choose?

For introverts the choice is simple. Respecting yourself always wins over being liked. For many extraverts the choice is equally simple. Being liked wins over principle every time. Extraverts excel at being charming rogues. However, many other extraverts suffer on the horns of this dilemma. They know what is the right thing to do and they want to do it, but they can't give up their longing to be liked.

This is not to say that introverts are invariably more morally upright than extraverts. An introvert's need to respect himself can involve avenging an injury with murder, or proving strength by carrying out a crime. Moreover, we all, introverts and extraverts, have a capacity for self-delusion. It's very easy to persuade yourself that you're acting with the best possible motives. Politicians and criminals of all kinds are past masters of this.

Two people can do the same thing but for very different reasons. An introvert and an extravert might work together on an insider trading scam, the introvert following the principle that as a superior person he is above the law, the extravert wanting to please the introvert and to get the money with which to impress other people and earn their liking.

On the other hand, people can behave in ways which surprise us or merit our condemnation.

Many of us would feel that there is no doubt that Ferdinand and Imelda Marcos plundered their country, yet, without having answered the some 298 charges against her, Imelda, after Ferdinand's death, returned to the Philippines where her loyal supporters elected her to parliament. Loyalty is a problematic virtue. Should you give unquestioned loyalty to another person or a cause?

When you're a child you want your parents to be loyal to you because they're all you've got between you and the dangerous world. When your parents side with other adults against you, as adults are prone to do, you feel alone and bereft. In an attempt to make restitution to yourself you can decide to be loyal to others in the way your parents should, you feel, have been loyal to you. Thus you choose to make loyalty the prime virtue and, if you are unlucky, spend your life being loyal to someone who, like your parents, betrays you. This, I guess, was the experience of some of Robert

Maxwell's supporters who had been turning a blind eye or excusing his megalomaniac conduct.

Don't the marriage vows imply loyalty? At the height of the Nick Leeson scandal I had several women journalists phoning me to ask whether Lisa Leeson was a fool or crazy to remain loyal to Nick. From the way they framed their questions it seemed that they had already made that painful journey through love, loyalty and betrayal. They knew that for a woman it's best to get out fast from such a relationship. From what I've learned about Lisa from newspapers and television it seemed to me that she had built her life around Nick. Caring for him was her purpose in life. Moreover, as a good introvert, she could not let herself down by being cruel and disloyal. He was her only hope, just as Imelda was the only hope of the Filipino poor, and she could not betray him.

Loyalty provides one of the reasons why people who reveal that certain colleagues are guilty of unethical behaviour are themselves so often punished while the guilty go free. In these cases loyalty is seen as more important than honesty.

One man's vice can be another man's virtue. In Anglo-Saxon communities the words 'bribery' and 'corruption' go hand in hand, like pepper and salt. In Italy bribery is a way of life. Explaining this, a Milanese businessman talking to me about bribery and the Italian political scandals said, 'You must remember that Italy hasn't been a country for all that long. The people here have never learned to trust a government. We were ruled by the Austrians and before that the Spanish. People had to protect themselves. They withdrew into family groups and did whatever was necessary to protect the family. They think of the government as the enemy and they protect themselves.'

Italians have another reason for distrusting the government. I had asked Francesco, a lawyer, and his wife Maria, a teacher, to read what I had written about the choice of values in Italy. They pointed out that many Italians have another reason for distrusting the government. They remember the Fascist government under Mussolini and how the idea of nationalism was used then. Many Italians are afraid of a return to Fascism and thus, unlike Americans, they have a dislike of nationalist ideas.

According to the Protestant churches, sin and guilt must be borne by the individual until death and the day of judgement. Catholics can confess and repent again and again throughout their lifetime. Professor Franco Ferrarotti of Rome University, the holder of the first academic chair of sociology in Italy, saw the attempts being made in Italy to reduce the amount of bribery and corruption in public life, which resulted in some of the biggest names in Italy being charged and in some cases convicted, as arising 'not from any moral sense but rather from the fact that the big Italian economic interests couldn't afford any more to pay the additional costs of bribes when they came face to face with international competition.' He described how in the Mediterranean culture 'stealing is not considered a serious offence, especially if you do it with manual dexterity. Corruption, if it does not entail physical offence to the persons involved, is rather considered a fine art. The same thing applies to lying, which is considered very serious in the Protestant countries. Here it is considered expedient: part of the way of life. An important American President – Nixon – lost the presidency because he told a lie. If we were to apply that principle to Italy, we would soon be without any kind of political leader whatsoever.'

He went on to explain that 'The Catholic institution of confession is crucial in Italy. First, you sin, then you confess. Then you get absolution and you sin again. It's a virtuous cycle of vice. Repentance doesn't mean that you aren't going to sin again. If you didn't, the institution would go bankrupt. Confession is a Mediterranean institution that is difficult to understand for outsiders. It really is basic to the understanding of the Inquisition, the Red Brigades and all the dark aspects of Italian history.'[11]

Francesco and Maria did not agree that Catholicism had had such a marked effect in Italy. They said, 'Italy is no longer a Catholic country.' When every Italian felt compelled to follow Catholic practices confession might be used in the way Franco Ferrarotti described, but now only those people who wish to attend church go. Church attendance in Italy has dropped like the birthrate, the lowest in Europe.

However, they did agree that the decision by the law to prosecute those involved in bribery and corruption, which meant taking on the powerful Mafia, stemmed from the big firms not being able to afford to pay the bribes demanded. Also, the firms wanted to trade in Europe, while the excesses of the eighties had left the government running out of money. I would guess that the change in attitude to religion meant many changes in the choices people made about values.

The change in attitude to the Church must have many causes, but an important one must have been the organization of education. Schools in Italy are no longer the province of the Church. Nowadays there are a few private Catholic schools, but most are state-run and classes in religion are optional.

Educating all children in the same system is the most effective method of breaking down class, racial and religious barriers. The Australia I grew up in was just like Northern Ireland, divided into two communities of Catholic and Protestant who did not mix and did not tolerate one another. There were two education systems, State and Catholic, and Catholic parents were forbidden by the Church to send their children to State schools. However, by the early sixties the Catholic schools could not cope with the influx of Catholic migrants and the ban was lifted. Within a decade the separation of Catholics and Protestants into hostile groups had virtually disappeared. Tragically, in Northern Ireland the Catholic bishops insist on the maintenance of Catholic schools and the British government has done little to promote integrated schools.

I examined further different attitudes to corruption by talking to a company manager in advertising who had had extensive experience overseas. I told him that in my years in the UK I had not observed the politicians being involved in financial scandals with anything like the frequency of their Australian and American counterparts. I asked, 'Is there less corruption in the UK, or is it simply a matter of avoiding publicity?'

He said, 'It is difficult to be absolutely sure about that. I started working in the seventies and corruption was not something that you encountered. In the advertising business there was certainly something called sharp practice which some people capitalized on, but corruption *per se* I don't think there was. Having come back to this country after being in Japan and the USA I find that corruption has reared its ugly head because the controls were relaxed and there was more money floating about. That's when people start behaving in ways that they shouldn't. In Japan there is much more institutional corruption. Bribing people is par for the course. My job in Japan was to spend money in the media. In the UK and the USA, the more money you spend the better deals you can do because you can use what's called volume discount which is shown on the invoice. In Japan, because the system developed differently, these discounts weren't automatically rebated. Instead, the money arrived at the company president's office once a month in a brown paper bag full of cash. Japan, of course, is a cash society. In the late seventies there used to be something called settlement day one day a month when literally thousands of people would be walking around Tokyo with bags full of cash to settle their bills. So there is far more scope for corruption in Japan and it is much more accepted.'

There might not be people walking around the City of London with brown paper bags full of cash, but bribes can be made by calling them something else. BBC Television's *The Money Programme* on bribery and the market described how large bribes can be hidden in company accounts. They can even be made to look like tax deductible expenses. The bribes can take the form of equity in a company, or contracts of employment, or offers of employment to the relatives of the bribed, or even real estate.[12] Those who do the bribing need not bear the guilt and sin because they can persuade themselves that what they do is for the good of the company. Both the Protestant and the Catholic conscience thus employed would feel no need to heed the exhortations to virtue by those economists who see an end to our economic woes only through a change to virtuous behaviour.

The first problem in getting people to change their wicked ways is to get them to admit that their ways are wicked. Surveys of people's attitudes always reveal the presence of the P-factor, the piousness which ensures that the majority of people will report that they put family and friends way ahead of money in importance, and that nothing concerns them more than the state of the environment.

Researchers don't usually have the opportunity to ask a supplementary question which will reveal the hollowness of such claims.

Nick Ross on his BBC Radio 4 programme *Call Nick Ross* has developed a very sharp line in supplementary questions. One morning when the topic under discussion was the possible increase in tax paid by middle income earners, one man rang to say that he was very concerned with the limited government funding of schools and teachers and that he would be willing to pay more tax to bring about improvements. There was nothing in his tone of voice or what he said to suggest that his motives were anything but sincere. Nick then asked, 'If an accountant looked at your last tax return and told you that you'd paid too much tax, would you want to get your money back?'

At first the man was too surprised to reply, and then, fumbling for an answer, he said, yes, he would want his money back. He was too shocked to think of an answer along the lines of being willing to pay more tax provided all the middle and upper income earners did, but actually he had precluded himself from taking that stance by having earlier assumed the high moral ground.

The operation of the P-factor can turn every activity, however dubious, into a virtue. When the eminent political economist Goldwin Smith was presenting his inaugural lecture in Oxford in 1859 he said,

> To buy the cheapest and sell in the dearest market, the supposed concentration of economical selfishness, is simply to fulfil the command of the Creator, who provides for all the wants of His creatures through each other's help; to take from those who have abundance, and to carry to those who have need.[13]

This economist was speaking just ten years after the famine in Ireland. In 1841 the population of Ireland was 8.2 million. By 1851 it had fallen to 6.5 million. At least a million people died of starvation and disease and millions who survived emigrated under appalling conditions to America. There was little evidence of those with abundance giving to those in need.

However, there has never been any difficulty in associating money with virtue. Amongst English essayists one of the sharpest eyes cast upon our behaviour was that of Jill Tweedie. In her weekly column in the *Guardian* she made us laugh and she made us think. In 1978 she wrote,

> What I do find hard to bear is money in its role as the coinage of virtue and that, I sometimes think, is its biggest role in our society. Many people have protested about advertising and media images that make people feel inadequate. The perfect Mum using the perfect washing powder or producing the perfect meals with perfect ingredients causes other, normal Mums who also go out to work, an unjustified anxiety and sense of failure. The perfect Dad, covering his family with layers of insurance, does much the same things to men. But these messages do more than create inadequacies. They constantly, though much more subtly, correlate money – through possession – with being a good person.
>
> The woman in the ad may be wielding a box of Magic Formula X and a silly smile but behind her and around her lies her real virtue – a (£3,000) fitted kitchen, (£1000) worth of kitchen equipment and a glimpse beyond of wall-to-wall carpets and Dralon upholstery . . . Take women's magazines, ostensibly dedicated to the average and virtuous homebody, cooking her heart out on a shoestring. What do we actually see in the glossy, full-coloured photographs? Delicious food, certainly, but served in casseroles that a moment's thought tells us cost (£40) a throw and laid on tables of a pine's antiquity worth a month's salary . . .
>
> Worse follows. Our little screens bring frightfully nice people into our homes, telling us of their high ideals, their devotion to vitamins or bread-making or some such virtue-ridden occupation and there they are, surrounded by gently glowing rosewood, sunk in velvet sofas, framed by hugely expensive potted palms and hunting prints that cost a grand a go . . .
>
> Thus we learn, Pavlov-style, to associate everything we have been taught to respect – concern for others, good housewifery, good motherhood, hard work, moral excellence – with a background of sumptuous living such as most of us cannot hope to reproduce . . .
>
> A woman once confided in me her distress that her daughter was living with a married man. 'I am a Christian woman,' she said, 'and find what she is doing wrong. Besides, they have no carpets and they sleep on the floor.' Which sin do you suppose distressed her more?[14]

Unlike the present crop of media moralists who have read nothing in psychology other than the 70-year-old writings of Freud and the 30-year-old writings of R. D. Laing, Jill read new psychology texts. She would home in on the one gem which might be embedded in a desert of psychologist-speak. Thus when a group of psychologists in the UK and Holland carried out an extensive but carefully constructed experiment on tax evasion they had, of course, to report their methods of working and their analysis of the results, but the gem in their work was abundantly clear. They had looked at aspects of behaviour like alienation, social orientation and competitiveness, but what correlated directly and strongly with tax evasion was simply the opportunity to evade. If we see the chance we take it.[15] Indeed, many of us, as we fill in our tax return, might well exclaim as did Robert Clive, when charged with turning to his own use huge sums of money belonging to the East India Company, 'By God, Mr Chairman, at this moment I stand astonished at my own moderation.'

The universality of less than virtuous behaviour is never more clearly revealed than in the amazement shown when someone behaves decently. Such a person receives admiration to the point of sainthood.

Thus did Aaron Feuerstein, owner of the Malden Mill textile plant in Massachusetts, become an American hero. When, two weeks before Christmas, his plant burned down, many people assumed that he would collect the insurance money and depart. Instead he told his staff that he would keep them on full pay and give them a Christmas bonus. When his generosity became known, people sent gifts and money in a deluge. President Clinton invited Aaron to his State of the Union address where he proclaimed him an American hero. This was much to Aaron's surprise because, as he said, 'I haven't done anything. I don't deserve credit. Corporate America has made it so that when you make as much money as I do, it's abnormal.'[16]

Decency is what is abnormal.

To explain our general lack of decency in terms of an inherent wickedness or the machinations of the devil is just lazy thinking. Such explanations neither take account of what actually happens nor provide a basis from which change can be made. You can't make a better car unless you understand how the present car functions, and you can't make a better human being unless you understand how the present one functions.

Understanding our lack of virtue does not require delving into the Freudian id or the Jungian shadow and collective unconscious, nor into the imaginary genes which are supposed to control complex behaviour, all concepts which explain little and predict nothing. It is simply a matter of observing what happens to us and how we interpret what happens to us.

Behaving decently or behaving badly usually refers to our relationships with others. We either help or injure others. Of course we can injure ourselves by lying to ourselves or being greedy for food or mind-altering substances, but we usually think of such behaviour as stupid rather than wicked. Morality is concerned with how we behave towards one another.

What makes behaving decently towards other people so rare is that we have to look after ourselves because other people are dangerous. Trusting them is perhaps the most difficult of all the virtues.

Will Hutton in his book *The State We're In*, his Channel 4 television series *False Economy* and his essays and lectures stressed how an increase in trust between different sections of society is necessary if we are to create a more fair and equitable society no longer beset by our present economic woes. The question is, how can we learn to trust one another?

We each came into the world as a newborn baby filled with unself-conscious self-confidence and completely trusting the world and everyone in it, but, just as we lost that self-confidence, so we withdrew our trust. Even the most caring and competent mother will fail to meet all her baby's needs, and most of us had mothers who were not particularly competent even if they were caring. We cried, and she did not come to comfort us; we felt pain and she did not take the pain away. Then we met other people, adults who made promises which they did not keep or who teased us and laughed at us, other children who hurt and bullied us. Our parents' warnings about strangers were not always enough to keep us safe from bewilderment and hurt. To survive both as a person and a body we had to become wary of other people.

Where we did trust people we circumscribed that trust. We might, say, trust our mother to provide our food but not trust her to respect our privacy. When someone betrayed our trust we were devastated, but, having learnt that our trust can be betrayed, we betrayed other people's trust in us. Other people limited their trust in us.

The market operates on such circumscribed trust. Such trust can be generated by appearances alone. Writing about the City in the nineteenth century Andrew St George said:

> There was such a danger as overspeculating on oneself. 'If in private life,' mused D. Morier Evans, a great City writer, 'a man live in a mansion, maintain a large establishment – servants – an equipage, and all the outward appearances of wealth, few people care much to inquire whether or not he possesses the reality – credit, almost without limit, is at his command and without question.'[17]

The same situation pertains today. Outsiders wanting to gain a favourable reputation in the City can use an extravagant display of wealth to create the impression of trustworthiness. Many people were greatly impressed with Asil Nadir's possessions and life-style, but few realized how little actual money he had to maintain the vital cash flow in his businesses.

Insiders in the City, coming from a shared background of family, school and traditions, can be more accurate in their assessments of one another's creditworthiness, but such trust is actually very circumscribed. A public school education emphasizes conformity, not self-knowledge, 'ought', not 'is'. A City chap might know that he can trust a colleague with his money but not his wife, yet not know why he is trustworthy in one case but not in the other. He knows that his colleague is a philanderer, but doesn't know whether this is because the man is trying to maintain his sense of existence through sexual relationships, or is driven to prove his personal worth through his most prized possession, or seduces a colleague's wife as a way of doing the colleague down, and so on. He might not even ask himself why his colleague does what he does, yet unless we know why someone does what he does we cannot know that person, and if we don't know that person we are foolish to trust him.

The trust which Will Hutton advocates is the kind that develops only with self-knowledge. If we know ourselves we can know other people. For some years now managers have been told to 'empower' their employees, and many managers use the language of empowerment, but most, as the research shows, do it this way.[18]

Managers can't empower employees if they don't trust them, and they can't trust them if they don't know them. Similarly, employees can't trust their managers if they don't know them.

Knowing one another requires more than sharing a works canteen and abseiling together down a cliff. We need to be consciously aware of the theory we use to assess other people and how well that theory explains what we observe and predicts what the other people will do. A theory is a tool, and if you don't start off with good tools you won't get the good result you want.

One of the reasons I often don't enjoy large parties is because they're the kind of events where I meet someone who, on discovering that I'm a psychologist, asks, 'Are you analysing me?' Occasionally I feel sufficiently energized to give a little lecture on how each of us, whenever we meet someone, analyses what that person is saying and doing. We each have our own theory about why people behave as they do.

Some people have theories which are very simple. There are men who operate on 'Male/my race/my nationality = good; female/under thirty/sexy = available; the rest = waste of time'. Some people have theories which bear a relationship only to their fantasies and not to reality. Such theories are usually based on notions of astrology, and New Age and Jungian magic. Then there are the people who are actually interested in other people, who have thought about how we operate, and who try to relate their theories back to real experience. Their theories might use concepts from psychology, or literature, or simply the concepts embedded in the language. We all like to tell ourselves that we are good judges of character, just as we like to tell ourselves that we have a good sense of humour, but only this last and rather small group of people have a chance of judging well.

We need to know what our theory is in order to test how adequately it explains why people behave as they do, and how well it predicts what they will do. Neither simple theories nor fantastic theories perform either of these tasks in any reliable and useful way. There are many complex theories of behaviour, either privately owned or enshrined in psychology textbooks, which explain only a little and predict even less. These theories usually have ignored salient features of behaviour, or failed to change when experience required change, or they have implications which militate against explanation and prediction.

All theories, simple, fantastic or complex have at their centre a model of a human being. This model might be of a person divided into body and soul or spirit, or of a mechanical puppet worked by the levers of instinct or genes or planetary influences, or of the person as an agent, doing and choosing. (The model I use is that of an agent busy creating meaning.) Whatever the model, it contains an essence of goodness or badness. Some people have a model which says that people are, in essence, good, and some people have a model which says that people are, in essence, bad.

Theories which use a model of a person as essentially good incorporate ideas about how this goodness can be brought out. Theories which use a model of the person as essentially bad incorporate ideas about how this badness can be controlled or contained. The argument which rages about teaching methods is between those people who see children as basically good and therefore requiring teaching individually tailored in order to bring out the best in that child, and those people who see children as basically bad and therefore requiring teaching methods which establish the obedience, order and discipline necessary to keep this badness under control.

Moral exhortations usually reveal whether the person doing the exhorting is using a model of intrinsic goodness or badness. Will Hutton's exhortation to the privileged to give up their privileges seems to imply that it would be possible for them to discover and bring forth their intrinsic goodness to create changes which would benefit us all. I don't know which model Hamish McRae uses, but the Protestant work ethic was certainly based on the Christian belief that we are all sinners who were born in sin. Only by working hard, being honest, upright, God-fearing, and despising the follies of pleasure could a person keep that essential sinfulness under control and, perhaps, attain salvation.

Actually, there is no little kernel of goodness or badness nestling inside a newborn baby. Goodness and badness are simply ideas which we impose on the hapless child and on ourselves. If only we would remember this we would be more keenly aware of the implications of our ideas.

Those of us who use a model of essential goodness find it easier to trust other people than do those of us who use a model of essential badness. The effects of each kind of model holding are the same as the effects of being an optimist or a pessimist. Believing in basic goodness means that you go along feeling reasonably safe with other people but occasionally suffering the pain of betrayal and disappointment. Believing in basic badness means you go along being wary and alone, but occasionally are surprised into joy with someone's goodness. The surprised reaction by so many Americans to Aaron Feuerstein's common decency suggests that most Americans actually use the basically bad model, even though the belief in the American dream, which says that if you have a dream and work hard your dream will come true, seems to imply a belief in basic goodness. Still, Americans are, on the whole, a religious lot, and the basis of Christianity in all its forms is that we are all sinners in need of salvation.

Believers in the essential badness of human beings are more likely to claim that human nature never changes. Of course they fear change because any change could unleash the intrinsic badness to wreak havoc on the world. The only changes they are likely to support are those which impose controls and sanctions. A return to Protestant rectitude is likely to appeal to them more than the democracy and opportunity of Will Hutton's stakeholder society. Much of the huge stream of scorn and derision which has been directed at Will comes from this source, even though it is couched in political terms.

Believers in the essential goodness of human beings aren't likely to be afraid of any change which might bring forth that essential goodness. Ideas of democracy, freedom and equality do appeal as long as those ideas don't have effects which threaten the believers' interests. Those rich people who are currently supporting Tony Blair's New Labour certainly intend to stay rich.

Whenever we project our ideas on to other people we need to remember that our projection itself can create what we expect. Quite often, when we find ourselves the recipient of another person's projection we act in the way that projection requires. Thus many mentally competent but physically frail old people, when put in a nursing home where the staff treat them like children, soon begin behaving like incompetent children. Experienced teachers know that children will become increasingly naughty the more they are treated as if they are always naughty. So, if you want to bring out the worst in people, treat them as if they are intrinsically bad, and, if you want to bring out the best in people, treat them as if they are intrinsically good.

There are, of course, many exceptions to this. Some people will continue to behave decently no matter how much they are condemned as wicked, and some people will see being treated as being good as an open invitation to further wickedness. The two conditions which are impervious to being treated as good in the hope of becoming so are greed and a lack of conscience.

The research file which five years ago I labelled 'Morality' is bulging with examples of both these conditions. There are stories about embezzlement, fraud and insider trading, stories retold in lengthy books, many of which I've read. There are stories about companies and governments which turn a blind eye to a country's human rights abuses in order to gain rich profits. Long-running stories include events in Indonesia and Burma. Despite the Indonesian government's cruel repression of the East Timorese and the absence of freedom of speech, in one year, 1995, Japanese companies invested £47 billion in Indonesia and British companies £9.5 billion.[19] In Burma Aung San Suu Kyi, released from house arrest by the State Law and Order Restoration Council, begs companies not to come to Burma and thus give support to the military junta which inflicts the most terrible abuses on the Burmese people. Following John Pilger's television programme on this subject, the *Guardian Weekend* received the following letter from Terry Evans, a businessman in Rangoon.

> As one of the international businessmen currently engaged in joint-venture investments in Burma, I feel compelled to counter the charges levelled by John Pilger (in *A Land of Fear*, May 4). All too often, businessmen in Burma are portrayed by the media as carpetbaggers who operate with scant regard for human rights. In truth, it is the international business community that is in the vanguard of liberalisation in Burma. The ruling military council (SLORC) has opened the economy to joint investment by foreign companies and is committed to privatisation of state-owned assets. These policies are improving the living standards of millions of Burmese citizens, not just 'a small sector at the top of society'.[20]

In the eighties Margaret Thatcher used to tell us about how all the changes she was making in the economy would result in the making of wealth which would then 'trickle down' to the poor. Ten years later very little of this wealth has trickled down to the housing estates where most of the people are poor and unemployed, and even less of the wealth created by big companies in Burma will trickle down to the poor of Burma. Big companies take most of their profits home, and what little remains in the country goes to dictators or politicians and their friends.

How refreshing it would be if such businessmen could say, truthfully, 'I'm here to make money and to hell with the poor!', but, even if such a businessman were not suffering from the delusion of piousness but speaking truthfully, his public relations managers, devoted to the P-factor, would not let him.

Some people engaged in lining their own pockets at the expense of others do so out of greed, and others out of greed and a lack of conscience.

We are all born lacking a conscience, not because we are inherently wicked, but because we lack the concepts necessary for a conscience, concepts of past and future and of other people with whom we can have relationships. Once we discover other people and have the chance to form a bond with one mothering person we soon acquire a conscience because we realize that to maintain this bond we have sometimes to relinquish our own needs and wishes and defer to someone else. We can no longer be totally selfish, though sometimes we might try.

Babies who do not have the opportunity to form a bond with one mothering person do not develop a conscience. Over the last thirty years this process has been well documented in research in child development and psychotherapy. What hasn't been discovered and, indeed, is virtually unknown, is whether this failure to bond can be overcome in later life and a conscience created. This research could have been done in our prison system with a captive group of subjects, but ignorant politicians and their supporters, motivated by short-term revenge rather than enlightened self-interest, have prevented it. As a result, individual families and whole societies continue to reel from the blows inflicted by such conscienceless people.

Only a small proportion of such people are seen from the outset as criminals. Most appear to be ordinary members of society. However, within the family the conscienceless one, untroubled by guilt and the knowledge that other people are different from objects in that they have feelings, becomes very powerful. One such woman, whom I have known for many years, at the slightest criticism explodes into a rage from which her family retreat in fear but continue to do what she wants. In the workplace, people with consciences and who see lying as a dangerous and disreputable occupation, become helpless and fearful in the presence of someone who not only blatantly lies but who does not even acknowledge the necessity of repentance when the lie is revealed. I have seen senior managers in the NHS rendered speechless by the lies told by one consultant whose research speciality, would you believe, was psychopathy. To do his research he only had to look in the mirror.

This kind of helplessness sometimes seems to be carried over to the law courts, especially when the sums of money involved are large.

> ITEM: According to Home Office research, 40 per cent of people found guilty of theft under £200 are sent to prison by the Crown Courts.
> ITEM: A pregnant mother was this week sentenced to five days' imprisonment for failing to come up with a £55 penalty for not paying her television licence. She was only saved from jail when two solicitors had a whip-round to pay the fine.
> ITEM: Yesterday Roger Levitt, founder of the Levitt Group, which crashed in 1990 owing £34 million and who ploughed nearly £900,000 belonging to Frederick Forsyth, the author, into his doomed business instead of buying bonds, walked free. Mr Levitt, who admitted lying to the City watchdog body to keep his debt-ridden company afloat, was ordered to serve 180 hours' community service – though whether anyone would want this discredited fraudster anywhere near them, even on community service, remains to be seen.[21]

The capacity for conscienceless lying seems to be correlated with the ability to make a miraculous recovery from devastating illness, particularly those illnesses which afflict a businessman charged with the embezzlement of large amounts of money. Ernest Saunders was found guilty on counts of theft and false accounting and sentenced to five years, but was released after ten months because doctors found he was suffering from Alzheimer's disease, an irreversible and terminal condition. He miraculously recovered and became, again, a company director. Similarly, Alan Bond in Australia made a miraculous recovery from the depression and brain damage which struck him during his first trial.

People with a conscience, other aspects of self-interest not pertaining, can see the error of their ways and wish to change. If we are to change society we need, first, to understand ourselves and others, and, second, to take account of those members of society who do not wish to change or are incapable of change. Moral exhortations will not achieve this. We have yet much to learn.

8

A Choice of Futures

> We must live within the ambiguity of partial freedom,
> partial power, and partial knowledge.
> All important decisions must be made on the basis of
> insufficient data.
> Yet we are responsible for everything we do.
>
> Sheldon Kopp[1]

Money is an idea. This idea operates according to the meanings we attach to it.

We are free to create whatever meanings we wish about money, but the effectiveness of our own meanings is limited by the knowledge which informs our meanings and by the meanings which other people create. People are free to think what they like, though what they say and do are subject to necessity, and so we have no control over the meanings that other people create.

Everything that happens arises from an infinitely vast network of causes. Thus when we make a decision we can never know all that we need to know.

Much of what happens to us is not in our control. What is always in our control is how we interpret what happens. We are free to choose the meanings we create, and so we are always responsible for how we interpret what happens. It is our interpretations which determine what we do. Thus we are always responsible for what we do.

To live safely and satisfyingly we need the information which will provide a wide array of choices from which to choose our meanings.

If you can't add and subtract you'll make bad choices when you become involved in the market. If you can't work out probabilities you'll worry about unlikely events and be surprised by those that are likely. It's tough being a child because you know so little and thus your interpretations are chosen from a limited array which might have little relationship to what actually happens. Many adults live in uncomprehending misery because they think that what they experience is fixed and real.

What we need in order to survive and to give ourselves the possibilities of security, happiness and success is the understanding that what we experience are the meanings we've created, and the skills to test our meanings against a reality which we can never know directly. To form interpretations which measure up against reality we need knowledge of the world around us and the world inside us, that is, the meanings we have created and how we create them – our own individual truth.

While you have been reading this book you have probably noticed a certain refrain that something 'will lead to disaster'. Events like tidal waves and earthquakes usually lead to disaster, but, these aside, what most frequently leads to disaster is the way that we think, the meanings we create. These are the meanings that prevent us from having good, close relationships with other people, or lead us to hate ourselves or lose confidence in ourselves, or cause us to invest the world with fantastical features with the power to hurt us, or trap us in a prison from which we can find no escape. These are the meanings which prevent us from ordering our priorities in ways which promote security, happiness and success, and lead us to promote stupid rather than intelligent trades.

To avoid these disasters we need to understand how we create meaning, that is, to understand ourselves. The question is, are we capable of understanding ourselves? The fact that so many otherwise intelligent and educated people don't understand how we create meaning suggests that we may be incapable of understanding ourselves.

Edward O. Wilson, the renowned naturalist and founding father of sociobiology, considers that we have not yet reached the stage of being able to think about ourselves in a scientific way.

> To me it is remarkable that we do not live in a scientific age, as much as we might think otherwise. We live in an age in which we are – at least people in developed countries are – benefiting from remarkable advances in science and technology, but in our thinking, in our linguistic expression, in our way in which we deal with the universe intellectually, we are still prescientific. We might as well be agriculturalists in the Fertile Crescent, in terms of how we combine scientific knowledge with our daily idioms of thought, and I think that one of the great challenges, intellectually and in the immediate future, is to find a way of combining the best in scientific knowledge and thinking and concept and creativity, with the best of the humanities, and develop a scientific culture.[2]

The essence of science is not a body of knowledge but a way of thinking. It is a matter of being concerned with 'what is' and not with 'it ought' or 'I wish'. Scientists express their ideas in words and mathematical symbols, but in trying to understand 'what is' something else takes place. The zoologist Colin Tudge pointed out that 'human thought is clearly not dependent upon words'. We can have an idea 'in a flash', and then have to spend much time in putting that idea into words.

> Words, in short, are *not* the necessary raw materials of thought, as Descartes supposed. They trail behind the thoughts. The thoughts themselves flow in us like some dark river in the caverns of the brain (a very Coleridgean kind of notion), just as they must do in animals. Words merely *describe* those ideas. Or, as Ludwig Wittgenstein said, words *point* at ideas.
>
> But to describe ideas in words, to point at them, is not a trivial thing to do. In the language of computers or of librarians this ability allows the thinker to access his or her own thoughts. More: it enables us to monitor them, and to direct them.[3]

So we can think about the way we think, but it may be that we are not constructed to do this well. Colin Tudge went on,

> Among the many wise things that Marvin Minsky says in his excellent book *The Society of the Mind*[4] is that our brains are evolved organs which have been selected to observe and cope with the outside world and which emphatically have *not* been selected for the purpose of self-examination. In short, we are innately bad

at introspection. Our failure to perceive the nature of our own thinking, or the nature of consciousness that gives access to that thinking, or of the words that give order to that consciousness, are surely a manifestation of this ineptitude.[5]

I think that Wilson is right about the general level of our thinking about ourselves, and certainly Colin Tudge and Marvin Minsky are right in saying that as our brains were evolving hundred of thousands of years ago our ancestors, puny creatures in a dangerous world, had to pay more attention to what went on around them than to what went on inside them. The world is still a dangerous place, but most of these dangers have arisen because we don't think about what goes on inside us.

We have applied our scientific and technological thought to the world around us, not to the world inside us. If this way of looking outward is an evolved feature of the structure of our brain and not a habit which we have learned, then the exhortations from economists and others that we should change our way of living will be to no avail, and we shall continue on the path to self-destruction, a short-lived species with an in-built fault that has led us to over-populate the world, turn the land into desert, destroy the animal, insect and plant life that sustains us, pollute the air, change the climate and kill one another rather than co-operate. Dinosaurs lasted for many millions of years and Neanderthals for about a quarter of a million years, but homo sapiens has existed barely 100,000 years and is fast running out of time.

Dinosaurs became extinct presumably because they lacked the physical and mental equipment to overcome the problems presented by huge changes in the planet and its climate. In our brief history we have on occasions overcome our physical limitations. We weren't built to fly, but now we can. We cannot be in two places at once, but now with television we can see and be seen in a multitude of places. So perhaps we are capable of understanding how we think and therefore act.

It is difficult to think about thinking because we cannot find an objective position from which we can view our thoughts. If you're inside a big building it is hard to grasp the dimensions of that building. If you can't leave the building to see what it looks like from the outside, and if you've been in the building for a very long time, you might not be aware that you are enclosed by the building and that everything you do is limited by the way the building is constructed; you may think that you are experiencing the whole world, not just the interior of that building. Something similar can happen when you try to think about thinking. You think that your thoughts are free to go wherever they wish, and you do not realize that your thoughts are bounded by a framework of meaning which you/your thoughts have constructed early in your life.

This framework concerns how you have learned to see depth and distance (most people learn this through sight but some learn through sound and touch), how you have created a mental map of your position in relation to other objects (geographers' study of mental maps show that there are as many different maps of the world as there are people to hold them), how you have populated the space which you have learned to see, and what values you have created about your space and the people and objects in it. This framework is inside you, and you are inside it.

Each of us has our own individual framework. Our maps have one common feature. Each of us is at the centre of our own map. You can see examples of this kind of thinking if you look at the maps of the world drawn by geographers in different countries. I grew up with maps which had Australia in the lower centre of the page and the Americas and Europe/Africa on the edges. European maps have Europe/Africa at the centre, and American maps have the Americas at the centre. The *New Yorker* magazine once had a cover, now reproduced in countless posters and the idea adapted for other places, of the typical New Yorker's map of New York, with Manhattan at the centre, then past the Atlantic and far on the horizon, faintly, Europe. We each have a map just like that where we're at the centre, what's important to us is close by, and the rest of the world fades rapidly in the distance.

The *New Yorker*'s map featured skyscrapers, cars and people. Someone who grows up in a society where God and Jesus are continually mentioned is likely to create a space which contains that person's idea of God and Jesus, just as someone who grows up in a society where spirits are constantly mentioned is likely to create a space which contains that person's idea of spirits. Some such people will have a space that contains a benign God and Jesus, or benign spirits, while other people see their space inhabited by a wrathful God, a suffering Jesus, or impish, malign spirits.

The space is constructed by memory, and so we see in our space what we have learned to see as important. Just as certain advertisements, though in a multicultural society, feature only white faces, so do certain people see only white people, or only black people. We tend too to see people of our own generation. Children notice children, the middle-aged the middle-aged, and the old the old. Our memory selects other aspects of the space which we see as important and ignores the aspects we regard as unimportant. For the bicentenary celebrations in Australia in 1988 my sister wrote a chapter for a local history book in which she described a disastrous family holiday when I was about four. I remember the events extremely well. According to my sister's account I wasn't there. When I commented upon this she assured me that I hadn't been there, though I could not have been anywhere but with my parents. Some years later when a long lost relative returned unexpectedly my sister expressed surprise that I knew this person, someone who in my early teenage years was so immensely important to me that I kept his photograph on my desk in the bedroom I shared with my sister. I could only conclude that I do not feature in my sister's memory, a realization which brought a sense of being annihilated, a feeling that many of the participants in the Russian and Chinese revolutions must have had as they were written out of history.

The framework which is inside us and in which we are is not just a container. It determines what meanings we are able to create. If your framework contains only white people you are not able to create any detailed, empathetic meanings about people of other races. If your framework is dominated by an idea of God as the prime cause of everything that happens, you are not able to create any detailed, empathetic meanings about people whose framework contains no non-corporeal beings. If your framework is one where everybody competes with everybody else and to lose is, if not to die, to be annihilated, you are not able to create any detailed, empathetic meanings about people whose framework is one of co-operation and altruism. If your framework is one where everybody and everything has a price and only the price matters, you are not able to create any detailed, empathetic meanings about someone like my friend Ofra who says, 'Money is so boring!'

In order to change we need to become aware of the framework which contains all the meanings we have created and see it, not as an accurate representation of the world and everything in it, but as our own individual construction created in terms of our own individual experience. Being aware of our own limited view helps us appreciate the different, and also limited views of other people.

It is not just our framework which limits us. Within that framework we can create other prisons out of the meanings which we regard as absolute truths.

Many children grow up believing that, not merely to be accepted, but to be allowed to exist they must be good. 'Good' can be defined in a multitude of ways, but many women choose to define 'good' as 'kind, caring, responsible'. Any woman who applies this definition to herself but at the same time doubts her worth is likely to fall prey to an unscrupulous, selfish lover, male or female. I have known dozens of such women. A woman like this marries or remains tied to a man who treats her abominably. If the man leaves (always for another woman) she soon finds another man who is just as much a scoundrel as the first. Friends offer her escape routes, which she does not take because she is trapped in a prison of her own making. This is how it is constructed (see Figure 1).

The only way she can escape from a relationship which causes her such pain is, in her definition, to become a bad person, and this she will not do. Many women fail to be as successful in their careers as they might be because they have created such a prison and included in their definition of 'bad' the terms 'ambitious' and 'competitive'. Thus they cannot challenge their bosses, or compete with their colleagues, and are very likely to remain tied to a bad or inadequate boss.

Another popular prison is one where the person has defined one other person as the sole giver of affirmation the person sees himself needing in order to feel worthwhile, acceptable, good. Many men

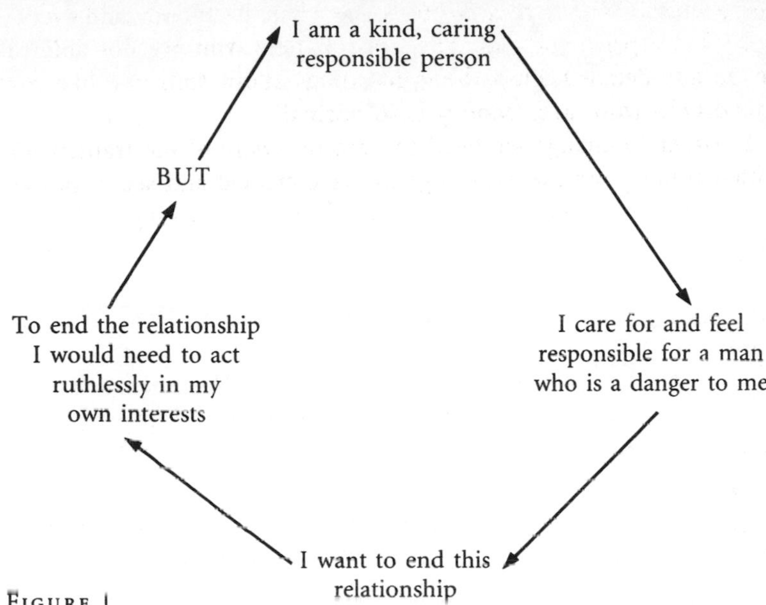

FIGURE 1

have in childhood given this power of affirmation to their father. If the father has set standards which are within the power of the boy to reach, and if the father shows his approval and love, then the boy enters adult life brimful of self confidence, and is very likely to succeed at what he undertakes. But if the father has set standards which are beyond the boy's capacity, and if he cannot bring himself to praise his son, the boy enters adult life full of self-doubt, and trapped in a prison which prevents his success no matter how great his ability. (See Figure 2.)

Many people, men and women, spend their entire lives believing that a parent's affirmation and only a parent's affirmation can give them the right to exist and to live freely.

These kinds of prisons become prisons only because the person has used definitions which she or he regards as absolute truths. If the woman changed her definition of 'good' to 'On the whole I try to be kind, caring and responsible but occasionally I must be unkind in order to protect myself', and the man changed his definition to 'It would be nice if my father approved of me, but if he doesn't it's

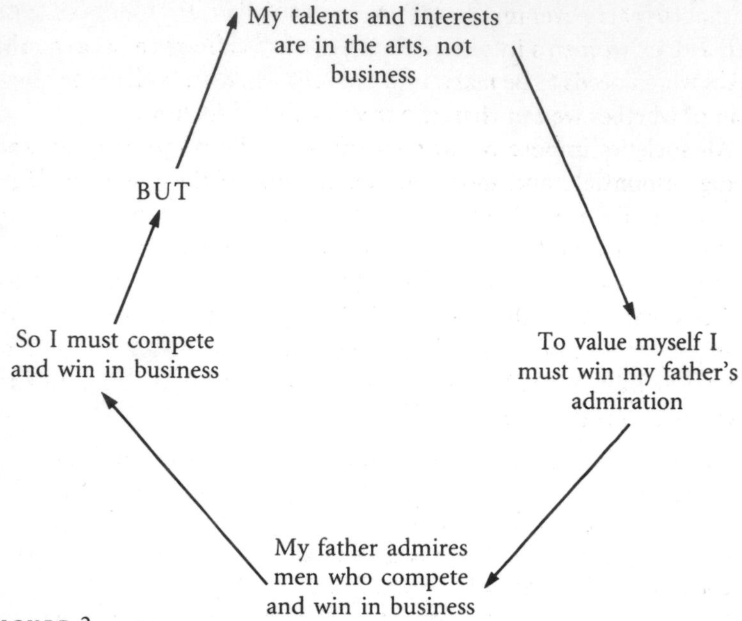

FIGURE 2

not important because other people whose opinions I value approve of me', the prisons would vanish.

The shared beliefs of groups of people can form similar prisons. The hard men of the Republican and Loyalist sides of the conflict in Northern Ireland have created such prisons, as have the hard men of Serbia and Croatia and every other conflict across the globe. It is much easier to fight over old disagreements about absolute beliefs than to face present problems.

Such prisons become the whole way of life and the reason for existing. Offer to take the prison away and the person resists, preferring to suffer rather than have to face again the question, 'What shall I do with my life?'

This issue of creating prisons out of beliefs which are mistakenly seen as absolute applies equally to men and women. However, when the question of exploring the nature and history of such beliefs arises women, on the whole, are more prepared than men to attempt it. This is not to say that women are skilled explorers of their internal world or that they are never imperceptive or never fall for the lure of magical beliefs like 'women's intuition', but there is a difference between the sexes which needs to be taken into account when we look at the question of whether we can change our ways and, if so, how.

All societies impose on women the necessity of growing up and being responsible and most women do so. To the question 'How old do you feel inside?' women usually answer in terms of late teens and early twenties. Men are more likely to give an earlier age, feeling that inside they are still children. When the *Guardian* ran a series of interviews under the title *The Seven Ages of Man*, Nick Hornby, that perceptive chronicler of male life in Britain, was despatched to interview John Kinsella, a 57-year-old retired accountant, a steady, responsible family man.

> An awareness of one's own mortality is not necessarily accompanied by a corresponding sense of maturity. John Kinsella is, to all outward appearances, a mature man, but he is precise about how old he feels: '10.' I laugh. 'Seriously, I really don't feel as though my mentality has changed at all in the last 50 odd years. I feel sorry for the women: they are the ones who mature. Men just stay struck.' It is hard to see the ten year old under the tie and V-neck and the clouds of Senior Service smoke, but the observation is a familiar one, and is probably the closest we will ever come to a one-line explanation of the terrible state of the world.[6]

Children are delightfully playful, but they don't manage their lives well because their sense of time passing is still developing and they are not skilled in seeing the full consequences of their actions. They use play not just as a means of exploring the world but as a way of distracting themselves from worries about what goes on in the world around them, as Alton Mort showed in his cartoon (see over).

There's no use in a woman commenting on this. Men will only say she's a nag, a shrew, and what would she know about it? Yet, at the same time, men want women to set limits to their behaviour, even though women find doing so tedious and unpleasant and eventually despise men for being so incorrigibly childish. And however much men want women to limit their games, they see this limiting as a challenge to their manhood which they must resist. So

" I have devised this remote control so that when I am concerned, upset or stressed about world population, environmental damage, the ozone hole, I point the " remote " at my head and – zap – I start thinking of Sport – Sex – and Money "

the games get bigger and bigger and more and more dangerous, and there's no way a woman can play mother, coming out of the house in the evening, calling the boys and telling them, 'That's enough now. Come in and have your tea.' There's no one to say that the game must come to an end except the men themselves, and if they cannot or will not end the game then the game will end us for ever and ever.

Man the game player is not man the wise.

The market operates, not as a process to meet our needs, but as one big game. Games follow the rules of competition, not the rules of trust and co-operation except within a team which is pitted against another team. Yet, according to Will Hutton, it is trust and co-operation which are needed to establish a better society than the one we have.

Will Hutton, the economist John Kay, Professor John Grey and the Labour Party's authority on social services Frank Field wrote,

> Any civilised community should be justly concerned to create as much wealth as it can, to ensure that income and wealth are [sic] fairly shared and that centres of private and public power are properly accountable. The aim must be to build a free, moral, socially cohesive society based on universal membership, social inclusion and organized around the market economy. This is what we mean by the stakeholder economy and society . . .
>
> A willingness to create trust and to co-operate . . . is fundamental to the capacity of firms to produce and the ability of the economy and society to function without extensive state regulation.[7]

These are all fine principles, but what these four men are saying will prove to be nothing but hot air if they cannot at the very least recognize the question which follows what they say. How can we create trust and co-operation in a world where men make the rules about the market and the rules, especially the unstated rules, are all about competition, not co-operation?

To look at this question they don't have to go off into the woods, bang a drum and get all upset because their daddy didn't love them. All they need to do is to apply their fine minds to the question of why we are so unskilled in understanding why we do what we do.

They could begin by looking at the seven main reasons why most people, and especially men, do not wish to inspect their own private logic and its origins, and see the connection between private logic and public action.

1 Believing that correct behaviour keeps private logic private, even from yourself

In a society where there are many rules about correct and incorrect behaviour and where any lack of conformity is punished it is imperative to keep your thoughts to yourself because your thoughts do not always meet society's rules. In such a society people protect one another by refraining from asking personal questions (such protection is not extended to children who are taught that they must always tell an adult the truth) and indeed not asking personal questions becomes one of this society's rules. Thus children can grow up knowing only what they ought to think, and lacking any skills in exploring their thoughts and feelings.

Of course, unattended-to thoughts and feelings do not disappear. They have a habit of revealing themselves at the most inappropriate moments. So people have to find ways of distancing themselves from their thoughts.

One method much favoured by the English upper classes is to remove the words 'I', 'me', 'my' and 'myself' from their vocabulary and replace them with 'one', 'one's' and 'oneself'. To me 'one' always sounds so isolated. 'I' always stands in relation to 'you', 'he', 'she' and 'they', but what does 'one' stand in relation to? 'A multitude' or 'nothing'?

Another way of distancing yourself from the personal is to use the passive voice. Instead of saying, 'Mary baked a cake' you can say, 'A cake was baked by Mary'. Then the reference to the person can be dropped altogether, as in 'Land mines are being planted in increasing numbers.' To become a psychologist you have to learn to write a research report entirely in the passive voice. Such reports give the impression that the experiments did themselves. They also protect psychologists from having to reveal just how fallible they are.

If it becomes imperative to say who did what the personal can again be avoided by using an abstract noun. This is a form of distancing which so amused Samuel Brittan when he was a schoolboy.

> I have been a methodological individualist since I was in short trousers, long before I became aware of the words. It was in foreign rather than economic policy that I first became aware of it.
>
> When we were school boys my brother and I used to find very comic the practice of some bombastic Central Europeans we knew who showed their contempt for the ineptitude of western foreign policy by saying things like, 'Russia is laughing' or 'Germany will gobble them up'. They failed to appreciate that entities like Russia, Germany or Britain are complex entities, not superbeings.[8]

Worse, just as a ship is 'she', a country becomes a 'she'. On Radio 4 Michael Portillo, when Minister for Defence, said of Japan, 'She is reducing her armed forces.'[9] Who is this she? A photograph of the Japanese parliament shows a sea of male faces. The Emperor of Japan is always male, the Empress and Crown Princess can be nothing but mute, obedient dolls. But then, as a politician and Minister for Defence, Michael Portillo would find it extremely difficult to follow the rule of honest speech, 'Own what you say.'

If you don't own what you say, how could I ever trust you?

2 Being frightened to introspect for fear of what might be found

If, as a child, you've been surrounded by adults who always imply and sometimes tell you that you are, in essence, bad, you can grow up believing that at your very core there is something dangerous and evil, some bestial instincts, which must be locked away and never disturbed lest, if let loose they destroy the world, or, at the very least, destroy your sense of existence. If you're an extravert you can keep your eyes firmly fixed on the world around you and keep yourself busy there. If you're an introvert you can spend your time in your internal reality, creating theories about this and that and never thinking about why you do this. Either way, you can avoid exploring your thoughts and feelings.

This might be an effective way of maintaining your sense of existence, but it makes you basically untrustworthy. You don't trust yourself, so how can I trust you? Moreover, it might be that at my core I have something dark and dangerous, so how can you trust me?

3 Being frightened to reveal anything of oneself because that would mean being found out

To trust one another we have to get to know one another, which means revealing something of yourself to another person. You have to put yourself into a situation where you are vulnerable to rejection and ridicule, even humiliation. Even if you know yourself very well and accept and value yourself you can still be hurt by the person to whom you reveal yourself. You have to risk trusting before you can trust.

If you think of yourself as being basically bad, or if you feel that you put on a confident front to hide inner weakness and inadequacy, you fear being found out. How can you risk letting anyone getting to know you?

4 Lack of the ability to think in terms of how people think and act

Getting to know another person means being interested in that person. That means being interested in what interests the other person, even though those interests have not previously appealed to you. I know about *Star Trek* solely because my son has always enjoyed it. A good measure of friendship is how much the other person knows about your interests and treats them with respect.

However, when we don't value and accept ourselves we are so absorbed in thinking about ourselves that we don't have any time, much less interest, to observe other people and learn about how they see the world. There are many people like this, and many people, while valuing and accepting themselves, who hold firmly to the view that anything that does not interest them is, in the whole scheme of things, not important. Thus there are many men who regard as totally unimportant women's interests such as maintaining the continuance of the human race by having and raising children, and there are many women who regard as totally unimportant men's interests in the means whereby the human race survives, things like food production, building, engineering and finance. I am acquainted with a large number of people, men and women, who pride themselves on their understanding of human nature, indeed they make their living from such skills, yet they dismiss out of hand vast areas of human experience on the grounds that they aren't interested in it, therefore it is not important. They complain about the changes made by the government in the National Health Service, but refuse to be interested in politics. They worry about their incomes, but refuse even to attempt to understand the global functioning of money. If they read, it's novels, not newspapers.

People who work in human resources management and public

relations will say they always get to know the interests of their staff, clients and the people their clients wish to impress. However, if this is done in a mechanical, routine way and not with genuine concern, the whole process is nothing but an empty charade that impedes rather than enhances good relations. What could have been more chilling than the sight of Margaret Thatcher enacting 'genuine concern'? Such displays do not promote trust.

To understand another person's interests we have to be able to understand the difference between persons and objects. Objects don't have interests. They just exist. Persons are agents. They are in the business of making sense of what is happening and acting according to the sense they have made.

As I have described earlier, there are people who have not learnt how to distinguish people from objects. They see the outside of people and do not wonder about what goes on inside. To them cars move and people move. Televisions talk and people talk. What's the difference? Try to explain to one of these people how that person has hurt your feelings and soon you will be floundering in a wild sea of confusion while the other person ignores your accusation, produces a version of events completely different from your own, and, rather than apologizing, treats you with contempt.

In dealing with such a person you can often be left with the feeling that you aren't dealing with a real person, just an empty shell. Inside no one is at home. Of course inside there is a person, but it's a person who does not use memory to maintain a sense of identity. Many of these people, as they damage or destroy the lives of those people who get close to them, earn the diagnosis of psychopath because they show they learn nothing from their experience. Instead, each act in the drama of their lives is a repetition of all previous acts. They create an identity in response to what they see as the advantages to them of the situation in which they find themselves, act without fear of guilt or remorse, and, when they have drained all the advantages and grown bored, or brought everybody and everything crashing down, with one bound they are free, to be born again in a new place with a newly invented identity. When Robert Maxwell was reported to have died many people believed the rumour that it was not his corpse floating in the sea and that he was somewhere else inventing a new life. As Linda Grant, in her splendid novel about memory and growing old *The Cast Iron Shore*, wrote, 'If you re-invent yourself perpetually, you are unburdened by morality.'[10] Just how unburdened by morality Robert Maxwell was was not seen until he died and the edifice of his empire crumbled.

No matter whether we call such people psychopaths or great leaders, they have little interest in the past so they have little interest in the future except for what advantages it might bring them in the short term. Enlightened self-interest means nothing to them because such a concept is based on the understanding that what in the long run matters most is good relations with other people. (If you are surrounded by loving friends, poverty, illness, loss and old age become bearable. Riches do nothing to assuage the pain of being alone and lonely.) Notions like 'making the future safe for our children' is to such people quite meaningless because their notions of survival and success relate to them and them alone.

People who cannot distinguish persons from objects have always been most at home in the market and in positions of power. However, their numbers, I would guess, are increasing at a rate that puts our future even more in jeopardy.

To acquire the ability to distinguish persons from objects a baby needs to be cared for by one mothering person who has the inner resources to give the baby continual attention, concern and love. To be able to do this the mothering person needs security and the support of other people. These necessary conditions are less likely to pertain in the lives of refugees than in the lives of people who are secure in their right to live where they do. How many millions of people are now refugees? How many of their children will grow up not knowing the difference between persons and objects?

Many of these children will become fighters in the endless wars and know no other life or even the possibility of another life. Others will become the power brokers, the politicians, the money makers who trust no one but themselves. They know the language of trust but not its meaning. How can we trust them? How can they learn to trust us?

5 *Fearing to recognize the multiplicity of points of view*

As Calvin found (see over),

Refusing to acknowledge the multitude of perspectives, insisting on the rightness of your own views and defining any deviations from your views as being mad or bad might bring the comfort of a spurious certainty, but this way of thinking cannot promote trust. Trust requires the recognition and acceptance of difference in the perspectives of different people.

Yet all these different perspectives are not equally valid and useful. Some will arise solely from a person's idiosyncratic fantasies which no other person shares or could even imagine. Perspectives arising solely from personal fantasies can be transmuted into art which can enhance the lives of other people, but only if the fantasies are amenable to forms of art which other people can recognize and if the artist can deal with the practicalities, like mixing paints to get the right colours, or coping with the vagaries of publishers and editors.

Even when different perspectives are tested using the methods of science and shared logic, there is no absolute standard against which they can be measured. It is all a matter of judgement, and judges rarely agree completely. Sometimes their differences arise from what level of probability is deemed by individuals to be acceptable. Not everyone in the UK thinks that a one in fourteen million chance of winning the lottery is a good bet. Sometimes the differences concern personal interests. An increasing number of scientists might agree that the world's climate is changing and producing global warming, but certain scientists, employed by those large industries which might be adversely affected if governments required a significant reduction in the production of airborne pollutants, insist that global warming is not happening.[11]

Trusting one another means trusting one another's judgements. To trust you I need to believe that you are a good judge of probabilities and that your judgements are not based soleiy on your selfish interests. To trust me you must believe the same about me.

calvin and HobbEs
by WATTERSON
UH-O

OH NO! EVERYTHING HAS SUDDENLY TURNED NEO-CUBIST!
COMICS

IT ALL STARTED WHEN CALVIN ENGAGED HIS DAD IN A MINOR DEBATE! SOON CALVIN COULD SEE BOTH SIDES OF THE ISSUE! THEN POOR CALVIN BEGAN TO SEE BOTH SIDES OF EVERYTHING!

THE TRADITIONAL SINGLE VIEWPOINT HAS BEEN ABANDONED! PERSPECTIVE HAS BEEN FRACTURED!
THE MULTIPLE VIEWS PROVIDE TOO MUCH INFORMATION! IT'S IMPOSSIBLE TO MOVE! CALVIN QUICKLY TRIES TO ELIMINATE ALL BUT ONE PERSPECTIVE!

IT WORKS! THE WORLD FALLS INTO A RECOGNIZABLE ORDER!
WATTERSON 6-17

YOU'RE STILL WRONG, DAD.

6 Wanting the impossibility of being both secure and free

I have often been told that some people find my books scary. When I have the chance to ask why the answer is that it was shocking to find what the person thought was solely private, personal experience actually being described there on the printed page. Many people find such an experience delightful – indeed, we read books in order to read about ourselves – but those people who find my books shocking do so because they fear that if they continue to read about themselves they will lose the dream that somehow, someday, their life will become what they want it to be. If understanding yourself means losing that dream, they don't want to know.

Different people have different dreams about what they want their life to be, but the common core of these dreams concerns freedom and security. We want to be a free, independent adult, carving out our future, and at the same time we want the security of being a member of certain groups, a family, a firm, a society, a culture, which over time stay very much the same.

Because all that we can ever know are our constructions of meaning we like things to stay the same. We don't like the hard work and anxiety of trying to create constructions that keep up with change. Shopping is so much easier if our local supermarket never changes its layout of goods, and it's so much easier to get along with people if you always know how they are going to behave.

However, every construction of meaning and every event has good implications and bad implications. You can feel very secure being part of a family or a firm where no one ever says or does anything surprising, but such a family or firm is very boring. When everything stays the same we know what the available choices are and what their outcomes will be. Sooner or later such security starts to feel like a prison, and we long for freedom because freedom gives us different choices. Yet a multitude of available choices means a multitude of possible outcomes; such uncertainty creates anxiety, and so we long for security.

This paradox of freedom and security, stated here in such general terms, applies to all of us. However, in terms of individual experience we each differ in how we define security and freedom and the amount of freedom and security we each can tolerate. I have heard a number of Muslim women argue that, within the Islamic rules which apply to them, women enjoy great freedom, yet to me these rules would be as stifling as the grave.

A certain situation might seem to an outside observer to be very secure, yet to the person in that situation those aspects which seem to create security actually threaten to overwhelm and annihilate the person. Introverts, no matter how much they enjoy the company of family, friends and colleagues, must have space and time to themselves, and extraverts, as much as they need to feel connected to other people, recognize that to avoid being annihilated by their vital connections they must spend some time alone. Thus apparent security can create a terror as great as a completely insecure situation.

The meanings we each give to security and freedom play an important part in the creation of trust. No matter how much we want to be trustworthy, when we are frightened we act entirely in our own interests. Certainly when our fear is in response to the threat of bodily death some of us can still show concern for others and even sacrifice ourselves for others, but when we are gripped by the fear of being annihilated as a person we act with utter selfishness.

Sometimes this fear rises when we have suffered a disaster which everyone can see – an unexpected and massive fall in the stock market, the loss of a job, the death of loved ones – and sometimes it arises when, in the privacy of our own thoughts, we look at our life and think, 'Is this all there is?', and see in utter clarity the certainty of our death.

As children we gave up being ourselves in order to be good and, armed with the promise that such a sacrifice would bring the most satisfying of rewards, we entered adulthood. We studied diligently, we worked hard, we entered married life and accepted its responsibilities because we believed that this was how life ought to be lived and it would be satisfying. One day, usually as we enter those years called middle age we look at our life and ask, 'Is this all there is?' Even the promised rewards of economic security, status and power do not fill the hollow inside us, and death looms close by. We feel very frightened. Most people turn this unnamed fear into anxiety about growing old. They become very conscious of changes in their bodies and in their physical and mental abilities. They contrast themselves unfavourably with those younger than themselves, and often, out of envy, act vengefully towards those over whom they have power. Managers going through this experience can make the lives of their staff sheer hell.

Some people, in the grip of this fear, panic and flee. Some give up their high-powered jobs and retreat into the simple life. Some desert their loyal partners in marriage and take younger lovers in the hope of proving themselves to be still young. Others turn to embezzlement and fraud. All selfish escapes, but none so selfish and so painful as the fall into anxiety and depression where every thought and action is absorbed in the defence against the overwhelming fear of annihilation.

This is an explanation of such selfish behaviour. It is not an excuse.

If you want to be able to trust yourself you need to know the conditions under which you would feel threatened with annihilation. To trust another person you need to know the conditions under which that person would feel threatened with annihilation. Thus, if you were an extravert maintaining your sense of existence through a network of relationships and I an introvert maintaining my sense of existence through a self-generated pattern of achievement, organization and control, we would each have to respect the other's order of priorities and be aware when danger threatened. For instance, as your business partner I should not expect you to forego family holidays, and you should not ride roughshod over my office organization. Moreover, when disaster strikes and you have been rejected or abandoned by those whom you hold dear, or I have lost control of part of my life, the one who is untouched by the disaster should not expect the other to maintain the steadfast trustworthiness of happier times.

Trusting one another should not be just a matter of maintaining the status quo. If we understand our sense of existence and fear of annihilation we can identity the conditions which allow us to enhance our sense of existence. Such an enhancement would be for an extravert to increase the number and variety of relationships and get to know not just family and friends from a narrow circle but people from many different backgrounds. For an introvert it would be to increase the range and variety of possible achievements.

However, if you're an action man attending only to what goes on around you and always valuing thought over action, you are still less than the person you might be. If you're a thinker devoted to creating theories about market processes, or the nature of black holes, or the functioning of God's will, and you haven't got time (that is, you don't know how) to have a friendly chat with anyone you meet, you are less than the person you might be.

The greatest enhancement of our life comes from learning the skills of the other, for extraverts to learn how to explore their inner reality of thoughts and feelings, and for introverts to acquire good social skills. In my book *The Successful Self* I tried to show how all the successful selves I interviewed had done just this. These were people who were successful in their work and in themselves.

However, it is impossible to create these enhancements if you don't value and accept yourself.

In the therapy and counselling market there are always fashionable ideas which are sold as the panacea for all of life's problems. Of recent years the idea of self-esteem has traded well. Ask why did you lose your job/get divorced/drink too much, and the answer will be, 'You have low self-esteem.' Ask how you can get a job/make a good relationship/stop drinking, and the answer will be, 'Get high self-esteem.'

Self-esteem is spoken of as a commodity which can be acquired by talking to the right therapist/buying the right self-help book/ talking to yourself in the right way. Of course all of this is nonsense.

There is no such thing as self-esteem. 'Self-esteem' is an abstract noun which is no more than a jargon label for all that we think, feel and do with regard to ourselves. Labels can be useful shorthand, but they can also be easily reified, that is, turned into a thing which is talked about as if it were real. This process is rather like buying a pound of coffee, putting the beans into a glass jar, writing on a sticky label 'COFFEE', putting it on the jar, and then, every time you want a cup of coffee, you tear off a piece of the label, put it in a cup, pour hot water on it, and drink the water/label mixture while believing that you're drinking coffee.

The language we use to talk about ourselves is riddled with words which, when we use them, mean that we are doing the equivalent of drinking a water/label mixture and thinking it is coffee. Words like 'intelligence', 'personality', 'traits', 'depression' and 'schizophrenia' are merely labels for different kinds of thoughts, actions and feelings. They do not refer to entities which lurk inside us. So it's best to avoid such abstract nouns and look at what we actually do.

We have ways of thinking, feeling and acting with regard to ourselves which lead us to feel secure within ourselves and to face the world with courage and optimism. We also have ways of thinking, feeling and acting with regard to ourselves which lead us to feel uncertain and confused in ourselves and to face the world with fear and despair. When I write about this part of our experience I use the words 'valuing' and 'accepting'. Occasionally I use the term 'self-confidence' because, although this is an abstract noun, it is fairly closely tied to the behaviour we describe as 'confident'. I never use the term 'self esteem' except to say that there is no such thing. It's just one of those terms which psychologists and therapists use to con you into believing that they know something that you don't. The therapy and counselling market is full of confidence tricksters.

The self-esteem industry has generated a great deal of business with self-help books, seminars, workshops, and programmes of self-improvement. Like all confidence tricksters the purveyors of self-esteem make it sound so very easy. It's just a matter of thinking the right thoughts and saying the right things and you can swap your low self-esteem for high self-esteem.

Parents and teachers are instructed to make sure that the children in their care acquire high self-esteem by always telling the children that they're wonderful and everything they do is great. If children (and adults) aren't told, when appropriate, that what they have done is imperfect and that they could do better, how can they ever learn from their mistakes? The skill parents and teachers need is to be able to point out errors in an encouraging way.

However, like all confidence tricks, the self-esteem trick overlooks an essential part of reality: words are cheap. You can tell yourself over and over that you are the greatest, and your loved ones can praise you to the skies, but if in your heart of hearts you are convinced of your essential unworthiness, or if the political and economic conditions of your country show you that there is no recognized place for you in society, words alone will not change how you feel about yourself. If you're unemployed the words you want to hear are not, 'You're wonderful,' but, 'We're offering you this job.'

When someone whose opinion we value praises us we can, but not always, feel a burst of confidence, and we can, when quite self-confident, ignore our critics because we know that, 'Anyone who disagrees with me is a fool,' but day by day we need other people to show us by their actions, not by their words, that they value and accept us. A managing director, having done a course in self-esteem, might praise his staff and say that he values their opinions, but if he then proceeds to make changes in the firm without any consultation he shows that he does not value his staff, and they in turn do not trust him.

We learn to value and accept ourselves when other people show by their actions that they value and accept us. Any intelligent species, knowing this about themselves and knowing that how they value and accept themselves is central to everything they do, would organize their society to promote mutual acceptance and worth.

We have done the opposite. We have created a society where some people are regarded, and regard themselves, as being more valuable and acceptable than others. We have created a market where those intelligent trades which by their very nature promote acceptance and worth and create the conditions whereby we can enhance our lives cannot operate efficiently, choked as they are by the stupid trades which now dominate the market and which do nothing but diminish and destroy our lives. As part of this, we have developed ways of bringing up our children which ensure that they grow up confused and conflicted and unable to trace and rectify the source of their pain.

7 Not wanting to remember, much less understand, your childhood

In every society children are expected to revere, obey and never criticize their parents. Thai children kneel before their parents. In traditional Chinese families all honour is given to the old. The Bible is full of stories about children being sacrificed for their parents. There is not one story about parents sacrificing themselves for their children.[12] In Western societies the old may be tidied away into nursing homes by their adult children, but usually with great feelings of guilt and anxiety about what people will think. Putting a parent in a home, just as getting angry with Mother or resenting Dad, is something no thoroughly good child would do. The Christian ethos means that we are always mindful of the Fifth Commandment which is not simply the instruction to honour our parents but, 'Honour thy father and mother, so that thy days will be long in the land.' Criticize your parents and you're dead.[13]

This is why so many people are reluctant to look at their childhood with an adult eye, something which is an essential part of coming to understand yourself. Good experiences in therapy can enable someone to do this. The differences between those people who have escaped the heavy hand of the Fifth Commandment and those who have not is very striking.

In one of the workshops I ran for a mental health association most of the participants, being counsellors, were well used to exploring their childhoods. However, there were three participants, women who worked for a local charity, who were attending their first group. The topic of our workshop was 'Anger, Revenge and Forgiveness', and in the first part of the morning I asked the group to consider how anger had been treated in the family in which they had been a child. The counsellors fell upon this task with great enthusiasm. Each told the group about the peculiar behaviour of their nearest and dearest. As ever in such exercises there was much laughter and much sadness.

The families so described fell into three groups. One group was where the adults got extremely angry and lashed out verbally and physically at the children who grew up, not surprisingly, terrified of anger. The second group was those families where nobody ever got angry. The adults got migraines and stomach upsets and fell into silences which lasted for days or weeks, and they punished any hint of anger by a child with expressions of shock, horror and rejection. From this the child drew the conclusion that anger was the greatest sin. Not surprisingly, the child entered adulthood quite unable to deal with anger in any form.

The third group of families was that of the three charity workers. Their childhoods were ones of undiluted sweetness and light. Anger was never a problem because nothing ever happened which would give rise to anger. The counsellors, who had been busily questioning one another about their experiences, fell silent. They did not even question the statement by one of the women that her mother kept a leather strap behind the kitchen door but never had to use it because the children were so well behaved. The vastly superior moral status of the charity workers was there for all to see. At this point these women ceased to be participants and became voyeurs, and in their answers to the feedback questionnaire they deplored the fact that they had learned so little because the workshop was so subjective when they were in need of objective facts.

At least these women did attend a workshop aimed at providing tools for the exploration of our meaning structure. Legions of men never go to anything like that. In the workshops I've been running for the last 25 years the ratio of men to women has always been no better than 1 to 10.

However, at this workshop there was one point on which all the participants agreed. Never, in the whole of their childhood, had their parents, when calm and rational, talked to the children about how to handle anger, their own anger and other people's anger. Just think about that. The time and effort we parents put in teaching our children how to cross the road safely, not to talk to strangers, to wash their hands and clean their teeth, how to read and write and come in out of the rain, a vast multitude of things, but we never teach them, except by our own bad example, how to deal with the most natural and swift reaction by all human beings, the emotion which arises when we are frustrated.

Yet we all live in groups and frustrate one another all the time.

Like everything else in life, anger has good implications and bad implications. We are puny creatures in a world indifferent to our existence, but when the world frustrates us our anger can give us the energy to overcome that frustration. Anger can help us survive, but it can also kill us.

Many parents, one way or another, teach their children that anger is wicked. This ensures that such children cannot deal with anger because it frightens them. They expect to be punished for their own anger and harmed by the evil of another person's anger. Thus, if you and I are business partners, and you have adopted your family's style of never ever showing anger and I have adopted my family's style of responding to all frustration by flying into a rage, we can never trust one another because my rages lead you to think that I could kill you, and your dissembling and silences lead me to think that you hide things from me and do not tell me the truth.

Adults tell children that it is wicked to get angry, and then proceed to get angry with the children. What could be more ridiculous, and more wrong, than hitting a child in order to teach the child that violence is wicked? Impressed by the discrepancy between what adults say and what they do, many children conclude that children aren't supposed to get angry but it is all right for adults to get angry. Thus when these children enter adulthood they can distance themselves from the pain they suffered in childhood and proceed to do to children what had been done to them. Such cruelty is easily cloaked in sentimentality.

Cruelty and sentimentality go hand in hand because in both the subject is treated, not as a person, but as an object on to which the ideas and feelings of the torturer or the sentimentalist are projected. What country is more sentimental about children than the USA, the home of Disney, and what country is more cruel?

> In the richest nation in history, a child dies from poverty every 53 minutes. The statistics are chilling. One in five US kids live in poverty, the highest in any industrialised country in the world, while the number in 'extreme poverty' – with a family income less than half the official poverty level – has doubled since 1975 . . .
>
> The heart of the problem is the same one which afflicts much of American politics: voters say they want action to protect children, but they also want less government spending and lower

taxes. They can't have both and, in the ensuing struggle, children have one major disadvantage: they don't vote.[14]

An equally chilling account could be written about the children of every country. In some countries the emphasis would be on the exploitation of child workers, and in others on the alienation and loneliness, often with drug addiction, of children from affluent families where the parents lavish money on their children but not love and acceptance. In some countries the emphasis would be on abandoned children scavenging in rubbish tips, and in others middle-class children whose sole purpose, according to their parents, is to fulfil the parents' needs and aspirations. Many children are loaded with the expectation that they be a credit not just to their parents, but also a credit to their country. The one thing they cannot be is themselves.

There are a few parents who make every effort to treat their children as persons in their own right, but even if these children are able to retain their trust in people who treat them in this way, once they enter the school system they fall into the hands of people who exploit their trust by teaching them that there are absolute truths which cannot be questioned. Such supposed truths concern religious and political dogma and the 'facts' which must be memorized and reproduced. Such 'facts' are an impediment to clear understanding. When I was a child I was taught that there was only one way of counting. Everlasting and absolute numbers existed in some heavenly state, and I was being made privy to them. No one explained to me that the way we counted was a historical accident and that other ways of counting could be just as useful. As a result of this stupid teaching, when I entered high school and encountered algebra, I found it quite baffling until I realized that numerical systems are simply sets of ideas. I remember feeling angry because I had been deceived. Episodes like this in my schooling and my observations of the discrepancies between the absolute rules which the adults taught children and the adults' actual behaviour left me, like many children, entering adulthood unable to trust those adults I saw as filling parental roles. A consequence of such experiences is the widespread distrust of politicians which, unfortunately, most politicians do nothing to dispel by a display of honest, upright behaviour which matches their rhetoric about morality.

Children are exploited by their teachers because the teachers are part of a system set up by State and Church to keep these institutions in power. Of course there are many fine teachers who see their task as creating the conditions necessary for each child to develop as an individual, but such teachers are always under attack. The *Daily Mail* uses the term 'child-centred' as a term of abuse.[15] Helping children to develop as an individual means encouraging them to develop as a clear, logical, independent thinkers, well aware that we each have our own way of seeing things. Clear, logical, independent thinkers are always a threat to the Church and the State, and so such a kind of education must be eradicated.[16] Stephen Webster, a science teacher, writing about the new UK national curriculum in science, said,

> Children get hooked into science when they start to wonder what is out there in space, or there inside the body. The facts come along later. If the imagination hasn't fired, forget it . . .
>
> Now we find ourselves with a curriculum that doesn't believe in questions. This prejudice is implicit rather than explicit, and works subtly: it favours the measurable and penalises the equivocal. Facts learnt by children can be measured, whilst their questions cannot be and so are neglected. The results will soon be with us – school-leavers will turn away with relief from science. It is bound to happen. Their questions about the natural world will have withered long before.[17]

We are born with a brain whose powers far exceed the powers of our puny body. Most regrettably, psychologists for over half a century persuaded us that we were each born with a fixed amount of intelligence. The psychologists' test results were a function of the tests used, not a reflection of reality. Now the research shows that good nutrition, a great deal of varied stimulation and practice in the hard process of thinking produce huge increases in ability and increases in brain complexity, something that can happen right through the age span.[18]

In the studies which produced these results the subjects were given tasks which encouraged the clarity of thought which would bring the task to a successful conclusion. Tragically, many of us carry mental lumber from our childhood which impedes clarity and makes us more stupid than we need be.

When we are small children trying to learn how to fit into a strange world, puzzled by the discrepancies between what adults say and what they do, we are also being introduced to the religious beliefs held by our family and teachers. In Christian and Muslim families God or Allah is talked about in much the same language as that used for talking about the family. God or Allah is our father and we are his children. Our parents tell us they love us and then they punish us, a contradiction that puzzles and hurts us, but which we are expected to accept without question. We are told that God loves us and that he will punish us if we are wicked. We are certainly not encouraged to ask questions in the hope of getting our confusion resolved.

Many children, faced with such confusion, simply stop thinking. They give up trying to make any coherent sense of their experience, and thus grow up to be much more stupid than they need have been. It is possible to live and not think about what we are doing, but when disaster strikes our lack of thought can make the disaster much worse. Here are two examples which I have encountered recently.

I first met Rachel when she was an accountant married to a very successful lawyer and leading a very comfortable life. Now whenever we meet she brings me up to date with her battle against rheumatoid arthritis. It had started not long after the birth of her second child, but the doctors were slow to diagnose what was happening and, rather than support her through this trauma, her husband had fled, leaving her in near penury and with two sons to raise. Now, ten years on, she was facing her second knee operation. Speaking of her illness and her husband's defection, she said, 'I've always seen it as God's way of punishing me.'

I asked her what she could possibly have done to have merited such a punishment. 'You've always done your best,' I said.

'My best isn't good enough,' she replied.

I asked her why God should single her out for such a cruel punishment when the world was full of villains who flourish like the green bay tree. Doesn't God ever go to the City or Wall Street?

Rachel smiled. 'I've got a personal relationship with God.'

So she had her own personal tutor in life. But aren't the best teachers the ones who know that they'll get the best results by giving encouragement, rewarding the right responses and ignoring the wrong? Alas, God doesn't seem to read the research on how his creatures learn.

And God's encouragement can be misunderstood. When Bill's wife Louise died after a particularly long drawn out and painful illness Bill was released not just from the pain of witnessing such a death, but from a stormy marriage with a dominating woman. Bill loved to speculate with his money but Louise had watched every penny. Within a month of her death he'd invested in a business venture, sold to him by someone he'd met at his club, which promised riches. All went marvellously at first and Bill looked forward to tremendous profits. Then came the crash.

Later I asked why he had not been more suspicious of such a venture and particularly of the man whose idea it was. Bill said, 'I believed everything he told me. I thought it was God's way of making up to me for all I'd been through.'

Whoever said that God was a reliable investment manager?

In this book about money I have talked a lot about God. Money and God are not disparate subjects but sets of ideas by which we try to create certainty in an uncertain world. Some people try to keep the two sets of ideas entirely separate, giving to Mammon what is Mammon's and to God what is God's. Some people see both sets of ideas forming one overarching whole, and find in the functioning of money God's purpose in the world. Again, other people see the set of ideas relating to money as relating to something real, while the set of ideas relating to God are only fantasy. Even these people cannot separate themselves from the society in which they live, where individuals who may adhere to ideas which lack any relation to reality can act on those ideas and produce effects which are only too real. You might dismiss astrological investment advisers as charlatans, but those people who interpret human behaviour in terms of the movements of the planets guided by God's hand will buy and sell according to these interpretations. And what greater evidence of the interaction of our ideas about money and our ideas about God than Hamish McRae's solution to our economic woes, that we all should adhere to the Protestant work ethic?

However, with money and religion, whenever we try to pin everything down and make everything certain, we encounter even greater uncertainty. Why not stick with the uncertainty which seems to be the natural state of our existence? Not the implacability of divine rewards and punishments which are mirrored by parental rewards and punishments, but instead the uncertainty of chance. You can be unlucky, and you can be lucky. Here's an example.

The markets in Adelaide in South Australia stay open until after nine on a Friday night. Families come there to shop and to enjoy an evening out. Around the markets the restaurants are simple but wonderful.

Leaving a fish restaurant one evening, I passed a young family, mother, father, a sleepy three-year-old in a push chair, and an argumentative five-year-old. She was tired, and she wanted her father to carry her home. He was tired too, too tired to carry a five-year-old who didn't realize how big and heavy she had become.

This could have turned into one of those nasty scenes where the child, whining and complaining, impervious to her parents' explanations and offers of later compensations, so raises their ire that they shout at her and slap her, reducing her to a state of humiliation and impotent rage which she can direct only at the favoured sibling. Not so with this family. The young mother had an alternative.

'I'll toss you for it,' she said. 'Heads you walk, tails daddy will carry you.'

Now the odds were even. The overbearing, unfair power of the adults was removed. In the world of chance she was her father's equal. If the coin came up heads, it was the luck of the spin, not the impotence of children, which forced her to trudge her way home.

Trying not to disclose my interest, I walked on by. When I felt it sufficiently prudent to stop and look, I saw a tired father hoisting a triumphant five-year-old on to his hip. Next time, perhaps, he'll make the lucky call.

Now let's suppose that you have decided that you do want to

become acquainted with your private logic. You have decided that you can abandon the idea that correct behaviour keeps private logic private, that you're prepared to risk the searching of the nooks and crannies of your private logic, that you can risk other people knowing your dark secrets, that you want to improve your understanding of other people, that you'll face the fear of a multiplicity of points of view, that you'll give up wanting to be simultaneously secure and free, and that you're prepared to cast a critical eye over your childhood. What will you do next? Will you venture into the therapy market and see what you can buy?

Years ago when I was travelling in North Africa I was told that the most dangerous market in the world was at Fez in Morocco. Tourists were known to have disappeared into the souk, never to be seen again, perhaps only one of their number, months later, stumbling naked from its furthest edge, stripped of every possession and every memory. Nowadays the therapy market is much the same.

Therapy is based on an idea as old as the human race. It is the idea of the story, a meaning which has a beginning, a middle and an end. Indeed, nothing is fully meaningful to us until we have embedded it in a story. For instance, you look up into the sky one night and see there a collection of lights in a pattern you've not seen before. Just saying, 'There's some lights up there' doesn't satisfy you. You have to put the lights into a story, what the lights are (a plane, a flying saucer?), where the lights came from (air force base, another planet?) and what will become of them (return to base, invade?). Not knowing the beginning or the end of a story is always disturbing. We'll invent a beginning or an end just to ease our discomfort.

Our most important story is our life story because our life story is our identity. We feel our identity to be confirmed when we tell our story to an attentive listener. This helps us clarify and understand our story, and such an understanding can change the beginning of our story (how we remember our past) and the ending of our story (how we plan our future). Listening to other people's stories helps us understand our own.

An attentive listener to our life story (or to one of the stories within the whole story) does four things.

First, the listener pays careful attention to what we are saying. The listener looks at us and not elsewhere, does not doze off or change the subject, but speaks only when appropriate to ask a question or to exclaim in sympathetic encouragement.

Second, the listener offers comfort – 'That must have been terrible for you', 'You poor dear, how you suffered' – with the occasional touch of a hand or a hug.

Third, the listener helps understanding by asking for clarification – 'Would I be right in thinking that this is what you mean?', 'Could you tell me how you felt about that/why that was important to you?'

Fourth, the listener offers encouragement – 'I'm sure you're wise/strong/brave/intelligent enough to face what needs to be faced.'[19]

If we really cared about one another this is what we would do for one another all the time, but we don't because, having never been listened to in childhood, we have not learned how to listen. If we want to be listened to, what do we encounter? There'll be those, usually men, who will engage in conversation only if the topic offered for discussion is one which they deem to be important to themselves. If you insist on being heard they'll tell you you're over-reacting. There'll be others, usually women, who'll exclaim, 'I find people so interesting!' and then proceed to talk at length about themselves. If you insist on being heard they'll say, 'I know exactly how you feel,' and go on talking about themselves. And then there'll be all of them, men and women, who, if you pin them down and force them to listen to what you have to say, will insist on interrupting you and, brooking no argument, tell you where you went wrong and what you must do. Our nearest and dearest usually specialize in such non-listening.

Good listeners are a scarce commodity, and scarce commodities invite a market.

The idea of selling the promise of a peaceful mind through some kind of listening is hardly new. In past centuries the Catholic Church sold indulgences to relieve people of their worry about their sins, and all organized religions have been happy to exchange the assurance of an eternal life for the faithful's prayers and worldly goods. However, while a scarce commodity can be one of the most life-enhancing possessions, once it becomes subject to the market and all that that implies every grace and virtue that it has can be lost.

Consider the history of the Great Abbey at San Galgano in Tuscany.

Its story began with Galgano Guidotti who was born in 1148, and who, like many saints, led a dissipated life until faced with the question, 'Is this all there is?', whereupon he became a hermit and retired to the hill of Montesiepi where he built a circular hut of branches. However, as the guide book says, 'the life of a hermit is not an easy one',[20] and he died within a year. Five years later he was canonized, and a group of Cistercian monks set up a monastery and built the Great Abbey in the valley below Montesiepi. The guide book records:

> Economic ties with the Sienese government were quite strong. The Abbey was located in the centre of the Republic, and traffic from pastures, the mines and the sea would stay the night on Abbey property under the protection of the monks, who in turn organized important trade fairs. Several of the monks were named managers and administrators of the State Treasury, positions of extreme responsibility.
>
> All this spiritual, cultural and economic splendour underwent a rapid decline, caused by many factors. Mercenaries in the pay of the Florentine Republic organized a series of raids aimed at the Abbey in 1364. But the worst evil was the so-called 'commenda', a commission that many an abbot would demand on business transactions that took place at the Abbey, or on the Abbey's properties. From the middle of the fifteenth century onwards, the Commendatari, abbots who cashed in on the Abbey's income, concerned themselves solely with exploiting the profits of worldly goods, to the detriment of monastic life and the upkeep of the buildings. Around 1550 Girolano Vitelli neglected the upkeep of the estates, sold precious and non-precious objects, including the lead from the roof of two churches. Life in the monastery suffered the ill effects of such a situation; by 1550 only five monks remained. In 1600 there was only one, so badly dressed as to kindle the indignation of a visitor.[21]

The bell tower collapsed, the roof fell in, and now the Great Abbey lies open to the skies, an empty shell in a vast, lonely landscape, lacking the cosy green swards, the car parks, the picnic areas and ice cream vans that the great English abbeys of Fountains and Rievaulx, plundered by Henry VIII, now enjoy.

In the turbulent centuries that followed the fall of the Roman Empire the abbeys offered islands of sanctuary and peace. Within their walls a traveller on life's journey might find comfort, a clarification of the story of his life in terms of the biblical stories and the lives of the saints, and encouragement in terms of finding salvation by leading a good life. The orders of monks and nuns who ran the abbeys were, on the whole, founded by people very mindful of Jesus' scorn for money and Saint Paul's view of the love of money as the root of all evil. However, out of their poverty came great wealth, partly from the unpaid work of the monks and nuns and partly from the gifts of money left to the abbey by people who wished to store up treasure in heaven. Many of the monks and nuns were seduced by this money.

Money is seductive because it gives us the power to impose our own individual meanings on the world and to ignore the meanings which other people create. Money means you don't have to listen.

If there is a pattern to human life it is one of irony. Abbeys were created as centres of poverty, humility and listening, and became centres of wealth, arrogance and power. The art of listening requires no money, just care and humility on the part of the listener, and therapy has become a market where wealth, arrogance and power abound.

The moment listening became therapy money was on the scene. In his letters to Wilhelm Fliess where he chronicled the development of his theories about the unconscious sexual origins of neurosis, Freud also revealed his need for money. On 21 September 1899 he wrote,

> My mood also depends very strongly on my earnings. Money is laughing gas for me. I know from my youth that once the wild horses of the pampas have been lassoed, they retain a certain anxiousness for life. Thus I have come to know the helplessness of poverty and continually fear it. You will see my style will improve and my ideas be more correct if this city provides me with an ample livelihood.[22]

However, such an ample livelihood would not have been forthcoming if Freud had said to his potential customers, 'In return for a goodly sum of money I shall listen to you talk.' There had to be a touch of the Phineas T. Barnum, something magical and fantastic which only the salesman of listening could provide. Barnum brought creatures from distant realms where his customers could not travel. Freud invented another realm, the Unconscious, filled with the mystical beasts of id, ego and superego, atavistic instincts and powerful complexes, through which he could be the only guide who always knew more about the customer than the customer knew about himself. Freud made some important discoveries about how we structure the meanings we create, but these are simple ideas and simple ideas don't sell unless they come in a fancy wrapper that promises much more than the ideas themselves.

Such exclusivity is expensive. Some of Freud's followers sold (and still sell) their services with breathtaking chutzpah. They make those sharks of the business world, the firms which lease office equipment, look like amateurs. Lease a fax machine or a copier and you sign up for a specific term of years, but sign up for analysis and the term is life. Trying to leave analysis shows only that you need more. Try going on holiday and you'll find that, while your local greengrocer won't charge you for the fruit and vegetables you don't buy, your analyst will charge you for the hours you didn't attend.

Freud tried to corner the market in listening and so was exceedingly angry when some of his erstwhile disciples set up on their own. Not only did he lose trade but these renegades demonstrated to the world that anyone could set up as a listener. All they needed was a gimmick, and what a plethora of gimmicks there are now. The programme for the First Congress of the World Council for Psychotherapy in 1996 listed some 56 different kinds of psychotherapy (give or take a few depending on how you count the names), and these did not include therapies like Reike System of Natural Healing, Spiritual Astrology, Reflexology, Aromatherapy, Soul Alchemy, Kinesiology, and the work of Deepak Chopra who will 'give you the ability to create unlimited wealth with effortless ease, and to experience success in every endeavour'.[23] Now there's an offer you can't refuse!

Amongst all this expensive dross are a few gems of listeners, like David Smail, a psychologist and therapist whose book *How to Survive Without Psychotherapy* shows just how to do that.

To find someone like David Smail you need to be able to identify the different kinds of dross. It isn't a matter of one theory or one school of therapy being better than another but of the basic attitude presented by each individual therapist which forms the basis of the kind of therapy each sells. There are six different attitudes which are dangerous to customers and should be avoided.

1 'I have the Secret of Life'

Therapists with this attitude are found in great numbers amongst analysts and those who hold some religious or spiritual belief. This attitude is dangerous because it is a lie. The secret of life is that there is no secret.

2 'I and I alone have the power to make you happy and successful'

Such people can be found operating as spiritual gurus, various kinds of cognitive therapists, holistic therapists, management consultants and hypnotherapists. The competition amongst them is intense. Their followers have given up thinking, so they don't discover until too late that no one has the power to make anyone happy and successful. Being happy is something we have to do for ourselves, and being successful depends on how we each define success, what cards we've been given in the game of life, how we play them and what happens by chance.

3 'Confess your sins and repent. Only then will you be saved'

This basic attitude has been immensely successful in the USA where most people are familiar with the game of being saved. Here the preacher rides into town, gathers the populace around him, preaches hellfire and damnation, names everyone a sinner, lists the sins, and calls for the sinners to come forward, confess their sins, repent and be saved. Some do and some don't, but everyone has a good time.

There's lots of scandal and drama for everyone to enjoy, all the self-proclaimed sinners can revel in some minutes of fame, reformed sinners like the preacher can claim the special status of having been wicked (how deliciously dangerous!) and now good (what virtuous superiority!). Fortunately the saved don't stay saved because that would deprive the preacher of his livelihood.

Adapting this game to therapy, therapists have invented new sins like the Cinderella complex, or loving too much, co-dependency, an unacknowledged inner child and, most lucrative of all, addiction. You can get addicted to anything, and the good thing is you're not responsible. You can spend your days shopping or take one lover after another, and it's not your fault. It's the way you were born. The particular gene which determines your addiction will be discovered any minute. You're not a spendthrift or a philanderer as unkind people might say. You're an addict. And, if you confess your sin (how a genetic defect can be a sin is not explained), you can go into recovery, a delightful state where you can talk endlessly about your problem and excuse yourself for your bad behaviour. There's no end to this delightful state because being in recovery never leads to recovery because once an addict always an addict.

Meanwhile your therapist has a steady income and perhaps a fortune made from the sale of the books and videos which promote this particular kind of therapy. The self-help publishing industry is vast and maintained by publishers who don't want any book which renders therapy unnecessary and a readership who want to be saved again and again. Barnum, you should be living at this hour!

4 *'I can connect you to magic powers'*

The basic model for this kind of therapy is one with which we're all familiar, the priest who mediates between a Supreme Power and weak mortals. The priest occupies that most enjoyable of states, power without responsibility. Whatever the priest demands of his flock, it is not the priest's demands but the demands of the Supreme Power. Rich people who behave selfishly can be called to account, but people who claim a priestly role can deny responsibility for their actions while seducing, mistreating and defrauding their credulous flock.

Some such therapists reveal their priestly role from the start because the Supreme Power they claim to represent is not the usual God with whom we're all familiar. Others do not immediately reveal their priestly role, but use intellectual, psychological or theological terms to imply that you and the therapist agree on what these terms mean. If you hear the word 'spirituality' be on your guard. At the risk of revealing yourself as 'unspiritual', ask what the therapist means by 'spirituality'. Answers which imply a recourse to magic and to absolute truths show that you are being conned. You'll gain no clarity here.

The same applies if you hear the word 'transpersonal'.

5 *'Keep taking the tablets/herbal remedy/sitting in front of a bright light'*

If only by ingesting some substance or by carrying out some simple act all our troubles would disappear!

When you're depressed deciding to do something for yourself – talking to a kind doctor, following a healthy diet, taking time to relax – can be the turning point because you've actually changed from continuously being your own worst enemy to occasionally being your own best friend. Such a change in how you think about yourself and a change in what you do can be the means of finding your way out of the prison of depression. However, anyone who tells you that a tablet, a vitamin, a bright light will sort out your relationships and make you happy and successful, and who charges you for this advice, is a charlatan.

6 *'It's all in your genes'*

This is perhaps the greatest confidence trick of all because here the therapist is using the language of science to defraud customers ill-educated in science. The notion that some complex form of behaviour has one basic cause, a gene, is used by many people in different situations and usually for one very seductive reason. It absolves people of responsibility. You can be very aggressive, or drink too much, or withdraw into a depression every time life fails to be what you want it to be, and it's not your fault. It's the fault of the genes you were born with. Or you can ignore certain people, like the poor or the homeless, because their misery is nothing to do with you. It's caused by the genes they were born with.

However, one group of therapists have given this notion that a gene can cause complex behaviour a spurious validity and, indeed, base their profession of psychiatry on it. Psychiatrists say that certain behaviour, which they call mental illness, is caused by genes. There's a depression gene, a schizophrenic gene and so on. Any minute these genes will be discovered. The international Human Genome Project, which has now spawned the word 'genomics', plans to identify all the genes in the human collection and show their sequence and location. Psychiatrists expect that this project will discover the mental illness genes. An editorial in the *British Journal of Psychiatry* in August 1996 stated this clearly.

> The Human Genome Project is the enabling technology by which the genes contributing to the genetic aetiology of common familial disorders, including the major psychiatric disorders, will be identified. We may be uncertain precisely how quickly and by what means such discoveries will be made but there is little doubt that they will happen and that the knowledge gained will radically alter clinical practice. Moreover, insights from genomics are unlikely to be restricted to disease. It is likely that we will gain insights into the genetic basis of behavioural traits such as personality, cognitive ability and sexual orientation. The complex issues raised and their implications need to be considered now. The accuracy of diagnosis of major psychiatric disorders will be greatly enhanced and the complex interplay between environment and genotype will be increasingly understood. Ultimately we can expect that the drugs produced as a result of understanding molecular pathogenesis will improve management and prognosis.[24]

Of recent years psychiatrists have been forced to admit that the environment does have some effect on the way we behave, though few of them have actually grasped that it is not what happens to us which determines our behaviour but how we interpret what happens to us. Consequently they talk, like certain psychologists, about the relative functions of genes and the environment in the abstract entities of intelligence, personality, traits, and sexual orientation, and in doing so ignore the work of those scientists whose study is genes, the geneticists. What geneticists say is that there is no scientific basis for explaining (and excusing) our behaviour in terms of the causal effect of genes. Steve Jones, Professor of Genetics and Head of the Galton Laboratories at University College London, wrote,

> Most modern geneticists find queries about the relative importance of nature and nurture in controlling the normal range of human behaviour dull, for two reasons. First, they scarcely understand the inheritance of complex characters (those, like height, weight or behaviour which are measured rather than counted) even in simple creatures like flies or mice and even when studying traits like size and weight which are easy to define. Second, and more important, geneticists know that the perpetual interrogation – nature or nurture? – is largely meaningless. Its only answer is that there is no valid question.
>
> Although genetics is all about inheritance, inheritance is certainly not all about genetics. Nearly all inherited characteristics more complicated than a single change in the DNA involve gene and environment acting together. It is impossible to sort them into convenient compartments. An attribute such as intelligence is often seen as a cake which can be sliced into so much 'gene' and so much 'environment'. In fact, the two are so closely blended that trying to separate them is more like trying to unbake the cake. Failure to understand this simple biological fact leads to confusion and worse.[25]

Many people are prepared to put up with confusion if they can use it to absolve themselves of responsibility for what they do, and even more so if it gives them power and wealth. Psychiatry is now a huge profession, closely linked with the vast industry of pharmaceutical drugs, and invested by the State with powers to arrest and detain. If you get sent to jail you'll know when you'll be free again, but become an involuntary psychiatric patient and you are in the power of psychiatrists forever.

There are good therapists of all theoretical persuasions, but they can be hard to find because they aren't famous. Fame prevents a therapist from doing good work because, even if the therapist tries not to be changed by fame, clients expect the therapist to be something more than a humble companion on a journey of exploration. They expect an answer, and a good therapist knows that the getting of wisdom is not a matter of finding answers but of asking better questions.

The questions a client initially brings to a therapist are usually entirely personal, like, 'Why am I in pain?', 'How can I be happy?' A good therapist knows that better questions link the personal with the political. David Smail wrote, 'We will not significantly reduce the prevalence of emotional pain in the world through psychotherapy, which sees it as an essentially personal matter, but rather by coming to accept that it is a function of social organization, which is a political matter.'[26]

He concluded his book by quoting from Fernand Braudel at the end of his magnificent survey of the socio-economic history of modern times, *Civilisation and Capitalism 15th–18th Century*:[27]

> Jean-Paul Sartre may have dreamed of a society from which inequality would have disappeared, where one man could not exploit another. But no society in the world has yet given up tradition and the use of privilege. If this is ever to be achieved, all the social hierarchies will have to be overthrown, not merely those of money or state power, not only social privilege but the uneven weight of the past and of culture.[28]

We are in a trap where to change our society we have to change ourselves, and we can't change ourselves until we change society. However, individuals can start at one side of the trap and progress to the other. If enough people do this the trap might disappear. Already there are those people who begin by blaming themselves for being poor and jobless, then, realizing that there are political and social reasons for their misery, turn their energies to changing the political system. There are also those people, notably many economists, who begin looking for answer to economic, political and social problems in terms of economics, politics, and sociology and then, realizing that their answers are inadequate, reframe their questions in terms of individual experience. David Marquand wrote,

> For more than 40 years, the entire political class has taken it for granted that the central objective of economic policy is to promote wealth creation; that wealth can be equated with GDP per head; and that the rate of growth of GDP per head is, therefore, the litmus test of economic, indeed of national, success . . . [Meanwhile] the public knows that the equation between social well being and per capita gross domestic product has broken down while the politicians still stick to it.
>
> Yet the best economists are beginning to subvert the equation. Armatya Sen, once Drummond Professor at Oxford and now at Harvard, has shown there is no correlation between social performance, measured by life expectancy, and economic performance, measured by GDP growth. Life expectancy in Kerala, one of the poorest Indian states, is higher than in South Africa or Brazil. In terms of life expectancy, Harlem is worse off than Bangladesh. Between 1900 and 1960, improvements in life expectancy in England and Wales were inversely correlated. When the growth rate went up, life expectancy went down, and vice versa.
>
> The obvious conclusion is that the public are right and politicians wrong. A country may be rich in terms of GDP per head, but impoverished in terms of well being. Britain's failures are social, not economic; and our failure is the product of politics with which economic success has been pursued. The goal of public policy should be maximum well being, not maximum growth.[29]

However, well-being is more than a matter of life expectancy. The factors which encourage growth play a major part in well being. The *Economist* summed these up:

> Many studies show that 'market friendly' policies work best: secure property rights; reliable enforcement of contracts; a liberal trade regime; low taxes and public spending; a welcome of foreign investors. Economists argue about how much weight to attach to one factor or another, but most have come to agree with this broad proposition: the key to growth is granting producers and consumers the economic freedom to face and respond to incentives.[30]

Such an economic freedom for producers and consumers now has its own jargon term, 'stakeholding'. In a speech to the business community of Singapore in 1996 Tony Blair outlined what he called the Stakeholder Economy where he proposed shifting

> the emphasis in corporate ethos from the company being a mere vehicle for the capital market to be traded, bought and sold as a commodity, towards a vision of the company as a community or partnership in which each employee has a stake, and where a company's responsibilities are more clearly delineated.[31]

Tony Blair's enthusiasm for stakeholding seemed to fade as his need to win the 1997 election took over but the possibilities of stakeholding continued to be vigorously argued amongst those interested in politics and economics. John Plender, one of the leader writers for the *Financial Times*, wrote,

> The stakeholding solution offers a means of legitimizing the tempestuous mechanics of capitalism and of preserving human and social capital in the interests of competitive advantage ... The stakeholding solution ... is about responsible individualism. It accepts that uncertainty is a condition of life for the foreseeable future and that people who have been used to security in a paternalistic environment will have to develop a more robust sense of independence.[32]

Responsible individuals are those people who recognize the importance of relationships. Will Hutton, in his sequel to *The State We're In*, *The State to Come*, wrote,

> The word stakeholding has become so loaded with ambiguity and baggage that the intent behind it is overlooked. It is based on the notion that the same values that animate us to make our personal relationships work should also animate our wider economic and social relationships, and that the idea we are 'soft' at home but 'hard' at work is inadmissible. The same values should inform all our dealings.[33]

Stakeholding, then, recognizes that we are all individuals living in a network of personal relationships. As Samuel Brittan reminded us, *It is individuals, not collectives, who feel, exult, triumph or despair. It is this which distinguishes individual people from trees and makes the individual person the ultimate end of political and moral discourse.*

Each of us is an individual, but we all live together in one world.

It is clear that we cannot enjoy high levels of well-being while there are people living in poverty. No matter how rich we are, we cannot protect ourselves from the ills and evils that poverty bring. It is in our own selfish interests to promote the well-being and the wealth of the poor. This is the firmly held view of the *Economist*.

> For years the North wrung its hands about poverty in the developing countries and asked what could be done to relieve these countries' miseries. Now, for the most part, the North no longer feels guilty about its wealth, or anxious to see the South do better: Rather, it feels anxious about its wealth, and would prefer on the whole (but off the record) that the South stayed poor.
>
> So far as economic policy in the industrialised world is concerned, the first thing to be said about such thinking is that it is deeply misconceived. The lessons of experience, and all we know about economic principles, teach that when poor countries grow richer, it is not at rich countries' expense. If anything, the opposite is true: rich countries will prosper more if poor countries do well than if they do badly.[31]

The experience of the individual and the politics of the many are part of the one whole. The point at which the political becomes personal and the personal political is the need each of us has to survive both as a body and as a person. Put in moral terms, it is the question of selfishness. We can all enjoy noble, unselfish, long-term aspirations when our survival as a body or as a person is not threatened, but once it is threatened we usually act in short-term and often mean and selfish ways. Our actions are determined by how we have interpreted what we deem to be a threat. For us to act differently we need to understand our interpretations, how we created them and what their implications are.

It is our inability to understand ourselves which lies at the root of an uncomfortable fact now emerging from the research into the factors which promote growth. Economic freedom promotes growth but political freedom can impede it. Richard Thomas reported,

> There is mounting evidence that political freedoms do, at some point, compromise economic growth. In an article for the new *Journal of Economic Growth*,[32] Harvard economist Robert Barro

concludes that economic growth rates are negatively associated, albeit weakly, with greater democracy.

Surveying 100 countries between 1960 and 1990, he shows that while economic freedoms – free markets, rule of law, strong property rights and limited corruption – are powerful determinants of growth rate, political freedoms appear to have the opposite effect.

Although some democracy does better than none, lots of democracy – more frequent votes, at more levels, on more issues – is worse than some. You can have too much of a good thing.

There are two reasons why this is so. First, voters don't know what is good for them. They want to feel good now, not tomorrow. Even if at some level we know that a recession is necessary, we would rather put it off. And because politicians know this, the economy is run in line with our short term, greedy wishes.[33]

It seems that we have a choice of futures.

We can go on as we are, solving few problems and creating even greater disasters.

Or

We can give up much of our political freedom by giving the power to a few unelected people who we hope can make the hard, long-term economic decisions which we refuse to make. However, if we give up those political freedoms which took such time and effort to acquire, we are being no more than little children not wanting to take responsibility for ourselves and wanting Daddy to look after us. We need to remember that throughout history dictators do not have a good track record.

Or

We can take responsibility for ourselves. This means making the effort to understand what we do and why we do it.

This means standing at the junction of the political and the personal, looking both ways and creating a unity. Understanding ourselves means understanding politics and economics, and understanding politics and economics means understanding ourselves.

To do this we have to take responsibility for ourselves. We are on our own and we have to look after ourselves. We have one marvellous resource. We have one another. However, to make the most of that resource we need to be much better at understanding and accepting one another.

There is in our lives a basic insecurity. It is not just the insecurity of living on a planet and in a universe where the unexpected can always happen. It is a basic insecurity resulting from how we function as living beings. Everything which is alive on this planet functions in the same way, interpreting what happens and responding, not to what has happened, but to how each individual life form interprets what has happened. As human beings our liberation and our burden is that we can reflect upon the interpretations we have made. That is what consciousness is. We not only know what we do but we can reflect upon the wisdom of what we have done.

Yet to live in a world where all we can know for certain is what we feel and think is to live a life full of uncertainty. We can comfort ourselves with fantasies of certainty, but these are just fantasies and they bring in their train some terrible implications. However, we can make some amazing journeys with a special kind of imagination. Instead of creating self-absorbed and self-serving fantasies, we can reach out and imagine ourselves into the world of another person. Provided our childhood experience has not robbed us of this skill, through the leap of empathy we can find ourselves close to other people, and out of this closeness can come the resolution, optimism and courage which will enable us to deal with the uncertainties and dangers of our lives.

Such closeness can be the closeness which gives us the strength and mutual trust to build a better society. It is this closeness which has a value far beyond that of all the money in the world.

NOTES

PREFACE

1 *Moral Sayings* (1st c. BC), 656, trans. Darius Lynam, in *The International Book of Quotations*, Penguin, London, 1976, p. 596.
2 *Elegies* (c.28–c.16 BC), 3.7.1, *ibid.*, p. 596.
3 *Yiddish Proverbs* (1949), ed. Hanan J. Ayalti, *ibid.*, p. 597.
4 Crispin Tickell, *The Doomsday Letters*, BBC Radio 4, 12 December 1995.
5 Jack D. Schwager, *Market Wizards*, HarperBusiness, New York, 1989.
6 Jonathan Cape, London, 1995.
7 Vintage, London, 1996, p. xi
8 *Op. cit.*, p.xiii.
9 *Ibid.*, p. 24.
10 *Ibid.*, p. 326.
11 *American Scientist*, 1975, reproduced in Daniel Dennett, *Consciousness Explained*, Penguin, London, 1993, p. 38.
12 *The World in 2020*, HarperCollins, London, p. 269.
13 *Ibid.*, p. 273.
14 *Ibid.*, p. 274.
15 *Ibid.*, p. 275.
16 *Ibid.*, pp. 264, 265.
17 *Ibid.*, p. 265.
18 *Ibid.*, p. 267.
19 Sinclair-Stevenson, London, 1996.
20 *Op. cit.* p. 23.
21 *Ibid.*, p. 29.
22 *Ibid.*, p. 138.
23 *Ibid.*, p. 139.
24 *Ibid.*, p. 142.
25 *Capitalism with a Human Face*, Edward Elgar, Aldershot, 1995, p. 17.
26 *Ibid.*, p. 89.
27 *Ibid.*, p. 97.
28 *Ibid.*, p. 31.
29 *Ibid.*, p. 29.
30 *Ibid.*, p. 268.
31 *Ibid.*, p. 37.

1 THE LOGIC OF THE ILLOGICAL

1 Dostoyevsky, *The Brothers Karamazov*, trans. David Magarshak, Penguin, London, 1957, p. 755.
2 Andrew St George, *The Descent of Manners*, Chatto, London, 1994, p. 209.
3 Methuen, London, 1930, p. 45.
4 *Guardian*, 6 July 1992.
5 *Guardian*, 19 September 1994.
6 'It's a Mad, Mad, Mad, Mad World Money Market', *New York Times*, 8 May 1994.
7 BBC TV, 2 February 1995.
8 *Guardian*, 17 February 1995.
9 *The State We're In*, p. 12.
10 *Living with the Bomb: Can We Live Without Enemies*, Routledge, 1986.
11 *Op. cit.*, p. 24.
12 George Smoot and Keay Davidson, *Wrinkles in Time*, Little, Brown, 1994.
13 Oxford University Press, 1995, p. xii.
14 Dorothy Rowe, *Choosing Not*

Losing, HarperCollins, London, 1988, p. 33.
15 Dorothy Rowe, *Beyond Fear*, HarperCollins, London, 1987, pp. 255ff.
16 *Ibid.*
17 Mike Oaksford, Frances Morris, Becki Grainger and J. Mark G. Williams, 'Mood, reasoning and central executive processes', *Journal of Experimental Psychology: Learning, Memory and Cognition*, March 1996.
18 *The Market Wizards*, p. 278.

2 WHAT DOES MONEY MEAN?

1 Daniel Dennett, *op. cit.*, p. 24.
2 James Ring Adams and Douglas Frantz, *A Full Service Bank*, Simon & Schuster, New York, 1992, p. 14.
3 *Guardian*, 1 July 1993.
4 *The Money Culture*, Coronet Books, London, 1991, p. 114.
5 Gregory J. Millman, *Around the World on a Trillion Dollars a Day*, Bantam Press, London, 1995, p. 74.
6 *You and Me*, Penguin Books Australia, Ringwood, Victoria, 1995 (unnumbered pages).
7 *Sidelights on Relativity*, trans. G. B. Jeffery and W. Perrett, Methuen, London, 1922, p. 28.
8 Quoted by Karl Popper in his essay *Sources of Knowledge and Ignorance*, British Academy Proceedings, Vol.46, 1960–61.
9 Oliver Sacks, *An Anthropologist on Mars*, Picador, London, 1995, p. 108.
10 W. H. Freeman & Co., New York, 1995.
11 Oxford University Press, 1995, p. 13.
12 *Guardian Weekend*, July 1994.
13 Ian Stewart, *Guardian*, 19 June 1992.
14 Susan A. Greenfield, *Journeys to the Centers of the Mind*, W. H. Freeman & Co., New York, 1995, p. 112.
15 *Ibid.*, p. 9.
16 Stuart Kauffman, *At Home in the Universe. The Search for the Laws of Self-Organization*, Penguin, London, 1996, p. vii.
17 R. R. Llinás and D. Pare, 'Of dreaming and wakefulness', *Neuroscience*, 1991, 44, pp. 521–35.
18 Oliver Sacks, *op. cit.*, pp. 53–4.
19 *Economist*, 4 February 1995.
20 James B. Stewart, *Den of Thieves*, Simon & Schuster, New York, 1991.
21 Daniel Dennett, *op. cit.*, p. 357.
22 New American Library, New York, 1972, p. 18.
23 *Ibid.*, p. xiv.

3 THE PUBLIC MEANING OF MONEY

1 Thomas Merton, *The Way of Chang Tzu*, New Directions, New York, 1965, p. 67.
2 *A Short Histoy of Financial Euphoria*, Penguin, London, 1994, p. 13.
3 *Purity and Danger*, Routledge, London, 1966, p. 68.
4 *What Shall We Do?* trans. Leo Weiner, 1904, in Kevin Jackson, *The Oxford Book of Money*, p. 261.
5 *A History of Economics*, Penguin, London, 1991, pp. 38–9.
6 *Independent on Sunday*, 28 September 1993.
7 *USA Today*, 4 August 1993.
8 *Guardian*, 29 December 1994.
9 *Money and Class in America*, Weidenfeld & Nicolson, New York, p. 65.
10 *Guardian*, 12 September 1992.
11 *Economist*, 20 August 1994.
12 1 January 1994.

13 *South China Morning Post*, 7 January 1994.
14 4 January 1994.
15 *Liars Poker*, Coronet Books, London, 1989, p. 116.
16 *Op. cit.*, p. 63.
17 Gregory J. Millman, *op. cit.*, p. 105.
18 'Money': Microsoft Encarta 96 Encyclopaedia. 1993–1995 Microsoft Corporation Funk and Wagnalls Corporation.
19 'The price of a dollar', *Independent on Sunday*, 7 November 1993.
20 J. K. Galbraith, *Money: Whence it Came, Where it Went*, André Deutsch, New York, 1985.
21 Gregory J. Millman, *op. cit.*, p. 32.
22 Paper money display, Design Museum, London, 12 July–19 October 1995.
23 *Traces of Guilt*, BBC2, 2 February 1996.
24 *Economist*, 28 November 1994, p. 25.
25 *Guardian*, 2 February 1996.
26 From *Second Hymn to Lenin and Other Poems*, in *Complete Poems* Vol.1, ed. Michael Grieve and W. R. Aitkin, Martin Brian & O'Keeffe, London, 1976, p. 550.
27 *The Utopia of Sir Thomas More*, 1516, trans. Ralph Robynson, 1551, J. H. Lupton, 1895, Clarendon Press, Oxford, 1895, p. 304.
28 *The Book of the New Moral World*, in Kevin Jackson, *op. cit.*, p. 456.
29 *News From Nowhere*, 1891, in *ibid.*, p. 465.
30 Hougton Mifflin, 1888, in *ibid.*, p. 465.
31 *Economic Possibilities for Our Grandchildren*, 1930, in *Collected Writings*, ed. Donald Moggridge, Cambridge University Press, 1989, Vol.IX. pp. 321–2.
32 Judith and Garfield Reeves-Stevens, *The Making of Star Trek Deep Space Nine*, Pocket Books, New York, 1994, p. 33.
33 *Star Trek: The Next Generation*, Paramount Pictures Corporation, 1988, pp. 42, 53.
34 Gollancz, London, 1986.
35 Dave Marinaccio, *All I Really Need to Know I Learned from Watching Star Trek*, Crown, New York, 1994, p. 87.
36 Quark as told to Ira Steven Behr, *The Ferengi Rules of Acquisition*, Pocket Books, New York, 1995.
37 *Guardian*, 25 September 1992.
38 *Religion and the Rise of Capitalism*, John Murray, London, 1927, p. 43.
39 *Economist*, 25 December 1993–7 January 1994, pp. 107–9.
40 Chapter 24, verse 20.
41 *The Arabs*, Random House, New York, 1987, pp. 109–11.
42 Dan Atkinson, *Guardian*, 9 April 1994.
43 23 April 1994.
44 *Guardian*, 16 June 1994.
45 *Economist*, 7 August 1993, p. 57.
46 *Hong Kong Standard*, 1 January 1994.
47 *The Bulletin*, 7 February 1995, p. 78.
48 *Ibid.*, p. 77.
49 *Sunday Times*, 14 November 1993.
50 *Op. cit.*, p. 7.
51 Jonathan Cape, London, 1990.
52 *Op. cit.*, p. 627.
53 24 February 1996, p. 96.
54 *Guardian*, 2 February 1995.
55 Matthew Lynn, *Sunday Times*, 2 July 1995.
56 *Independent on Sunday*, 28 November 1993.
57 *The Bold Riders*, Allen & Unwin, Sydney, 1994.
58 *Australian Business Monthly*, October 1993, pp. 40–50.
59 *The Bold Riders*, p. 28.

60 Dan Atkinson, *Guardian*, 9 April 1994.
61 James Ring Adams and Douglas Frantz, *op. cit.*, p. 7.
62 *Observer*, 3 November 1996.
63 *Ibid.*
64 *Guardian*, 26 March 1993.
65 *Guardian*, 3 March 1995.
66 19 July 1995.
67 *Financial Times*, 16 March 1996.
68 *Guardian*, 30 November 1996.
69 19 July 1995.
70 11 March 1995.
71 7 July 1995.
72 *Guardian*, 29 February 1996.
73 *Guardian*, 28 February 1995.
74 *Financial Times*, 12 August 1996.
75 The Brookings Institution, 1987.
76 30 April 1994.
77 *Op. cit.*, p. 203.
78 *Ibid.*, p. 197.
79 *Ibid.*, pp. 7, 202.
80 *Economist*, 22 April 1995, p. 99.
81 *Ibid.*, pp. 100, 103.
82 Gregory J. Millman, *op. cit.*, pp. 207–9.
83 *Independent on Sunday*, 26 March 1995.
84 *Guardian*, 7 September 1993.
85 *Independent on Sunday*, 3 March 1996.
86 *Guardian*, 14 August 1995.
87 *Op. cit.*, p. 219.
88 *Ibid.*, p. 220.
89 *Guardian*, 9 February 1996.
90 September 1993, p. 25.
91 *Economist* , 20 August 1994, p. 66.
92 Millman, *op. cit.*, p. 102.
93 *Australian Business Magazine*, April 1994, p. 50.
94 *Economist*, 'Survey of Corporate Risk Management', 19 February 1996, p. 5.
95 With Edward Whitley, Little, Brown, London, 1996.
96 19 February 1996, p. 10.
97 *Guardian*, 4 March 1995.
98 *Guardian*, 24 June 1994.

4 THE PRIVATE MEANING OF MONEY

1 *Independent*, 7 September 1993.
2 *Op. cit.*, pp. 56, 57, 101.
3 9 October 1994.
4 *Observer*, 22 December 1992.
5 *Independent on Sunday*, 30 May 1993.
6 11 January 1993.
7 *Independent on Sunday*, 12 December 1993.
8 *Innumeracy*, Penguin Books, London, 1990, p. 14.
9 20 March 1995.
10 Dorothy Rowe, *Beyond Fear*, HarperCollins, London, 1987.
11 *The Successful Self* and *Dorothy Rowe's Guide to Life*, HarperCollins, London, 1989 and 1995.
12 *Op. cit.*, pp. 240–3.
13 Quoted in James B. Stewart, *op. cit.*, p. 35.
14 *Ibid.*, p. 94.
15 *Ibid.*, p. 32.
16 *Ibid.*, p. 37.
17 *Ibid.*, p. 223.
18 *Ibid.*, p. 470.
19 *Dance Magazine*, February 1995, p. 56, quoting from Otis Stuart, *Perpetual Motion*, Simon & Schuster, New York, 1995.
20 Kathy Balme, *The Cartoonist*, 1 April 1993.
21 *Observer*, 6 June 1993.
22 *Dance Magazine*, p. 56.
23 12 April 1993.
24 10 May 1994.
25 *Independent on Sunday*, 13 June 1993.
26 14 November 1993.
27 *Op. cit.*, p. 60.
28 *Op. cit.*, p. 6.

29 J.K. Galbraith, *The Culture of Contentment*, Sinclair-Stevenson, London, 1992, p. 2.
30 *Op. cit.*, p. 14.
31 *Ibid.*, p. 22.
32 Robert S. Samuelson, *The Good Life and Its Discontents: The American Dream in the Age of Entitlement*, Times Books, New York, 1996, excerpted in *Newsweek*, 5 January 1996, p. 45.
33 *Op. cit.*, p. 28.
34 *Op. cit.*, p. 278.
35 Fred Kaplan, *Dickens*, Hodder & Stoughton, London, 1988, p. 21.
36 *Ibid.*, p. 30.
37 'Like treading on eggshells: an account of a one-day workshop on money in counselling', *Changes*, December 1992, Vol.10, No.4, p. 294.
38 *Independent*, 8 June 1993.
39 *Against the Gods*, John Wiley & Sons, 1996, p. 1.
40 *Ibid.*, p. 272.
41 *Economist*, 10 December 1994, p. 85.
42 Quoted by John Allen Paulos, *op. cit.*, p. 49.
43 *Guardian*, 11 March 1996.
44 Graham Bates and Jane Chrzanowska, *Money and the Markets*, Thorsons, London, 1994.
45 *Op. cit.*, p. 33.

5 THE VALUE OF MONEY

1 *No Hidden Meanings*, Science and Behavior Books, Palo Alto, 1975 (unnumbered pages).
2 J. K. Galbraith, *The Good Society*, p. 29.
3 *Economist*, 11 September 1993, p. 104.
4 *Guardian*, 30 March 1996.
5 *Observer*, 15 January 1995.
6 *Guardian*, 11 March 1996.
7 *Ibid.* (OECD, Organization for Economic Co-operation and Development; EU, European Union; IMF, International Monetary Fund.)
8 Personal communication, 23 March 1996.
9 *Independent on Sunday*, 7 April 1996.
10 *Guardian*, 22 March 1996.
11 *Independent on Sunday*, 7 April 1996.
12 Personal communication, as above n.8.
13 *A History of Economics*, p. 24.
14 Channel 4, 4 April 1995.
15 *Guardian*, 4 April 1995.
16 'Art as a Commodity', lecture at the conference on *Art and Money*, Tate Gallery, 4 March 1995.
17 *Delight*, Heinemann, London, 1949, p. 133.
18 4 February 1994, p. 24.
19 *Economist*, 11 March 1995.
20 *Economist*, 5 August 1995.
21 12 December 1994.
22 *Guardian*, 10 October 1993.
23 *Guardian*, 9 February 1995.
24 *Guardian*, 10 January 1996.
25 *Guardian*, 11 February 1995.
26 Robert van de Weyer, *The Call to Heresy*, Lamp Press, London, 1989.
27 Dorothy Rowe, *Wanting Everything*, pp. 78–114.
28 Robert Lefever, 'The Flight to Freedom', *Independent on Sunday*, 7 April 1996.
29 5 January 1996.
30 Dorothy Rowe, *Breaking the Bonds*, HarperCollins, London, 1992.
31 'Depression: Challenge for the '90s', *The British Journal of Psychiatry*, December 1994, Vol.165, Supplement 26, p. 5.
32 Peter Breggin, *Toxic Psychiatry*, HarperCollins, London, 1994.

33 'Drugs and Hypocrisy', *Journal of The Mad Persons' Union*, No 3, 1993, p. 2.
34 G. Edwards *et al.*, *Alcohol Policy and the Public Good*, Oxford Medical Publications, 1994; E. Osterberg,'Do alcohol prices affect consumption and related problems?' in H. H. Holder and G. Edwards (eds), *Alcohol and Public Policy: Evidence and Issues*, Oxford Medical Publications, pp. 145–63.
35 *Deterring Democracy*, Verso, London, 1991, p. 122.
36 *Guardian*, 6 October 1994.
37 Isabel Hilton, *Guardian*, 19 June 1996.
38 *Op. cit.*, p. 119.
39 *Economist*, 13 November 1993.
40 BBC1, 6 September 1994.
41 *Ibid.*, 20 September 1994.
42 Simon & Schuster, New York, 1994.
43 *Ibid.*, p. 171.
44 *Independent on Sunday*, 12 February 1995.
45 2 March 1996.
46 Dorothy Rowe, *Time on Our Side*, HarperCollins, London, 1994.
47 *Guardian Weekend*, 13 April 1996.
48 *Guardian*, 23 May 1996.
49 p. 3.
50 p. 5.
51 p. 33.
52 p. 4.
53 WDM, 25 Beehive Place, London SW9 7QR, 1995, p. 5.
54 CAAT, 11 Goodwin St, London N4 3HQ, 1995.
55 *Guardian*, 16 February 1996.
56 *Ibid.*, 31 May 1982.
57 *Observer*, 9 July 1995.
58 *Ibid.*, 28 April 1996.
59 10 June 1995, p. 15.
60 *Guardian*, 3 October 1995.
61 *Ibid.*, 12 August 1995.
62 *Dispatches*, Channel 4, 1995, 1996.
63 *Economist*, 10 June 1995, p. 6.
64 *New York Times*, 22 January 1996.
65 *Observer*, 11 February 1996.
66 *Guardian*, 27 June 1996.
67 *Ibid.*, 12 December 1994.
68 *The Muslim Discovery of Europe*, Weidenfeld & Nicolson, London, 1982, p. 193.
69 Hodder & Stoughton, London, 1977.
70 Deborah Shapley, *Promise and Power: the Life and Times of Robert McNamara*, Little, Brown, Boston, 1993, pp. 225, 226.
71 Michael Crama (ed.), *The True Cost of Conflict*, Earthscan, London, 1994, p. 197.
72 Published by Routledge, London, 1984, but now available only directly from Dorothy Rowe via HarperCollins, 77-85 Fulham Palace Road, London W6 8JB.
73 *Op. cit.*, p. 336.
74 *Ibid*, p. 340.
75 *Economist*, 19 August 1995, p. 47.
76 'A perspective on unemployment', *op. cit.*, p. 219.
77 *Ibid*, p. 211.
78 *Op. cit.*, p. 16.
79 *Guardian*, 15 February 1995.
80 Ibid., 25 January 1996.
81 *Op. cit.*, p. 219.

6 THE MARKET AND ITS EXPERTS

1 *Guardian*, 24 January 1995.
2 *Business Age*, September 1993, p. 24.
3 Mervin Powers Wilshire Book Company, Hollywood, 1966.
4 9 September 1993, p. 6.
5 Jack Schwager, *The New Market Wizards*, HarperBusiness, New York, 1992, p. 123.
6 *Economist*, 14 December 1996, p. 7.

7 James Gleick, *Chaos*, Cardinal, London, 1988, p. 5.
8 *Observer*, 2 October 1994.
9 Ilya Prigogine and Isabelle Stengers, *Order in Chaos*, HarperCollins, London, 1985.
10 *The New Market Wizards*, p. 310.
11 *Guardian*, 11 November 1993.
12 *The New Market Wizards*, p. 160.
13 *Ibid.*, p. 177.
14 *Ibid.*, pp. 179, 183.
15 *Op. cit.*, p. 83.
16 *The New Market Wizards*, p. 107.
17 *Ibid.*, p. 155.
18 Bart Kosko, *Fuzzy Thinking*, HarperCollins, London, 1994, p. 5.
19 Geoff Howard, 'Intelligent Automatic', *The Audi Magazine*, TKM Automotive Australia Pty Ltd, Issue 15, 1996, p. 58
20 *Economist*, 9 September 1995, p. 103.
21 *Ibid.*, p. 105.
22 *The Market Wizards*, p. 129.
23 Gregory J. Millman, *op. cit.*, p. 98.
24 Macmillan, London, 1996.
25 *Observer*, 8 September 1996.
26 *Guardian*, 5 May 1993.
27 *Op. cit.*, p. 113.
28 Millman, *op. cit.*, pp. 111–12.
29 *Ibid.*, p. 9.
30 *Op. cit.*, p. 84.
31 *Ibid.*, p. 90.
32 15 April 1995, pp. 5, 33.
33 *The New Market Wizards*, p. 255.
34 *The Essential Anatomy of Britain*, Hodder and Stoughton, London, 1992, p. 80.
35 5 January 1996.
36 *Op. cit.*, p. 141.
37 *Guardian*, 5 January 1993.
38 *Greed and Glory*, a Fulcrum Production for Channel 4, 1992.
39 *Guardian*, 18 September 1992.
40 *Op. cit.*, pp. xxiii, xviii.
41 *Independent on Sunday*, 8 August 1993.
42 Edna Carew, *The Language of Money*, Allen & Unwin, Sydney, 1988, p. 24.
43 10 December 1993.
44 Millman, *op. cit.*, p. xxii.
45 *The Market Wizards*, p. 172.
46 Dorothy Rowe, *The Courage to Live*, HarperCollins, London, 1990, p. 9.
47 *The New Market Wizards*, p. 67.
48 *Ibid.*, p. 410.
49 *Ibid.*, p. 247.
50 *Ibid.*, p. 266.
51 *Ibid.*, p. 64.
52 *The Market Wizards*, p. 318.
53 *The New Market Wizards*, p. 248.
54 *Ibid.*, p. 130.
55 *Ibid.*, p. 132.
56 *Ibid.*, p. 101.
57 New York Institute of Finance, Simon & Schuster, New York, 1990, p. xi.
58 *Ibid.*, p. 27.
59 *Ibid.*, p. 223.
60 *Op. cit.*, p. 74.
61 *Ibid.*
62 Faber & Faber, London, 1995, p. 33.
63 22 September 1994.
64 *New Internationalist*, No. 269, July 1995, p. 11.
65 *Australian Business Monthly*, February 1994, p. 126.
66 *Economist*, 10 February 1996, p. 102.
67 *Op. cit.*, p. 27.
68 21 October 1995, p. 121.
69 *Australian Business Monthly*, November 1993.
70 2 May 1993.
71 *Op. cit.*, p. 3.
72 3 June 1995.
73 20 May 1993.
74 *Financial Times*, 18 April 1996.
75 *A Short History of Financial*

Euphoria, Penguin, London, 1994, p. 87.
76 *Guardian*, 10 August 1994.
77 *Independent on Sunday*, 8 November 1992.
78 July 1994.
79 12 November 1995.
80 *Music and the Mind*, Channel 4 Broadcasting Support Services, 1996, p. 18.
81 *Op. cit.*, p. 4.
82 *Guardian*, 12 September 1994.
83 Tessa Morris-Suzuki, *A History of Japanese Economic Thought*, Routledge, London and New York, 1991, p. 171, quoting from Takamitsu Sawa, *Keizaigku to wa Nan Daro ka*, Iwanami Shinsho, Tokyo, and 'The paradigm of the high growth period', *Japanese Echo*, 1984, 11 (4): 37–47.
84 *Almost Everyone's Guide to Economics*, Penguin, London, 1978, p. 18.
85 *Economist*, 4 September 1993, p. 25.
86 *Op. cit.*, p. 36.
87 David Burningham (ed.), *Introducing Economics*, Hodder & Stoughton, London, 1991, p. 1
88 Alec Cairncross, *Introduction to Economics*, Butterworths, London, 1973, p. 6.
89 *Beyond Economic Man*, ed. Marianne A. Ferber and Julie A. Nelson, University of Chicago Press, 1993, p. 61.
90 *Economist*, 30 March 1996, p. 94.
91 18 October 1993.
92 *Guardian*, 29 June 1996.
93 *Ibid.*
94 *Guardian*, 23 March 1996.
95 *Independent on Sunday*, 3 January 1993.
96 *Keating*, Allen & Unwin, Sydney, 1988, p. 34.
97 April 1994, p. 8.
98 *Guardian*, 24 July 1995.
99 *Honest Opportunism*, Hamish Hamilton, London, 1993, p. 262.
100 *Guardian*, 18 May 1993.
101 *Op. cit.*, p. 61.
102 2 June 1966.
103 *Economist*, 16 July 1994.
104 *Guardian*, 7 March 1996.
105 *An Inquiry into the Nature and Causes of the Wealth of Nations*, 4th edn, Stirling & Slade *et al.*, Edinburgh, 1819, Book 1, Chapter 10, Part 2, p. 177.
106 *Ibid.*, Book 5, Chapter 2, Part 2, p. 278.
107 Robert Locke, *The Collapse of the American Management Mystique*, Oxford University Press, 1996, p. 229.
108 *Ibid.*, pp. 50, 52.
109 *A History of Militarism: Romance and Realities of a Profession*, Norton, New York, p. 11, quoted in Locke, *op. cit.*, p. 3.
110 *Ibid.*, p. 245.
111 10 February 1991.
112 4 October 1992.
113 10 November 1993.
114 15 July 1995.
115 HarperCollins, London, 1996, pp. 126–7.
116 *Independent on Sunday*, 10 July 1995.
117 *The Fish Rots From the Head*, p. 12.
118 *Guardian*, 1 September 1994.
119 *Observer*, 16 June 1996.
120 Richard Semler, *Maverick!*, Century, London, 1994.
121 *Op. cit.*, p. 4.
122 *Ibid.*, p. 1.
123 *Ibid.*, p. 210.
124 *Guardian*, 22 May 1996.
125 Graham Bannock and William Manser, *Dictionary of Finance*, Penguin, London, 1990, p. 100.
126 Edna Carew, *The Language of*

Money, Allen & Unwin, Sydney, 1988, p. 113.
127 *Australian Business Monthly*, January 1993.
128 Century Business, London, 1992.
129 Century Business, London, 1996, p. 189.
130 10 February 1996, p. 20.
131 *Op. cit.*, p. 182.
132 *In Business*, BBC Radio 4, 25 April 1995.

7 MONEY AND MORALS

1 Thomas Merton, *op. cit.*, p. 68.
2 David Barchard, *Asil Nadir and the Rise and Fall of Polly Peck*, Victor Gollancz, London, 1992, p. 256.
3 *Sydney Morning Herald*, 9 March 1995.
4 *Op. cit.*, p. 232.
5 3 January 1996.
6 *Guardian Weekend*, 15 June 1996.
7 *Guardian*, 18 June 1996
8 *Op. cit.*, p. 20.
9 *The Anatomy of Thatcherism*, HarperCollins, London, 1992, p. 33.
10 *The Successful Self.*
11 *Observer*, 14 November 1993.
12 3 December 1994.
13 Andrew St George, *op. cit.*, p. 217.
14 6 April 1978.
15 Paul Webley, Henry Robben, Henk Elffers and Dick Hessing, *Tax Evasion: An Experimental Approach*, Cambridge University Press, 1991.
16 *Guardian*, 25 March 1996.
17 *Op. cit.*, p. 184.
18 David Austin, *Observer*, 28 March 1993.
19 *Guardian*, 14 May 1996.
20 18 May 1996.
21 *Guardian*, 27 November 1993.

8 A CHOICE OF FUTURES

1 *Op. cit.*
2 *Naturalist*, Allen Lane, London, 1995, quoted in *Guardian*, 31 August 1995.
3 *The Day Before Yesterday*, Jonathan Cape, London, 1995, pp. 250, 251.
4 Simon & Schuster, New York, 1985.
5 Colin Tudge, *op. cit.*, p. 252.
6 *Guardian*, 6 December 1995.
7 *Observer*, 7 July 1996.
8 *Op. cit.*, p. 90.
9 8 January 1996.
10 Picador, London, 1996, p. 69.
11 *Economist*, 7 July 1996.
12 Alice Miller, *Thou Shalt Not Be Aware*, Pluto Press, London, 1985.
13 Dorothy Rowe, *Time on Our Side*, HarperCollins, London, 1994.
14 *Guardian*, 4 June 1996.
15 4 August 1992
16 *Wanting Everything*, pp. 82ff.
17 *Guardian*, 7 December 1995.
18 American Association of Science Report, *Guardian*, 10 February 1996, and *Economist*, 24 February 1996, p. 123.
19 David Smail, *How to Survive without Psychotherapy*, Constable, London, 1996, pp. 39–48.
20 Vito Albergo and Andrea Pistolesi, *San Galgano*, trans. Rosanna Cirigliano, Andrea Pistolesi, Firenze, 1990, p. 4.
21 *Ibid.*, p. 9.
22 *The Complete Letters of Sigmund Freud to Wilhelm Fliess*, ed. and trans. Jeffrey Moussaieff Masson, Harvard University Press, 1985, p. 374.
23 *The Seven Spiritual Laws of Success*, Bantam, London, 1996, p. 1.
24 Anne Farmer and Michael J. Owen,

'Genomics: the next psychiatric revolution?', *British Journal of Psychiatry*, 1996, 169, p. 135.

25 *The Language of the Genes*, Flamingo, HarperCollins, London, 1994, p. 226.

26 *Op. cit.*, p. 229.

27 3 vols, Fontana, 1985.

28 David Smail, *op. cit.*, p. 245.

29 *Observer*, 9 June 1996.

30 25 May 1996, p. 16.

31 8 January 1996.

32 *A Stake in the Future*, Nicholas Brealey Publishing, London, 1997, pp. 256, 261.

33 Vintage, London, 1997, p. 1035.

34 *Ibid.*

35 Kluwer Academic Publishing, 101 Philip Drive, MA 01061, USA.

36 *Guardian*, 8 August 1996.

INDEX

Page numbers in bold denote major section/chapter devoted to subject

Abbey National 101
abbeys 418
Abedi, Agha Hasan 83, 84, 89
absolute truths 14, 19, 213, 214, 352, 360, 410
  prisons created from 284, 388–91
absolute values 345, 346, 347, 352
accountants **337–41**
'Act of God' bonds 105
acting profession 145, 146
Acuma 46
addiction 220, 221, 421
advertising 51
Afghanistan 347
AFL-CIO 335
afterlife 356–8
AI (artificial intelligence) 273–4
air quality 199
Akbar, Syed Ziauddin Ali 84 5
alcohol 217, 219–20 , 222
Aldiss, Brian and Wingrove, David *Trillion Year Spree* 61
Alison, Michael 346–7
Alistair 48, 49, 50–1
American Christian Coalition 320–1
amorality xi, xviii-xix *see also* morality
anger
  dealing with in childhood 407–9
annihilation, threat of
  effect of 30–2
  need for understanding of experience of 127–9, 137–8, 194, 203, 403
  warding off 32–4, 177, 179, 203, 402
Anti-Slavery International 233
anxiety 215–16
Argentina xiii
aristocracy 355
Aristotelian logic 8, 9, 24
Aristotle 71, 272
arms trade 7, 105, 180, 189, 197–8, **234–46**
  arguments for 237, 240
  and art market 207
  and Church 346–7
  and government 235, 236
  history 242
  land mines 239–40
  nuclear weapons 105, 241, 242
  poverty and suffering as outcome 243, 250
  rise in 242
  spending involved 241
  use of torture weapons by repressive regimes 240–1
artificial intelligence (AI) 273–4
arts 206–7
Ashdown, Paddy 85
Asia
  arms industry 241
  cigarette smuggling 221
Asimov, Isaac 35
asthma 189
astrology 174–5, 413
asylums 202–3

Atkinson, Dan 210–11
Attallah, Naim 122
Audi 272–3
Austin, David 287, 288f
Australia, xvi, 18, 54, 306
  banks 71, 75, 80–2
  economists 309
  gambling 49, 208–9
  housing 204
  Keating's vision of 322
  superannuation 97
  trade unions 335
Australia Reserve Bank 81–2
Australian aboriginals 204
Australian Business Monthly 323

badness 376–7
Baker, James 264
Ball, George 121–2
Bank of Credit and Commerce International *see* BCCI
Bank of England 15, 86
  and Barings collapse 89, 90
  and BCCI 85
  establishment 82
  role 82–3
banks **71–92**, 279
  central 15, 81–2, 109 *see also* Bank of England
  credit rating 76
  decline 90–1
  deregulation 75, 79–81, 82, 277–8
  function of commercial 74–5
  handling of small accounts 75–6
  and Internet 91
  investment/merchant 77–80
  Islamic 72–4
  safety of 71
  see also Barings Bank; BCCI
Barbarians at the Gate (Burrough and Helyar) 78–9
Barclays 333
Baring, Peter 86, 87, 88
Barings Bank 104, 112
  collapse 80, 86–9, 89–90, 110
  see also Leeson, Nick
Barkworth, Peter 117, 145–6, 163
bartering 53, 193
Bauman, Bob 235
BCCI (Bank of Credit and Commerce International) 83–5, 279
Becker, Gary 316
Belgium, xvi
Bell, Eddie 126, 319, 322, 323, 325, 328, 335
Bell, Steve 66, 68–9f
Bellamy, Edward
  Looking Backward 59–60
Bernstein, Peter L. 171–2
Bill 413
Billington, Michael 212
binary logic 272
birth control schemes 247
Black, Fischer 294
black economy 185
Black-Scholes pricing model 294, 295
Black Wednesday (1992) 4
Blair, Tony 85, 319, 426
Blake, Gil 297, 298
Boer War 284
Boesky, Ivan 131–3, 136, 281
Bond, Alan 381
Bootle, Roger
  The Death of Inflation 308
Bosnia 250
Bouchard-Sornette theory 294, 295
Bowen, David 331
Braudel, Fernand 425
Breggin, Dr Peter 219
Bretton Woods Conference (1944) 17
bribery 305, 365, 368
  in Italy 365–7
Brien, Alan 117
Britain
  attitude towards pound 53
  car industry 182
  departure from Gold Standard 56
  gambling 209–10
British Aerospace 235–6, 241, 340
Brittan, Samuel xvi-xviii, 250–1, 256–7, 308, 394, 426–7
Brown, Gordon 287

Brownian motion 294
Brummer, Alex 79, 112
Buddy 289, 290, 292
Buffett, William 96
building societies 76, 101
buildings
  and strengthening sense of existence 203–4
Burma 233, 278
Bush, President George 224
business schools 330, 332

Cambodia 239
Camelot 172
Campaign Against the Arms Trade 236
Campbell, Lady Colin 121
cannabis 222–3
capitalism 113
car boot sales 195–6
car industry 182
Carew, Edna 302, 322
Carey, George 346, 347
Carryer, Mary 75
casinos 176, 209, 210
Catholic confession 366
central banks 15, 109
  Australian 81–2
  see also Bank of England
chance 414
  inability to understand 173, 175–6
chaos theory viii-ix, 7, 67, 197, 264
charitable bequests 30–1
Cheung, Johnny 47, 48
Chicago Board of Trade 53, 104, 107
Child Poverty Action Group 248
childhood 158, 356
  demand from adults of obedience 244
  effect of bad experience of 259–60
  handling of anger 408–9
  influence of on attitude towards money 164–71
  loyalty to parents 364
  power of affirmation given to father 389
  punishment for being curious 187
  reluctance in understanding **407–12**
  reward for goodness 158, 402
children 391
  attitude towards money 152–3
  effect of wars and conflicts on 241–2
  inheritance of money 160–1, 162
  poverty of 248, 409–10
  and prostitution 229–30
China 54, 55, 56, 233, 237
Chinese 266
  eminence of old people 49–50
  gambling 49, 173
  managing of money 48–9
  talking about money 144
  use of superstitions/magic 47–8, 49, 50, 173
CHIPS (Clearing House Interbank Payment System) 279–80
Chomsky, Noam 222, 225
Chung Tzu 40, 285–6, 342
Church 214, 311
  and arms trade 346–7
  attitude towards money 51–2
  attitude towards usury 71–2
  and education 367
  and idea of perfect symmetry 270–1
  and politics 320
CIA 225
Cicchino, Buddy 273
cigarettes *see* nicotine
Citron, Robert 175
City of London 282–4, 285
CJD (Creutzfeldt-Jakob Disease) 172–3, 199, 321
Clark, Alan 327
Clarke, Kenneth 6, 83
Clinton, President 186, 237, 371
Clive, Robert 371
clothing trade **201–2**
CM Financial Analysis study 333
cocaine 224
coinage 54–5
collecting 139, 140f
commercial banks 74–5
Commonwealth Bank 71, 75, 81
Communism 63, 113, 321

company accounts 338, 340–1
competition 126–7
computers 66, 293
  fuzzy logic systems 272–3
  and market predictions 268–70
conflicts *see* wars
Conran, Shirley 169
conscience, lack of 378, 379–80
consequences 196–7, 257
Conservative government 94, 215, 236, 252 *see also* Thatcher, Margaret
Conservative Party 93, 318, 327
Continental note 56
Conwell, Rusell 52
Co-operative Bank 77
Coopers and Lybrand 87
Copernicus 270
COPEX (Covert Operations and Procurement Exhibitions) 241
corporation tax 318
corruption 305, 320–1, 365–8
counterfeiting 56, 57, 228
courage 362
credit card fraud 57
credit rating 76
Creutzfeldt-Jakob Disease *see* CJD
crime 325
Crisp, Quentin 121

Daily Telegraph 87–8
Daly, Emma 229
Davey, Brian 187, 192
Davidson, J.T.
  Talks with Young Men 100
Davies, Hunter 205–6
Davis, David 239, 240
Dawkins, Richard 183
de Camp, Catherine
  The Money Tree 34, 35
death 127
  and afterlife 256–8
decency, lack of 371–2
Deep Space Nine 63
Dennett, Daniel 11, 28, 33–4, 35
depression 218, 422
deregulation 75, 79–81, 82, 277–8, 280, 281
derivatives 7, 105, 106, **107–12**
  hedge funds 108–9
  history 107
  lack of understanding 109, 110–12
  uncertainty of 112
designers 268
DHSS 151
Dickens, Charles 165–6
Direct Line 102
directors **329–37**
  age 332–3
  attitude towards company money 120
  background 331–2
  distinction between managers and 334
  rewards 333–4
Dirty Money (television) 225–6
diseases
  threat of to rich 190
dissipative structures 264
Dostoyevsky 1, 7
Douglas, Mark 300
Douglas, Mary 44
'downsizing' 335–6
Downton, Christine 274
drugs 220
  cannabis 222–3
  pharmaceutical 217–19
  separation between legal and illegal 221–2
drugs trade 7, 197–8, **223–6**
  and money laundering 207, 226, 227–8
Dunblane tragedy 346
Dunne family 45
Dutch 95, 107

Eckhardt, William 271, 298–9
economic forecasts 306–8
economic growth 186, 426–8
economics 4, 310
  and politics 426
  seen as masculine profession 315–16

trend in theories 312
see also economists
Economist 79, 262
on artificial intelligence 274
Big Mac index 306
on company accounts 340
on derivatives 110
on economists 309–10
on mines 239–40
on pensions 95
on promotion of well-being 426, 427
study on economic forecasting 308
survey of international banking 91–2
on Wall Street 281
economists **302–18**, 426
claiming access to universal truth 312–13
and cognitive psychology 317
criticism of 303–4, 305, 311–12
definitions 302
failure in forecasting results 306–8
objectivity of 313–14
and politicians 310
predicting of future events 304–6
role as soothsayer 308–9
economy 184–6
and environment 186–7
and GDP 185–6, 187, 426
education **212–15**, 367
Egypt 250
Einstein 19
elderly 97 *see also* pensions
Elizabeth and Michael 136–7, 194–5
Emerson, Ralph Waldo 326
empiricist philosophers 20, 21
Employment Policy Unit 256
entitlement 154–8
environment 188–9
and economy 186–7
envy 150–1
'equestrian class' 155–6
ERM (Exchange Rate Mechanism) 4, 287
errors of judgement 125–6
ethics 193–4, 345
Europe 323–4
Evans, Dick 235, 236
Evans, Terry 378
evolution 183–4
Exchange Rate Mechanism *see* ERM
executives attitude towards company money 120
see also directors
existence
enhancement of sense of 403–4
maintaining a secure sense of **138–59**, 194, 203–4
see also annihilation, threat of
experience, past 123–4, 362
interpretations of 22–3
experts ix, 6–7, 17, **285–341** *see also* individual groups of
extraverts 138, 395
characteristics 128, 131, 139, 402
enhancing sense of existence 403–4
importance of relationships 128, 129, 139, 159, 298, 362
relationship with introverts 136–8, 363–4
Eysenck, Professor Hans 138

Falklands War 237, 238f
families 44–6, 81
Far Eastern Economic Review 305
Federal Reserve Bank 15
Ferengi 62, 259, 295
Ferrarotti, Professor Franco 366
Feuerstein, Aaron 371, 377
financial products 65–6, 106–7
Financial Times 332, 427
Finniston, Sir Monty 283
First Congress of the World Council for Psychotherapy 419
Fischer, Gus 123
Fliess, Wilhelm 418
Flynn, Paul 346, 347
food
and bodily survival 35–6
trade 199–200
football 205–6
Ford Financial 90–1

France 330
Francesco and Maria 365, 366
Franklin, Benjamin 12–13
fraud
  counterfeiting 56, 57, 228
  insurance 98–9
free market 260, **275–85**
freedom
  economic growth and political 427–8
  and security 63–4, 81, 113, 178, 179, 250, **401–6**
Freud, Sigmund 164, 174, 312, 316, 418–19
Friedman, Milton 276–7, 312
Friedman, Thomas L. 5–6
Frost, Sir David 125
fudging 351–2, 353
futures market 53, 66, 106, 107–8
  'hurricane' 104–5
fuzzy logic 272–3

Galbraith, J.K. xiv-xvi, 42–3, 44–5, 155–6,
  178, 193, 308, 313
Galeano, Eduardo 305
gambling 49, 173, **207–12**, 282
Gardam, Tim 5
Garratt, Bob 332, 333, 334
GATT (General Agreement on Tariffs and Trade) 276
GDP (Gross Domestic Product) 185–6,
  187, 426
GE Capital Services 90
GEC 346
General Motors 91
genes 105, **422–4**
George, Eddie 82, 90, 261
Germany 182, 329, 330
gifts 191, 192–3
Gimpel, René 207
G.M. Hughes Electronics 274
GNP (Gross National Product) 185, 186, 187
God 350, 352–3, 354, 412–14
Godley, Wynne 307, 309
gold, value of 65
Gold Standard 15–16, 56
Golden Guru Awards 307
Goldman Sachs 294
Goldsmith, Sir James 268
goodness
  belief in basic 376–7
  definition 388
Grand Design 173, 174, 175, 262, 354
Grant, Linda 232, 398
Great Abbey at San Galgano 417–18
Great Depression 16, 58, 71
Greece 54–5
greed 154, 184, 378, 379
Greenfield, Susan 21, 28
Greenhouse Effect 102, 105
Greenspan, Alan 264
Gregory, Richard
  Eye and Brain 21
Gross Domestic Product *see* GDP
Gross National Product *see* GNP
Guardian 143, 308, 391
Gucci 45
Gucci, Aldo 227

Haft, Herbert 45
Hannah, Professor Leslie 332
happiness 358, 359–60, 420
Harsanyi, John 316
Harvey Jones, Sir John 86
Hasbro 45
hawalah 226
Healey, Denis 66, 287, 304–5
health **189–90**
Heath, Ray 144
heaven 356
hedge funds 108–9
Henry VIII, King 14, 58, 59
Hermes 99
Herodotus 54
Hill, Napoleon 262
Hitachi 46
Hockney, David 121
Hoggart, Simon 260, 327
homeless 204
Hong Kong 47–8, 50, 144, 205

Hopkin, Sir Bryan 309
Hornby, Nick 391
housing 204
Howie, Lord 149–50, 171
Huff, Darrell
  How to Lie with Statistics 321
Hughes (G.M.) Electronics 274
Huhne, Christopher 307, 321
Human Genome Project 423
Hurricane Andrew 102–3
'hurricane futures' 104–5
Hussein, Saddam 105
Hutton, Will 186, 376, 377
  on amorality xi, xviii
  on banks 77, 90
  on inflation 6
  on pensions 92, 94
The State We're In x-xii
The State to Come 427
  on trust 372, 374, 392

Independent on Sunday 121, 331
India 51, 200
Indonesia 240, 278
inflation 6, 308
  control of 18
  and unemployment 250, 251–2
insecurity 7, 66–7, 429 *see also* security
Institute of Islamic Banking and Insurance 73–4
insurance **98–105**
  amount spent on policies 99
  fraud 98–9
  future problems for industry 105
  life 99–101
  mispriced risks in industry 102–4
interest 71–2, 73
International Year for the Eradication of Poverty (1996) 248
Internet 57, 91, 228
introverts 138, 395
  achievement and control 129, 131, 139, 298, 362
  characteristics 128–9, 131, 159, 402
  enhancing sense of existence 403, 404
  relationship with extraverts 136–8, 363–4
Investcorp 45
investment banks 77–80
Iran 74
Iran–Contra scandal 227
Ireland 314, 367, 369, 390
Islamic banks 72–4
Italy
  bribery and corruption 365–7
  education 367

Jackson, Kevin
  Oxford Book of Money 8–10
Japan 107
  corruption 368
  dirty money 46–7
  management 329, 330, 331
Johnson, Ross 78, 79
Jones, Adam Mars 278
Jones, Paul Tudor 275–6
Jones, Steve 424
journalism 5
Just World 67, 157, 174, 200–1, 211–12, 352, 354–5, 356

Keating, Paul 75, 97, 322
Kennedy, Douglas 117, 146–7
Kennedy, George 120, 319
Kevin and Hilary 195–6
Keynes, John Maynard 17, 60, 309, 312, 314–15
Kinsella, John 391
Kleinwort 80
Knutson, Kelly 57
Koran 72, 73
Kosko, Bart 272
Kravis, Henry 78, 79
Kwan, Joseph 48

Labor Party (Australia) 323
Labour Party (Britain) 319
Lamb, David 72–3
Lamont, Norman 4, 32–3, 287
land mines 239–40
language 41, 42, 43, 53

Lapham, Lewis H. 45–6, 52, 155, 156, 157–8, 162, 280
Laurance, Ben 5
Lawrence, Michael 285
Lawson, Nigel 79
Leeson, Lisa 365
Leeson, Nick 86–8, 110, 119–20, 129, 130–1, 365
leisure **205–12**
LETS (Local Exchange Trading Systems) 54, 58
Letwen, Shirley Robin 363
Leunig, Michael 18f, 343, 344f
Levine, Dennis 227
Levitt, Roger 380
Lewinton, Christopher 283
Lewis, Bernard 242
Lewis, Michael 14, 51–2, 154
life insurance 99–101
LIFFE (London International Financial Futures and Options Exchange) 106, 290
Lifton, Robert 337
Lilley, Peter 248, 260
Lipschutz, Bill 297–8
listening 415–16, 418, 419
Living with the Bomb (Rowe) 243
Llinás, Rodolfo 29
Lloyds Names 103–4, 139, 141
Local Exchange Trading Systems *see* LETS
Locke, John 15
Locke, Robert 330, 345
logic
  different kinds of 8–10
  see also private logic
lotteries 210 *see also* National Lottery
loyalty 364–5
Lucas, Robert 316
lying 366
  to oneself 348–5

McDiarmid, Hugh 58
McKay, Randy 299–300
McNamara, Robert 242
McNeill, Pat 169
McRae, Hamish xii-xiv, xviii, 63, 256, 414
Major, John 4, 85, 196–7, 237, 239, 287
Malaysia 74
management consultants 336–7
managers **329–31**, 335, 336, 374 *see also* directors
Manchester United 206
Manolas, Kerry 134–6
maps 386
Marber, Patrick 212
Marc 152–3
Marcos, Imelda 89, 364, 365
marijuana 222
market 38
  and computers 268–70, 293
  deregulation 277–8, 280, 281
  and experts 6–7, **285–341** *see also* individual groups of
  free 260, **275–85**
  government interference in 275–6
  operation as a game 392
  predicting viii-ix, 7, **261–75**, 293–4, 295–6
  Thatcher on 259
  and traders *see* traders
  and trust 373
Market Wizards viii, 262, 297
Markowitz, Harry 96
Marquand, David 426
Marshall, Alfred 315
martyrdom 296–7
Marx 174
Massow, Ivan 121
MasterCard 57
mathematics 311
Matthews, Professor Kent 185
Maxwell, Robert 80, 97, 397–8
MBA 329
meaning structure(s) 2, 3, 32, 49, 133, 171, 318, 408
  and competition 126–7
  creation 26–8, 29, 382–4, 386–8
  differences between individual 2, 37–8, 124
  and reality 124–6, 159

threats to 216
media 33, 51
Mendels, Joseph 218
mental illness 125
asylums 202–3
genes as cause of 423
use of tranquilizers 219
Mercer, Don 323
merchant banks 77–80
merchants 282, 283
metaphors 115–16, 162
metaphysical philosophers 20–1
Midland Bank 77
'militarism' 330
Milken, Michael 31
Millman, Gregory J. 288–9
mines, land 239–40
Minford, Patrick 307
Minsky, Marvic 384
Mohamed, Dr Mahathir 74
monarchs 14–15
Mondex credit card 57
monetarism 4
money
abolishment idea **58–64**
change in attitude towards 4–6
defined 54
different meanings for 13
early objects circulating as 54
errors in belief that money is consistent and unchanging 18–19
factors needed to arrive at true value of 179–80
future as reason for existence 43
history **53–7, 64**
importance of compared to other things 151–2
inconsistency in value of 13
and language of time 42–3
people's relationship with 116–20
power of vii
and realm of imaginary 64–6
and survival **24–39**
unreality of 119
money laundering 207, 225, 226–8, 279
Money Programme, The 368
morality xvii-xviii, 59, **342–81**
and Church 346–7
Just World *see* Just World
and politicians 326–7
reasons for straying from principles when money is involved 343–4
see also absolute truths; absolute values
More, Sir Thomas 58–9
Morris, Philip 221
Morris, William 59
Moseley, Hannah 121
Moss, Brian P. 88
mutual funds 90, 91

Nadir, Asil 343, 349, 350, 373
NAIRU (Non-Accelerating Inflation Rate of Unemployment) 256
Nash, John 316
Nasser, President 73
National Alliance for the Mentally Ill 219
National Health Service (NHS) 144–5, 281, 337
National Health Trusts 145
National Lottery 47, 172, 210–11
'new wealth accounting system' 186
New York Times 5–6
News International 123
Newton, Sir Isaac 15
NHS *see* National Health Service
nicotine 217, 220, 221, 222
Nigeria 240
Nisse, Jason 80
Nobel Prize (1994) (economics) 316
Norman, Montagu 15, 16
North, Oliver 225
Northern Ireland 367, 390
Norwich Union 101
Nuclear Test Ban Treaty 241
nuclear weapons 105, 241, 242
Nureyev, Rudolf 139, 141

object permanence, gaining of 41–2
offshore banking 226
O'Kane, Maggie 347
old boys' network 89, 331, 332

organized crime 305–6
Ormerod, Professor Paul 264, 314
The Death of Economics 303–4, 306, 311–12, 314
Owen, Robert 59

Pacioli, Luca 337–8
Pakistan 233
Panos Institute 224
Pareto Partners 274
Pasley-Tyler, Robert 153–4
past experience *see* experience, past
Paul 194, 253
Paulos, John Allen 122–3, 176, 270
P.E.H. 49–50, 144
Pension Fund Guarantee Corporation 96
pensions **92–8**, 99
perfect symmetry, idea of 270–1
personal construct theory xvi, xviii
Personal Equity Plans (PEPs) 90
pharmaceutical drugs 217–19
philosophy 20–1, 22
pilfering 350–1
piousness 368–9
Plato 20, 21, 58
Platts, Richard 121
Plender, John 427
Plutarch 58
politicians 6, 39, 277, **318–28**
'career' 325
distrust of 410–11
and economists 310
and Europe 323–4
lack of understanding of constituents 324–5
and lying 327–8
and morality 326–7
understanding business 318, 319
understanding economics 321–2
pollution 189, 191
Polycrates of Samos 55
poor 247–50
disparity between rich and 188, 191, 246, 249, 250
promotion of well-being 427
pornography **229–33**
Portillo, Michael 395
possessions 151–2
seeking of security through 139, 141–2
poverty *see* poor
prices 261
pride 32, 33
Priestley, J.B. 208
Priestman, Jane 133–4, 149
Prigogine, Ilya 264–5
prisons 324, 326
Private Eye 88
private logic 2–3, 8–10, 16, 36–7, 49, 318, 415
logic of ideas within 24, 33, 39
and politicians 39, 324
and public logic 9, 171
reasons for not wanting to inspect **393–413**
private pensions 94–5
probability 176
prostitution **229–33**
Prudential 99, 101
Prufrock 154
psychiatrists 339, 423–4
psychology (psychologists) 310, 312, 313, 314, 316, 411
psychotherapy 336, 419, 420
Ptolemy 270
public logic 8, 9, 17, 171, 318

Queens Moat 333
Quran 72, 73

Rachel 412–13
racism 355
Raeburn, Anna 163–4
Railtrack 274
Raschke, Linda Bradford 265–6
Ray and Julie 170
Reagan, Ronald 363
reality and meaning structure 124–6, 159
relationships 258
between introverts and extraverts 136–8, 363–4

destroying of by borrowing and lending 162–4
extravert's attitude towards 128, 129, 139, 159, 298, 362
and money 44, 160
need for 43–4
relationships (contd)
power 231–2
wistakeholding 427
wills and family 160–2
repentant sinner theory xvi, 420–1
rich 248
charitable bequests made by 30–1
dangers affecting 188–91
disparity between poor and 188, 191, 246, 249, 250
people's definition of 121
Riddell, Peter 325
Riley, Thomas 110
risk, assessment of 171–3
RJR Nabisco 78, 79, 221
Roach, Stephen 335–6
Robertson, Paul 311
Robinson, Jeffrey
The Laundrymen 227–8
Roddenbury, Gene 60, 61, 62
Rogers Jr, James B. 298
Ross, Nick 369
Rotblatt, Joseph 244
Rowe, Edward 134
Royal Commission on Environmental Pollution 321
Ruanda 250
Rubython, Tom 101
Russell, Bertrand 32
Ryle, John 100–1

Saatchi, Maurice 95–6
Sacks, Oliver 20, 21
Saferworld 243
Sagan, Carl 244
Sampson, Anthony 283
The Arms Bazaar 242, 244
Samuelson, Robert J. 156
Saudi Arabia 240
Saunders, Ernest 380–1
Sawa, Takamitsu 312
Schartz, Marty 10
Scholes, Myron 294
Schwager, Jack 262, 265–6, 267, 269, 297
science 312, 384
scientists 286, 303, 304, 384
secrecy 1–2, 23, 142–5, 146, 147, 148–51
Securities and Futures Authority (SFA) 87
security and freedom 63–4, 81, 113, 178, 179, 250, **401–6** and money **64–71**
seeking of through possessions 139, 141–2
self-esteem 404, 405–6
Sellar and Yeatman
1066 and All That 4
Selten, Reinhard 316
Semler, Ricardo 334
Sergeant, Carol 89
SERPS (state earnings related pensions) 94
service sector 256
sexual relationships 230
and money relationships 164
Seykota, Ed 296
SFA (Securities and Futures Authority) 87
Shakespeare 62
share owning 5
Sharpe, William 96
Shaw, George Bernard 157
Sheehan, Paul 108
shelter **202–4**
Shepperd, John 309
silver, value of 65
Singapore 97, 306, 426
single European currency 53
sins, repentance of xvi, 420–1
Slaughter, Joanna 97
slavery **233–4**
Smail, David 420, 425
Smith, Adam xviii, 210, 252, 259, 276, 329
Smith, Dodie 146

Smith, Goldwin 369
Smith, Jeannie 175
Smith, Terry
  Accounting for Growth 339–40
smoking 217, 220–1, 222
Smullyan, Raymond 174–5
Social Darwinism 248
Soros, George 90, 268
South China Morning Post 50
South Korea 174
Spear (J. and W.) 45
Spencer, Herbert 248
Spens, Lord 85–6
Sperandeo, Victor 282, 297
St George, Andrew 99–100, 373
Stakeholding 426–7
  relationships in 427
Star Television 50–1
Star Trek 60–3, 295
Star Trek V: The Final Frontier 62
state earnings related pensions *see* SERPS
statistics 269–70, 271
Stewart, Ian 170, 211–12
Strassman, Diana 315
style 134
Successful Self, The (Rowe) 404
Sullivan, Kevin 147–8, 148–9
superannuation funds 97
Supreme Power 421, 422
Switzerland 207
Sykes, Trevor 80–1
symmetry 270–1

Taliban militia 347
tardive dyskensia 219
Tawney, R.H. 71–2
tax evasion 371
teachers 410–11
telephone banking 57, 76
Terence 138–9, 160–1, 161–2, 167–9, 196, 295–6
terrorism **189**, 191
Thales 107
Thatcher, Margaret 75, 93, 250, 255, 363,378
  on market 259
  on politicians' understanding of business 318
  and 'value for money' 38, 122, 180
theories 3–4
  used in assessment of people 374–6
therapy 415–17, 418–25
Third World 247
Thomas, Richard 427–8
Thompson, Christopher 88–9
Thomson, Richard 331, 332
Tim 207
Time on Our Side (Rowe) 116, 142
tobacco 220, 224
tobacco companies 220–1
Today (radio programme) 51
Tolstoy, Leo 44
Tony 150–1, 167
Torture Trail, The (television) 241
trade 191, **192–8**
  consequences of 197
  and history of City of London 282–4
  intelligent and stupid 196, **198–246**, 407
  outcome of stupid **246–57**
  people's enjoyment of 194–6
trade unions 335
traders 10, **287–302**
  addictiveness 299
  background 292
  behaviour 289, 290–3
  diagram of head 290f
  dress code 291
  exclusion of women 289
  feelings about money 296
  image 288
  mathematicians and 293–4
  qualities needed for success 297–9, 299–301
  search for self-knowledge 295
tranquilizers 218–19
Trout, Monroe 267, 271
trust 372–4, 395, 398, 399, 402, 403
tuberculosis 190
Tuckey, Andrew 87
Tudge, Colin 384–5

Tumin, Judge Stephen 326
Tweedie, Sir David 341
Tweedie, Jill 369–71

unemployment 250–4, 256–7
  and Great Depression 16
  and inflation 250, 251–2
Unicef 241–2
United Nations
  Trade and Development Report (1993) 306–7
United States xv
  accountancy 338
  arms industry 237, 241, 242
  banks 74–5
  changes in attitude towards money 5–6
  chief executives' pay 333
  church and money 51–2
  and Continental note 56
  corruption in politics 320–1
  'equestrian class' 155–6
  gambling 209
  'managerialism' 330–1
  and markets 52, 275, 295
  pension funds 96
  politicians 319–20, 326–7
United States (contd)
  poverty of children 409–10
  severing of link with gold 56
  trade unions 335
  Wall Street 280–1
usury 71–2, 73

'value for money' 38, 122, 180–2, 187
Vatican 56–7
Veblen, Thorstein 141
virtue 361–3, 365
  association with money 369–70
  reasons for lack of 371–3
Visa 57

Walden, George 324
Walker, Patric 175
Wall Street 280–1
Walter, Christian 294
war
  effect of 241, 243
  inevitability of 242–5
  suggested rules for 245
Warburg 80
water trade **200–1**
Webster, Stephen 411
Weiss, Al 269
Welchman, Kit and Dorothy 166–7
well-being 426–7
Westpac 75
Wetherill, Eddie 76
Wheen, Francis 335
White, Harry 17
William III 82
wills 160–2
Wilson, Edward O. 383–4
Wilson, James 314
winning 38
women 388
  and economics 315
  education of in Third World 247
  exclusion on trading floor 289
  exploring of nature of absolute beliefs 390–1
  men's view of 233–4
Woollacott, Martin 236, 320
work 254
World Bank 112, 186, 247
World Development Movement 236
World Trade Organization (WTO) 276
writers 146–7

Xenophanes 19–20, 21

Yugoslavia 250

Zimbabwe 224